Rebecca Lowe is a freelance jo̶ rights and the Middle East. Sh̶ ̶̶̶̶̶̶̶̶, BBC, *Evening Standard*, *Indepe̶* ̶̶̶̶̶̶̶̶*mist*, *Sunday Times Magazine*, *Daily Mail*, *Huffington Post* and IranWire, as well as numerous travel publications. She was previously the lead reporter at the International Bar Association, where she focused on human rights and the rule of law and wrote extensively about the Arab Spring. She is a Fellow at the Royal Geographical Society and holds a BA in English Literature from Cambridge University and an MA in journalism from Stanford University, where she was awarded a scholarship.

Praise for *The Slow Road to Tehran*

'A terrifically compelling book, bursting with humour, adventure and insight into the rich landscapes and history of the Middle East ... Lowe recounts the beauty, kindnesses and complexities of the lands she travels through with an illuminating insight. A wonderful new travel writer.'   Sir Ranulph Fiennes

'Beautifully capturing the joys of solo adventuring ... highly entertaining and impressively valiant.'
                                      Caroline Eden, *Financial Times*

'[A] funny and freewheeling account ... Lowe, a freelance British journalist, has a forthright confidence that brings to mind those earlier Middle Eastern adventurers Freya Stark and Gertrude Bell.'   James Barr, *The Times*

'By cycling solo across the Middle East for 11,000 kilometres, Rebecca Lowe has achieved a remarkable feat. Her account of this grand journey is admirably observant, unfailingly humane and humorously self-aware to just the right degree. She shows sensitivity to the uniquely Middle Eastern lives she encounters while also maintaining an eye for their chaotic opera of quotidian dramas. This is a book that makes you laugh, gasp, cry and learn something about the many peoples of the Middle East.'

Arash Azizi, author of *The Shadow Commander: Soleimani, The US, And Iran's Global Ambitions*

'The book is a fascinating ride through entire cultures, with the diversity and vibrancy of south-east Europe and the Middle East fully on show ... For all cycling enthusiasts, those interested in the culture and history of the Middle East, or just those impressed by feats of endurance, Lowe's tale is a must-read.'

Adam Becket, *Cycling Weekly*

'The idea of cycling from England to Iran seems to me completely barmy – heroically barmy, magnificently barmy, in the style of the great travellers of the past who walked on foot to the South Pole or rode on camels to China. Not even straight to Iran, but by way of Egypt and Sudan, the Sahara and the Persian Gulf – 11,000 kilometres – a whole year balanced on two wheels, held upright and propelled only by her own muscle-power. Over impossible mountain ranges, on uncyclable roads, through states where being a foreigner or a woman is discouraged. She writes about it with wonderful vividness and self-mockery. And she is a real traveller. She stays, eats, and drinks, one way or another, with local people, and for brief, intense moments shares a little of their lives. She knows an extraordinary amount about the history and current politics of everywhere she goes, always complex and usually painful, with problems often shamingly rooted in the colonialist inheritance. Everywhere she discovers a reciprocal friendliness and curiosity, and a changing world that often belies the expectations that outsiders have of it.'

Michael Frayn, author of *Noises Off* and *Copenhagen*

'Here's a book in the great tradition of the British lone traveller – those spirited individuals who set off to explore Foreign Lands with an open heart, determined against all odds to see what joys they might find. Rebecca Lowe is a cross between her two illustrious forebears, Eric Newby and Dervla Murphy. Her carefully woven tale is insightful, delightful – full of gusto and grit, and always entertaining.'

Benedict Allen, author of *Explorer* and *Into the Abyss*

'This is modern travel writing at its very best, full of vim and vigour, painstakingly researched, laced with wry humour, political (without being *too* political), adventurous and rich with anecdote. As Lowe checks in her beloved, much dented and repaired bicycle (nicknamed Maud) at Tehran's airport, I couldn't help but whisper: bravo!'

Tom Chesshyre, *The Critic*

'Rebecca has pulled off an astonishing feat, both in terms of her journey but also with her book, which is both thought-provoking and highly entertaining. Refreshingly free of anguish and navel-gazing, she instead turns her focus on the people and stories of the Middle East while expertly weaving in the salient aspects of Britain's often nefarious relations with the region. This elegant blend of adventure, politics and history forces the reader to face up to some uncomfortable truths but always keeps us pedalling on a wild, colourful ride through blistering deserts, chaotic cities and lonely highways. All this, served with a good dose of self-deprecation and excessive drinking, makes for a highly readable book that will stay with you long after you roll into Tehran, weary, saddle sore, but triumphant on her behalf.'

Lois Pryce, author of *Revolutionary Ride: On the Road in Search of the Real Iran*

'Lowe is a witty, worldly travelling companion with a hawkish eye for detail and whip-sharp turn of phrase. She pedals across deserts with steely thighed grit, deftly weaving humour with serious journalism. A life-affirming read that will have you dusting off your derailleur and hitting the open road. Bravo!'

Antonia Bolingbroke-Kent, author of *Land of the Dawn-Lit Mountains*

'From now on, whenever anyone asks me about solo women travel in the Middle East, I'll point them to Rebecca Lowe's book. This was an audacious journey, written about with humour and humility alongside a good understanding of the region.'

Leon McCarron, author of
The Land Beyond and *Wounded Tigris*

'*The Slow Road to Tehran* is packed full of wit, warmth, razor-sharp insights and a spirit of fiery adventure. It's also a book full of hope, recognising the challenges faced by one of the world's most misunderstood regions, and wishing on it the same spirit of freedom that drives the book's irrepressible author.'

Nicholas Jubber, author of *The Fairy Tellers*
and *Drinking Arak Off an Ayatollah's Beard*

'Lowe, whose winningly self-deprecating tone persists through adventures and misadventures alike, is no naif. A veteran journalist with a focus on human rights, Lowe is clear-eyed about the fraught history of Western adventurers in the Middle East, with a reporter's knack for depicting the vivid characters she encounters.'

Jen Rose Smith, *Washington Post*

'I laughed out loud, gawped in awe at Rebecca's wordsmithery and magic, and marvelled at her understanding of complex situations and ability to distil them with such elegance. I read the book slowly, as life demands, and savoured drawing it out and out and out. The writing was deft and insightful and expertly (seemingly effortlessly) hewn.'

Sarah Outen, filmmaker and author of *Dare to Do*

'[Lowe] is a perceptive writer who finds new ways to think about the complex peoples, histories and politics of the countries she journeys through.'

Ben East, *Observer*

'Already familiar with Rebecca Lowe's work, I was expecting *The Slow Road To Tehran* to be good. But I didn't anticipate just how good. Brilliant, in fact. It's everything you could want from a travel book: beautifully written, warm, compelling, exciting, and funny as fuck. The sheer quantity and quality of research is exceptional, and there was something new and fascinating to learn on every page. I have so much admiration for this wonderful book, and suspect it will soon become a travel literature classic.'

Charlie Carroll, author of *The Lip* and *The Friendship Highway: Two Journeys in Tibet*

'*The Slow Road to Tehran* is the very best of modern travel writing. It contains wonderful descriptions of faraway places and hilarious encounters on the road, as well as of the grit needed to cycle across continents by oneself. But it is much more than that. Rebecca Lowe's narrative brings out the humanity of the Muslim peoples of the Middle East whose lands she crosses, as well as the contrasts between their countries and the very different situations in which they find themselves today. This book gives you an inkling of why things are the way they are.'

John McHugo, author of *A Concise History of the Arabs* and *Syria: A Recent History*

'I have read so many books that are ostensibly just like this one. However, nothing comes close to this seminal and definitive work. Every male should read this book, then atone. Every female should read this book, then take heart. Rebecca Lowe has created a truly "cannot-put-down" read and we are all richer for it. This is clearly the most important travel book of the last five years: a true milestone in combining cultural adventure with geopolitical wisdom.'

Austin Vince, curator of The Adventure Travel Film Festival

'Illuminating, gripping and often funny.'   *Wanderlust* magazine

'Absolute page-turner. An inspiring traveller tale full of surprises right to the end.' Reza Pakravan, explorer and filmmaker

'I am a huge fan of cycling odysseys and *The Slow Road to Tehran* by Rebecca Lowe, recalling the incredible 11,000km solo ride she took across Europe and through the Middle East, couldn't be more relevant, featuring her epic exploits and the colourful varieties of people she encountered.'
Iain MacGregor, author of *The Lighthouse of Stalingrad* and *Checkpoint Charlie*

'Simply brilliant. Lowe pulls off the feat of combining deep knowledge of the Middle East with insight, humanity, a cracking good bike ride, rich and unexpected stories from the road, and an (almost) unwavering sense of humour. I couldn't put it down.'
Kate Rawles, author of *The Carbon Cycle* and *The Life Cycle*

'A delightfully thoughtful tale, bursting with people, adversity, adventure and kindness. Roads unwind with welcome snatches of history and politics, and roadside chatter, which reveals so much. This is an outward-looking, open-hearted book. People make the place, it seems, and the humble, slow-going bicycle is the best way to find them.' Stephen Fabes, author of *Signs of Life*

REBECCA LOWE

THE SLOW ROAD TO TEHRAN

A REVELATORY BIKE RIDE THROUGH EUROPE AND THE MIDDLE EAST

CONTENTS

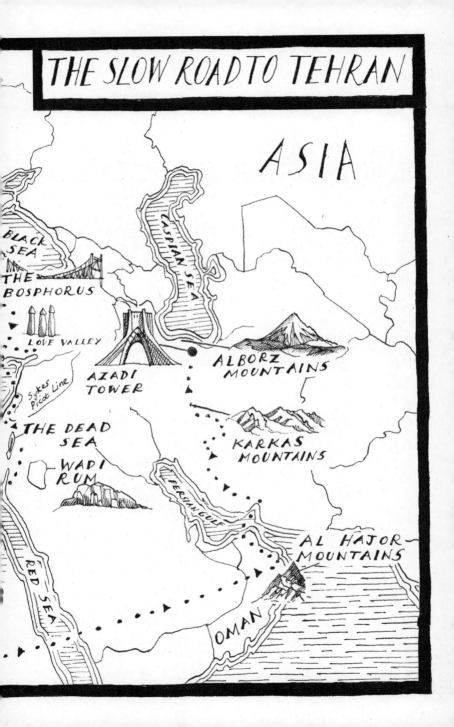

To Dad, *whose generosity of spirit was an inspiration in life and beyond – and who might actually have read this book if only I had completed it on time.*

And to my baby daughter, Frankie, *whose birth finally made me realise what I put my poor parents through. Sorry Mum (and Dad, if you're listening).*

PROLOGUE

'For it is not death or hardship that is a fearful thing, but the fear of death and hardship.'
Dervla Murphy, *Full Tilt* (1965)

I can see the road clearly, threading its way between the mountains and the sea. I trace my finger along it. At times it is distinct and solitary, at others it disappears into the darker line of the motorway or the crease of a coastal ravine. I look up, expectant.

'See,' I say. 'Here.'

The man seems unimpressed. He rubs a hand down his chin and I hear the quiet rasp of stubble against flesh. For the first time, I notice the smudge of grey beneath his eyes. He looks older than his twenty-seven years.

'There's no road,' he repeats. He doesn't acknowledge the map. The map is irrelevant because he knows this country well.

'But look,' I tap my finger. 'It seems to go all the way, no?'

Finally, he glances down. I notice he has tufts of grey at his temples too. The poor man, I think. He is not a fixer by trade but an electrical engineer. I recruited him to help me because he was known about town. Samer, the man who connects people; the guy who gets things done. But so far our relationship hasn't gone well. First, he kept me waiting for three hours due to a 'minor gas explosion' at home. Then there was the flyover incident with the forklift truck that nearly killed us both, and which went some way towards explaining the grey smudges and tufts.

And now this. You might have thought, considering Samer's somewhat relaxed approach to traffic signals, that a quiet coastal track would appeal to him. But he seems determined to put me off this route.

'There *is* a road,' he concedes. After all, there's no real denying it. 'But it's bad.' He stabs at the pale, shaky line, crushing four villages beneath one plump digit. 'There's sand. And cracks. Bad for cars. Bad for bikes.' His eyes flick to the bulky three-gear contraption leaning against the wall, its royal blue frame tarnished russet at the joints. On the handlebars, a dayglo zip-bag declares 'BEIRUT BY BIKE' beside a logo of a rather athletic cyclist in a jaunty bandanna doing a wheelie. Having been cycling around the city for several days now, I admit it's not an image that I recognise. 'Bad for *that* bike.'

I put down the map, resigned. The truth is, I've already made up my mind to cycle up to the border in the north. It is December 2014 and I've come to Lebanon to report on the worst refugee crisis the region has ever known, as millions of displaced Syrians flee the devastating war at home. For the past week, I've been in Beirut interviewing politicians, activists and aid workers to try to gauge the impact of the conflict on Syria's smallest and most vulnerable neighbour. But my report feels dry and lacklustre. To understand the issue fully, I'm aware I need to access the tented camps beyond Tripoli on the coast. I need to speak to the people living and surviving on the front line.

How to get there poses a challenge, however. Taxis are expensive, while buses have a frustrating tendency to dawdle for hours or neglect to turn up at all. In a sudden eureka moment, it occurs to me that a bike may be the solution. To Tripoli, it is under ninety kilometres door-to-door, so doable (just) in a day. And the road looks ideal, hugging the shoreline and unspooling like Ariadne's magic thread all the way to the north. From Beirut, it seems to me that I should be able to travel the entire route without once having to navigate the madman's gauntlet of the motorway.

Plus, I admit the idea excites me. I have cycled in a few

interesting places before – India, Mexico, the Balkans – but never the Middle East. For this reason, the thought also scares me, and I've spent the past few hours trying to find someone to accompany me on the ride. So far, however, I have failed.

'You shouldn't go to Tripoli anyway,' Samer says. 'Jihadists are still fighting. You could be shot. Or ...' He hesitates.

'Or ...?'

'Worse.'

'Worse?'

'Yes, worse.' He seems irritated now, as if talking to a child. 'Kidnapped, tortured. Worse.'

I look at him, unsure how to respond. A lengthy silence passes as he finishes one cigarette and lights up another. The Cedars packet is a similar colour to my bike, and probably equally as life-threatening. 'So you don't want to come, then?' I ask finally.

He blows out a long, slow trail of smoke, then stands up and reaches for his leather jacket. It is heavily worn at the elbows and smells wholesome and musty, like damp wood. 'No, Rebecca,' he says, and I know from his tone that our conversation is at an end. 'I'm afraid you're on your own for this one.'

After Samer leaves, I think long and hard about what he has said. He is not the first person to caution against cycling the coastal path or travelling to the northern governorates alone. And the bicycle has admittedly seen better days. Even the men at the rental shop laughed when I suggested taking it outside Beirut, presuming that I was joking.

But my instincts suggest it will be okay. Friends in Tripoli have reported that, despite pockets of unrest, the city streets are safe. And if the road proves unrideable, I can always just try another tack. So, after lengthy consideration, I decide to ignore Samer – and Mohammed, and Midhat, and Halifa, and all the other locals who seem to see cycling through their country as a mark of mental illness – and take the plunge.

* * *

Escaping Beirut isn't easy. Extricating myself from the city's noodle-like tangle of ring-roads and overpasses feels like fighting off an attack by a many-tendrilled cephalopod. But once I've finally wrested free, my entry onto the coastal path is all the sweeter. From that moment on, it is a thrilling, beautiful ride. The road, doubted by so many, is indeed sandy and uneven, but also quiet and pleasant and almost perfectly designed for a bike. Following an early puncture – repaired for free by a passer-by, who charitably risks his young son's life by sending him on his BMX down the eight-lane motorway for a repair kit – the trip is smooth and straightforward. For several hours, I dip up and down the cliff edge, through whitewashed villages that blaze with reflected light, brushed by a crisp winter breeze seasoned with jasmine and spice. Wisps of music drift from hidden fishermen's coves and I recognise Fairuz, the 'Jewel of Lebanon', and Mohamed Mounir, the 'Arabic Bob Marley'.

By the time I reach Tripoli, I'm in a relaxed, buoyant mood. The Sunni and Alawite militia groups reportedly operating in the area are nowhere to be seen, and I make it up to the border without incident.

This uneventful mini-adventure teaches me several important things. First: always carry a puncture repair kit when cycling. Second: Lebanese people are astonishingly helpful. Third: Lebanese drivers are homicidal maniacs. Fourth (most importantly): never trust people who say things can't be done. Of course, *some* things can't be done. I couldn't have cycled to the moon, for example – or even realistically beyond Lebanon itself, which is hemmed in by a warzone in the north and its long-time adversary Israel in the south. But there's measured risk and there's recklessness, and I feel that often the two are confused. Activities that many may judge as foolhardy frequently transpire to be nothing of the sort, the dangers illusory and overblown.

Following this brief coastal junket, the thought occurs to me: if I could cycle across Lebanon when so few seemed to think it feasible or wise, could I not go further? Across a larger country, perhaps? Or even a continent? Could I – possibly, at a push, with enough chamois cream and a good tailwind – make it from my home in London *all the way through the Middle East?*

The idea seems absurd. But it comes on with a rush, as if the notion has been sitting there all along just waiting to be found. I will travel with nothing but the barest essentials and speak to local people to understand their concerns. I will peel back the layers of artifice and prejudice to unearth the human stories underneath. And I will do this, like Patrick Leigh Fermor, not as a vagrant or tourist, but as a roaming sage or cognoscenti with an eye to revealing the truth.

At least, this is what I'll tell my mother. Lacking Fermor's earnest romanticism, I harbour few illusions. I am more Sancho Panza than Don Quixote, and arguably more Rocinante than either: ageing and unqualified and – in sporting terms, at least – undoubtedly past my prime.

Like Fermor, however, my destination isn't in doubt. For him, it was the 'mysterious and lopsided' Black Sea and the 'levitating skyline' of Constantinople. For me, it is the dark burgundy foothills of the Alborz, where a city shrouded in mystery lies in a pool of violent sun.

The thought is immediate and unambiguous. If I go anywhere, I know Tehran should be the prize.

INTRODUCTION

'I am neither of the East nor of the West, no boundaries exist within my breast.'
Rumi, thirteenth-century Persian poet

My interest in the Middle East began aged ten with a journey down the Nile.

I remember the trip vividly. My family and I were booked on a boat that would take us from Aswan to Cairo over the course of a week. Each morning, we would rise at 4.30am to reach the temples and tombs before dawn, then return five hours later for a pot of hydrating milky tea. Those early alarm calls felt exhausting, as we were herded blindly onto the coach in the dark – but there was no way around it. By 7am, the sun was already high overhead, gleaming like the blade of an executioner waiting to strike. It felt like a completely different sun from any I'd ever known, not warming or life-affirming but keen-edged and cruel. Among the ruins, clammy tourists in straw fedoras clustered in islands of shade as if shipwrecked and awaiting rescue. Meanwhile, my brother and I would dash from shadow to shadow, pretending the sunny areas were crocodile pits or briny swamplands determined to suck us into their grasp – neither of which felt like such a stretch of the imagination.

For me, the most enjoyable parts of these excursions were the trips underground. Entering the burial chambers felt like being transported into a new world – not a descent into a fiery abyss but into a cool Elysium of gilded sarcophagi, frescoed tombs and beautifully baffling hieroglyphs engraved from ceiling to floor. Here, away from the heat and tumult of the surface, was a subterranean wonderland that glowed in silent splendour; a place where power seemed etched into the earth itself and humans walked shoulder-to-shoulder with the gods.

'Egypt in Arabic is called *Misr*, which means "frontier",' our guide, Abduh, told me one afternoon. I had just escaped a thrashing at table tennis by the loss of our final ball over the balustrade and was sprawled on my belly scouring the water for crocs. 'This suits us, I think. Long ago, we were the great gateway to Africa and Asia. Maybe one day, *inshallah*, we will be again.'

Or this is how I imagine our conversation might have gone based on the spidery mess of jottings in my diary. I kept a journal every holiday until my mid-teens, but the one from Egypt is the most detailed: a tumescent *magnum opus* bursting with Polaroid photographs, primitive hieroglyph sketches, scraps of papyrus and declarations of unrequited love for Abduh, whose great marmot of a moustache and dominance on the ping-pong table more than qualified him in my eyes as husband material.

Egypt fascinated me. What happened to these imposing monuments, I wondered, now eroded and shattered by time? Or to the pharaohs who created them, whose souls were considered divine? It had never occurred to me before how power shifts through the ages, and how empires rise and fall. To me, Britain had always been Great, its position as enduring and inevitable as the air that we breathe. But 5,000 years ago, we were forging homes from dung and willow rods while Egypt was erecting limestone pyramids on foundations the size of ten football pitches. And when Egypt was celebrating its first female leader, it would be another three millennia before we would feel ready to do the same.

Before we parted ways, Abduh gave me a dried lotus flower for my diary. 'You seem to like our country,' he said, as I hastily shut the book so he wouldn't see his name plastered in tiny scarlet hearts across the page. 'Make sure you return. You've only visited a small part of it – the safe, easy bits – and there's so much more to see.'

I promised him I would. Twelve years later I kept my word, and from then my interest in the Middle East grew steadily. Over the next decade, I returned several times to Egypt, both for work and leisure, as well as to elsewhere in the region: Lebanon, Turkey, Oman, the UAE. Each visit revealed more of this cryptic corner of the globe, while exposing how little I truly knew. These places confounded me, each a bewildering Gordian knot of cultures, faiths and histories spanning back far beyond the beginnings of my own native land. As an outsider, I knew that there was a limit to how much I'd ever understand. But I felt a growing desire to at least fulfil my pledge to Abduh: to look beyond the 'safe, easy bits' and see the place raw.

On my return from Lebanon, I immediately began preparing for my journey to Tehran. When asked about it, I told most people I would be 'touring the Middle East'. But this was a quick answer to a complex question because there are many Middle Easts to choose from. There's the one stretching from Morocco to Pakistan and the one from Egypt to Iran. There's the one involving Turkey and Sudan, and the one excluding both. There's the one focused on Arabia and the (rare) one embracing the 'Stans. The lines of this difficult patch of land have never been firmly drawn. Or, more accurately, they've been drawn too many times and never from within. The term itself reveals the problem: middle of what? East of what? Certainly nothing relating to the people who actually live there – people who may justifiably be perplexed by the criteria of this club into which they've been cast.

The idea of the Middle East is a relatively modern phenomenon. In the nineteenth century, Western diplomats preferred a more binary approach, splitting the East into 'Near' and 'Far'. The Far East largely referred to countries beyond India, while the Near East designated a hazy tract of land between India and Europe focused chiefly on the territory ruled by the Ottoman Empire. 'The limits of the Near East are not easy to define,' British historian Arnold Toynbee wrote in 1916. 'On the north-west, Vienna is the most conspicuous boundary-mark, but one might almost equally well single out Trieste, Lvov or even Prague. Towards the south-east, the boundaries are even more shadowy ...' Following World War I, the epithet became fuzzier still, as well as increasingly redundant. Why have a collective term linking parts of Eastern Europe to Western Asia, after all, when the common denominator (the Ottomans) had collapsed?

Meanwhile, the area between Turkey and East Asia was swiftly assuming greater strategic importance. The British soldier and diplomat Thomas Edward Gordon was not the first to label this zone, but in 1900 he became the first to commit the moniker 'Middle East' to paper and therefore into the history archives. For him, the region was centred around Iran and Afghanistan, which he saw as crucial buffers against Russia. Two years later, US naval officer Alfred Thayer Mahan referred to the 'middle East' (sic) to indicate approximately the same area, echoing Gordon's concerns and calling on Britain to strengthen its naval fleets between Suez and Singapore.

Nowadays, this sprawling land of soft borders continues to change shape with the seasons. The US, EU, UK and UN all employ different definitions, each nominally conclusive, their smudgy uncertainties disguised. The frontiers of the so-called 'Middle East' remain so pliable, in fact, that commentators sometimes choose to ignore it and employ more useful, concrete names. The 'Arab world' is one, although this excludes Israel and Iran, both of which most Westerners would see as distinctly 'Middle Eastern'. The 'Islamic world' is another, but this extends far beyond the region into Africa and Asia, with Indonesia and India between them accounting for a quarter of all Muslims across the globe.

So what *is* the Middle East? Nobody really knows, it seems. And yet everybody knows. In the West, its form rises before us, fixed and inviolable, splashed daily across the media. It suggests chaos and repression, conflict and terror. It appears alien and menacingly 'other', with values that clash wildly and incontrovertibly with our own.

It wasn't until recently that I truly began questioning this image. In 2011, as murmurings of protest grew into mass revolt across the region, I was working at the International Bar Association (IBA), a global legal organisation with a tenacious Human Rights Institute. As the IBA's lead reporter, I covered the Arab Spring extensively, with a focus on human rights violations, military abuses and constitutional crises. For the Arab people, this was a time of profound hope and acute despair, as dictators tumbled like dominoes and new devastating forces rose unstoppably in their wake. Every day, the press was filled with reports of gross atrocities almost impossible to imagine – yet what was often missing, I felt, was context. Where had this unrest come from? What was the driver? With two-thirds of its population aged under thirty, the Middle East has long been a young region ruled by old men, so why were these demonstrations happening only now?

The answers to these questions frequently appeared glib. This was a world of simple dichotomies – tyranny versus terror, democracy versus dictatorship, East versus West – while the voices of the people, trapped between the extremes, seemed rarely to be heard at all.

The Middle East has always been a difficult place for Western journalists to cover. It is too thorny, too delicate, too detached from our own immediate concerns. And prejudice is pervasive. Since 9/11, the region has largely been reduced to a troika of incendiary tabloid bullet points – *Bombs! Burqas! Bigots!* – which both reflect and perpetuate bigotry at large. 'It is no coincidence that racist violence is on the rise in the UK at the same time as we see worrying examples of intolerance and hate speech in the newspapers,' Christian Ahlund, chair of the European Commission against Racism and Intolerance (ECRI), said in 2016.

His comments followed an ECRI report that was particularly critical of the *Sun*, *Daily Mail* and *Daily Express* for 'fuelling prejudice against Muslims' with 'reckless disregard'.

More recently, the outgoing chair of the Independent Press Standards Organisation, Alan Moses, echoed these concerns. 'I have a suspicion that [Muslims] are from time to time written about in a way that [newspapers] would simply not write about Jews or Roman Catholics,' he remarked in December 2019. In fact, he said, the portrayal of Islam had been 'the most difficult issue' he had faced during his five-year tenure as head of the watchdog.

It is not just the British media exhibiting these worrying trends. In 2015, a study by the universities of Illinois and Arkansas reported that 81 per cent of domestic terrorists presented on US news broadcasts were identified as Muslim, despite the fact that – according to FBI data – Muslims only comprised 6 per cent of all domestic terror suspects in reality. Likewise, research by the consultancy firm 416 Labs found that only 8 per cent of *New York Times* headlines about Muslims from 1990 to 2014 were about positive issues, while 57 per cent were negative. Its investigation concluded that the average reader is 'likely to assign collective responsibility to Islam/Muslims for the violent actions of a few'.

In recent years, far-right Western leaders such as Donald Trump, Viktor Orbán and Andrzej Duda have done their best to fan these flames, bolstering the strength and legitimacy of Islamophobia throughout the world. With such powerful voices shaping the public narrative, it hardly seems surprising that most Europeans have come to view Syrian and Iraqi refugees as a 'major threat', even though their chance of being murdered by a jihadist is roughly the same as being struck and killed by lightning. Or that three-quarters of Americans say they're too scared to travel to the Arab world because of its perceived dangers – despite the fact that eight in ten cannot even identify the region on a map.[1]

[1]   Survey data from the Pew Research Center (2016) and YouGov (2017).

While covering the Middle East, I wrestled with how to cut through this bombast. Was there a way to depict the region with a clearer lens? The problem was not simply the bias in the media, I knew, but the nature of journalism itself: an industry led by crises and conflict – 'if it bleeds, it leads' – because this, on the whole, is what people want to read. Dominated by stories of violence and villains, the media inevitably paints a deeply distorted image of the world in which dangers are magnified and the very worst events come to appear as the norm.

What was needed, I felt, was a new type of reporting – one that shifted the focus away from politics and bloodshed to the everyday lives that lay beyond. One that depicted the region not as a homogeneous sphere of chaos and fanaticism but as a sweeping, splintered mosaic, often as different from itself as from those looking in from elsewhere.

What I needed, I knew after my brief jaunt through Lebanon, was a *bike*.

When I told friends and family that I planned to cycle alone from London to Tehran, the response was mixed. Many were supportive, several … less so. Most people's concerns focused on three core personal traits that, notwithstanding some tremendous good luck on my part, would in all likelihood prove my undoing: being a woman (vulnerable to sex pests); being a Westerner (vulnerable to terrorists); and being a journalist (vulnerable to tyrants).

'We think you'll probably die,' one friend helpfully informed me, looking at me with the kind of wary fondness usually reserved for unruly toddlers or puppies that have soiled the carpet. 'We've put the odds at about 60:40.' Others were less optimistic. A family member with a particularly unfortunate sense of humour sent me a copy of Rudyard Kipling's 'If', stressing the importance of keeping my head 'when all about you / Are losing theirs', while a man in the pub described me as a 'naive idiot who'll end up decapitated in a ditch – at best'.

My mother took it well, all things considered. At least, she didn't burn my passport or call the local sanatorium to have me committed. She did write me an email, however, to clarify her feelings in case there had been any ambiguity on the matter. 'You cannot imagine how devastated I feel ...' it began, before launching into a calm and measured analysis of the potential pitfalls awaiting me along the way. The words 'dangerous', 'reckless', 'hostile', 'juvenile', 'dangerous' (again), 'terrible worry', 'risking life and limb', 'robbed and raped' and 'family disintegrating' were all used to persuasive effect, alongside a restrained smattering of a dozen or so exclamation marks to emphasise the most salient points. In response, I'd done what any loving daughter would do in such circumstances – I'd hugged and kissed and reassured and comforted ... and continued to do exactly as I pleased without another thought.

It was my boyfriend, however, who was likely to be affected the most. P (as I'll refer to him here) and I had been going out for three years and living together for two when I told him of my plan. It wasn't a request for permission; it was a statement of fact. And he accepted it, albeit grudgingly, and put up no serious objection. It wasn't until later that it occurred to me how unreasonable I'd been, and how in his situation I may not have been quite so understanding. While I've never been good at compromise, even for me this level of blinkered obduracy was extreme. I loved my boyfriend, yet I had a driving compulsion to do this trip, however foolish or ill-advised to some it may have seemed.

It didn't help matters that I was leaving at the height of the Syrian War, when Islamic State was at its strongest and the refugee crisis at its most severe. By the end of 2015, nearly five million people had fled Syria – double the number of the previous year – and jihadist killings were mounting. In the months before my departure, ISIS captured Ramadi in Iraq, Palmyra in Syria and Sirte in Libya, and claimed responsibility for the murder of hundreds of civilians across Syria, Iraq, Turkey, Egypt, Kuwait, Tunisia, Yemen and Saudi Arabia.

Because of this, there seemed to be an assumption by some that I was courting risk simply for the thrill of it; that the threat of death or disaster was, at some level, part of the point. But I am no adrenalin junkie, and I was in fact keen to survive the endeavour. In my mind, as with the Lebanese trip, the risks were measured. The jihadists, far from running amok across the region, were in reality circumscribed and avoidable – and I fully intended to avoid them. I would not be entering live warzones, such as Libya or Syria, or terrorist hotspots, such as the borders of Syria or Iraq. A handful of courageous journalists were risking their lives by reporting from such places, but that wasn't what my journey was about. My journey was about the people outside these areas who comprise the vast majority of the Middle East: the silent 99.9 per cent who are stifled by the deafening minority every day.

It was a refrain I repeated to my mother on regular occasions but one that also happened to be true: I wasn't doing the trip because I believed it would be dangerous; I was doing it because I was convinced it would be safe.

There were problematic aspects to my plan, I knew. Though well-meaning in intent, it carried the weight of history with it. Europeans have been venturing to distant shores for hundreds of years for personal and political gain, inspecting the world much as a zoologist might scrutinise specimens in a lab. The history of exploration is bound up with exploitation, from the early seafarers who sought riches and fame, to the later cartographers, Arabists and spies who worked in the shadows of empire. Even someone such as Wilfred Thesiger, the famous British officer and explorer who travelled to connect rather than conquer and spent years living among the Marsh Arabs and Kurds, was the product of the imperial system ('He seemed ... as though he'd just been awarded his First Field Colours,' he once pompously replied to a student when asked his opinion of a murderous Danikil tribesman, in reference to a sports prize given out at Eton).

These people may overwhelmingly have been men – and

wealthy, public school men at that – but there was no denying that, as a white British traveller journeying through the Middle East, I would be following in some controversial and insalubrious footsteps. My trip may not have been incentivised by money or power, but there was undoubtedly more than a whiff of vanity about the endeavour. I wanted to learn about the region's history, culture and people, yes. But I also wanted to prove myself, to have an adventure, to enjoy as absolute a sense of freedom as possible without sprouting a pair of wings.

The journey, I knew, would be an exercise in privilege. Due to the lottery of circumstance, I would be whisking in and out of places where others were trapped, enjoying a personal liberty that many couldn't share. I would return home to accolades and applause – and the publication of this book, itself an emblem of privilege – while those making far more courageous journeys would face abuse, resentment and arrest. All of this couldn't help but leave a sour taste in the mouth. It also made me more than aware of the irony when people warned me of the potential perils of the trip. Could I really be worried when I was the one, ultimately, in the position of power? When I, with my pallid skin and purple passport, symbolised one of the greatest threats ever to impact the Middle East: namely, the hegemony of the imperialist West?

I couldn't change my heritage. But perhaps, I felt, I could use the journey to take a good look at myself. I could try to improve my understanding of the connections between our worlds, and of my complicity in the difficulties facing the region today.

The reality is that the Middle East cannot shake the past because it continues to bear the scars. Long before oil was discovered, the region was a battleground for global power struggles between East and West, each jostling for dominance with little concern for the people over whom they fought. It is no coincidence that the largest 2011 protests occurred in countries with a recent colonial legacy, where dictators had risen from the ashes of empire either to challenge Western supremacy (Muammar Gaddafi, Bashar al-Assad) or to collaborate and benefit from its largesse (Hosni Mubarak, Ben Ali, Ali Abdullah Saleh). In both situations, homegrown tyrants became a kind of mirror image of the imperial powers they replaced, maintaining control largely through violence, coercion and fear.

Through their autocratic allies, Western powers have been able to maintain their influence in the Middle East to the present day. Colonialism may have ended, yet colonial-era policies continue to impact the region through diplomatic meddling, military intervention and a global economic system that benefits kleptocratic regimes over the public at large. In the lead-up to the Arab Spring, fiscal reforms imposed by institutions such as the International Monetary Fund and World Bank helped to rip apart societies that did not have the transparency or accountability to support them, redirecting public funds into the hands of a cosy nepotistic elite. Meanwhile, the West remained characteristically blind to the consequences of its actions. In 2010, as Egypt creaked under the most severe inequality it had experienced since the feudalistic 1950s, the World Bank was branding the country its 'top Middle East reformer' for the third year in a row and praising Mubarak's 'bold' and 'prudent' governorship. A few months later, the country erupted in flames.

The protests, therefore, were not simply a call for a more 'Western' way of life, as they have so often been portrayed. They were also, just as clearly, a rejection of the West-sponsored injustices that have beleaguered the Middle East for so long. In this way, the West could be seen as both cause and cure of the Arab Spring: a paradoxical symbol of *liberté*, *égalité* and *fraternité* on the one hand, and exploitation, expedience and hypocrisy on the other.

Tragically, despite the courage of the participants, the bulk of the revolutions failed (in the short term, at least); Syria, Libya and Yemen descended into civil war, while Egypt found itself tightly bound in fetters once more. In the meantime, paranoid despots used the unrest as an excuse to crack down on civil rights across the region, from the harassment of local activists and journalists to the expulsion of foreign aid workers and NGOs. Indeed, it is this suffocation of freedoms, and not Islamic State or al-Qaeda or any of the other fanatical groups who consistently dominate the news agenda, which constitutes the main threat facing the region today.

And it would be this heavy repression, as stifling as the summer heat, which – beyond terrorists, criminals, perverts, poor drivers and all the other manifold risks I was warned about before I left – I would most come to fear and resent during the twelve months I spent on the road.

My route, which was designed to cross as much of the Middle East as possible on my way to Iran, ultimately comprised twenty countries: the UK, France, Switzerland, Italy, Slovenia, Croatia, Bosnia, Montenegro, Albania, Serbia, Kosovo, Bulgaria, Turkey, Lebanon, Jordan, Egypt, Sudan, Oman, the UAE and Iran. But why pick Tehran as the finish line, you may ask? Well, Iran more than any other nation in the region has arguably experienced the most devastating impact of Western interference in recent times. A direct line can easily be drawn between the MI6- and CIA-sponsored coup that ousted the democratic leader Mohammad Mosaddegh in 1953 and the 1979 Revolution that ushered in the oppressive Islamist regime that remains in power today. Since this time, Iran has been vilified by the international community as a dangerous, fanatical backwater – and Western travellers have largely stayed away.

Yet the more I read and wrote about Iran, the more this image began to appear both simplistic and flawed. The Islamic Republic seemed to me a tale of two countries, starkly divided between the conservative, insular ruling clerics on the one hand, who viewed the outside world with scorn, and the more progressive, outward-looking populace on the other, who embraced it with warmth. This somewhat crude, bipartite analysis had problems of its own,

I was sure. But this apparent disconnect – between politics and the people – fascinated me. As my plans for the trip began to take shape, I knew my journey could only end there.

But endings, of course, need beginnings ... So, with no further ado, let me leave these introductory notes here and kick this story off. I very much hope that you enjoy the ride.

Chapter 1

THE LURE OF THE UNKNOWN

Western Europe

*'The door to the east lies open: O you who strive
after leaving, enter it with a glad greeting! Seize the
chance of freedom from the cares of the world ...'*
Ibn Jubayr, twelfth-century Arab traveller

First, a confession. I am not a cyclist. I am, at a push, someone who cycles.

My apologies, therefore, to anyone who bought this book under false pretences. But if you're hoping for rousing tales of sporting prowess or pushing the limits of physical endurance then I advise you to stop reading here. Likewise, if you're after an informed analysis of the difference between cantilever and caliper brakes, or the pros and cons of an internal gear hub, this probably isn't the book for you. No hard feelings – just drop it back and request a refund. We'll pretend you were never here.

The truth is, examining my credentials in the run-up to departure, I was not an obvious contender to attempt an 11,000-kilometre, year-long bike ride halfway across the world. I was not particularly fit, had no sense of direction and held uncharitable views about people in spandex. It was at least six years since I'd last cycled up a hill.

While I rode my bicycle almost every day in London, I did so on a light carbon racer that I mainly used to commute: a round trip of precisely fifteen kilometres. Prior to departure, I clocked up a total of zero hours of training (why waste time trying to get fit in advance, I reasoned, when I could just do this on the road?) and instead focused on purchasing equipment, researching the route and organising logistics. I had at least done one semi-long cycle before, I consoled myself: a London-to-Paris charity event I'd undertaken as a reporting assignment in 2009 alongside twenty-four strapping policemen. Admittedly, I'd been in Team Rhino, the slowest of the three groups (later re-christened 'Team Wino' for reasons I found deeply unfair), and was travelling baggage-free courtesy of the support vehicle that accompanied us. But these, I felt, were mere details. I had completed the ride without injury or disaster, and that surely was what counted.

I set my leaving date as 20 July 2015 – in the (ultimately vain) hope that this would give me time to make it through the Sahara and Gulf before the searing heat of spring – and, as this day approached, I tried my best not to focus on the magnitude of the endeavour in front of me. Nonetheless, I could feel the tension lurking inside, coiling tightly about my chest and gut. Nights were the worst, when my worries broke free from their daytime shackles and beat about my head like bats in a cave. The same thoughts circled endlessly: *why am I doing this? Should I be doing this? Am I able to do this?* And the unsettling notion that every person is forced to confront at some point in their lives: *what if my mother is right …?!*

It didn't help my nerves that I didn't have a bicycle. While I had generously been donated one by Kona, it was coming fresh off the production line and wasn't due to arrive until the day before departure, meaning I wouldn't have time to practise on it or have it adjusted to fit my body. This, however, felt like a small price to pay for the privilege of owning a beautiful new tour bike – one that I knew would not only be a strong and reliable companion on the road but the name of which added a frisson of excitement to the idea of having it nestled between my legs for a year: the Kona Sutra 2016.

I have long been an advocate of diving in at the deep end. When we were toddlers, my parents taught me and my brother to cycle by running alongside our bikes holding our handlebars and then abruptly letting go, at which point we would crash with brutal predictability into a prickly shrubbery or onto the concrete flagstones. It was a painful, chastening experience that seared itself long onto both my memory and my cranium, and it strikes me now that a period with stabilisers might not have been such a bad idea. But the method was an effective one. It didn't take long before we both realised it was in our best interest to stay upright, veering away from the rocks and thorns like a workhorse cowering from the whip.

The mind and body are astonishingly resilient things when put to the test. Ability is overrated, I've always felt; it is proclivity that counts – the instinct and readiness to succeed. So I resolved just to get on my bike and deal with the trivial problem of having no idea what I was doing once it was too late to back out from actually doing it. There are few things harder than setting off, after all: that sharp, bracing blow when the floor is pulled out from under you or the safety catch released.

After that, surely, half the battle would already be won?

The night before I'm due to leave, I am already regretting this course of action. I feel chronically underprepared and wish fervently to delay. Having left my job only three weeks ago, I've spent every minute since then scouting for sponsors, tying up loose admin and purchasing gear – leaving very little time to pack.

At 9pm, the living room is carpeted with a colourful medley of bike tour 'essentials', from a mini-tripod and inflatable chair to a collapsible wine glass and silver-plated hipflask. In my 'electricals' pile alone, I have three cameras (a DSLR, Go-Pro and camcorder), a laptop, a Dictaphone, a solar-powered battery charger, a normal battery charger, a Kindle, a travel speaker, a satellite tracker – bought by P and my parents as a safety measure – a mini-iPod and an iPhone 4. Beside this heap is a knotted lump of cables the size of a basketball that I feel obliged to include because I removed all the wires from their respective boxes and now have no idea which ones go with which pieces of equipment.

And in the centre, perched with elegant insouciance against the armchair, sits my most prized possession: my ukulele.

It does seem rather a lot of things when they're laid out like that, I admit. But I console myself that my haul at least pales in comparison to the items ferried by camel train across the desert by the explorer and Arabist Gertrude Bell in the early 1900s, which included folding tables with linen tablecloths, a trunk of hats and parasols, a Wedgewood dinner service, a canvas bed and bath, and as many pieces of weaponry as she could strap to her stockinged calves beneath layers of lacy undergarments.[2] That was a different era, of course, and I've no doubt that even Ms Bell would have discarded the odd chaise longue or two if she'd been forced to carry everything herself. But there's sadly no time to distil the cargo now. By the time everything is squeezed into my four panniers, rucksack and bar bag, the total load including the bike weighs nearly ten stone. And that's before my bottles of water and gin are added, and my hardback copy of Miss F.J. Erskine's *Lady Cycling: What to Wear & How to Ride*: a must-read for any serious female tour cyclist ('Wool above, wool below, wool all over, such is the Medes and Persians hygienic rule for cycling,' the author counsels wisely. 'It is essential to have well-cut knickerbockers in lieu of skirts ...').

Having never cycled with panniers before – especially ones swollen and bulging like a blocked water main – I wonder whether it might be prudent to take a test ride. However, it is already dark outside, so instead I place the bike on its side and practise trying to pick it up. Ten minutes later I call for P, and together the two

---

[2] Even Bell could not rival the baggage eccentricities of Lord Byron, however, who, on one of his journeys, reportedly carried a pair of geese to cook for food, but was forced ultimately to take them home with him when he couldn't bear to have them killed.

of us manage with some difficulty to heave it upright and rest it awkwardly against the wall.

'Feeling prepared?' P asks, a little unkindly.

'Yes,' I say. 'I'll get used to it.'

'You definitely need a whole litre of chamois cream? That's a lot of chafing.'

'You never know.'

'And seriously, a ukulele? Who do you think you are? Laurie Lee?'

The romantic in me protests vehemently, while the cynic concedes he may have a point. Aged thirty-plus, with a mortgage and long-term partner, I can no longer claim to operate in Lee's 'swinging, weightless realm' of endless unmapped potential, 'when the body burns magic fuels, so that it seems to glide in warm air, about a foot off the ground'. My gliding days are over, and my fuel tends to be the kind you purchase from crooked roadside mechanics in Karakalpakstan. However, I admit I struggle to discount this image entirely. In recent weeks, I cannot deny having entertained the occasional quixotic vision of the road ahead, in which I've imagined myself in some kind of meadow or bucolic pastureland, strumming a plaintive folk ballad while local herdsmen and wildlife gather around to listen. In these passing fancies, people would be clapping and cheering, birds swooping and singing, and nearby fauna would be looking on with that wistful poise we all know from classics such as *Watership Down* and *Bambi*.

P, however, appears to see things differently. 'Well, at least it'll act as a good deterrent,' he says, handing me an enormous goblet of red wine. 'A few bars of "The Lancashire Hot Pot Swingers" and no self-respecting thief or murderer is likely to hang about for long.'

My alarm sounds at 6.30am. Then 6.45am. Then 7am. Getting up feels like a momentous effort. The day looms bright and fierce, ablaze with a lifetime of anticipation. With my eyes still closed, I flex my left arm, my last remaining hope for delay. Since having my typhoid jab a week ago, I've felt like I've been having daily wrestles with Tyson Fury. Lying in bed each night, I've passed the sleepless hours imagining myself as the heroin addict in *Requiem for a Dream*, my bicep turning mushy and gangrenous as I cry out deliriously, heroically, that I'm leaving no matter what, only to be dragged off by medics and sedated.

But it isn't to be. My arm feels fine. I feel fine. The weather is perfect. So, summoning all the willpower I possess, I finally drag myself up, change into my cycling gear – sleeveless top, shorts, padded underpants, sports sandals – and prepare a modest breakfast of cornflakes, three crumpets, two bananas, a blueberry muffin and three cups of tea, drawing out these final moments of comfort and familiarity as long as I can. It is fortunate, perhaps, that this initial ride is going to be easier than the rest, as P has offered to drive my panniers to my sister's house in Bolney, West Sussex, where we're due to meet my parents before I board the ferry to France. So I will enjoy the shameful indulgence of cycling the first few hours David Cameron-style, with accompanying support vehicle and entourage.

The day begins well. The sun is a pale lemon disc, warm but not hot, and my doubts and restlessness fall away as I weave my way south around cars trapped in rigid jams. *This is easy*, I think, conveniently forgetting that I'm carrying about a tenth of the weight I should be. *What was all the fuss?*

Then I enter Croydon – and I hope I never have to say those words again. Does it ever end? It reminds me of Montana, which I once travelled through during a Greyhound bus trip around America, hoping to be as enamoured with the 'land of the shining mountains' as John Steinbeck had been during his (admittedly largely fanciful) journey through the state five decades earlier. Instead, I recall falling asleep at the border and awaking what seemed like several months later to exactly the same fields of wheat and skipping tumbleweed, wondering if this was where time went to die. Croydon feels the same. It is also necessary to climb a gruesome hill to escape it, which may explain why so many people end up staying there.

The hill is truly fierce. As I edge my way up in fitful wheezes and gasps, it occurs to me that cycling on a slope is an entirely different proposition to cycling on flat ground. A different sport altogether, in fact. Ridiculous as it may sound, it never occurred to me to examine the terrain between here and Iran; instead, in an act of hubristic folly, I pored over the map like a giant or god, teleporting myself with seamless ease from one point to the next. Because of this, I have no idea what lofty horrors might lie in store – and I find myself suddenly gripped by panic. Could I plot a route that bypasses all but the most meagre of gradients, I wonder? Would that not be a feat admirable in itself, for its creative cartography, perhaps, if not its athleticism?

For now, however, I have no option but to continue. If nothing else, the idea of having crossed Croydon for nothing is unconscionable. So I press on, exhausted, and eventually make it to the top of the hill and onwards to Bolney by lunch. The meal is a jolly affair. Over champagne and fish pie, I am treated to a hamper of generous gifts from my sister – including two rape alarms ('one for convenience, one for volume') – as well as useful advice on how to dislocate a man's thumb if attacked ('bend, twist and pull!').

Then, before I know it, it is time to say goodbye and I find myself enveloped in a series of smothering bear-hugs. 'Please be careful,' my father cautions. Aged eighty-seven, he recently began a course of chemotherapy for chronic lymphocytic leukaemia, although as ever he's doing his best to appear spry. 'Remember: call if you need *anything*. BLAST [the 'Becky Lowe Action Support Team', founded by my long-suffering parents two decades ago] will be waiting!'

'And don't speak to any strange men,' my mother adds. 'Unless they're very handsome, of course.'

P and I say our goodbyes at the dock. It will be two months before we meet again, although it doesn't feel like it. All day long

I've felt an odd sense of detachment from my surroundings, as if it is not me going away but someone else entirely. Rather than fear or excitement, all I feel is a tremor of adrenalin low in my abdomen, like the whirr of a generator gently powering me on. It's as if all extraneous emotion has been harnessed to the challenge ahead, just as oxygen is channelled to the core muscles of long-distance runners to help spur them towards the finish line.

'Call me when you arrive,' P says, giving me a hug. 'And try not to get lost between here and Dieppe.'

'It's just a direct ferry ride,' I reply.

'Yes. I know what you're like.'

On the boat, a couple spot me with my bike and ask where I'm going. They seem impressed when I say Iran but immediately assume that I'm single and searching for love on the road. It is a response I'll come to know well. Male travellers generally require little rationalisation, I find, while women are often suspected of having an ulterior motive: mending a broken heart, perhaps, or soothing a troubled soul. Perhaps there's some truth to this – but what of Dervla Murphy or Gertrude Bell, who carried souls as tough as bootstraps? Or Hester Stanhope, Freya Stark, Mary Kingsley, Nellie Bly?[3] Or the growing number of female pioneers today, whose aims and hopes and fears are as disparate as any of the men who've gone before?

I have already outlined my reasons for doing this trip. But these are really only the justifications. Beyond them lies a deeper urge far harder to explain. George Mallory famously climbed Everest because it was 'there'. Wilfred Thesiger was drawn to Arabia for 'the lure of the unknown'. Ibn Battuta relished the

---

[3] Interestingly, few of these women would have described themselves as feminists. Bell and Stark were even allied as young women with the anti-suffrage movement, and both openly preferred the company of men to women. Yet they were clearly feminists in action if not intention, carving out independent, intrepid careers that arguably did more to inspire generations of women than the most fervent of placard-wielding activists.

idea of turning from speechlessness 'into a storyteller'.[4] Ask any traveller and their answer will most likely be infuriatingly vague: both everything and nothing; to go mad and stay sane. It's a black hole of obfuscation where some see eternity and others a dead star. In this way, travellers are the ultimate paradox. They crave knowledge and secrets, enlightenment and bewilderment. They want both to decipher the mystery and delight in it; to expose the world, while mourning, in the words of Robert Macfarlane, 'the diminishing limits of the unfamiliar'.

In the ferry lounge, I buy a bottle of 2010 Chateau Lieujean Haut-Medoc and watch as the Newhaven shoreline slips quietly between the sky and the sea. Soon the tremor in my gut begins to settle and the brittle reality of the venture ahead assumes a softer glow. *I can do this*, I think. And for the first time, as the cool sea air turns from white to gold to violet to silver-grey, I think that maybe I truly can.

My relationship with the Dieppe hotelier gets off to a bad start. This is perhaps unsurprising, as I startle her awake at 11pm by crashing through the door with my big dirty *vélo*. She is wearing a cotton nightgown and is small and angular, all elbows, knees and nostrils. She twists into the room like a spindle, hisses at me to *taisez vous* and disappears again with a dismissive swipe of her hand. *So French!* I think delightedly.

The next morning, I rise early to pack for departure. But without a bicycle stand, attaching the bags to the luggage racks proves a challenge. First, I rest the bike against a sturdy-seeming potted plant, which promptly collapses. Then I try the hedge. But hedges are thorny, hateful things and not to be trusted. This one gives a veneer of helpfulness before rearing up on its bushy haunches and swallowing my bike whole. It isn't until 10am, two

---

[4] Ibn Battuta was a fourteenth-century Moroccan explorer who spent twenty-nine years travelling 75,000 miles across the Middle East and North Africa: five times the distance covered by Marco Polo.

hours later than planned, that I am finally ready to leave – but this poses some difficulties too. Rather than cycling directly from the hotel, where I fear I may have witnesses, I instead walk a hundred yards down the lane, where I mount my steed with what I hope may be mistaken for a nonchalant swing of the leg. Then, with a sharp push, I veer away from the fence, launch myself erratically off the kerb and collide with the side of a Vespa. Glancing around, I'm relieved that nobody seems to be watching except a herd of enormous cows. They stare at me disdainfully. I try again and stagger with inevitable futility into the path of an oncoming van. *Ah yes*, I remind myself. *People drive on the right in France.*

Disheartened, I stop for a rest. Cycling with panniers already feels exhausting. I've made progress, at least: about ten metres, to be precise. I do some calculations. At this rate it will take me approximately fifty-eight years to complete the trip. And P, I suspect, may have got bored of waiting.

Eventually, however, many failed attempts later, I achieve a kind of unsteady rhythm – even if this rhythm, as it turns out, is largely misdirected. For the next few hours, I circle and backtrack along a muddled contortion of backroads, often arriving after twenty or thirty minutes in broadly the same spot as where I started. By the time I locate the highway, I feel almost ready to give up for the day. But here I finally begin to make good progress, the weight of my bike propelling me over its soaring undulations like a bowling ball aimed at the pins.

The miles start to flash by, although I'm mindful of overdoing it. 'It is important that ladies should only go moderate distances at first,' the ever-perspicacious Miss F.J. Erskine advises. 'Any day's work over forty miles is too much.' I take her words to heart. By 5pm, having covered an extravagant forty-*three* miles, I pull into Forges-les-Eaux flush with elation and relief. Relief that I'm alive; relief that I can steer; relief that my bags, which seemed so uncompromisingly cumbrous on the ground, can move – *and efficiently* – when annexed to the body of the bike. Keen to celebrate these ostensibly minor but momentarily earth-shattering achievements, I take a turn about town to see what it has to offer. Known primarily for its thermal waters, Forges-les-Eaux has a large central square and pretty river with a green, pearlescent sheen. But limited life can be found today. Some cafés and *bartabacs* are open, but most places are closed. And nowhere has wifi except the tourist office, which is also closed.

Admitting defeat, I buy a Camembert and baguette and return to the town periphery to find somewhere to camp. After a little exploration, I discover the ideal place – a beautiful meadow bathed in buttery sunlight, accessed by a slender track choked by dense foliage – and I feel a wave of pure contentment as I erect my tent and shake off the rigours and strains of the day.

Then, with a jolt, I realise I forgot to pack my gin – and immediately my mood shifts. Here I am, alone, exhausted and inescapably sober, with nothing to soothe my nerves as the chill of night descends. For the next few hours, I lie shrink-wrapped in my sleeping bag, ice-cold and alert, every sound and shadow as sharp as the prick of a knife. My mind drifts: to the derelict farmhouses I passed today, which reminded me of the psychopath's lair in the film *Wolf Creek*; to the jungly vegetation outside, which initially seemed so enchanting but in the dark of a moonless night calls to mind the carnivorous algae in the novel *Life of Pi*; to every faintly disturbing story, book and movie I've ever encountered, which rise from my subconscious like steam from a gutter, haunting my thoughts and permeating my dreams.

I feel uneasy and lonelier than I've ever been. And – *by god* – I still have 11,000 kilometres left to go.

'We're not Poland or Hungary,' the shopkeeper says as he fills paper bags with cherries in the central *arrondissement* of St Germain, Paris. 'Muslims are *pas de problème*. But if they cannot accept our *liberté*, then we have problem.'

Around one in fourteen people in France are Muslim, making it the most Islamic country in the West. Many are second- and third- generation immigrants whose families arrived from the former North African colonies several decades ago. Historically, public attitudes to these communities have been fairly positive. Surveys suggest that the French view Muslims more favourably than any other European country except Germany and Britain, while Muslims have affirmed their sense of attachment towards France. When I arrive in Paris, however, tensions are clear. The brutal ISIS attacks that left 130 people dead are yet to occur, but the *Charlie Hebdo* shootings and a series of smaller attacks, including a beheading near Lyon, have shocked the nation.

'We *absolument* condemn these attacks,' a young Muslim cleric says after approaching me outside the Great Mosque. The pearly white Moorish building was built in 1922 in memory of the Muslim *tirailleurs* killed fighting for France during World War I and was later used by the Algerian imam Si Kaddour Benghabrit as a refuge for Jews during the Nazi occupation. 'This isn't Islam. These men don't come to mosque. Their ideas are from *la propagande*.'

The further from the centre I cycle, the more the city seems to unravel, and the *Périphérique* ring-road feels like a frontier between worlds. The air seems denser on the other side, the light duller, while Brutalist concrete blocks clog the skyline, pockmarked and cinereal grey. Soon, I find myself passing through La Grande Borne in the southern *banlieue* of Grigny. Designed initially as a socialist utopia but inhabited mainly by impoverished residents of Arab or African origin, *cités* like this are now places of 'geographic, social and ethnic apartheid', according to the former French prime minister Manuel Valls. Today, the only people I encounter are an elderly Chinese man fiddling with his moped engine, which coughs and spews black smoke, and two young men on a side street smoking weed. Nearby, broken bottles lie heaped beneath a torn Givenchy poster on which the 'e' has been transformed into a noose with dashes of khaki paint.

I approach the two men and ask directions to strike up conversation. They are both dressed in grey tracksuits and one has a *hamsa* (hand of God) tattooed on his arm. They speak broken, hesitant English.

'He *idiot*,' the one without the tattoo, Benjamin, says when the conversation turns to Amédy Coulibaly, an Islamic State sympathiser from La Grande Borne who killed five people in the wake of the *Hebdo* attacks. 'Always in trouble.'

'You're Muslim?' I ask.

'Yes.'

'Kind of.' His friend, Hakim, smiles. 'We try.'

The boys, both eighteen, grew up here, though Benjamin's family originates from Morocco and Hakim's from Algeria. I ask if they enjoy living in France and they glance at each other.

'Yes,' Hakim says.

'No,' Benjamin says.

They both grin nervously.

'We love France, but ...' Hakim pauses to pass me the joint. 'Here we have – how you say? – *laïcité* [secularism]. Some people see us as threat. And then some Muslims get angry.'

'Angry?'

'In words, I mean. But sometimes – *boom boom*!' He mimics shooting a gun.

'No, she'll think we're terrorist!' Benjamin turns to me. 'We're not terrorist. We're rappers.'

I laugh, but he's serious. 'No, *c'est vrai*. Music is our passion.'

I request a performance, but they both turn shy. Instead, I ask where they think of as home. 'France? Morocco? Algeria?'

'France,' Hakim says. 'But my parents maybe *Algérie*. We speak Arabic at home. My grandfather knows people killed by France in the war.'

France has long tried to suppress troubling aspects of its colonial history. Yet in the *banlieues* the ghosts of the past continue to rise. A focus of France's 'civilising' mission abroad, Algeria was under French rule from 1830 to 1962 and only achieved independence following a brutal eight-year conflict in which atrocities were committed by both sides. Textbooks are sparse on the details, however, and while President Macron recently took the ground-breaking step of acknowledging wartime crimes, wounds from the period remain raw.

Relations with Morocco, a former French protectorate, are similarly sensitive. 'What does Morocco mean to a Frenchman?' George Orwell asked scathingly in his 1939 essay 'Marrakech'. 'An orange-grove or a job in government service. Or to an Englishman? Camels, castles, palm trees, Foreign Legionnaires, brass trays and bandits. One could probably live there for years without noticing that for nine-tenths of the people, the reality of life is an endless, back-breaking struggle to wring a little food out of an eroded soil.'

Plagued by conflicted identities and frustrated by years of neglect, North African migrants have sporadically taken to the streets to protest and riot in recent years, while extremism has steadily grown. Born into a Malian immigrant family, Coulibaly was reportedly radicalised by an Algerian in prison, where – although official records don't exist – estimates suggest an astonishing half of all inmates are Muslim.

Hakim tells me he has been arrested twice and has several friends in prison 'for no reason'. 'The government doesn't care about us,' he says. 'There's no *égalité* here.'

'You don't feel you can progress?' I ask. 'Get a good education? A good job?'

'Good jobs are for people from the right neighbourhoods. If I apply for work, I never say where I live.'

Neither of the boys believe any of this is an excuse for violence, however.

'You can't blame France for Coulibaly,' Benjamin says. 'He is – how you say ...?' He flicks the dead joint over a hedge. '*Psychopath.*'

France is familiar terrain, yet on a bike it feels vast and unconquerable. Days turn into weeks as I labour across the rich, rolling farmland that dips and crests with gentle constancy.

Villages appear and recede, each a rustic idyll of cobbled lanes, stone homesteads and ivy-clad barns. Flowers sprout everywhere, on walls and windows, balconies and balustrades, and I am saturated by smells: honeysuckle, cinnamon, lavender, manure.

Most nights I wild camp, although it's a skill that needs to be learnt. More often than not, I leave my search for a site too late, culminating in a panicked dash into the undergrowth as if I were Jonathan Harker trying to escape the Carpathian mountains before sundown. Eventually, however, I begin to develop an instinct for finding the best spots: somewhere close to civilisation, ideally, yet also tucked away from view. Riverbanks are my favourite places, allowing me to wind down in restful solitude accompanied only by the soft murmur of water and the occasional inquisitive mallard.

Through the deepening summer heat, I progress slowly southeast. By mid-August, the mercury has climbed to 37°C and, unused to such temperatures, my body struggles to cope: my lower back burns, my right hand goes numb and my Achilles tendons creak ominously. One afternoon, I collapse wearily on the roadside after a long, sweltering ride, and – to my immense and enduring shame – adopt an unconvincing Keyser Söze-esque limp in order to hitch a lift to the next village in a truck of topless farmers.

Adding to my discomfort is my Brooks saddle, which appears to be constructed from some form of steel-reinforced granite. While I've been reliably informed it will 'soften up' eventually, at this stage I hardly see how that's possible short of performing *La fille mal gardée*'s clog dance on it every morning. The day it transforms into a sugary puff of clouds and fairy-dust will certainly be a day of celebration, and will no doubt go down as one of history's greatest scientific marvels.

None of these ailments and irritations would feel so onerous if only I could share them with someone. But it is August and France is almost entirely empty. Cafés and restaurants are closed, *patisseries* and *boulangeries* abandoned. In a *commune* called Sens, I meet a retired oil-rig worker named Remy who believes

France is now a ghost-town due to a recent crackdown on drink-driving. 'They've killed the country,' he tells me – before adding, perhaps unnecessarily, 'like Mussolini.' As if to compensate, he and his friends appear to be drinking enough for the rest of France put together. Remy is clearly the ringleader of the group and turns out to have travelled extensively across the world. He likes Iran the most 'because of the people', he says, and Britain the least because he ''ates the Eenglish'. Why, I ask? 'I'm just joking!' he responds jovially. 'Though actually I do 'ate them. Not really.'

I ask him about people's attitudes to Islam here. 'People like to make *amalgame*,' he says. A conflation of terrorists with Muslims. 'I think we go in a dangerous direction.'

'Dangerous? Really?'

'*Oui!* Here, secularism is *idéologie*. People are easily scared.'

After three weeks crossing rural France, Geneva feels intimidatingly dynamic. Trams rattle by, everyone speaks English and chain stores hum with industry and excess. The place feels reassuring yet discomforting, as if I were already half feral and best suited to a life in the wild.

I stay with my friend Keira. As soon as I enter her house, she lets out a shriek. 'My god!' she cries. 'What happened to your *legs?*'

At first I assume she's talking about my magnificent thighs, now the girth and texture of two baby elephant seals. But it turns out she's actually referring to the huge mottled patchwork of bruising around my knees – the consequence of my bike falling on me repeatedly and painfully as I load it up each morning. It is for this reason that I've decided to christen the bike Maud, in fact, after a sociopathic donkey I recently discovered in an old *New York American* cartoon who violently attacks everybody she meets. I mention this to Keira and she nods.

'Yes, I like it,' she says. 'It does look like you're in some kind of abusive relationship, to be honest.'

From Keira, I learn more about Switzerland's eccentricities. I've always found it a curious place: a living oxymoron of ethical extremes. As the global headquarters of diplomacy and human rights, it is home to the UN, Red Cross and Geneva Conventions; yet it has also long been a favoured hub for offshore wealth, enforcing strict banking secrecy laws that have facilitated mass criminality and inequality across the world. The country reminds me of a rich, philanthropic uncle whose charismatic exterior belies a trove of unsavoury secrets – not to mention a strikingly conservative set of social values. Women are heavily discriminated against in the workplace, Keira tells me, and Islamophobia is widespread. In 2009, the far-right Swiss People's Party (SVP) campaigned for a ban on new mosque minarets by releasing posters of niqab-clad women standing beside minarets that resembled missiles and ultimately won the referendum by 57.5 per cent.

It seems a sad counterpoint to the Schengen ideals. National borders may dissolve, yet new fiercer ones emerge between people, races, tribes. In Switzerland, the number of Muslims has quintupled in the past thirty years, and attitudes appear to be hardening. A 2017 survey by *SonntagsBlick* newspaper revealed that over a third of Swiss people felt threatened by Islam, despite the fact that Muslims comprise only 6 per cent of the population and just one in eight of them are citizens.

'Switzerland is still one of the most tolerant countries in Europe,' Keira stresses. 'But the SVP are gaining support all the time and racism is growing. If I were a Muslim migrant, I'd be worried.'

My ascent into the Alps begins gently, past rivers the colour of mown grass and plunging valleys sheathed in spruce, larch and pine. Pastel limestone outcrops reflect the cumulus swirls overhead, and the bold Romandy sun is replaced by a mellow amber disc. Every breath feels invigorating, as if the atmosphere comprised pure oxygen. Here, in the passport-free Schengen Area, no country borders exist to bridle the sense of space and I flow from Switzerland back to France as if buoyed on currents of air.

In Chamonix, however, I receive a shock. After pitching my tent in the shadow of Mont Blanc, I discover several missed calls from my brother. When I ring him back, the news is devastating.

'I'm sorry to tell you this by phone,' he says gently, 'but Dad had a bad reaction to the chemo. He developed a blood infection that reached his heart and brain.' He pauses, his voice strained. 'Doctors say he may only have six weeks to live.'

His words hit me like a physical blow. Early the next morning I take a train to Milan, where I leave Maud with a friend and catch the first flight home. Over the next week, I stand vigil at my father's bedside. He is weak and delirious, though has moments of lucidity. 'You're meant to be cycling!' he declares sporadically. 'Why are you here?'

I find it hard seeing my normally indefatigable father so helpless. There is talk of palliative care and home nursing and hospices, but none of it seems quite right associated with him, whose light has always burnt so bright. Undeterred, the family and I focus on gaining further medical opinions; there is a specialists' meeting coming up in which his case will be discussed, and we all cling to this small seed of hope.

During these long days at the hospital, staring through sterilised blinds onto a sombre car park, I think of all my father has given his family in the seven decades since he first became a parent. A butcher's son from Lancashire, he was expected by many to forgo higher education in order to continue the Lowe family trade. But he was a bright boy, and after winning a coveted spot at Bolton Grammar School, where his flat Lancastrian vowels were expelled like demons in an exorcism, he went on to Bristol University. There, he swiftly made his mark – though less through scholarship, it should be said, than fecundity. By graduation, he was not only married but had a baby boy. Ten years later, having wasted little time, the couple's brood had ballooned to six.

In 1978, my father and his first wife divorced, and shortly

afterwards he met my mother: a vivacious Hungarian émigré, eighteen years his junior, who had fled a life of penury under Soviet rule. Two more children followed, my older brother and myself, growing up in the same house in the same region of industrial Middle England as our half-siblings had before. The location – a grammar school catchment area – was no accident. As with all my father's decisions, it stemmed from love, pragmatism and an unyielding sense of familial duty. Lacking the funds to put his ample offspring through private school, it enabled him to provide (in his eyes, at least) the best education that money couldn't buy.

Now, watching his torso rise and fall as he sucks in shallow breaths, I am struck by the sacrifices my father made to give his children the life and liberty we enjoy today. From a young age, he limited his own choices so he could expand our own, working relentlessly to raise us, feed us, shelter us, support us. All so we could have the opportunities he never had. All so we could survive and fend for ourselves. All so we could attend decent universities and embark on good careers – and, if we so chose, leave our friends and family behind to go on capricious junkets across the world.

A week passes. On the seventh day, I am sitting in my usual chair, beside the sterilised blinds, staring out at the sombre car park. The newspaper is full of articles about the Syrian War and the surge of refugees pouring into Europe. In the *Guardian*, an open letter from twenty-three academics condemns Assad's massacre of a hundred civilians in the Damascus suburb of Douma, adding to the tens of thousands who have perished already. As I am reading, the registrar enters the room and asks to speak to me outside. She opens the blinds and, as she turns, a ribbon of light catches her brow and her eyes appear to shine. We walk into the corridor but already, somehow, I know what she will say. The new drugs seem to be working. They will know for certain tomorrow, but for now the signs look good. And I can tell from her tone that this is the turning point, the miracle, for which we all hoped.

The world goes on. The war in Syria continues. People lose

their homes, their families, their lives. But I have a father again, and for that alone right now I am grateful.

A week later, I am back in Milan. Dad improved rapidly from the antibiotics, and although the future remains uncertain – no more chemotherapy is possible and the level of leukaemia in his system is yet to be confirmed – I cannot help but feel optimistic. He was dragged to the brink but fought an impossible battle and won. What other obstacles or ailments could possibly vanquish him now?

Revitalised, I continue my journey east. The Italian landscape is pleasant but not as beautiful or unbounded as France. It is also laden with intimidatingly aerodynamic cyclists who continuously whizz past me on the road, leaving me floundering helplessly in their wake. Particularly prevalent are droves of ancient men vacuum-packed in Lycra, their flesh brown and wizened, their nuts and bolts hoisted with wishful elasticity. One such character tells me he has cycled 1,000 kilometres from Catanzaro, despite having a wife and newborn baby at home. Didn't they mind him leaving, I ask? '*È complicata!*' he cries. 'My wife – she *molto difficile!*'

As August bleeds into September, every day is a learning curve. I learn not to put loose bananas in my bar bag or poorly wrapped chocolate in my rucksack. I learn that Camembert should never be left in a hot pannier overnight, and certainly nowhere near my underwear. I learn not to wear my rape alarm to the toilet, where it's at risk of falling into the bowl and going off for ten minutes, attracting the frenzied attention of half a dozen strangers and an off-duty policeman.

Most of all, I learn that visiting Italian cities at the height of summer is a kind of madness, their beauty choked at source by the crowds that ooze and swell about the streets. Many of the visitors are British and reflected in them I see myself, like a grotesque fairground hall of mirrors. Watching these wretched creatures waddle about with their ubiquitous rucksacks and selfie sticks, I am reminded of the Moroccan explorer Ibn Battuta's description of the *Afranj* (Western Europeans) who visited al-Aqsur in the fourteenth century. '[They] are unparalleled as to ugliness,' he wrote in his exuberantly titled *A Gift to Those Who Contemplate the Wonders of Cities and the Marvels of Traveling* (more commonly known as simply *The Travels*). 'Most of them are tall and fat, with straw-coloured hair and white faces tinged with redness ... Most of them also carry on their backs saddlebags both small and large, in the manner of pack animals ... It is a most undignified sight.'

In Venice, the mob is overwhelming. Here, tourists have become both the lifeblood and death knell of the city; they provide the income while simultaneously inflating prices and stifling local industry. Even *vaporettos* are now reportedly being imported from Greece. Without intervention, Venice is at risk of slipping from cultural idyll to commoditised relic – if it is not too late already. In 2009, the native population fell below 60,000 and a coffin was borne down the Grand Canal to symbolise the death of the great Venetian republic.

And yet, despite these issues, the city's prodigal beauty still glows beneath the pelt of visitors clogging its waterways. In every crack and crenellation, every glittering channel and inflected arch, there lies evidence of Venice's former imperial might. Threading my way from island to island, I pass ageing Byzantine mosaics, ornate Gothic traceries and High Renaissance balustrades that dazzle and delight the eye. What mainly interests me, however, is not the Western heritage but the Eastern: the clock towers, cupolas, caravanserais[5] and other remnants of Islamic culture that comprise the foundations of the metropolis we see today.

Without Muslim commerce, Venice is unlikely ever to have developed beyond a fishing village. At the height of the Republic's

---

[5] The word caravanserai (rest house) comes from the Persian *kārvān*, for caravan, and *sarāy*, for palace. They would traditionally be spaced at intervals of sixteen miles: the average day's walk for a camel.

powers, income from the Islamic world comprised half its revenue, allowing it to monopolise eastern sea routes for over four centuries. Textiles, spices, pearls, dyes, peacocks and precious metals were imported from Arabia and Persia, in exchange for amber, coral, cloth, wood, salt and slaves. The scale of trade was spectacular. In the fourteenth century, the poet Petrarch witnessed convoys of ships the size of 'floating mountains' leaving the Venetian quay en route to Alexandria, Tripoli and Beirut, while Venetian caravanserais sprang up from Spain to China to house the streams of travelling merchants. Accompanying this growth in East–West mercantilism was a blossoming of cultural exchange, as translations of Arabic and Persian texts flooded European markets, including the first printed copy of the Qur'an.[6]

Islamic influence did not simply form an additional layer to this already culturally stratified city but comprised a core part of its bedrock. Look deeply and it can be seen in the pattern of the streets, the layout of the *palazzos*, the richness of the painted facades. St Mark's Basilica is a microcosm of Venetian diversity, its 'cross' design derived from classical Greece, its cupolas reminiscent of Cairene minarets, its golden frescoes influenced by Persian epic poetry. 'It possesses the charm of colour in common with the greater part of the architecture ... of the East,' John Ruskin wrote of the church in his treatise *The Stones of Venice*. 'The Venetians deserve especial note as the only European people who appear to have sympathised to the full with the great instinct of the Eastern races.'

---

[6] Italy's first encounter with Islam actually came far earlier, however, when the Arabs took over Sicily in 902 and stayed for 200 years. During their rule, the Muslim caliphs exerted pressure on the *dhimmi* (Christians) to convert but did not demand this by force. In the meantime, they improved irrigation, trade and agriculture, and allowed the arts to flourish. Long after they had been ousted, their influence continued to be felt across the artistic and scientific spheres, while numerous Arabic terms were absorbed into the Sicilian language, including *cassata* (cake), which may derive from the Arabic *qashatah*, and *mafiusu* (bravado) believed to be from the Arabic *mahyas*.

Venice today retains much of the aura of cultural exceptionalism established during its heyday. The city, famed for its biennale, has distinguished itself as an enclave of liberalism within a nation shifting markedly to the right – and yet, despite its Islamic heritage and the presence of several thousand Muslims, the historic centre does not appear to contain a single working mosque. An exhibition submitted for this year's biennale, which involved building a mosque inside a derelict Catholic church to raise awareness about the lack of Islamic places of worship, was even reportedly shut down due to 'security concerns' and objections from the Catholic diocese, clearly by authorities with a blind spot for irony.

When I arrive at the church, the Santa Maria della Misericordia, the door is firmly locked. In a nearby café, I ask a group of portly middle-aged men about the mosque but none have heard of it. 'A mosque?' one of them says, clearly perplexed by the question. 'That's not something we want around here.'

'Why?' I ask.

'We are not a Muslim country. We like drinking.' He laughs: a shuddering *haw haw haw* that jiggles his domed belly, revealing a provocative strip of pink midriff. 'And sex with *donne bellissime!*'

As I cycle across northern Italy, the mental strain of the journey begins to take its toll. For hours each day, I am stranded with a stream of long-repressed thoughts and emotions that bubble to the surface as though a stopper has been released deep inside. Regrets and recriminations spume thick and fast: people I've hurt; mistakes I've made; opportunities I've missed. Much of this takes me by surprise as I had no idea it was lurking down there at all, biding its time for resurrection. But now there is no avoiding it. With nothing to distract me, it rises in whorls and draperies, impossible to ignore.

And yet eventually, as I ride, I start to feel better. Cycling becomes a kind of catharsis, dredging up the sediment and filtering it for release. Each day is exhausting yet exhilarating as my muscles and mind pulse with a steady drumbeat of energy. I have never felt so alive, so focused or so free. I can go where I like, see who I like, stop where I like. I can travel, in the words of Freya Stark,[7] by 'SA' (the seat-of-my-arse) – both literally and figuratively – carrying my home as a tortoise hauls its shell.

It isn't long, in fact, before I begin to understand why so many people become fanatical about this simple, self-propelled form of transportation. Fast enough to be invigorating, slow enough to be immersive, cycling is a wonderful way to experience the world. On a bike, it is not about the destinations but the parts in between: the uncharted cracks where the gridlines fall away. Here, embedded in the contours of the earth, no pretence is possible. Nobody expects you, so nothing is fluffed or curated or preened; everything is laid out, wild and raw, in a state of guileless undress. And you are too. As a cyclist, you become as much a participant in your surroundings as an observer of it, befriended and accepted as a mirror image of its vulnerability. You're not an imposter but an equal; not a tourist but a guest. You're a quaint curiosity, unthreatening and endearingly unhinged, and are welcomed into people's lives.

Indeed, it comes as no surprise to learn that, two centuries after their birth, bicycles remain the most popular form of transport in the world. They are healthy and non-polluting, accessible and cheap. With engine and passenger acting as one, they're the most efficient form of transportation ever devised, helping people cover double, triple, *quadruple* the distance they

---

[7] Born into poverty with a sickly disposition, Freya Stark never let her upbringing or illnesses hold her back. Fiercely intelligent, eccentric and egotistical, she travelled extensively across the Middle East and became a celebrated explorer, cartographer, writer, mountaineer, Arabist and propagandist. Though an avowed imperialist, she eventually came to question the ethics of empire and believe that Britain should have a purely cultural role in the region rather than subjecting it to direct rule. 'I have been thinking with more and more certitude on the wrongness of all our ways on becoming utilitarian at the expense of human relationships,' she wrote in 1943. 'The human relationship is what counts.'

could achieve on their own. In this way, a bike performs a kind of magical metamorphosis, spinning gold from straw. It works as both machine and metaphor, showing us what we might be capable of if only we had enough support, drive and momentum to help propel us along our way.

But bikes are even more than this. Their value is not just practical but also political, psychological and symbolic. From farm labourers in the nineteenth century to Black Lives Matter (BLM) activists in the twenty-first, these humble devices have been used to push boundaries, physical and conceptual, and promote socio-political reform. In Germany, one of Hitler's first acts in power was to confiscate bicycles used by anti-Nazi protesters, while police during the BLM demonstrations in the US were ordered to 'focus on the bikes'. In Victorian Britain, men tried their hardest to disempower the new wave of velocipedestriennes (yes, a real word), from specious scaremongering about the risks of gout and tuberculosis to bad-mouthing any lady who replaced her skirt with a subversive pair of bloomers.[8]

Cycling is hard work. My arse burns, my limbs ache and my chamois cream is disappearing at a far swifter rate than I feel comfortable admitting. But it is wild and thrilling and joyful too. And as each day passes, I feel it seeping deeper and deeper into my blood.

---

[8] In 1895, American mother-of-three Annie Londonderry became the first woman to cycle (and more often sail: she was a terrible cheat) alone around the globe. The twenty-four-year-old wore a heavy skirt and corset, and carried only a change of clothes and a gun. A true inspiration to us all.

Chapter 2

BORDERLANDS

The Balkans

'There are no foreign lands. It is the traveller only who is foreign.'

Robert Louis Stevenson,
The Silverado Squatters (1883)

Ljubljana surprises me. Just twenty-five years after Slovenia separated from Yugoslavia, its capital seems to bear few scars of communist rule. Instead, it appears dynamic and progressive. A public wifi network spans the city, bike lanes wreathe across the roads and pavements, and recycling bins can be found on every street corner. Even the graffiti has a kindly edge, crying 'refugees welcome!' and 'stop repression!' With the exception of its morally questionable policy of serving wine in 100ml thimbles, it feels close to my perfect city.[9]

High on a hill in the centre stands Ljubljana Castle. As I look out across the parapet of this medieval fortress, I can just make

---

[9] I should probably note that, as a matter of course, I've started carrying round a thermos of wine to ensure I have a cool *aperitif* on hand after a day's ride. This may seem like an indulgence, but it is in fact highly abstemious compared with the likes of some – such as mountaineer Albert Smith, who on his climb of Mont Blanc in 1851 reportedly carried with him sixty bottles of *vin ordinaire*, six bottles of Bordeaux, ten bottles of St George, fifteen bottles of St Jean, three bottles of cognac and two bottles of champagne.

out the site of the new city mosque in the distance, tucked between the railway station and a sea of red-tiled rooftops. At present, all that seems to exist is a dusty framework of scaffolding, yellow cladding and skeletal minarets framed in piping and cement,[10] but the very fact of the building's existence feels significant. A whole century has passed since the last mosque was built here – by Bosnian Muslims (Bosniaks) drafted into the Austro-Hungarian army during World War I – and the Italians destroyed it long ago.

The Ljubljana Mosque is the consequence of fifty years of petitioning by Slovenia's tiny Muslim community, most of whom arrived in the second half of the twentieth century from Bosnia, Albania and Kosovo, or in the 1990s as they fled Serbian persecution. Slovenia's first contact with the Islamic world came five centuries earlier, however, when the country formed an unwilling buffer between the Ottomans and Europe, creating a lingering association between Islam and militancy that remains embedded in the Slovene psyche today. 'In the Middle Ages, our ancestors were attacked by Muslim soldiers, and they did bad things here,' city councillor Mihael Jarc declared in 2004 during his failed campaign to oppose the mosque. 'This is in our historical subconscious.'

Outside Ljubljana, the stark lines of industrial suburbia gradually give way to the toy-box hues of the countryside. Apple-green hills glow under a translucent sky, while terracotta roofs litter the fields like flecks of spilt paint. The landscape is drier than in Britain, yet brighter too, as if it's been touched up in technicolour. The ride is beautifully tranquil, and I arrive in Novo Mesto at the centre of the wine-growing Krka Valley as the sun dips towards the hills and gilds their crowns with amber. Settling in a bar beside the cobbled main square, I make a casual enquiry about regional wines and moments later find myself presented with four enormous complimentary 'taster' glasses by the waiter.

---

[10] The mosque, which cost a staggering £30 million to build, opened in February 2020.

These include the local speciality, Cviček, which is just 10 per cent alcohol and is said to be one of the few wines in the world made from both red and white grapes. It is dry and dark pink, and worryingly drinkable. Predictably, the French hate it.

Two hours later, after knocking off the wine alongside a tumbler of *'miš-maš'* – a cocktail of claret and Fanta that has the complexion of a bloodied urostomy bag – I retrieve Maud to cycle the last few miles to Otočec. It occurs to me, as I lurch unsteadily out of the square, that the final drink might not have been entirely necessary. But, suddenly finding myself in an uncommonly good mood, I fly with wild, cackling abandon out of the village and into the coal-black countryside beyond, veering bumpily along rutted tracks and gravelly lanes with a bike light the wattage of a glow-worm. 'Come on, Maudy!' I cry, slapping her torso as I ride. 'Let's see what you can do!'

By the time I reach the campsite, breathless and ruddy-faced with adrenalin, the barrier is firmly locked. This proves to be nothing a little limbo and light trespass can't solve, however, and within minutes I have erected my tent, eaten three Gorenjka chocolate bars and passed out, sated and exhausted, in bed.

As I approach Croatia, the landscape becomes both more idyllic and unkempt, as if shaking itself loose from its neat Western moorings. Houses blend into barns and cattlesheds, gardens into allotments and arable land, and the viscid scent of mulch and cow dung hangs heavy and low in the air. Feeling chipper, I am just ruminating on the remarkable feat of a borderless Europe when a policeman steps out and halts me in my tracks with a bark.

'Oi!' he cries, blocking my way with his not inconsiderable girth. 'How get here?'

'Why, is there a problem?' I ask pleasantly. I got here by squeezing through a row of concrete bollards that had a convenient, bike-sized opening in the middle. But I decide not to go into detail.

'This not border! Passport?'

Despite being in the EU, Croatia is not part of the Schengen zone, it turns out. Unlike Switzerland, which is confusingly in the zone but not part of the EU. This means I have entered the country illegally, marking my second inadvertent criminal foray in the past twelve hours. I prepare to be interrogated, or at least admonished – but being a woman, with our innate foolishness and incapacity for following simple directions, can often, I find, be quite useful in such situations.

'I'm sorry,' I witter, giving what I hope to be a convincing smile of silly-me contrition. 'The signs were just so very confusing ...'[11]

Twenty minutes later, following a few brusque instructions, I have made it successfully through the correct crossing to the other side – though sadly my triumph proves short lived. The route here is far from smooth, and I soon find myself on a series of craggy cross-country paths that gradually get muddier and lumpier until they are almost entirely mud and lump with no path at all. Eventually, ragged and sweaty, I pull up at a restaurant on the outskirts of Zagreb, where a garrulous barista serves me potato broth while cleaning the ale pipes and unburdening his soul. Life is difficult, he explains. 'We didn't fight for independence, we fought for privatisation. The tycoons arrived and swept everything up. *Everyone* is corrupt.'

I ask about refugees and he tells me that they often pass this way at night. 'I see them sometimes, sleeping in the fields.'

'Do people mind?'

---

[11] Men beware: women have been using such tactics for centuries. One of Freya Stark's 'seven cardinal virtues for a traveller' is the ability 'to use stupid men ... with equanimity'. During her first excursion into Druze country in 1928, she proved her skills in this regard by convincing the French gendarmerie that she had accidentally stumbled into the territory due to 'inaccuracies in her Thomas Cook guidebook', despite the fact she was 90 kilometres outside Damascus and riding a donkey at the time. 'The great and only comfort about being a woman,' she once wrote, 'is that one can always pretend to be more stupid than one is and no one is surprised.'

'Some. But I remember when we Croats were just like them, trying to escape the Serbs. So if I see a refugee, I'll help them.'

It is now mid-September and Hungary has just strung razor-wire across its border with Serbia. Rather than travelling through the northern Schengen states, refugees are now being channelled west through Croatia and Slovenia. At this time, the Croatian government is being heralded as a beacon of altruism. They take migrants in, tend to the sick and provide transport across the country; they insist their borders will remain open. Yet just a week later, after 13,000 people arrive in just two days, all but one of Croatia's crossings with Serbia are closed.

'Europe was wide open, a place of casual frontiers, few questions and almost no travellers,' Laurie Lee wrote in *As I Walked Out One Midsummer Morning*. His journey through England and Spain in 1934, he said, 'coincided with the last years of peace'. Are we now at war again, I wonder? Not between armies or states but between those who flee their homes and those who fortify them?

Desirous to avoid more of Croatia's fecund grasslands, I instead engage in a little suicidal experimentation with the motorway. When I exit several miles later, relieved and somewhat surprised to have survived the ordeal, I find myself surrounded by grey. The sky is grey, the road is grey and the horizon is filled with tenement blocks, all a dour, wretched grey.

I haven't just crossed nations but seasons too, it seems. Slovenia has stolen the summer and cast its shadow over the south.

In Zagreb's old town, bars and cafés rumble with the honeyed laughter of their well-heeled clientele. A 'vintage festival' is in full swing, exhibiting old rusty bicycles, overpriced antiques and classic MGB Roadsters. My Couchsurfing[12] host, a young journalist called Mirko, seems at ease in these crowds, although

[12] A membership website that connects travellers with local hosts offering free accommodation.

he can afford few of the prices. Until recently, he lived in a cramped flat with his parents and four siblings, sleeping on the living room sofa – although now, courtesy of his grandparents, he has an apartment all to himself.

In the main square, we spot former prime minister Jadranka Kosor, the first and only woman to hold the office since independence. The capital is small and it's apparently quite normal to see senior politicians freely wandering the streets. 'You cry "fuck you!" and they cry "fuck you!" back,' Mirko explains. 'It's like a form of hello.'

We make our way to a cabin in the mountains where a group of Mirko's friends have gathered. Apple and pomegranate trees litter the garden, while grapes dangle with languid grace through a wooden trellis overhead. The young men – a trader, hairdresser and archaeology graduate – all feel depressed about the state of their country. 'Even the refugees don't want to stay,' they quip, as we drink herbal tea from beer tankards and look out over rolling hills cloaked by a shaggy mantle of conifers. 'That's how bad it is!'

Inside, the villa is covered in a creative array of Christian crosses, some forged from metal and ceramic beading, others from sugar icing and cookie dough. I ask about relations between Catholics and Muslims, the latter of whom comprise just 1.6 per cent of the population, and am told they're 'okay'. 'We have a few mosques in Zagreb,' Novak, the archaeologist, says. 'One of the biggest in Europe, I think.'

However, historic tensions remain, he concedes. Battered by Ottoman raids throughout the 1500s, many Croatians in the occupied south-east fled north or abroad, while churches were destroyed or converted into mosques. Then, a century later, the tide turned. A surge of nationalistic zeal across the Balkans saw the Turks expelled, the mosques and madrasahs destroyed, and the Muslims exiled, killed or enslaved.

'We were the last line of defence against the Turks,' Novak says. 'Their empire ended here, inside our country, so some still see us as the great defenders of Christianity. That's why refugees aren't always welcome.'

'There's a Slovenian philosopher, Slavoj Žižek,[13] who says people should be less idealistic about refugees,' Mirko adds, passing me a glistening bowl of pomegranate seeds. 'He says we should accept their values are different and that they're not perfect people.' Žižek is not anti-refugee, he stresses. 'He means we should help them anyway, good or bad. Otherwise, it's only the bad guys, the *fašisti*, who talk about such things. And that's a real problem.'

By October, I've become a wild camping aficionado. I can construct and dismantle my tent with military efficiency and am often awake and away by dawn. I've perhaps become a little too obsessive-compulsive about it, however, as everything must have its place. If the stove is where the first-aid pack should be or a sock has snuck into the food compartment then I cannot continue until order has been restored. This kind of pathological attention to detail may seem excessive, but I worry about taking my eye off the ball. I've always been someone who swings from extreme to extreme, and I either oversee my chattels as a neurotic drill sergeant might supervise his troops or I know they'll end up scattered about the plains of Europe, never to be seen again.

There are times when my swiftness in setting up camp proves invaluable. Near the Bosnian border, I run over a squashed snake part-concealed in the roadside foliage and – as someone with a lifelong serpent phobia – I am immediately gripped by panic. *Oh god*, I think. *The fields are clearly swarming with them!* Desperate to avoid camping anywhere grassy and therefore inevitably reptile-infested, I pull into what appears to be a derelict building site, where I discover a mausoleum of rusted tractors and bulldozers parked on a large, dark mudflat. It is a barren, gloomy,

---

[13]   Žižek's book that explores this issue is called *Against the Double Blackmail: Refugees, Terror and Other Troubles with the Neighbors.*

spooky place, but the ground is dry and rock-hard, and almost certainly snake-free, so to me right now it seems like paradise. Within twenty minutes of arrival, I have erected my tent, poured a hefty nightcap and fallen fast sleep.

What seems like moments later, however, I am awakened by a terrifying roar. Scrabbling outside, I see the machines beside me coming alive, their engines bellowing, their headlamps piercing the dewy half-light of dawn. In a slow, funereal procession, a dozen of them roll by just metres from my door, their drivers staring in mild bewilderment at this peculiar, wide-eyed creature hunched before them in her underwear. It feels like a lot to take in before six in the morning and, shocked by the vehicles' proximity, I pack up and abandon camp in lightning speed before the moon has faded from the sky.

Crossing Bosnia takes several days. Around me, beauty and privation exist in uneasy harmony as I make my way first through the Serb-Orthodox region of Republika Srpska and then the Bosniak-majority federation of Bosnia and Herzegovina. The landscape shifts constantly, from golden pasture to bleak urbanism, from boundless valleys to Brutalist decay. Here, my easy ability to continue onwards, aided and embraced by communities caged by circumstance, feels like an affront. Every day I'm offered food, drink, friendship, warmth: a thousand little kindnesses I know I can never repay.

Most places feel sunny and peaceful, yet undercurrents of tension are clear. In Republika Srpska, I hear that ethnic clashes have been escalating since the twentieth anniversary of the Srebrenica massacre, in which over 8,000 Bosniaks were killed by Bosnian Serbs in 1995. Serb nationalism appears to be resurging throughout the Balkans, in fact, driven both by Russia and by local leaders seeking to scapegoat Muslims for their own failures. 'Are those refugees really just passing through?' a Serb military officer asks me as I try out a Zastava M84 machine gun at an army recruitment drive I stumble across in a park. Shooting, I discover, is a lot of fun. 'Or is Sarajevo secretly trying to increase the number of Muslims?'

Near Banja Luka, the *de facto* capital of Republika Srpska, I make camp behind a half-built church by the roadside. As darkness falls, I drift into a dreamless sleep – only to be rudely awakened once again by a thunderous racket just inches from my head. This time the noise in question belongs not to a battalion of reanimated farm machinery, however, but to two gruff workmen clutching a chainsaw and electric drill. One is stout and heavy-browed with a complexion of raw beetroot, while the other is skinny and pale and sporting a chin of prickly stubble. Both look like axe murderers. As I emerge from my tent, Beetroot strides over, grunting and revving his saw, and I feel myself stiffen with fear.

'*Dobar dan!*' he rasps. '*Da li želite cigaretu?*'

Hello! Do you want a cigarette? The men, it turns out, are not murderers at all. They're builders – and they've come to bring me breakfast. Alongside the cigarette, they produce an apple, two biscuits and what appears to the untrained eye to be a bottle of white wine. They both take a slug before passing it to me – and it doesn't take much for me to realise, swiftly and unequivocally, that it is not wine at all but some kind of devil's brew created from the flames of hellfire itself.

'*Dobro?*' Beetroot says encouragingly. Good?

I nod back, unable to speak. My lips are numb and my oesophagus seems to have dissolved.

'*Dobro,*' I croak eventually. 'Thank you, you're very kind.'

Sarajevo raises my spirits. After the simmering antipathies of Republika Srpska, the city skyline – a heterodox jumble of Catholic spires, Islamic minarets, Jewish cupolas and Orthodox belfries – feels like a celebration of inclusion. Particularly enchanting are the 'Sarajevo Roses', in which scars left by mortar rounds during the Bosnian War have been filled by scarlet resin to convert the traumas of the past into artworks of arresting beauty.

On Ferhadija, the main pedestrianised avenue, a 'meeting of cultures' sign provides a tangible marker of Sarajevo's schismatic character. Look east and you confront remnants of the city's Islamic past: Gazi Husrev-beg Mosque, built by an Ottoman governor who shaped Sarajevo into the most powerful city in the Balkans; Baščaršija, the old town, with its distinctive clay roofs, emerald domes and stone-vaulted bazaars; Slatko Ćoše ('sweet corner'), named after the traditional pastry shops that date back hundreds of years. Look west, however, and sleek shopfronts, rose-blush paintwork and decorative cornicing signal the arrival of the Austro-Hungarians. Walking this way, I pass bustling bars, fashion boutiques and the Sacred Heart Cathedral, where Romanesque belltowers crown a neo-gothic masterpiece that acts as the modern symbol of the city.

My host is an Austrian friend, Nikki, who is conducting research for a local thinktank. 'I'm examining how Bosnian women reconcile being Muslim with being European,' she explains over a pot of tea. 'What's interesting is that there isn't actually much conflict at all.'

Under Ottoman rule, Bosnia was one of the few European countries, along with Albania and Kosovo, in which large numbers converted to Islam and declined to convert back. 'The Islam practised here is more social than political,' Nikki tells me. 'It's influenced by Sufism but mixes in Bosnian customs. People don't practise polygamy or marry their cousins, and women don't always cover their hair. It's a special European type of Islam.'[14]

The main problems facing Bosnia are not religious, Nikki asserts, but economic: unemployment, corruption, inequality of

---

[14] In 1928, the grand mufti of the Bosniak community, Mehmed Džemaludin Čaušević, stated that the veil was a cultural, rather than Islamic, tradition. This argument was later picked up by the leader of the Islamic Community in Bosnia, Ibrahim Fejić, when the face covering was prohibited under Soviet rule. 'It is a sin in Islam to allow oneself what the religion forbids,' he said during a speech voicing support for the ban. 'It is as much a sin to forbid to oneself what the religion permits.'

wealth. However, these issues are reopening old sectarian wounds, she concedes. 'Boundaries were more fluid before the war. Now the country has lost its identity so people are searching for it in their race and religion. Politics and the media are drawn along ethnic lines, and all of it is dirty.'

From Sarajevo, I catch a bus to Podgorica, Montenegro. This wasn't originally part of the plan, but I've already fallen badly behind schedule and would otherwise miss my rendezvous there with P. At the bus station, I am told that only minibuses are making the treacherous journey across the ravine and it takes some persuasion to convince the sour-faced driver to squeeze a dismembered Maud into his boot. Finally he relents, however, and I celebrate by spending my remaining Bosnian notes on a packet of McVitie's Hobnobs.

I am just settling into my seat when the driver suddenly appears again. Maud will cost an extra four marks (£2), he declares, clearly making up the sum on the spot. Now out of cash, I try to offer some Hobnobs as compensation, but biscuits are clearly not viewed as acceptable *baksheesh* on Bosnian buses. The man simply stands there unmoving, pursing his gristly lips and waiting.

After a brief standoff, it seems clear he's not going to give in – so, with a scowl and spurt of muttered expletives, I begin to collect my bags to disembark. Just as I do so, however, an elderly woman sitting nearby stands up and stops me. She then reaches into her purse, pulls out some coins … and, to my immense astonishment and relief, pays the fee on my behalf.

Deeply touched, I feel momentarily lost for words. 'Thank you!' I eventually gush. '*Hvala lijepa!*'

She smiles and places her hand on her heart. Then she whispers a single word: 'Muslim.'

The journey through Tara River Canyon, the deepest gorge in Europe, is exhilarating and terrifying. We rattle down slopes, career around bends and graze plunging bluffs that overlook oceans of empty space. More than once I wonder if the brakes have failed or if the driver bears a grudge against any of the passengers on board. But I can't deny the landscape is extraordinary: a Jurassic, Janus-faced wilderness of verdant greens, saw-toothed greys and pools of peacock silk. A vast miscellany of trees surround us, and I recognise pine, beech and fir while cursing my arboricultural ignorance.

Part of me is disappointed not to be crossing this terrain by bike. Imagine the sweet madness of such a ride! But how much I would have enjoyed it in reality, I'm unsure. Shielded in my metal cocoon, the fierce wildness of the world around me appears irresistible. Outside, exposed to the elements, however, I may well have felt differently. 'When danger or pain press too nearly, they are incapable of giving any delight,' Edmund Burke wrote in his treatise on the sublime. 'But at certain distances, and with certain modifications … they are delightful.'

Due to the driver's giddy alacrity, I am able to disembark and cycle to the airport before P arrives. I am very excited to see him, and as we greet each other I feel my mind and muscles decompress with an urgency that surprises me. I hadn't realised before how tense I was. 'You made it!' he exclaims, genuinely surprised. 'You remembered to turn right at Zagreb then?'

Together, P and I spend a lovely few days exploring Montenegro. The country is minuscule, with a population similar to Glasgow. Yet crushed inside is a dense abundance of natural wonders, from golden beaches and freshwater lakes to limestone gullies and glistening fjords. Both a blessing and a curse, the country's searing beauty attracts visitors and investment and the avarice of powerful men. Rows of shorefront tower blocks expose the soiled underbelly of unregulated construction, while glossy yachts anchored in the marina provide a worrying hint of what's to come. This is an idyll on borrowed time, as tax breaks doled out to the likes of Oleg Deripaska and the Rothschilds help transform it into a tourist mecca for the super-rich.

The break passes in a flash, and on the final day I notice my thighs beginning to tingle. It feels like a warning sign to return to the saddle before they revert to their former supine selves, like the collapse of a soufflé removed too soon from the heat. While losing P again so soon is hard, he softens the blow somewhat by making perhaps the most generous gesture he has ever made over the course of our five-year relationship: he offers to take the ukulele with him.

My delight when he says this can hardly be expressed in words. The ukulele and I haven't been getting along well, I admit. The problem is that bicycles aren't really designed to carry ukuleles; they're designed to carry sturdy, docile things that stay where you put them and lack an independent spirit. But ukuleles aren't like that. They're fickle and flighty and have pretensions of grandeur far beyond their station. 'I could've been a star!' I would hear it holler. 'Jammed with George Harrison! Plucked by Pearl Jam! But instead here I am, bound and gagged beside your rump, forced into a life of humiliating depravity.' At which point the instrument would issue a rousing war cry, throw off its manacles and pitch itself headlong onto the road – where it would lie, stunned and subdued, until it was whisked back up and lashed with punitive impropriety against my arse again.

Now, wonderfully, we both have the liberty we crave. I just wish that P had never talked me into bringing it in the first place.

Following the curve of the Cijevna river, I make my way high into the mountains. The vegetation grows bright and bold under the midday sun, as lush and green as a fairytale. I pass a graveyard draped in orange garlands and a moss-coloured brook overlooked by a limestone hut, while around me the hills expose stripes of layered sediment like the ancient growth rings of a tree.

After around twenty-five kilometres of climbing, I feel my legs begin to tire. I press on, sensing that I'm close to the Albanian border – when suddenly, with shocking abruptness, the road stops. Dead. In front of me, as clear as day, there is nothing. The track simply ends, as if sucked into the mountainside and swallowed by the bracken and pine groves beyond.

Nearby, I notice a woman standing outside a house. Dashing up, I enquire about the crossing. 'Ah,' she says, shaking her head. 'Border no built.'

'Not built?' I stare at her in horror. 'What do you mean?'

'No. Built,' she repeats, slower this time. Her expression – a mixture of condescension and pity – is one I know well, and I feel a sudden jolt of homesickness for my mother. 'Go Lake Skadar.'

Lake Skadar?! That involves retracing my steps almost twenty kilometres! I look around frantically for someone who may be able to help – but it's futile. There is nobody else here and no solution except to return.

Two hours later, I arrive back at the lake, exhausted. There, a man advises against crossing the border so late in the day. 'Albania is dangerous,' he says. 'Nobody goes out after dark.' He is far from the first person to issue such a warning; almost every Montenegrin I've met seems to live in a state of permanent terror concerning their southerly neighbour, as if much of each day is spent beating back armies of bloodied savages sweeping across the Albanian Alps. Such sentiments are nothing new, it seems. 'No nation are so detested and dreaded by their neighbours as the Albanians,' Lord Byron wrote in 1811. 'The Greeks hardly regard them as Christians, or the Turks as Muslims … Their habits are predatory …'

The next morning, undeterred, I set out early for the Lake Skadar border crossing. The closer I get, the more the landscape appears to shrivel and blacken, as if wilting beneath the sun. I pass a crooked sign reading 'SHITEN PLLACE' and a tiny boy with bare feet clutching a packet of Marlboro. At the checkpoint, the guard seems discordantly cheery in relation to the dourness of the surrounds. 'Wilcome!' he trills, stamping my passport with a grin. 'Watch out for the rain!'

Albania immediately feels both poorer and prettier than the Montenegrin borderlands. I pass huddles of scrawny cows and goats, and climb into ochre hills that pierce wisps of drifting cloud. Crosses are strewn everywhere – on cars and trellises, windows and fences, and even as a huge chalk outline that adorns the far side of the dale like a puritanical Cerne Abbas Giant.

And then, with a gasp, I see the road. It rises steeply from the valley floor in a terrifyingly sheer zigzag, marking the start of the Prokletije ('Accursed') Mountains.

The name is depressingly apt. It is the toughest ascent I've faced so far, and one for which I feel hopelessly ill-prepared. Hesitant to begin, I stall for twenty minutes to eat a carrot and listen to a man talk unintelligibly about his chickens. Then, finally, I set off – and it is agony from the start. My glutes burn, my back aches and every hundred metres I have to stop to rest and catch my breath. But I am determined not to dismount. It feels somehow significant, this hill. If I can manage it, I feel I can finally call myself a cyclist; I can stop feeling like a charlatan and develop an iota of self-respect. So on I go, slogging, sweating, slipping, swearing, until I'm amazed there can be any more hill left to climb. Every corner I turn, more mountain appears, until I begin to feel like Sisyphus condemned to heave his rock ever upwards, only to have it roll endlessly back down again to the bottom. I try to channel Ranulph Fiennes, as I generally do at such moments ('plod on, plod on, plod on'), but I quickly feel him slipping from my grasp – until, before I know it, I find myself screaming a two-word mantra of considerably less exalted origin, while the summit remains tantalisingly out of reach.

Eventually, however, three hours after I set off, I make it – and the reward is tremendous. Opening before me is a deep, winding gully, almost phosphorescent in hue, centred about the pea-green banks of a copper-tinted river. And to my left, snaking between me and the valley floor, are the most diabolical set of hairpins I've ever laid eyes on. After a short rest, I pitch myself onto them like a child on their first toboggan ride, and – eyes streaming, hair flying, rucksack straps buffeting like tickertape – I swiftly hit that shaky sweet-spot between controlled thrill and reckless folly, before skidding to a near-calamitous halt at the bottom among a herd of errant goats.

Afterwards, I feel elated. *I did it! I DID IT!!* This is what I love most about cycling: the payoff that follows the pain. Is there any sport more tightly wedded to the human condition, I wonder, both in terms of physics (what goes up must come down) and ethics (you reap what you sow)? I just wish I had more time to savour the moment. But I must make it to Vermosh before nightfall, seventy kilometres to the north – so, hastily, I push on.

The terrain quickly proves challenging. Heavy rain begins to fall, turning the ground from gravel to slush, and Maud's tyres slip and sink in the gloop. Pigs block my path, dogs howl and give chase, and gaping potholes turn the road into a kind of rustic steeplechase. Eventually, I give up. Maud is baulking at the steepening moguls like an recalcitrant Omani camel being coaxed through the Hadhramaut dunes, and I am too weak to force her on. Instead, I decide to find a lift. The people I approach don't seem to grasp what I'm asking, however, so they invite their neighbours around to consult. They have a better idea but are not fully confident of their analysis, so they phone a friend across the road who turns up with a wheelbarrow full of sheep. He stares at Maud, stares at me, rearranges his sheep and cries 'O Zot!' (My God!).

Finally, sometime later, it is decided. A local fish farmer will take me to the next village, where his friend will collect me and drive me onwards to Vermosh. Delighted, I thank him and offer money, but he refuses. The friend, Murat, refuses too, despite having already picked up three hitchhikers – a local man and Israeli couple – and despite being a treacherous Albanian who inevitably cannot be trusted. Instead, he offers us all sweets and fruit, and heroically keeps us alive during our nail-biting voyage along the narrow, rubble-strewn pass between the cliffs and barrier-free scarp as we're engulfed by an apocalyptic downpour that swamps the vehicle like a carwash.

I drift off to sleep, and by the time I awake it is pitch-black and we are sloshing through a series of shallow rivers. We could be anywhere, and it suddenly occurs to me that the Montenegrins might have been right after all. Was all this just an elaborate ruse? Are we being lured to some terrible torture dungeon to be robbed and left for dead? It doesn't help that the Israeli couple spend the final part of the journey cheerfully discussing gun culture in Albania, where shootings reportedly kill nearly twice as many people as in America. 'There's an ancient code of honour called the Kanun,' the girl explains. 'It's a tradition of gang violence that gained strength under the Ottomans, when Albania was basically left to run itself.' Kanun customs re-emerged after the fall of communism, she says, as corruption and lawlessness flourished. 'Everyone just takes justice into their own hands.'

Fortunately, however, there are no blood feuds between anyone in the truck. And Murat turns out not to be the homicidal type. He simply drops us outside a farmhouse, helps us unload our bags and leaves us to the care of a plump, homely couple with cheeks as pink as bubblegum. Moments later, with a convivial wave, he is gone.

We walk into a Christian shrine. Exhibited on the walls is an abundance of religious iconography, including a plaster model of Archangel Gabriel and a velvet tapestry of Jesus staring at the sky with a look of soulful omniscience. Albania's north-west is a Catholic stronghold within this Muslim-majority nation, it turns out, due to its remote location and history of autonomous governorship outside Ottoman control.

We settle in the snug oak-panelled parlour, where the air is thick with woodsmoke. A large cast-iron pot bubbles on the stove, emitting a rich aroma of lamb, rosemary and garlic. As we wait for our meal, I ask the Albanian hitchhiker, Peter, if he is Catholic like our hosts. No, he replies. 'Bektashi.' A moderate Sufi sect that arrived here from Turkey after being banned by Atatürk. 'But there aren't many of us left in Albania now.'

The Bektashis played an important role in the development of the Albanian nation, I later discover. When Albania was striving to break free from Ottoman rule in the 1800s, the sect declined to ally with its Islamic overlords and instead threw its support behind the *Rilindja,* or 'national awakening', which helped the country forge its own independent identity. Meanwhile, the Christians did their bit to help too, it appears, by putting national unity above religious allegiance and refusing to accept the West's characterisation of them as a crucial *Antemurale Christianitatis* (barrier state) against the Islamic East.

This prioritisation of statehood over faith appears to have endured. 'There is a rather beautiful characteristic of Albania,' Pope Francis eulogised during a trip here in 2014. 'I am referring to the peaceful coexistence and collaboration that exists among followers of different religions.'

Peter is not entirely convinced, however. 'Actually, tensions do exist,' he says, spooning a hillock of *shopska* salad onto his plate. 'Some politicians are quite critical of Islam. And the Christian clergy think it was forced on Albania against its will.'

'Are there concerns about extremism?' I ask.

'Well, some people get worried about the stricter Arabist Muslims, influenced by the Gulf states. But the Turkish Muslims, led by Fethullah Gülen,[15] are much stronger these days. They are more moderate and don't think the Arabists fit with Albanian values.'

He downs a *rakija* and shudders. 'What I don't get, if you don't mind me saying, is the West's great *fear* of Islam. I mean, it's so varied. It can be European and liberal, or Turkish and secular, or Saudi and hardcore, or anything. We're in NATO. We want to join the EU. We don't have sharia law. So when people ask if Islam and Western values can co-exist, I don't get it. They already do!'

I leave the farmhouse soon after breakfast. Outside, the building's metre-thick flint walls are hung with rusty garden tools and

---

[15] A powerful, moderate Islamist scholar, with millions of followers in Turkey and across the world, who fell out with President Erdoğan a decade ago and now lives in exile in the US.

plump bushels of onions, and its bright terracotta roof, slick with rain, blazes like a beacon in the hoary morning mist. As I load up Maud, pigs snuffle around a pile of giant, warty pumpkins nearby, while, in the distance, a gauze of white cloud forms a halo over forested hills.

Leaving proves tougher than expected. Beyond the yard I encounter a vast swamp of mud and floodwater, and I am forced to half-push, half-carry Maud across ice-cold streams and mushy fields for over an hour before we reach firm ground. Rain falls in a sheet and, after crossing briefly back into Montenegro, I slosh my way to a smear of a town called Berane, where I check into a motel that looks like a cross between a brothel and a correctional facility. From there, I set my sights on Rožaje, where £10 buys me a lambent fuchsia room with no curtains and a blocked toilet, plus a smattering of hair and blood on the wall for no extra cost.

Berane and Rožaje are both located in a sprawling, impoverished Muslim-majority region called Sandžak which straddles the Montenegro–Serbia border. Their poverty is not the kind you find written about; it is dull and unremarkable, a low, heavy hum. Long neglected by both Podgorica and Belgrade, and historically the victims of severe and persistent persecution, residents here tend to profess allegiance to Bosnia and Turkey (Muslims refer to themselves as Bosniaks, while the name 'Sandžak' comes from the Ottoman term for flag or district, *sanjak*), and a sense of gloom and ennui is clear.

From Rožaje, I take aim for Serbia. It is a glum ride, filled with rain, fog and a tag-team of howling dogs that chase me in a crazed frenzy as if they're being attacked by a swarm of bees. Car horns reach a crescendo and appear to develop an entire language of their own. Depending on its timbre and urgency, a honk seems to mean 'hello' or 'watch out' or 'bugger off' or 'nice arse', or all of the above, and they blather about me in a constant cacophonous swirl.

After passing through several pitch-black tunnels that seem perfectly designed for the eradication of surplus cyclists, I reach the Serbian border. Here, the guard takes my passport and flicks through it slowly and quizzically, before returning to the beginning to start the process again. Then, once he has tired of this somewhat tedious endeavour, he puts the passport aside, stares at me, smiles … and taps his knees invitingly.

Oh god, I think. He wants me to sit on his lap!

I am weighing up my options (slap him? Scream? Oblige, then crush him with my now-leviathan thighs?) when he reaches over and drapes a coat across my bare legs. 'Brrrrr,' he says, miming the cold – and immediately I'm flooded with relief. So not a sexual deviant at all, it turns out, but a considerate young man. Sometimes it can be so tricky to tell them apart.

And my legs *are* chilly, now he mentions it. It is mid-October and winter is snapping at my heels. My hope is to keep abreast of it until I hit sunnier climes to the south, like those heroes in films who outrun giant tornadoes or tsunami waves before being whisked miraculously to safety. But I clearly need to up my pace. Bearing this in mind, I push on and cross this slim sliver of Serbia in an hour to reach Kosovo's northern border, where the thread of the Ibar river dilates into a broad, misty lagoon.

The edge of Europe isn't far now. And, for the first time on this journey, it feels – just about – within my grasp.

My first impressions of the large Kosovan city of Mitrovica, noted in my diary, are alliteratively unequivocal: 'grey, grotty, grisly, grim'. Roads are blocked by rubble, heaps of litter clog the pavements and a dusty sign near the border reads 'Respect the Resolution 1244 Security Council' – a decree that mandated the withdrawal of Yugoslav forces from Kosovo in 1999 – alongside a picture of a large steel gunship.

I book a room at the first motel I find. This transpires to be a half-built, curiously cavernous place with hints of *The Shining*, run by a gnome-like man with a terrifying Adam's apple. My room is huge but filthy, and I force the man to have it cleaned. If nobody complains then nothing will ever improve, I find myself thinking, before catching myself with horror. Three months on the road and I've already turned into my mother.

Outside my window, an oblong park opens onto rows of bland high-rises that extend to a murky blur of foothills beyond. This is the southern side of the city, which is linked to the north via a bridge across the Ibar river. When I visit the bridge later, however, I discover it is blocked by broken slabs of concrete, armed guards and, situated right in the centre, a patch of thorny scrubland known euphemistically as the 'Peace Park'. It is a stark physical symbol of the great ethnic rift wrenching this city – this country – in two, and the image of it shocks me. 'Not many people cross the river,' a waiter tells me later. 'I've only crossed it twice in fifteen years, and only because my father got sick. They have better doctors over there.'

After dinner, I walk into a jungle. Albania has just beaten Armenia in the UEFA Euro qualifiers and everyone is celebrating. Horns screech, fireworks blaze and swarms of fans chant and howl with joy. The energy is intoxicating in its intensity, as people succumb to a deep primal urge to belong and exclude. It all seems harmless at this level. But when does this change, I wonder? When does the game become reality and beeping horns morph into bullets and blocked bridges?

Crossing the bridge feels like entering another country. Here, people speak Serbian, not Albanian, and use the dinar rather than the euro. Changing money is no problem, however; you can do it easily on the black market. In fact, you can do practically anything, according to my friend David, an NGO officer who has lived here for several years. 'Money laundering, stealing, driving unlicensed, you name it. The joke is that you have to shoot three times before the police turn up.' Plans to open the bridge are constantly postponed, he says, and hostilities simmer unchecked. 'They're two very different cultures. It's hard to see how they could ever fully integrate.'

Kosovo, which is over 90 per cent Muslim Albanian, unilaterally declared independence from Serbia in 1990, prompting a ruthless crackdown by Belgrade that ended with the intervention of NATO. During the conflict, the Serbs vandalised over two hundred mosques – including the nineteenth-century Ibar Mosque by the bridge, which is yet to be rebuilt despite campaigns by Mitrovica's Muslim population – as well as Islamic libraries, madrasahs and the five-century-old archives of the Islamic Community of Kosovo. In retaliation, Muslims attacked Serbs and ravaged dozens of Orthodox churches. Today, just over half of all UN members have officially recognised Kosovo as a country, but Serbia still refuses to do so – and part of me, I admit, feels sorry for this former powerhouse of a state. Once a dominant drill sergeant with a flock of pliant minions, the country now stands alone and embittered on the sidelines, weakly waving its fist. The dial of history has turned, and these bolshy jingoists – once the victims of renegade Ottoman commanders determined to impose their tyrannical rule over Belgrade – have been hoisted by the same nationalistic petard that drove them to expel the Turks a century ago.

'I find these long ethnic struggles fascinating,' David remarks. 'I mean, who do you blame? The Serbs? The Turks? The Crusaders, even? After a while, the origins of a conflict get lost and the spiral of repression and revenge develops a momentum of its own.'

What's important to note, he stresses, is that ethnicity and religion may fan the flames of conflict, but they rarely provide the spark. 'Take the Russians,' he says. 'Since Catherine the Great, they've positioned themselves as the great protectors of Orthodox Christianity, but this is just a pretext. Their true aim, of course, is power.'

I think of Kosovo itself: Europe's most Islamic country, yet, at the time of writing, only recognised by thirty-one of fifty-seven Organisation of Islamic Cooperation member states due to its alliance with the US.

I mention this to David, and he smiles. 'Exactly! Religion is just a tool. Politics trumps faith. Every. Single. Time.'

* * *

The Kosovans are hardly reticent when it comes to expressing their affection for America. Indeed, their fondness seems to verge at times on infatuation, like a lover ever-indebted to their brawny paramour for saving them in their time of need. In Pristina, I walk down George Bush Boulevard, past a towering bronze statue of Bill Clinton clutching a sheaf of documents dated 24 March 1999 – the first day of the NATO strikes against Belgrade – and into a boutique named 'Hillary' filled with an alarming array of monochrome trouser-suits. Nearby, a hotel is crowned with a diminutive Statue of Liberty, while kiosks along the main shopping precinct are packed with t-shirts declaring 'THANK YOU USA' and 'WE LOVE YOU CLINTON', alongside a panoply of Stars and Stripes paraphernalia.

As I wander, I struggle to get a handle on the essential psyche of this nascent capital. At first, it strikes me as an attractive, progressive city with few signs of the precarious instability at its core. Yet it feels oddly sandblasted too: of structure; identity; history. Only scattered remnants of the city's rich Ottoman past remain, while in the centre an eclectic imbroglio of buildings can be found thrown together like clothes at a jumble sale – partly a result, I am told, of the unregulated, mafia-run construction industry.[16]

For dinner, I meet a lawyer friend on 'small café street' – when not naming their roads after US presidents, Kosovans clearly prefer more topographical monikers – who tells me that, despite Pristina's seeming erasure of its Islamic heritage, the religiosity of the city is growing. 'Kosovo has over 800 mosques and new ones every month. Hijabs and prayer mats are sold everywhere. Things are changing fast.'

'Too fast?' I ask.

---

[16] Indeed, corruption is severe in Kosovo and goes right to the heart of government. In confidential NATO reports leaked in 2011, the president and former Kosovo Liberation Army leader, Hashim Thaçi, was identified as one of the country's 'biggest fish' in organised crime.

'For some, yes. But, personally, I'm not worried.' He looks at me. 'I mean, which Middle Eastern country do you think Kosovans most identify with?'

I consider. 'Palestine?'

He smiles. 'No – Israel. They're surrounded by enemies too, and have America fighting their corner. They also have World War II links, when the Albanians protected Jews from the Nazis.' Nationalism here is a far greater concern than religion, he believes. 'Kosovo is young and doesn't know who it is. It's that vacuum of identity that could cause problems down the line.'

The Bulgarian border is a disappointment – though what I was expecting exactly, I am unsure. Some glorious Ozymandias-style relic, perhaps? An allegorical snarl of barbed wire heralding empires' inevitable decay? Whatever it was, there seems little sign of the Iron Curtain now. Instead, all I encounter is an entirely nondescript checkpoint manned by a group of affable guards who unsportingly let me through with barely a second glance.

I stop for the night in Tran, a neat, pretty town paved in pastel. It dawns on me that I've arrived in my twelfth country of twenty, and I am excited to mark the occasion with the discovery of the best guesthouse I've stayed in so far: a luxury palace that not only boasts clean sheets, working lights and a real live *towel rail*, by god, but a pleasing lack of grime and pubes in the bathroom.

After a long, celebratory shower, I go to the restaurant and order a bottle of Domaine Peshtera 2011. It costs just £3 and I drink it at the bar alone. An hour passes, then two, and I begin to discern contours around the room I never noticed before, while the cretonne drapery exhibits a delicacy of pattern and form I find oddly intriguing. The waiter's pale, oval face hovers nearby like a full moon, occasionally disappearing behind a cloud or looming abruptly into view just inches from my own. I order a *rakija*, then another. Then, without warning, I find my head filled with Deep Thoughts, so I go outside for a cigarette – because, although I no longer officially smoke, I often struggle to give these kinds of thoughts (my best kind) my full attention without one. On the doorstep, I watch the rain gushing off the awning and forming a nacreous stream across the road. The future appears as an ashen blur on the horizon, like a fog that's yet to clear. But there are shafts of light too, and perhaps a trace of blue. I squint harder; it's so hard to see from here. Is it blue or just further layers of grey?

Inside, I try to change my euros into Bulgarian lev, but I am convinced the waiter short-changes me. Our quarrel swiftly escalates until a woman with a parboiled face intervenes to mediate. Voices rise and fall in fragments. 'No time,' one man seems to cry. 'We must squeeze juice from the trees.'

I order a final *rakija* and go upstairs to bed.

The next morning, I wake up and have no idea where I am. I don't mean I'm hazy about the town or hotel; I mean I don't know what *country* I'm in. For a few seconds, my surroundings seem entirely alien, as if someone has plucked me from my home and randomly dropped me like a pin on a map. My mind flicks through the options: Albania, Montenegro, Serbia, Kosovo ... all countries I've passed through, some more than once, over the past ten days ... before alighting with a kind of *aha!* on Bulgaria. And then, scanning the room, it all falls into place: the empty Marlboro pack and shot glass; the heap of soiled clothes; the clumsy buffalo blundering about my skull. Rolling with a whimper out of bed, I open the curtains and the darkness of the room barely changes. The sky is black as coal dust, the world a damp smudge. The rain has continued all night and now cascades in torrents as if a pipe in the heavens has burst. My padded underpants, draped over a chair, remain moist.

Downstairs, I spend an exciting twenty minutes wrapping my belongings in plastic bags before venturing tentatively outside. Moments later, I venture back in again. It's like cycling through a washing machine. I can't see anything through my glasses and my underpants are instantly sodden once more. As this is almost certainly the state in which I'll be spending my dotage, I'd rather not start now. Instead, I decide to wait it out.

When I finally depart after lunch, a thick fog has descended. It is still drizzling, and the only life I encounter is the occasional pallid face emerging from the brume like a body washed up by the tide. By the time I reach Sofia, shivering and ill-tempered, it is dark once again, and I arrive at the home of my Warmshowers[17] hosts to find a flat in disarray. The couple have a baby and sociopathic toddler and are clearly struggling to cope. She is exhausted and barely able to speak, while he is doing his best to prevent the infant eating the curtains and destroying the parquet floor with his plastic Triceratops. 'Sorry, don't mind Tommy,' the man, Ewan, cries, reaching down to unpeel his clammy son from my leg, where he has fastened himself like a limpet. 'He just so *loves* guests!'

Later, I learn that the couple are not only keen cycle-tourers, but – to my considerable astonishment – even regularly do trips *with the children in tow*. To me, this sounds like the worst kind of self-inflicted torture possible, unless they're able to harness the cherubs like huskies or use them to hunt for food – but each to their own, of course. And I find I can't help but warm to this genial, chaotic couple with their beatnik edge and unkempt charm. Ewan, a Welshman, tells me he moved to Sofia after marrying his Bulgarian wife a few years ago but is yet to understand some of the country's 'quirkier' customs. 'For example, people shake their head to say yes,' he says, 'except those who have been abroad, who tend to nod.' As a result, the country exists in a perpetual state of unresolved ambiguity, which may explain why nothing has really been achieved over the past thirty years. 'Bulgaria is really in the mire. It's the poorest EU country and corruption is crazy. Nobody can afford to plan for anything so they just spend everything they have and take each day as it comes. There's

---

[17] Warmshowers.org is a couchsurfing website aimed at cyclists.

even a word for it – *prshosnik* – which means, literally, turning everything into waste.'

Among those most afflicted by *prshosnik* is the Islamic community, it seems. With its shared border with Turkey, Bulgaria was ruled by the Ottomans for centuries and is home to the highest percentage of Muslims in the EU. Many live in poor, remote regions of the north-east, Ewan says, and speak Turkish as a first language. 'They act as useful scapegoats for the ultranationalists, who have a lot of support. And Syria's made everything worse, of course. You hear refugees referred to as "scum" and "vermin" in the media, and the Orthodox Church even recently accused them of "invading" the country. It's pretty unpleasant stuff.'

As is the case elsewhere in the Balkans, such attitudes have a long lineage. In the latter days of the Ottoman Empire, uprisings across Bulgaria were savagely crushed, and a revolt in the Rhodope Mountains resulted in the slaughter of up to 15,000 civilians. 'I have supped full of horrors,' the US correspondent Januarius Aloysius MacGahan reported after witnessing the aftermath of the assault. 'We looked again at the heap of skulls and skeletons before us, and observed that they were all … women and girls … [They] had all been beheaded.' MacGahan's reports sparked outrage across Europe and contributed to Britain's decision not to support the Ottomans in the 1877–78 Russo-Turkish War. The Eastern Orthodox coalition went on to triumph, Bulgaria won its independence and around a million Muslims fled. In 1989, following years of communist oppression, a further 360,000 ethnic Turks left the country – and, in light of recent times, their stories sound chillingly familiar: divided families; abuse by border guards; perilous journeys across impossible terrain.

'Millions of Muslims were killed or driven from the Balkans in recent decades,' Ewan says, collapsing into an armchair and pouring himself a pint of cold red wine after finally settling his son in bed. Looking around, I suddenly understand what it must be like to survive an earthquake or tornado. 'In the past they ran east. Now they run west. And people wonder why some may bear a grudge ...'

The temperature has dropped to near-freezing by the time I leave Sofia and I am forced to don a pair of socks with my sandals to prevent my toes going numb. It's a powerful look, though not one I suspect the world is quite ready for yet, so it is perhaps fortunate that I am making my way out of the city and into the country's rural hinterlands. For several days, I cycle along cratered roads and mud-cracked paths, past wonky timber farms and tumbledown shacks. I encounter Roma on donkey carts, farmers on tractors and hunched old crones who I estimate to be somewhere between 300 and 400 years old. The sky brightens as I ride, and the bracken kindles in the sunlight from teal and puddle-green to vermilion, apricot and gold.

In the traditional village of Koprivshtitsa, a Frenchman approaches me to warn me about dogs. I should be careful, he explains, as they can be dangerous. However, they generally only attack if provoked. Since he arrived in Bulgaria five years ago, he says, he only knows two people who've been killed by them.

'Sorry,' I reply. 'Killed?'

Yes, he confirms. 'But they were both quite old, so there's no need to worry.'

Now extremely worried, I continue my journey at a somewhat brisker pace. But today it isn't the homicidal mutts I need to beware of, it turns out; it's the donkeys. Having ignored the warning of a passing motorist – *Achtung, die Straße ist sehr schlecht!* – I am coasting down a hill a little too speedily when I spot a handsome, furry mule on a grassy verge, momentarily distracting my attention. Then, out of nowhere, an enormous crevasse appears in the road before me, too wide to avoid. Maud bucks like a wild filly, I am catapulted from the saddle and, before I know what is happening, I find myself flying in a high looping arc over her handlebars, baggage in tow, before smashing into a painful, crumpled heap on the ground.

Badly winded, I remain spreadeagled on the asphalt for some time. But when I finally, gingerly, peel myself off, I am relieved to discover that both Maud and I have suffered only surface wounds. The only serious casualty seems to be my laptop, in fact, which short-circuited after being doused by an exploding carton of milk – and once again I berate myself for not heeding Miss Erskine's sagacious advice. 'Milk alone, when taken in quantities *is dangerous*,' she advises (her emphasis). Unless, of course, it is mixed with eggs and 'a teaspoonful of whisky' first.

After tending to Maud's injuries as best I can (bent handlebars, dislodged brakes, broken pannier racks), I plough on miserably to the nearest motel, which is large and pink like a blob of blancmange and located in the middle of a forest as if part of a sinister fairytale. I am the only guest, and a stooping, grizzled old man who may or may not be a scion of Nosferatu leads me to my room, which is the size of a toilet cubicle and already inhabited by a family of friendly cockroaches. To lift my spirits, I go to the murky dining room and order a bottle of 2006 Zagreus Premium Reserve Cabernet Sauvignon, which is thick and strong like blood, and tastes at this moment like a true nectar of the gods, whether Bacchus or Dionysus or Radegast or Sucellus or whichever intemperate deity currently holds sway over the Bulgars' deep and multi-layered soil.

As I sit there, feeling cheerier by the moment, the old man shuffles into the room. 'What would you like to eat?' he asks in German (the only language I've ever spoken with any proficiency but which I've sorely neglected for over a decade). 'What do you have?' I reply. 'What do you want?' he repeats. 'Pasta?' I say. 'We don't have pasta,' he says. 'We have sausages and potatoes.'

Four minutes later, he reappears with a plate of dry beef and chips. 'We didn't have sausages,' he explains. 'Now, what would you like for dessert …?'

* * *

We walk across a large, bleak courtyard and then past a compound of densely packed, corrugated metal cubes. That's where asylum seekers used to be housed, I am informed, though the structures are empty now. We arrive at a second courtyard flanked by a vast concrete block the colour of bruised cartilage. Its walls are veined with cracks and a pool of sour yellow light spills from the open doorway. 'Welcome to paradise,' the man beside me whispers as we enter. 'Home sweet home.'

Inside, we pass a filthy bathroom where water is running from a broken tap and overflowing onto the floor. A half-disembowelled washing machine sits in the corner wrapped in torn plastic sheeting. 'Careful of the rats,' the man, Hashem, calls encouragingly as I examine one of the blocked drains. 'They're as big as dogs.'

We go upstairs. There are several bedrooms, each with multiple bunkbeds. Hashem shares his room with five other men, though there's barely space for two. The mattresses are soiled with wear and mottled stains cover the walls like a kind of fungoid growth. The air smells of sweat. Several duffle bags are heaped in the corner and a young man in a Nike hoodie sits texting on his bed. Just standing there for a moment feels stifling. Then Hashem gestures that we've got to go, and we swiftly dash back out the way we came before the next team of security guards arrives at the main gate for their shift.

'Right,' Hashem gasps as we emerge breathless into the street. 'You owe me a drink!'

I have made it to a border-town called Harmanli, where I came in the hope of gaining entry to the local refugee camp. Bulgarian camps are notoriously secretive, so I wasn't confident of success. However, soon after I arrived I was fortunate to meet Hashem, a camp resident, who – in exchange for a beer – helped me to sweet-talk the guards.

Hashem leads me to a smoky, rancid-smelling bar, where he requests a Staropramen. It is the first drink he's ever been bought by a woman, he tells me. He would reciprocate, but he's just gambled away €12,000 and is waiting for his family to send him money. 'Bulgaria gives us nothing,' he says. 'But that's okay. We're men. We're survivors.'

The refugee crisis hit Bulgaria hard. In 2011, the country had 1,000 asylum seekers; in 2015, it was 20,000. There were no facilities to cope with those numbers and integration centres were overwhelmed. Now, however, many camps – including Harmanli – sit near-empty. Most residents have fled to Germany, Hashem says: a favoured destination due to its recent scrapping of the controversial Dublin Regulation.[18]

As he drains beer after beer, Hashem tells me his story. A Syrian Kurd, he fled to Turkey in 2012 due to the war, and in 2013 he made it to Germany via Bulgaria, Serbia, Hungary and Austria. After applying unsuccessfully for asylum, he travelled to the Netherlands, where he remained for a year before being deported back to Bulgaria under the Dublin rules. 'Europe's my only hope,' he says. He cannot return to Turkey as he was caught there with a fake Norwegian visa and absconded. 'I'm trying again tomorrow. It'll be my last chance for a while.'

I cannot say I warm to my new friend. There is something shifty about him, and it doesn't help that his story later changes. He has never actually lived in Syria, he confides, although his parents are from Qamishli on the Turkish–Syrian border. His uncle killed someone over a blood feud and his family was forced to leave. 'Life is cheap for Kurds,' he says with a shrug. 'You run or you die.'

---

[18] This regulation allows EU states to deport asylum seekers to their first port of entry to the bloc, thereby placing a disproportionate burden on countries located on the front line. Despite widespread opposition to the rule, attempts to overhaul it have failed. What would seem to be the fairest proposal – a quota mechanism whereby asylum applications are distributed more evenly across Europe – has not gained widespread support. Britain's response to the crisis has been particularly woeful: by 2020, we had only resettled 20,000 Syrian refugees (0.02 per cent of our population). Germany, conversely, has taken in nearly a million (1.2 per cent).

We go to a petrol station, where some of Hashem's friends are drinking orange juice on the forecourt. All of them have shaved heads and tattoos, and wear Adidas and North Face t-shirts. They are open and friendly and buy me a drink without asking. As we sit there, a black 4×4 Mercedes with tinted windows pulls up and a man climbs out and nods in our direction. He is a local 'chief', Hashem whispers – a trafficker – although I hardly need to be told. In his acrylic shell-suit, gold chain and luminescent yellow trainers, he is clearly from the Jimmy Savile school of conspicuous criminality. I ask how much I'd need to pay him to get me to Germany and am told 'up to £750' to cross the Serbian border and 'thousands' for the journey as a whole, depending on my ability to pay. It is harder now than it used to be, they explain, due to increasingly militant guards, closed borders and physical barriers such as the thirty-kilometre wire fence recently erected between Bulgaria and Turkey.

The conversation moves on to Syria and the men tell me they hate Islamic State and Bashar al-Assad equally. This comes as little surprise. The Kurds are the largest ethnic minority in Syria, Turkey and Iraq, and one of the largest in Iran, and have long fought for greater autonomy in the face of severe persecution. Under the Ottomans, there was even an eyalet marked 'Kurdistan' on the map. But after World War I, when the Middle East was being sliced up like a celebratory *génoise* between the imperialist powers, the Kurds found themselves unceremoniously fractured among competing nation states, their dream of a homeland shattered.

Since then, the idea of Kurdish statehood has lain buried but far from dormant, simmering with quiet fervour beneath the tangled faultlines overhead. 'It'll happen,' Hashem says. 'We're stronger now than ever. We're beating Daesh (Islamic State) when nobody else could.'

As we return to my hotel, however, Hashem's macho tone shifts. His money hasn't arrived, he murmurs. Could he have 20 lev (€6) for the bus tomorrow?

'Okay,' I reply, feeling oddly uneasy. 'Sure.'

The next morning, I receive a voicemail. Hashem overslept and missed the bus. And he's also in love with me: his 'angel'. His nerve enrages me, and I spend the day exploring the town while ignoring his increasingly persistent calls. Harmanli is an unsettling place, charming in parts but with a stale inertia at its core. Young men stand hunched in dark corners, their identical black leather jackets worn with age, their faces brittle and blanched like crackling twigs at first frost. Everything feels suspended here, in this shadowland of stray souls – desire, movement, joy, hope – and I find myself suddenly desperate to escape and move on.

Back in my room, I am packing my things when somebody knocks on my door. It's Hashem. 'Where have you been?' he demands, his eyes bulging and bloodshot. 'Why haven't you answered my calls?'

'I didn't want to talk to you,' I say, shocked he has found me. Swaying on his feet, he reeks of cigarettes and booze. 'I don't think you've been honest. I thought it was important that you left today?'

To get rid of him, I agree to have a final drink in the bar next door. When we arrive, he slumps at a table and demands a double vodka. He tells me again that he loves me, before somewhat undermining the sentiment by saying he loves 'all British women'. Gradually drunker and more incoherent, he says he respects me deeply. And wants to sleep with me. That's sweet, I reply, and will never happen in a million years. Eventually, I stand and walk out, but he follows me in a rage. 'I will kill you! And have sex with you!' he shouts – in that rather macabre order – and I race back to the hotel and into my room as he stumbles unsteadily through the foyer behind me.

A few seconds later, I hear crashes and a scream. And then silence.

Later, I discover that he lashed out at the receptionist and was arrested. At first, I feel guilty. He is not a malicious man, I think, just a desperate, misguided one. He is also clearly bright, with a talent for languages (he speaks four). But I needn't have worried, it transpires. A week later, I receive a message. He reached Munich after all – and he's sorry. I ignore him, but on some level I find that I'm pleased. Maybe, at last, he can get his life back on track.

After this experience, the complexities of the refugee crisis become clearer to me. Not all migrants are saints and not all are honest. I find myself thinking of Mirko's words in Croatia: '*We should help them anyway, good or bad ... Otherwise, it's only the bad guys, the fašisti, who talk about such things. And that's a real problem.*'

From Harmanli, I embark on an ambitious 118-kilometre venture to see a ghost-town called Matochina. The roads are badly pitted and hilly, and the final fifteen kilometres are spent juddering along an almost impassably muddy track through endless fields and pastureland.

Then, just as I emerge on an elevated ridge above a valley, I see it rise high and hazy before me: an odd, entrancing ember of a town glowing a deep, phantasmagorical pink.

From afar, the place looks eerily alive. But I'm aware that what I see is merely a mirage of vitality, a cadaver enlivened by an embalmer's brush. Only a handful of residents remain now and most of the buildings are boarded up. I visit the old school and museum, both shuttered and overgrown, and the ruined Bukelon fortress, which reportedly formed a key part of Rome's defences during the fourth-century Battle of Adrianople. The conflict resulted in a devastating victory for the Goths and is said to have marked the start of the decline of the Western Roman Empire.

After my brief reconnoitre, I re-join the road towards a town called Shtit, where I've heard there may be a guesthouse. As I depart, however, my way is blocked by five dogs baring their fangs and barking in a deafening chorus. They are a sinewy, cruel-looking pack, and as they encircle me I try desperately, without success, to forget the Frenchman's ominous warning in Koprivshtitsa. 'Bugger off!' I holler, lobbing a rock that bounces off one of their leaden skulls. 'Scram!' But my cries only enrage them further, and they growl and creep closer until they're standing just a few feet away. Then, just as I feel myself starting to panic, a swinging crook appears from nowhere and a shrill banshee cry fills the air. *Ahlooahlooahlooahh!!* Barrelling to my aid are three toothless shepherds, swiping and warbling for all their might. The pack retreats, I am saved, and I throw myself into my bemused heroes' arms in an adrenalin-fuelled rush of relief.

Night has descended by the time I finally leave the village, and I struggle to avoid the endless holes and cracks along the ink-black country lane. It is exactly the kind of place I don't want to get my first puncture – and barely has this thought, this enticement to the fates, entered my mind when I hear the dreaded *pffffft* and feel Maud stagger below me as if shot. Now, I rage? *Now?!!* Cursing, I pull over and dismount … and it's then that I hear the jackals, cackling with maniacal glee. *Oh god*, I think. *I'm going to die here. I'm going to end my days as some crass horror movie parody, en route to a town called Shtit.* I dig out my thermos and have a swig of emergency Cabernet Sauvignon Khan Krum. I feel better and have another. *What to do …?*

And then, as if by magic, I am saved for the second time today. A man in a truck pulls up and kindly offers to give me a ride – and twenty minutes later, I am safely ensconced at a guesthouse down the road, where an octogenarian cowboy with a striking resemblance to Freddie Mercury serves me a hearty meal of bourbon and tripe soup while showing me his treasured collection of steel weaponry, stuffed fish and paintings of bosomy women being violently massacred on the battlefield.

I leave at dawn for the Turkish border. Near Elhovo, I meet a British expat who tells me that, until recently, refugees would regularly pass through his village. 'The police sometimes beat them up, robbed them and dumped them back in Turkey,' he says. 'There were some real horror stories. Two guys had their legs broken and later froze to death, and I heard an Afghan was shot and killed.'[19]

I continue on. The road to the border is featureless and fringed by colourless grasslands. Occasionally, a yellow sign appears crying 'DANGER ZONE' and I wonder what gruesome terrors might be waiting for me on the other side, on that sweeping Anatolian plateau where two great worlds collide. *Ten kilometres ... five ... one ...* Europe spins out behind me like an unfurling thread. Europe: a beacon of hope for so many. A place of stolen dreams. Three months on the road and I still struggle to define it, this region of blurred identity that stands as a bulwark against the East.

Much of my route has followed the path of the first Crusade, which marked the birth of two centuries of bloody combat between ostensibly bipolar worlds – but how much has changed since then! A thousand years ago, Europe was stumbling in darkness, while the Middle East was bathed in light; the Christians were the dogmatic barbarians, the Muslims the enlightened savants. Now the world has turned and the West is centre stage once more – but for how much longer, I wonder? What are the values that unite us? Where are our liberal ideals now?

Borders are a pragmatic necessity. They impose order on confusion and create a framework for effective rule. But they are not real. They are not fixed. And the higher you fly, the fainter they become, until all you see is horizon and the endless white of the sky.

---

[19] I look up the incidents later. The first involved two Iraqi Yazidis who were fleeing Islamic State, while the Afghan was killed by border guards. The latter was shot accidentally due to a 'bullet ricochet', the officer responsible claimed, and all charges were dropped.

Chapter 3

BETWEEN THE CROSS
AND THE CRESCENT MOON

Turkey

'Perhaps an interface between East and West is the bicycle, the machine which makes us all brothers and sisters.'
American *Pedal Power* manifesto from the 1970s

At the border, a barbed wire fence forms a black, serrated scar through the hills. On the far side, a seven-kilometre queue of lorries snakes into the distance, pressed like dammed water against the checkpoint gates. It is easy to feel dismayed at such a sight, which seems to expose the brutal self-interest beneath humanity's burnished veneer. Yet I am buoyed by the human warmth on show too, as the drivers maintain their spirits with tea parties and shows of camaraderie on the roadside.

Pre-warned about the police, terrorists and traffic, and with Freya Stark's comments about the 'extreme' virility of Turkish men lurking at the back of my mind – 'it's almost frightening to feel so unsafe, even at my age!' she trilled to her agent, perhaps a little too enthusiastically, while travelling through the country aged fifty-nine – I begin this leg of my journey with caution. But it's not long before I relax. Crossing the border feels like switching from sepia into technicolour; everything appears brighter, sunnier, sweeter. Strains of the *azan* (call to prayer) drift from cafés and car radios, while customers smile and cry *merhaba!* as they see me pass by. The roads are a pleasure too. They no longer buckle and cleave beneath my wheels but run in straight, smooth lines towards the horizon. As in the Dark Ages, moving eastward feels like moving forward, as if emerging from the wilderness into the light.

From the highway, I turn onto a country lane. Cars are gradually replaced by tractors, and buildings by outhouses and farmyard shacks. Men in flat caps idle in doorways, while feral dogs gnash their teeth and give chase. And all the time the wild thought endures: *I've made it all the way to Turkey! I've finally reached the Middle East!*

Though I haven't really, in truth. Despite its Eastern trappings, this breakaway fragment of the country, which emerges from the great Anatolian steppe like a solitary lilting rose, is traditionally regarded as part of Europe. Not until I reach Istanbul can I truly claim to have crossed an entire continent by bicycle. There, at the Bosphorus, the powerful counter-currents of Europe and Asia funnel to a point just thirty-one kilometres wide, separated by a hairline fracture of a strait that feels far from capable of keeping these two vast behemoths apart.

Historically known as Eastern Thrace, this littoral outgrowth doesn't feel like it should be part of Turkey at all. Craning up towards the Balkans, it is suctioned onto Bulgaria and Greece with far greater fidelity than its fragile attachment to Anatolia. And, once upon a time, Thrace was indeed a united whole, spanning a broad landmass between the Bosphorus in the east and modern-day Sofia in the west. Renowned as fearsome fighters, the Thracians of Greek mythology are said to have descended from Thrax, son of the war god Ares, and to have been ruled by a series of mad and homicidal kings – several of whom, inadvertently or otherwise, allegedly killed or ate their own children.

Bearing in mind the warnings I've received about Turkey, one might be forgiven for thinking that little has changed in the generations that have elapsed since. As I cycle, I am half expecting to encounter warring fiefdoms, hostile clansmen and gangs of gladiatorial mercenaries rampaging majestically across the prairielands. But if such things exist, sadly they pass me by. The shirtless, heathen hordes, oiled and primed for battle (please allow me this short reverie), must be taking the day off.

There is one ancient tradition that seems to live on, however. To relax after a tiring day's slaughter, the heirs of Thrax reportedly enjoyed knocking back a few goblets of wine, and Eastern Thrace remains one of Turkey's main wine-producing regions today. It's *good* wine, too: strong and rich and spicy (which, coincidentally, is just how I like my gladiatorial mercenaries). I discover this in a village called Süloğlu, although the place looks unpromising at first. The main street is grimy and tired, with no obvious shops, restaurants or lodgings, so I make my way to the police station, where I am greeted with a mixture of befuddlement and alarm. Two hapless young chaps mutter and look mildly distressed, then fetch their colleague, who proceeds to scratch his nose and walk in harried circles around the room. Eventually, somebody who seems to be important arrives and tells me I am welcome to sleep in the basement – currently occupied by a huddle of ancient Honda motorcycles, three resplendent orange sofas and a thick layer of dust – and, grateful to be saved from the cold, I accept.

After our inauspicious start, the police turn out to be excellent hosts, not only providing constant rounds of tea and cigarettes but even my very first authentic Turkish döner. This, for me, is a special moment. As a long-time kebab obsessive, being surrounded by socially acceptable döner meat feels like a kind of dream. I've always secretly feared the 'Turkish kebab' might be some outmoded custom or puffed-up tourist propaganda, like dancing Masai warriors or Cairene papyrus painting. But the stories, thank goodness, are true.

It is, for this reason, a heavenly introduction to the country – if not exactly an exhilarating one. The responsibilities of the Süloğlu police force do not seem onerous. For hours, the men smoke and chat and shuffle papers in endless rotation, as their radios crackle with static and their firearms hang limp and idle by their sides. The incongruity between their listless apathy on the one hand and their overloaded artillery belts on the other feels both comical and sinister; Turkey is swiftly making the transition from conservative semi-democracy to autarchic security state, and even the most parochial of greenhorn patrolmen is now dressed like the Praetorian Guard.

I am just finishing my fourteenth cup of tea and wondering how to extricate myself politely from my cordial but lacklustre hosts and make my way to bed when the local pharmacist, Yusuf, appears, whom I met earlier in town. 'I told my wife about you and she insisted you come and stay,' he announces – and I don't need to be asked twice. Within an hour, I have relocated and am sitting in the couple's living room, which is modest and beige and garnished with traditional Turkish frills and curlicues. 'You drink wine?' Yusuf asks, pouring me a glass before I can reply. 'We have best in world.'

'Kayra Kalecik Karasi, the local pinot noir,' his wife, Elena, adds. A Greek national, she is plump and pretty with a slanted, laconic smile. 'Turkey's a big wine country and nearly half comes from here. It's a surprise, no?'

'It's a surprise seeing a Greek drinking Turkish wine,' I say.

'A Greek married to a Turk!' she laughs, punching Yusuf on the arm. 'What was I thinking?'

'We're doing our bit for world diplomacy,' Yusuf says, shielding himself from another blow. 'Unfortunately, the Greeks are very violent, so it hasn't been easy.'

The couple met in Athens, they tell me, and it was love at first sight. But it wasn't easy convincing Elena's grandfather, who saw the union as a betrayal of the countries' mutual enmity nurtured over generations. Embittered by centuries of Ottoman rule and desirous of securing former Ottoman territory, the Greeks invaded Anatolia in May 1919 in expectation of a swift victory. Instead, their forces were demolished and around 1.5 million

Greek Orthodox Christians found themselves evicted from their ancestral Anatolian homes.

'It was a monkey that lost us the war, you know,' Elena says, pulling out a sofa-bed for me in the dining room. 'One attacked and killed our king during the conflict, so his father, Constantine, took over. But his heart was never in it.'

'Please, not the monkey!' Yusuf cries, throwing up his hands in mock despair. 'Greeks are sore losers.' He pulls Elena over and kisses her. 'And they are mad.'

'The strange thing was, he said, how they screamed every night at midnight ... We were in the harbour and they were all on the pier and at midnight they started screaming. We used to turn the searchlight on them to quiet them. That always did the trick.'

In his short story 'On the Quai at Smyrna', Ernest Hemingway recounts the harrowing closing stages of the Greco-Turkish War. In September 1922, Turkish soldiers poured into Smyrna, while the survivors of the onslaught clustered on the dock in terror. Many were massacred, including women and children, and corpses formed a grey pontoon on the water. Nearby, in the Greek and Armenian quarters of the city, a fire broke out that killed tens of thousands.

Meanwhile, rising above it all, was the siren song of the hunted. When Hemingway – then a cub reporter for the *Toronto Star* – spoke later to witnesses, this is the memory that endured. This, and the women and babies. 'They'd have babies dead for six days. Wouldn't give them up. Had to take them away finally ...'

In 1821, the Greeks had fought for independence like a tiger caught in a net. Now it was Turkey's turn – and nothing was left to chance. Villages were pillaged, women raped, civilians slaughtered. The two sides battled hard; butchery was met with butchery, flames with flames. But by September 1922, it was over. Smyrna, once heralded as a pinnacle of diversity, had been crushed into homogeneity. No Greeks remained, all driven out, deported or killed.

And the British, who promised Greece the land but pledged it to Italy too? Who forged the treaty that enraged the Turks, inciting them to fight? Who orchestrated the assault but barely lost a man?

Well – we threw in the spark, and then we watched it burn.

One afternoon, I meet a couple of genial Antipodeans on the roadside. Matt is a Kiwi lawyer, Mel an Australian accountant, and we slip quickly into the easy banter of those who share linguistic and cultural roots. Together, we ride up and down hills, through wheat fields and pumpkin patches and small shabby towns with jarringly elegant mosques. We get along extremely well and I am delighted to have the company. With them, my energies are shifted to interaction rather than introspection, and our sense of communal purpose helps to rouse and spur me on.

One night, we stop in a village called Subaşı, where we've heard rumours there may be a guesthouse. It seems preposterous at first that such a small, dingy hole of a place would have one – but, after a cursory search, what a guesthouse it transpires to be! It is, by any standards, enormous. The size of a small school. From a distance, it appears magnificent, although the closer we get, the more blemishes appear, until it begins to look less like the gilded *palazzo* we originally imagined and more like the kind of faded holiday resort you find in ageing coastal towns such as Blackpool or Skegness. Outside, a swimming pool the colour of pea soup is overlooked by the type of stone gargoyles almost certain to come alive at night, while inside, under a web of lurid fairy lights in the dark mahogany foyer, a cluster of human-sized mannequins stare at us through waxen, horror movie eyes.

The receptionist is not a friendly chap. I suspect it may have been quite some time since he's had to welcome any guests here – eighty or ninety years, at least. To break the ice, I gesture to a portrait on the wall that depicts a man in a traditional *kalpak* with a flinty gaze and well-groomed moustache.

'Atatürk,' I say, as if he may not have noticed. 'A great man.'

'Yes,' he replies.

'You like him?'

'Of course.' He turns a page in the Qur'an, which is open on the desk before him. 'He stopped Turkey being slave.'

I nod. It is the answer I was expecting. Turkey's former leader is revered by citizens of every persuasion, from young, secular progressives to old, pious traditionalists. At the same time, it is one of Turkey's many paradoxes that the man almost singlehandedly responsible for creating one of the largest Muslim democracies in the world was neither a Muslim nor a democrat. From this gaping, multifaceted landmass, Mustafa Kemal Atatürk forged a country from the fog of war like a god moulding man from clay – and, where he was concerned, there was no room in politics for faith.

The hotelier hands me my key, and I am walking to my door when I hear Mel holler from down the hall. 'Might be a night for sleeping bags,' she cries. 'I think something in my blanket just moved!'

Istanbul, it turns out, is almost entirely bike-proof. Between the outskirts and the centre lies a labyrinthine mass of urban barbarity designed to vanquish even the hardiest of wayfarers: an Escher-like confusion of ten-lane roadways, vertical hills, jet-black tunnels and inconvenient cats. This assault course takes several hours to complete, and by the time the Ms and I finally make it through, bruised and stunned by the ordeal, a crimson flush is spreading low across the sky. Here, at the eye of the storm, the centre of the maze, I half expect to see the brawny form of the Minotaur rise from the shadows with a heap of ravaged cyclists at its feet. Instead, from the brow of a hill, we look out at an umber glow of corporate high-rises and neon kebab houses, breezeblock huts and *simit* food carts, Turkish flags and Ottoman minarets. Couples wander by hand in hand, while flower-sellers in *şalvar* trousers ply their trade with painted smiles. It all feels beautifully calm – and very different from the last time I was here, in November 2013, when the muddied imprint of baying crowds was still fresh upon the ground.

Being here now, on this finespun filament of land where two continents collide, should be a seminal moment. Finally, after three months and 4,200 kilometres, the first leg of my journey is complete: I've arrived at the gateway to the East. I've made it through *my* motherland, *my* culture, *my* people, and next it will be over to *them*, the ones who speak differently and think differently and worship different gods. However, it doesn't feel like a watershed; it feels like a progression. Another link in the chain. After all, what's truly changed? I've crossed Muslim states before: Bosnia, Albania, Kosovo. I've visited places that use different alphabets and fought on different sides in wars. I've met people with whom I have nothing in common and those who I hope will be friends for life. What alien singularities could Anatolia have in store that I haven't encountered already?

In some ways, Turkey has more in common with the West than the West does with itself. It has been knocking on the door of Europe for generations, after all: militarily, culturally, politically. A hundred years ago, the Turks, Slavs, Pomaks, Bosniaks, Greeks, Kurds and many others besides were all a single entity, caught in the same imperial net. Decades before Atatürk, reformist Ottoman sultans were lauding European politics, science and art, while acting as caliphs to Muslims across the world.

As I stand in the gloaming beside Gezi Park, I don't feel exhilaration. I feel exhaustion. And a desperate need for a drink. So, after tracking down our accommodation, Mel, Matt and I shut the door, crack open a bottle – and vow never to cycle in Istanbul again.

'Erdoğan works for the rich, but bribes the poor into supporting him,' Selim tells me. 'He gives them money and coal before elections and pretends he cares about God.'

I found Selim on Couchsurfing.com and have moved to his flat in Şişli, a commercial district in northern Istanbul, after saying an emotional farewell to the Ms. Over a sizzling lamb döner, the thirty-year-old banker explains how the president has gradually tightened his grip over Turkey. 'He's a classic dictator. He steals our freedoms, then distracts everyone with big shiny things. We now have the fourth-longest suspension bridge in the world and a presidential palace thirty times bigger than the White House.' He spears a juicy ribbon of meat with his fork. 'He named the palace *Cumhurbaşkanlığı Külliyesi*, can you believe it? It means an Islamic religious centre.'

I ask about the May 2013 protests and his eyes light up for the first time. They brought everyone together, he tells me: the young and old, rich and poor, progressives and conservatives alike. 'It was like Woodstock. There were medical tents, poetry groups, people clearing trash ... People even queued!' This isn't normal in Turkey, he stresses. 'We help friends and family all the time, but doing something for society is different. It felt like a real revolution.'

In Britain, it often feels like the opposite is true, I remark. People are generous in civic terms – queuing, recycling, giving to charity – but are perhaps more detached on a personal level. 'We're very individualistic. We like to keep to our private cocoons.'

'Yes,' he nods. 'Your civil society is strong, built up through history. You don't need to rely on each other so much because the system is good. It works. Here, it's different.'

Around 3.5 million people took part in the unrest, which began as a rally against the redevelopment of Gezi Park, one of the capital's few remaining green spaces, but swiftly expanded into a nationwide protest encompassing broader issues such as corruption, inequality and Erdoğan's growing autocracy. Demonstrations with echoes of both the Arab Spring and global Occupy movement erupted across Turkey with no central organisation or figurehead. When the police cracked down, 8,000 people were injured and more than a dozen killed. But the park was saved – and a new spirit of defiance was born.

'Was it worth it?' I ask. 'Has anything changed?'

'Well, the country's more divided than ever and Erdoğan's more paranoid and crazy,' he replies. 'But people have changed inside. I feel like we've lost our fear.'[20]

Istanbul is a city of smells. Some cities are places of colour or music or light, and Istanbul is certainly all of these things. But mainly, to me, it's a city of smells. There's the brackish tang of Galata Bridge, where anglers cast their lines for bluefish and bonito in the over-fished straits. There's the smoky sweetness of the *nargile* pipes that drifts in gyres from gaping mouths. There's the briny waft of the *midye dolma* stuffed to bursting with spices and rice. There's the zest-smell of the sea and the pepper-smell of the streets; the steam-smell of the hammams and the earth-smell of the mosques; the toast-smell of *simit* and the grease-smell of exhausts. These aromas nestle in every furrow like an olfactory footprint. Pursuing their scent, I pace about like a bloodhound, following the ancient jumble of passageways and plazas that overlook the Bosphorus in a bid to locate the city's elusive beating heart.

'Sadness,' the man with the gopher moustache says. 'That's what this building smells like. Once it was hope, but now it's sadness.'

Berat is a tour guide who approaches me to advertise his services. We're standing outside the Hagia Sophia, the dusky pink walls of which enclose the dense mass of 1,500 years of history. Built by the Byzantines in 537 CE, this stunning edifice embodies both East and West, its geometry based on an Orthodox cross, its dome a homage to the Levant, its marbled walls influenced by the Moors, Greeks and Celts. Constructed originally as a church, then transformed into a mosque under the Ottomans and a museum

---

[20] Erdogan's crackdown against civil society worsened following a failed coup in July 2016, which he blamed on Fethullah Gülen. Since then, he has fired hundreds of thousands of soldiers and public employees, condemning many to a life of penury.

under Atatürk, the structure has long stood as a powerful icon of inclusion. Now, however, Erdoğan looks set to reconvert it to a mosque once more.[21]

The Hagia Sophia feels like a fitting metaphor for Turkey as a whole, which has long strayed from bank to bank like a boat adrift, its contrary ideals acting as a kind of self-corrective tugging it back towards the centre. Two decades ago, there was hope it had found its sweet-spot under Erdoğan: a steady, moderate leader who evoked both Atatürk and Allah in a broad populist drive that blended patriotism, modernism and Islamism. In recent years, however, patriotism has turned to alt-nationalism and democracy to demagoguery – and hope has ebbed away.

'Or maybe it's the smell of fear,' Berat continues, warming to the theme. 'Erdoğan wants to take us back to the Ottomans. It's scary.'

I nod, although I can't help but feel he's doing the old imperialists a disservice. The Turks may have been 'agents of the devil' to Martin Luther, 'barbaric usurpers' to Voltaire and bloodthirsty 'baby-killers' to the Hungarians, but the society they created was arguably more tolerant and just than the Byzantine feudalism that came before. Like their Arab predecessors, the Ottomans generally prized pragmatism above piety and preferred to tax Christians and Jews heavily rather than force them to convert against their will.[22] Indeed, in the mid-1800s, the Ottomans demonstrated a remarkably progressive spirit, outlawing religious discrimination, banning slavery, introducing secular education and – astonishingly – decriminalising homosexuality more than a century before British lawmakers followed suit.

This spirit can be felt particularly strongly in Istanbul, which has thrived for generations in its pluralistic, patchwork skin.

---

[21] He finally did so in July 2020.

[22] 'You venture to call Ferdinand a wise ruler,' Sultan Bayezid II reportedly said in 1492 after welcoming the Jews and Arabs driven out by Catholic Spain. 'He who has impoverished his own country and enriched mine!'

Soaring high-rises loom alongside fifteenth-century minarets; the *muezzin* competes with the thump of punk and hip hop; unlicensed bars serve secret vodka to a farrago of polyethnic revellers. While tensions clearly exist, and the expat crowds are not always looked on kindly by more traditionalist locals, there remains an undeniable aura of inclusivity about the place. The city feels like a haven of interwoven polarities, where the pull of contrary impulses has created a community of prodigious character, like the knotted warp and weft of the rugs for which the country is renowned.

The city's changing names are a testament to its cosmopolitan heritage. Called Byzantium by the Romans, this was a Latinisation of the moniker given to it by its Ancient Greek settlers. It was then renamed Constantinople, from the Greek 'Constantinopolis' ('City of Constantine'), after the king declared it the new Roman capital in 330 CE. Finally, after falling to the Ottomans in 1453, it became known as Istanbul, a Turkish interpretation of the Greek *stim'boli* (to the city). So, as a pagan city, it had a Latinate version of a Greek name; as a Christian city, it had a Greek version of a Roman name; and as an Islamic city, it had a Turkish version of a Greek phrase. In the 1920s, there were even calls to change 'Istanbul' to 'Gazi Mustafa Kemal', endowing an Islamic title ('Gazi', or 'warrior') on a secularist state.

Istanbul's multiculturalism feels all the more impressive when one considers that it has borne witness to two of the greatest political and religious schisms in history: first, the collapse of the Western Roman Empire in 476 CE; then the split between Constantinople and Rome in 1054, after which the Christian world was cleaved into its own micro East–West divide. The latter conflict came to the fore in 1204, when the papal armies made a detour to Constantinople during their Fourth Crusade and proceeded, in a shockingly gratuitous assault, to smash the place to smithereens. The attack had cataclysmic consequences for both the city and Christendom as a whole. While the Byzantines eventually managed to wrest back control, Constantinople would never be the same again – and, just two centuries later, would prove easy prey for the Turkic *gazis* lurking in the wings.

The Ottomans had brought Islam to the door of Europe. And there it would remain, powerful and emboldened, for the next 469 years.

In 1993, over the course of three months, the Kurdish lawyer Tahir Elçi was beaten, stripped, doused in iced water and electrocuted on the genitals. Some days he was taken for mock executions, where the bullets shot at him would be so close that he could smell the burning metal.

Held on baseless terrorist charges, Tahir was accused of having links to the Kurdistan Workers' Party (PKK): a left-wing Kurdish militia group that has been fighting for greater rights and autonomy in Turkey since the late 1970s. He and the fifteen lawyers arrested with him took their case to the European Court of Human Rights, where they were awarded £25,000 compensation. The case had no immediate impact, he says. But in the years that followed, torture was employed by the security agencies less and less frequently. 'They know they can't get away with those tactics anymore,' he tells me over tea in a Beyoğlu café. 'Now their methods are subtler: harassment, bribery, surveillance.'

Renowned for his fearless human rights work, Tahir's clients include the Kurds and other marginalised groups, and he often acts as a mediator between the state and the PKK. Violence continues to escalate, however, and he is critical of both sides for failing to reach a resolution.

'The Kurds' success against Daesh is partly to blame, as it has fired them up and got Erdoğan worried. He's openly admitted that the PKK is the "primary threat" to Turkey, while Daesh is only "secondary".' That's why the president provided logistical support to Daesh at the start of the Syrian War, Tahir believes. 'He hoped they'd be useful against the PKK. But he helped create a monster.'

Erdoğan has always denied assisting Islamic State, but many

others have echoed Tahir's claims. In 2014, Columbia University's Institute for the Study of Human Rights compiled a damning dossier of media reports alleging complicity between the president and ISIS, while a video published by *Cumhuriyet* newspaper in 2015 allegedly showed Turkish aid trucks carrying weapons across the border. Erdoğan vowed the journalists who publicised the footage would be punished – and, true to his word, the editors were swiftly convicted and jailed.[23]

Tahir has been similarly harassed throughout his life. Just a few weeks ago, he was arrested for claiming that the PKK is not a terrorist organisation. 'I don't call them terrorists because they no longer target civilians,' he responds when I ask about the incident. 'But I've always said its violence isn't legitimate. Now we have the Peoples' Democratic Party, so we have democratic tools.'

This is the last time I see Tahir. Two days later, during a speech outside a mosque in the eastern city of Diyarbakir, he is killed during a shootout between the police and PKK.[24]

When I hear the news, it shocks me deeply and takes some time to process. Tahir knew the risks, yet had no fear. And I continue on my way, untouchable and immune, my passport strapped like a shield about my waist.

In Istanbul, the weather seems to skip a season. When I arrived, it was 25°C and balmy. Now, a fortnight later, there is frost on the ground and my breath puffs like smoke in the glacial morning air. Despite the strides I've made as a trailblazer of bicycle fashion, I

---

[23] More reporters have been jailed in Turkey than in any other country in recent years, and it currently ranks a dismal 153rd out of 180 countries on the World Press Freedom Index: lower than Pakistan, South Sudan and Russia.

[24] No official independent investigation was conducted into the shooting, and no arrests were made. Later, however, Forensic Architecture, a London-based research group that uses digital technology to investigate cases of state violence, analysed the incident and narrowed down the suspects to three police officers. They, along with a PKK militant, were finally charged with the killing in March 2020 and at the time of writing remain on trial.

decide it may finally be time to replace my socks and sandals with some proper shoes, so I purchase a cheap pair of trainers alongside some thermal leggings, gloves and a fleece. Now, dressed in my new all-black ensemble, I look less like a middle-aged Bavarian backpacker and more like a kind of mad cycling ninja.

On the ferry across the Bosphorus, I watch Europe melt to a coppery haze and disappear. As I do, I have an odd sensation of continental drift, as if it were not just me moving away but Anatolia as a whole. After years of pulling closer, Turkey and the West now seem more disconnected than ever. Talks with the EU have stalled, and for the first time since it laid siege to Vienna half a millennium ago, Turkey appears content to turn to the east and let its dreams of European integration slip gently away.

When I disembark, I feel an immediate sense of calm. The Asian half of Istanbul seems more sedate and less choreographed than the European, with fewer expats and oat-milk lattes and a greater sense of space. I only wish I could stay longer. But time is short, so I cross the Marmara Sea and push onwards through pastureland, prickly foliage and olive groves to Bursa – where a sallow-faced semi-alcoholic named Orhan introduces me to the local 'Iskender', the kingpin of the kebab world, which comprises a heavenly medley of lamb döner meat, tomato sauce, yoghurt and chopped pita bread – before continuing along a narrow, dun-coloured river towards the foothills of the Marmara peaks.

The university town of Eskişehir emerges like a lodestar through the fog, humming with industry, intellect and charm. In the historic district of Odunpazari, cobbled streets weave among jettied, timber-framed houses, their multicoloured facades gleaming between dark, cantilevered beams. With Christmas approaching, I stop in the crafts market to buy some gifts for home and am overwhelmed by the dazzling array of silverware, textiles and ornaments moulded from meerschaum – a pearly white, buttery-soft mineral native to this region – spilling from tables and shelves.

As I examine them, I realise there's something distinctly Persian about the exquisite intricacy of these artworks. There's something distinctly Persian about Turkey as a whole, in fact: in its food, its culture, its architecture, its warmth. At first, I assume this is simply the result of neighbourly exchange over generations – but then I learn about a formidable group of Turkic tribespeople, the Seljuqs, who subdued a sweeping expanse of territory between Egypt and China a thousand years ago and spread Persian culture across the span of their domains. 'There's no Turk without an Iranian,' a famous eleventh-century proverb declared, 'just as there's no hat without a head!'[25]

In order to stay on schedule, I must cross the vast blustery tundra of central Turkey within a fortnight. This entails covering at least 100 kilometres a day, and leaves little time for detours from the stale, relentless highways that criss-cross the country like latticework. Most journeys are efficient but rarely enjoyable, as I cling to the hard shoulder and judder over roadkill and rubber scraps and shards of broken glass. Meanwhile, the temperature continues to drop, transforming my body into an uncomfortable mosaic of microclimates: furnace-hot at the centre; frosty on the surface; glacial at the extremes.

As I ride, my emotions shift hour by hour, day by day. Yet what I like to imagine as existential angst borne of a refined and sensitive psyche can often, I note with some dismay, be cured by a bag of Skittles or a simple change in terrain. Happiness is not freedom or love or the poetry of the open road, I soon realise. It is a downward slope with a full belly and tailwind.

I arrive in Sivrihisar in a funk. Under a surly sky, the streets of this moth-eaten dishrag of a town meander listlessly between gruel-coloured tenement blocks, while the only café, located at

---

[25] It was an offshoot of the Seljuqs, in fact – the Sultanate of Rum – which laid the groundwork for the Turkey we see today. After the Seljuqs defeated the Byzantines in 1071, these Muslim warriors founded their own autonomous state formed from a confederation of *beyliks*, one of which ultimately grew into the Ottoman Empire.

the centre, has the sterile, starkly lit ambiance of a youth hostel or village hall. Walking inside, I encounter a murmur of unsmiling men dealing cards, while a pair of teenage girls play backgammon in tight-lipped silence nearby. Nobody looks my way as I enter, and I sit down in a dark corner alone.

Moments later, however, a young policeman arrives and things start to look up. After I have explained my predicament, he not only heroically buys me a lamb köfte out of his own pocket, but then goes to considerable trouble to find me accommodation for the night with one of his colleagues. Within an hour, I find myself sitting in a cosy one-bedroom flat eating a delicious second dinner of homemade beef stew and *dolma* (stuffed vine leaves), my feet clad ('because they look cold') in a pair of giant furry slippers shaped like lions.

As I am eating, the first policeman rings me. We talk through Google Translate, him speaking English, me Turkish, pronouncing each word slowly and haltingly.

'You. Are. Okay?' he asks.

'*Evet, teşekkür ederim!*' Yes, thank you!

'Good. I am … happy.' A pause and a cough. Then: 'Madam. How old?'

'Sorry?' I revert to English, surprised.

Another cough. 'You, please … How old?'

'How old am I? Why?'

'You like …?' I hear him tapping the words out on his phone. 'Yes?'

'You like … sex? With me? Tonight?'

My stomach lurches. 'What?' I splutter in horror. 'No!'

Shocked by the sudden twist to what I thought was a pleasant, sleaze-free conversation, I throw down the phone and direct a venomous glare at my host, Ugur. 'Your friend just asked me to have sex with him!' I blurt. 'Is this how you treat guests here?'

He stares blankly at me, not understanding. Then he shrugs and gestures to my plate. 'Good?'

'*Lezzetli,*' I say curtly. Delicious.

We eat in silence and I try to order my thoughts. Am I angry or amused by this young libertine? Here are two extremes of Turkish culture in a nutshell: the warmth and hospitality on the one hand, the sexism and opportunism on the other. I can't deny feeling annoyed by the exchange. But I also wonder who, ultimately, is the greater victim in this equation? The young man may have a disrespectful view of women – not to mention an optimistic view of their lack of discernment in the bedroom – but he is also a small-town stripling in a deeply repressed country that even lacks its own native term for 'sex' (*seks*). His request, I suspect, was motivated more by frustrated hormones than gender power-play – even if the impulse derived from a broader patriarchal culture in which all men, arguably, could be said to be complicit.

He did ask politely, after all. More importantly, he bought me a kebab – and for that I'll forgive almost anything.

'I want love,' Ugur tells me later when I ask why he's not married. Aged twenty-eight and a committed Muslim, he is quieter and sweeter than his friend, and I trust him not to try anything. How many sexual deviants have furry lion slippers, after all? 'Most friends marry, but I picky.'

The conversation drifts onto politics. Communicating over Google Translate, I ask his thoughts on Islamic State, and immediately his manner changes. 'Murderers,' he writes. 'Terrorism has no race or religion.' After several more ISIS-related questions, he visibly bristles. 'Why ask?' he types. 'You clearly don't understand real Turkey.'

He is right, of course. Is there even such a thing? Adela's attempt to find the 'real India' in E.M. Forster's *A Passage to India* results in a nervous breakdown and a ceaseless echo that drives everyone half-deranged. But there are certainly unreal Turkeys, or less real ones: the Turkey found in Antalyan beach resorts, perhaps. The Turkey found in balloon rides and dervish displays and boxes of Turkish Delight. The Turkey mined and crafted like meerschaum, created for foreign eyes (and wallets) alone.

'That's true,' I respond. 'But I promise I'm trying to learn.'

Before bed, Ugur writes down his contact details for me. Beside his name, 'Ugur Bulut', he draws a picture of a cloud. This is what Bulut means, apparently. It was chosen by his great-grandfather in 1935, when citizens were required to adopt surnames as part of Turkey's mass-modernisation drive. Most chose place names, personal descriptions or noble abstractions such as 'justice' or 'faith'. The president was given his name by parliament: Atatürk, Father of the Turks.

'You admire him?' I ask, nodding at the familiar portrait on the wall.

'Of course,' he says, almost misty-eyed. 'Without him, no Turkey. He is hero to us all.'

Atatürk undoubtedly left a towering legacy. Outraged by the punitive terms of the Treaty of Sèvres imposed by the Allies of World War I on the Ottoman Empire in 1920, which left Turkey with just a meagre sliver of Black Sea littoral, he roused the country to nationalistic fury, routed the European armies, abolished the Ottoman Caliphate and established a socially liberal, secularist state. His reforms were radical and long-lasting. A Western civil code was introduced, religious courts closed, polygamy outlawed and the Islamic calendar replaced with the Gregorian. Women were granted the vote, the hijab was banned in educational establishments and the day of rest was switched from Friday to Sunday. Most groundbreakingly, the alphabet was converted from Arabic to Latin, forcing schoolchildren and grandparents alike back into the classroom to relearn how to read and write.

The Father of the Turks didn't stop at that, however; he also wanted to change how people looked. One of his more controversial moves was to ban the fez: a hat rejected for being too Christian and foreign when it was introduced a century earlier but by then ironically deemed as Islamic and 'uncivilised' as the turban it originally replaced. Confounded, people did their best to guess what alternatives might be acceptable, leading to a rush on feathered berets, flowery bonnets and Fred Dibnah-style flat caps. A bemusing spectacle it must have been – though it was no joke at the time. Anyone failing to fall in line had a good chance of being hanged.

Bearing in mind the zeal with which this secularist conversion was enforced, it is perhaps unsurprising that the tide has now turned. Much like Iran, Afghanistan and Egypt – where similarly draconian dress-codes were introduced around the same time, prompting suppressed Islamists to rise in insurrectionary fervour and wrest control of each state in turn – Islam has only strengthened here through its subjugation. Atatürk's Turkey, united by force of personality alone, has long been coming apart at the seams.

'Imagine if Christians were treated like Atatürk treated the Muslims,' the young man says. 'They'd be outraged.'

I've arrived in the spa town of Haymana and am eating dinner with a twenty-year-old Sydney-born Turk called Alex. He befriended me after spotting me looking lost and hungry in the street (a look I have now perfected) – but he is clearly far from a committed Europhile.

'You don't like him?' I ask, surprised. Despite his staunch secularism, Atatürk for most Turks seems to embody a kind of human Rorschach test: a man of elastic credentials in whom everyone sees what they want to see. 'You're the first person I've met who doesn't.'

He throws his head back, clicking his tongue: the ever-confusing Turkish gesture for 'no'. 'People are idiots. Atatürk put pictures of himself everywhere, even though Islam prohibits this. He banned beards in universities.' His voices rises. 'We're an Islamic country. You can't ban beards!'

Alex doesn't actually have a beard, although he does have a light dusting of stubble that may or may not mark the beginning of more exuberant growth. In Turkey, such things are important, I've discovered; facial hair is not simply a question of fashion but comes weighted with social and political significance. Erdoğan went into politics, it is said, out of fury at being asked to shave his moustache while working at the Istanbul transportation authority and now sports a trim, almond-shaped number that allows for the Qur'an-mandated two millimetres of space above the lip. Meanwhile, opposition leader Kemal Kılıçdaroğlu prefers more luxuriant liberalist growth, the Gülen fraternity go clean-shaven, the leftists tend towards Marxist-style bushiness and the ultranationalists are partial to a set of drooping whiskers in the shape of the crescent moon.

'We're not Europe,' Alex says. 'We should be allowed to look how we want.' Have I heard about the reconversion of Hagia Sophia to a mosque, he asks? 'It's a sign we're not run by outsiders anymore.'

Alex recently returned to Turkey to study the Qur'an, he says, and 'undo the bad habits' he adopted in Australia. He shouldn't even be talking to me, apparently, although he admits he 'likes women' and hopes to get engaged soon. 'My parents will show me a girl's photograph,' he explains when I ask how the process will work. 'If I like her, we'll meet in person. If that works out, we'll get engaged.'

'You don't mind not choosing yourself?'

'No. I might be distracted by lust. If the woman is a good person, real love will come.'

I am just mulling on this rather beautiful thought when he adds: 'Anyway, if we meet and she's ugly then I can just dump her and try someone else.'

Later, he enquires about my own marriage plans. I confess I have none and he looks horrified. Everyone *must* get married if they want to enter Heaven, he stresses. And they *must* enter Heaven 'because it's awesome'. There is constant sex and drugs and virgins to cater for every whim. They need to be virgins, he insists, because their vaginas are tighter. That's also why he wants a virgin as his wife.

By now, I am beginning to suspect that Alex may not be the

enlightened Qur'anic savant I'd been hoping for. He certainly seems unusually preoccupied by vaginas, which crop up a few times during our conversation, often without warning.

'What about Hell?' I ask. 'What's that like?'

This, unsurprisingly, is a vagina-free zone. 'It's bad there,' he warns. 'Just huge pits of fire, as high as a house.' The fire burns the flesh from our bones, and when it's all burnt off, the skin regrows – only then to be all burnt off again. 'You don't want that to happen to you, do you?' he asks.

I admit I don't.

'Then you should convert!'

So this is how it ends, I think. Sprawled on a granite slab, rump aloft, being pulverised by a female sumo wrestler with a troubling sadistic streak. It's not quite how I imagined it, I admit. I'd rather not be completely naked, for a start. Or surrounded by a group of equally naked women, all eyeing me warily as I'm grappled into a series of undignified contortions. I'd also prefer it, in truth, if the women weren't all so disconcertingly enormous. This is a little sizeist of me, I know, but they truly are colossal. Not tubby. Not even fat. But unashamedly, relentlessly elephantine; a fleshy orgy of contour and crevasse. They lord over me in my torment, voluminous and aloof, like a clique of imperial blancmanges.

Why I'm here is a mystery. Following my meal with Alex, I decided against a massage in the local spa – mindful of the fact that almost every one I've had to date has ended badly, including an incident in Uzbekistan that almost certainly should have resulted in a criminal prosecution – and opted instead for the more innocuous-sounding 'deep clean'. It's a decision both I and the hammam drainage system swiftly come to regret. As I'm brutishly scoured and buffed, torrents of inky sludge sweep across the tiled floor like some kind of faecal magic porridge. Before a dozen pairs of increasingly alarmed eyes, I morph from brown to grey to red to pink and lose about two-thirds of my body mass.

By the end, I'm a pale shadow of my former self, lying raw and spindly on my granite plinth like a boiled baby langoustine.

Overall, it's a sobering and somewhat degrading ordeal. It's also, as it turns out, exactly what the doctor ordered. I've never felt so obscenely violated and extravagantly sanitised in all my life. Sadly, this newfound purity seems unlikely to stand much of a chance against my £8 hostel, the graffitied Marquis de Sade-style walls of which are worryingly reminiscent of a cell for the criminally insane – but I vow to enjoy the sensation while it lasts.

I hit the road at daybreak. Around me is a land of lost contours, barely visible through the mist. The hills are steep and exhausting, the wind bitingly cold. The mercury reads just −6°C.

And then I get a puncture … swiftly followed by another.

Each one takes twenty minutes to fix, my fingers numb and swollen like frozen chipolatas. Then onwards I trudge, past a vast salt glacier streaked in foliated shades of pastel orange and pink, and ramshackle towns that appear to have been fly-tipped by the roadside. I see odd space-age mosques with tinfoil domes and endless bisque-yellow buildings with terracotta roofs. I stay the night in Şereflikoçhisar, a cheerless urban smudge that proves as unattractive as it is unpronounceable, and am gifted a pair of earmuffs to protect my poor pillar-box lobes.

As I approach Ürgüp, Cappadocia, the terrain turns craggy and russet like the surface of Mars, and feels almost as cold. Fortunately, my host turns out to be a wonderful chap who instantly wins my heart by whisking me off to a restaurant famed for its metre-long kebabs. As we tuck in, he voices a desire to leave Turkey for Britain. 'British people are so nice,' he says. 'Much nicer than Turks.'

'Really?' I reply, as I devour my third *lahmacun* and realise that Alex was wrong. *This* is surely what Heaven must feel like. 'I definitely feel the opposite!'

He laughs. 'I guess, as you British say, the grass is always greener.'

I think about his comments afterwards. Romanticising foreign cultures is an easy trap, just as passing acquaintances are often treated with greater leniency than live-in relatives whose bad habits and bodily functions have long destroyed any illusion of respect. People welcome me here, but is it truly me they welcome or what I represent? Am I a person or exotic oddity? As a traveller, after all, I pose no threat to custom or routine. I cut deeper than the average rubbernecker, I hope – yet there is no denying the cloak of civility that surrounds me, muting and softening the world that I see.

Cappadocia is extraordinary. Situated on a high volcanic plateau, its improbable landscape was sculpted several million years ago by a heady amalgam of lava, wind and time. Ash and water formed 'tuff', which was later covered by a layer of basalt, and over the aeons the different rock types were carved into a forest of distinctive, top-heavy buttes. Dubbed 'fairy chimneys' by the prudish, these towering pinnacles can really be interpreted as one thing and one thing only: enormous, tumescent, thunderously erect cocks.

The effect is a priapic, preternatural dreamscape: a kind of Narnia meets Mordor meets Spearmint Rhino, where I half expect to encounter a host of horny troglodytes clad in nipple clamps and chains. Instead, I have to make do with a hirsute Canadian history professor called Martin, who I bump into outside my guesthouse in Göreme.

'See that?' Martin remarks, once pleasantries have been exchanged and we've decided we're both tolerable enough company to take a stroll together through town. He is gesturing to a Turkish flag emblazoned with the crescent moon in a tourist shop window. 'Where do you think that came from? That symbol?'

I consider. 'The Arabs?'

'No,' he smiles. 'The Greeks.' It was the logo of pre-Christian Istanbul – Byzantium – in honour of the lunar goddess who protected the people, he explains. Legend has it that the founder of the Ottoman Empire, Osman I, had a dream about a crescent moon that stretched across the sky, which he interpreted (presciently) as a sign that his kingdom would one day dominate the Earth. 'Later, when the Ottomans conquered Constantinople, they adopted the flag of Byzantium because of Osman's dream. It's remained the icon of the Islamic world ever since.'

I find something pleasing about the fact the Islamic crescent doesn't stand in opposition to the Christian cross but seems instead to act as a kind of bridge between the two worlds. However, Martin isn't finished. 'What about jihad, or holy war?' he asks. 'Where do you think that idea came from?'

'The ... Turks?' I venture, more weakly this time, feeling like the child at the back of the class who hasn't done their homework. Martin may be a terrible pedant, but he has a certain charm. Half-Persian and made up of considerably more hair than face, he has the air of an avuncular ayatollah.

'The Romans!' he cries, barely able to contain his glee at exposing the bottomless pit of my ignorance. In the early seventh century, the Persians were all-powerful and seized both Damascus and Jerusalem, he says. They were set to move on Constantinople, but Heraclius managed to whip up a religious frenzy against them. 'By framing the battle as a conflict between Christians and infidels, he managed to rouse his troops and keep the Persians at bay.'

The Prophet Muhammad was almost certainly influenced by Heraclius, he says, in the same way that he was inspired by Christianity and Judaism. 'For years, Western missionaries had been drilling into the Arabs that there was one God, that Christ came from a virgin birth, that they were all descendants of Ishmael, etc. Muhammad adopted and developed these ideas. That's why these faiths all have so much in common.'

'It does seem odd that Jesus is always portrayed as blond and blue-eyed,' I remark, shivering into the wind. Around us, cobwebs of snow lie like frozen doilies across the rocks and scrub. 'He was from Palestine, after all.'

'Yes, exactly!' Martin responds, and I feel a surge of scholar's pride that I've finally said something intelligent. 'People forget that Christianity was originally a Middle Eastern religion. When Islam arrived, there were far more Christians in Asia than Europe. There weren't the same stark geographical divisions we have now.'

It is difficult to conceive the magnitude of the Arabs' success in the seventh century. From humble beginnings, they spread both east and west across the globe, conquering Roman provinces and Persian satrapies alike with startling ease and efficacy. In just over a hundred years, the Muslim armies managed to establish the largest empire the world had ever seen, imposing a common language, creed and culture on a vast smorgasbord of domains stretching from Central and South Asia to Europe and the Maghreb.[26] And all this was achieved without resorting to the kind of barbarity employed by the Mongols and Timurids after them. 'The Mohammedans ... allowed the Christians to be perfectly free, provided they pay a tribute,' the Nobel laureate Bertrand Russell wrote in his essay *Reading History As It Is Never Written*. '[They] represented free thought and tolerance to a degree that the Christians did not emulate until quite recent times.'

For Mostafa, my brooding guide through Cappadocia's 'Love Valley', the reason for the Arabs' success is clear. 'Islam is the best religion,' he says. 'Better than the rest!'

'How so?' I ask.

He gestures to the quad bikes we've just ridden around this thicket of orgiastic erosion. His is plump and shiny with an engine the size of a cruiser tank. Mine is rusty and wizened with all the torque of a tin opener. 'Your bike Christian. Small, slow, weak. Mine Muslim. Big, powerful, better!'

---

[26] At its height under the Arabs, the Islamic Caliphate covered a colossal 11,000,000 square kilometres: more than twice the size of the Roman Empire.

Satisfied that he has explained the complex intricacies of the issue, he leans back on a particularly strapping manhood to roll a cigarette. For several centuries after the birth of Christianity, Love Valley was a powerful monastic stronghold, and hundreds of colourful, frescoed churches can still be found hewn deep into the rocks. For me, there's a gratifying irony in Cappadocia being a site of such religious fervour despite its somewhat smutty credentials. Perhaps for the monks, I ponder, there was an implicit symbolism in hollowing out these stout, self-assured shafts and sanctifying them in prayer.

'But you don't seem a very good Muslim,' I say, nodding at the cigarette. 'This is *haram* [forbidden], no?'

'Not *haram*. Not good, but better than drinking.'

'But surely it's even worse for your health?'

'It was not problem when Qur'an was written.'

'I thought the Qur'an was timeless?'

'Well, it does say, "Don't let your hands help your destruction." So some say smoking is banned.' He grins. 'But I don't.'

'I see. So you don't drink then?'

He laughs. 'Actually I do. But ...' He shrugs. '*Burasi Türkiye*.' This is Turkey.

I ask Mustafa's opinion of Erdoğan. Considering his somewhat *laissez-faire* approach to Islam, I expect him to disapprove of this vehement teetotaller who has cracked down hard on alcohol consumption in recent years. But I'm wrong. Mustafa is a fan, it turns out.

'I used to wake up and my money was worth half what it was the day before,' he says, stubbing out his cigarette and gesturing that it's time to go. 'Now I can afford things.'

We both climb onto his superior Islam bike for what he has disconcertingly described as a special 'loop-the-loop' section of our ride. 'Hold tight,' he cries. 'And whatever you do, don't ...!'

We plunge into a chasm and his voice is lost on the wind.

* * *

Snow is falling when I leave Göreme. Dressed like the Michelin Man in almost all my clothes – a vest, jersey, fleece, hoodie, gilet, jacket, leggings, trousers, gloves and three pairs of socks – I spend the first thirty kilometres crawling up a succession of vertiginous hills whipped by floes of Siberian wind. Leaden and stiff, I am galvanised by the knowledge that stopping would mean either instantly freezing to death or being devoured by one of the many neurotic hounds on my tail. So I push miserably on.

The dreariness is unremitting. For hours, I cycle in a shroud of white, past a wishful sign reading 'Panorama', barely visible through the haze, and pale sketches of foliage that line the road like bloodless phantasms. Eventually, as the sun begins to lilt overhead, I start to look for a place to stay – although my options appear depressingly limited. No towns or villages are to be found, and I begin to steel myself for a long, chilly night camping alone in the snow.

After a couple of hours of fruitless searching, I finally turn into a small dirt road marked with a cracked, rusty sign stating 'Ovacik'. The place doesn't look promising. For thirty minutes, I pedal among a wasteland of dung heaps, tractors and cement huts glazed with frost, hunting for signs of life. And then, just as I'm on the verge of giving up, I discover the entire male population packed inside a small, whitewashed hut reminiscent of a train station waiting room, the windows of which are clouded with steam, cigarette smoke and grime.

This, it turns out, is the village café. Its primary function appears to be to provide a space where men can escape their wives – and my arrival, it is fair to say, comes as a surprise. As I enter, a hush descends and three dozen stubbly mouths drop open in mute astonishment. For a moment, nobody says anything; we just gawk at one another as wild animals might do if thrown in a cage together at a zoo, and I suddenly worry that I've misjudged the situation terribly. Caught in this stark testicular glare, my ovaries feel painfully exposed. Have I stumbled into some malignant, exclusionary backwater, I wonder, where visitors enter but rarely leave?

No, it turns out. An hour later, I am eating a kebab courtesy of the village mayor and being regaled with stories about the last foreign cyclist they hosted here back in 1997. Since then, it seems, they've been waiting on tenterhooks for the second like some kind of messianic oracle – and now, *boom*, here I am. Whether I am precisely what they'd been expecting, he is too polite to say, but the novelty of my arrival soon appears to wear off. The men return to their tables, talking, smoking and staring into space, while a boxy television hums with chatter and static in the corner.

Eventually, after what feels like an appropriate amount of time, I begin to manoeuvre my troops for attack. First come the hints about my lack of accommodation ('Could you recommend any nearby hotels?'), followed by the false protestations of stoicism ('Camping is fine – I barely feel the cold!'). Then, once these blows have landed, I finally deliver my killer *mien*: a look of such pitiful, long-suffering forbearance that only the truly stone-hearted could avoid falling victim to its spell. It all works, of course, like a charm. This is Turkey, after all, and these kindly sorts succumb at the first sortie. Barely have I licked my plate clean when I am being ushered to follow an old man outside … and within minutes, I find myself ensconced in his cosy bungalow being served a feast of beef stew, homemade feta and fermented strawberries by his charmingly convivial wife.

For the next two hours, I am seated like a chatelaine on the sofa while streams of neighbours drop by to examine this strange, zeppelin-thighed creature rescued like a stray from the snow. All glow with warmth, hugging me tightly and kissing and pinching my cheeks, while the younger women throw quickfire questions at me through Google Translate. 'American?' Thumb down. 'British?' Thumb up. 'Married?' Thumb down (a flicker of disappointment). 'Christian?' Thumb down (a flicker of confusion). 'Believe God?' Thumb middle. 'Like Turkey?' Two thumbs up.

After a wonderfully deep sleep on the sofa, I leave at first light for the Taurus mountains. The ice-fog is yet to clear and the road and sky meld into one, a white gossamer ghost. The slope is gentle at first, then gradually steeper, until my glutes and thighs begin to burn. When the inevitable *pffffft* occurs, I half expect it, but I struggle to contain my exasperation nonetheless. Maud is clearly desperate for new tyres, but I know I have no choice but to wait until Beirut to change them, another 500 kilometres down the road.

Then, just as I feel my body begin to flag, the mist abruptly clears. The sun beams down, warming my face for the first time in weeks, and I absorb its energy like a battery plugged in to charge. Suddenly, the snow-dusted peaks in the distance feel like outliers in this gilded land as a wash of honeyed light fills the valley and a shock of electric sky erupts like an answered prayer overhead.

It isn't far to the summit. Once there, I don't stop. I continue up and over like a rollercoaster car, teetering for just a moment before making my plunging descent. Down, down, down I race, the air growing warmer, the sky brighter and bluer, as I speed towards to the sea. I can almost smell it now. I can almost taste it in the air.

Not far to go, I think. And I fly on, unstoppable, beating my way into the wind.

Upon arrival, Gaziantep appears entirely innocuous. Comprised of seemingly endless rows of half-built tower blocks bathed in buttermilk sunlight, the town emits a curious, bland sterility. It takes some time before I become aware of a latent, throbbing pulse below the surface: the muffled creak of faultlines under pressure. This ancient city, once known primarily for its food and copperware, has been hijacked by a distant revolution. Now its identity lies fractured and disjointed as Syrians and Kurds, diplomats and activists, terrorists and traffickers, all mingle together in cagey coexistence.

From here, the Syrian border – controlled by Islamic State – lies just thirty kilometres to the south. At first, I am cautious of venturing so close to this jihadist stronghold; ISIS are said to operate sleeper cells in Gaziantep, and the Syrian journalist Naji Jerf is shot dead in broad daylight soon after I arrive. However, around 500,000 Syrians currently live in the city and a Canadian NGO worker called Ellie has agreed to make some introductions. She assures me the streets are safe.

'Just don't mention the PKK,' she murmurs when we meet in a café. 'It's sensitive around here.'

'Okay,' I say, glancing with suspicion at the only other people in the vicinity: an elderly couple wearing matching taupe cardigans. 'Noted. And ISIS?'

She groans. 'That's okay. But please let's not talk about them. It's all anyone's ever interested in.'

We order drinks – her an Americano, me a Turkish coffee, Yemeni by origin, which involves leaving the powder unfiltered to create a rich, crude brew – and she shows me some statistics. Of the civilian casualties in 2015, 14,653 were killed by the Syrian regime, according to the pro-opposition Syrian Network for Human Rights, while just 991 died at the hands of Islamic State.[27]

'It's obviously bad the war has become so sectarian,' Ellie says. 'But people forget how the whole thing began. Assad has spent his life stirring up religious tensions, promoting his Alawite[28] cronies and repressing everyone else. But lots of Alawites hate him too. If we see this as a religious war, we just play into his hands.'

I ask about the Free Syrian Army (FSA). Should the West have done more to support them? 'Yes, at first,' she replies. 'But

---

[27] Between March 2011 and September 2020, the figures stood at 199,939 (88 per cent of the total) and 5,023 (2 per cent) respectively.

[28] The Alawites are a mysterious Shi'ite offshoot who have historically been persecuted for their moderate, esoteric beliefs. Originally poor and uneducated, their fortunes changed in 1920, when the French recruited many Alawites to help them topple King Faisal of Syria. The sect subsequently came to dominate the military, paving the way for Hafez al-Assad to seize power in 1970.

it's too late now. They've become fragmented and corrupt.'[29] This contributes to the appeal of Daesh, she says. 'Many of its members are former Ba'athist generals who lost their livelihoods after the Iraq War, so they know how to run things. They know how to fight.'

Ellie works at an NGO that focuses on developing civil society networks both inside and outside Syria. At the organisation's headquarters, she introduces me to its founder, Rania, who projects a maternal steeliness and clearly commands the love and respect of her staff. I ask about her background and learn from Ellie that she lost fifteen family members in Idlib. However, she declines to talk about herself. 'Speak to the others,' she tells me. 'Their stories are far more interesting than mine.'

One such person is a woman named Nazife. Thirty-seven, with a pale, guileless face framed by a satin al-Amira headscarf, she comes from a town called al-Zabadani and says she used to be an 'artist and farmer'. After the revolution began, however, she stopped working and began calling for demonstrations. 'I helped to form a "peace circle" of women,' she recounts, as Rania translates. 'We encouraged civil resistance, so it wasn't long before we drew the attention of the regime.'

One day, al-Zabadani came under fire from the Syrian Army and Hezbollah.[30] Many residents fled, but the peace circle stayed behind to act as intermediaries between the regime and rebel militias. 'The men tried to broker a ceasefire and failed,' Nazife says. 'But we managed to secure one in forty days.' They also negotiated the release of five female detainees and got women removed from checkpoint blacklists, she continues. 'It was partly good timing, but we brought something different to the table too.

---

[29] A Human Rights Watch investigation in 2012 outlined a litany of abuses allegedly committed by the FSA, including extortion, kidnapping, torture and the murder of civilians.

[30] A Shia militant group and political party based in Lebanon and controlled by Iran.

We understood the community's needs. The officers listened as they wanted our support.'

Over time, however, the siege worsened. Nazife's house was bombed, so she and her family moved. They were bombed again and moved again. Eventually, there was nowhere else to go. 'My son's shoulder was burnt. My daughter had shrapnel in her leg and my husband in his head. In August 2013, we knew we had to leave.'

Before they could escape, however, tragedy struck. Nazife's husband went to collect passports for the children and never returned. 'I looked everywhere,' she says, a gentle quiver entering her voice. 'But I never found him. Recently, I heard he may have been tortured and killed, but I'll probably never know for sure.'

After eventually securing passports for her children, Nazife put them on a flight to Lebanon. She stayed behind to search for her husband, but violence continued to escalate. 'Snipers were everywhere, and my neighbours were shot and killed. Then my sister was arrested, who has Crohn's disease. When I delivered her pills, the police threatened me. They said: "We know where you live and can get you any time." That's when I decided to leave.'

The checkpoints were now closed, so Nazife had little choice but to escape over the mountains to Lebanon, where the terrain was hazardous and patrolled by Hezbollah. If caught, she feared being detained – or even shot. 'The men had weapons to defend themselves, but I didn't,' she says. 'At one point, I had to hide for seven hours until the coast was clear. It was terrifying.'

Eventually, she made it to Lebanon and from there travelled to Turkey. Yet many of her friends remain trapped. In the neighbouring town of Madaya, the regime has implemented a full blockade. A kilo of rice costs $110. Milk costs $250. 'Twenty-two thousand people are starving to death,' she says. 'Babies are surviving on cornflour and adults are eating grass. It's desperate.'

Nazife rings her friend in the village. When she answers, she sounds delighted that Nazife has called, but she cannot disguise her fear. 'Our hunger is bad,' she admits. 'We can't continue like this much longer.' Just last week, six members of her family were killed by mines, while another five people had to have their legs amputated after getting injured collecting grain. 'We have a surgeon but little medication or equipment. He just does the best he can.'

I find it hard to process her words. The suffering is too great, too unfathomable. Her voice seems to come from another world. Yet it is calm and full of laughter, despite everything. 'It isn't all bad,' she chuckles. She's become a creative cook. 'I know all about apricot leaves. The tastiest part is by the stem, which you can steam or boil in soup!'

I ask where she finds her strength, and she falls silent for a moment. 'I don't know,' she replies finally. 'We're devastated but we know we cannot give up. We must protect and educate our children, and try to leave them a better future.'

Women in particular have suffered, she continues. But they've also thrived. 'We've found a new power we never had before. Through our struggles, we've found a voice.'

I've always found something innately reassuring about the sight of two old men on a park bench drinking tea. I watch the pair for a while, one with a moustache and flat cap, the other with white hair and walking stick, drinking and murmuring and waiting like Estragon and Vladimir, overlooked by the brindled walls of the Byzantine citadel. It is an image without past or future, peaceful and purposeless: a freeze-frame of soothing apathy.

If only time could always be stilled so easily. However, all around are hints of its busy onward march. Dig deep into the bedrock here and you'll discover layers of ancient history like a palimpsest of the past: the fortress foundations, constructed three millennia ago; the buried cities below, three millennia older still; the Neolithic pottery, Chalcolithic seals and Bronze Age tools; the Ottoman *bedestans* and Mamluk minarets; the pre-Christian rock-lodgings and medieval caravanserais. Located on one of the world's busiest thoroughfares, Gaziantep has attracted both settlers and invaders for as long as the history books can remember – the result of which, here in the 'old town', is a cultural potpourri of Mediterranean, Arabian and Anatolian influences that counters the insipid homogeny of the modern high-rises nearby.

Not far from the castle, past coppersmiths, cobblers and spice merchants plying ancient trades, I encounter a neoclassical building known as 'Liberation Mosque'. Its stripy, mismatched minarets at first strike me as a creative quirk of design; however, I soon discover they actually comprise a poorly conceived disguise. 'This was once a church,' a Russian tourist informs me. 'The base of that minaret was a church tower. The Armenians worshipped here before they were expelled.'

Now, suddenly, I see not a mosque but a mausoleum. During World War I, the Ottomans viewed the Orthodox Armenians as potential Russian collaborators and crushed them mercilessly. Over a million Armenians were murdered or sent on death marches into the desert. Thirty-two thousand came from Gaziantep.

'Why "Liberation Mosque"?' I ask.

The woman consults her guidebook. 'To commemorate defeating the French in October 1919.'

This feels like a devastating irony. When the French invaded, they were joined by their Armenian allies. The Turkish elite, many of whom lived in properties confiscated during the massacre, were concerned the Armenians would seek redress for the past and were therefore incentivised to rout them for good. The Turks won, Antep became Gaziantep, and the Holy Mother of God Church gained two minarets and a new name: Liberation Mosque. The building once associated with Armenian salvation was now a symbol of their brutal demise.

'I know what you need,' the woman says, catching my downcast expression as I consider the spiral of violence and vengeance in which our species seems forever embroiled. 'A taste of local baklava!'

She's right, as it turns out; it cheers me up enormously. Gaziantep's baklava is the best in the world. This isn't my opinion; it's objective fact. In 2013, the nutty dessert became the first Turkish foodstuff to be granted 'protected' status by the EU, and I am yet to meet a food connoisseur who doesn't rave about it. The locally grown pistachios that comprise the filling are so fêted across the country that they are even known as *Antep fistik* (Antep nuts) – meaning that the city's name, with its *gazi* prefix, can technically be translated as the wonderfully preposterous 'Muslim Warrior Pistachio'.

'Purest baklava in world,' the shop owner informs me. 'No flavouring. No lemon, cinnamon, rosewater.' I nod in appreciation, my mouth full. What he serves me is more than a dessert. It's an entire meal, both sweet and savoury, both dense and fairy-light. 'You like, I think?' His face erupts into a shaggy walrus of a grin. 'Then, please – it is on the house!'

'I hid in a sheikh's car boot,' the woman tells me while fending off the frisky onslaught of a passing conga line. 'Assad has killed most of the opposition sheikhs, so he was taking a huge risk. But it was my only hope of escape.'

I try to focus on the woman's story, but the music is loud and the conga increasingly combative in its passing sallies. We move further into the corner. She is now awaiting a German visa, she explains, and must leave Turkey every three months when her residency permit expires. 'Everyone goes to Cyprus. We're detained overnight and then come back. It's called "going on vacation".'

We're at the house of Nazgul, another NGO member, who is holding a party. It is Christmas Day, but unlike any I've ever known. Arabic songs are blasting out in lieu of carols, *mezze* and *kibbeh* replace turkey and trimmings, and alcohol is noticeably absent. Having awoken this morning feeling somewhat sorry for myself and missing the familiar comforts of home, I was delighted to be invited to this lively – if challengingly sober – soirée. Almost the whole NGO is here, and they act more like close family than colleagues; shoes are kicked off, hijabs abandoned, heads thrown back in wild hoots of delight. Everything sparkles with camaraderie. Dancing is done in pairs or circles, not alone as at home, and everyone seems to know the words to an endless array of traditional Syrian ballads, which fill the air until the early hours.

At 2am, one of the men walks me home. He used to work for the US Embassy, he tells me, but quit in disillusionment. 'Daesh, Daesh, Daesh. That's all they were bothered about. They didn't care about the Syrian people.'

'What's your feeling about Assad now?' I ask. 'Can he still be defeated?'

'It's difficult,' he concedes. 'But, whatever happens, I feel we've won. Before the uprising, there was no civil society in Syria. Now, everyone is an activist. We've seen a cultural revolution.'

Chapter 4

THE FRONTLINE OF TOLERANCE

Lebanon

'In Lebanon, it's never over for anyone. You cannot write off anyone or anything in this country.'
Saad Hariri, former prime minister of Lebanon

I feel a little queasy as I approach the Taşucu dock. The ferry, I've been told on many an occasion over recent weeks, doesn't exist. Nobody has heard of it, and nobody has believed me when I've told them about it. But, to my enormous relief, it turns out they were wrong. Because, as I turn into the harbour, there it is sitting incontrovertibly before me: one corroded, dirty-white vessel destined for Tripoli, Lebanon.

Around thirty people gather on the quayside, where we are kettled into a series of prison-style compounds. My bags are waved through security without checks, and my passport – along with everyone else's – is confiscated by the police. Almost all the other passengers are travelling to Syria to visit family members in camps and villages near the border, I am told, and this is a security measure designed to prevent them from absconding in Lebanon along the way.

The ferry leaves at 1am, five hours late. This is quite normal, apparently. We simply sit at the jetty, rocking gently, waiting for some unknown signal contingent upon some unspecified instruction. Meanwhile, the neon lights of the lounge keep the night at bay with grim tenacity. The male passengers pull their jackets around them and sprawl out languorously on the maroon faux-leather sofas, while the women and children retire to smaller, darker rooms elsewhere.

I cannot sleep and instead haunt the vessel in a somnolent torpor. The *QEII* it is not. It feels more like a cross between the *Mary Celeste* and a backwater YMCA. Eerily empty, its corridors are musty and cobwebbed and emit a mild odour of vomit. In one cabin, an overflowing ashtray and bottle of chemical blue aftershave stand beside a sink of sludge-brown water. Snores rattle through the hallways, while a plangent lament from an unknown berth coils eerily about my spine before drifting out into the night and across the open sea.

Up on deck, a man from Damascus introduces himself. He normally lives in Sweden, he says, but has moved temporarily to Antakya, Turkey, to be near his elderly mother, who is stuck at Atma refugee camp on the Syrian side of the border. 'The situation is desperate,' he tells me. Residents live in flimsy tents with little electricity or running water, and food deliveries from Turkey are often hijacked en route. Winter is bitterly cold, and rain turns the alleyways into gushing torrents of sewage. 'People have lost hope,' he says. 'All they have left is a drive for survival.'

As we stand at the balustrade, staring out into the blackness beyond, the man explains how he can never return to Syria because when he was last there, in 2011, he was arrested and detained for a month. 'They accused me, falsely, of being a spy. They hung me by my wrists and beat me with sticks. They wanted me to confess.' But he held his nerve, he says. He knew a confession could be his death warrant. 'They eventually released me after pressure from Sweden. But I still have the scars.'

Twelve hours later, I watch the Tripoli skyline expand from a tremulous shadow to a crust of pewter grey. The passengers all gather their belongings, awaiting permission to disembark. Another hour passes. One woman is distraught that she's being taken directly to Syria. 'I must collect money in Beirut!' she cries tearfully, but the guards pointedly ignore her.

At the immigration office, I am treated with brusque disregard. As I stand there, struggling to remain composed, I glance outside and see everyone else being herded like cattle onto a bus destined for the Syrian border. What must it be like for them, I wonder? It occurs to me that these people have not actively chosen a life of forbearance in the face of incompetence and indifference but have had it imposed upon them through a thousand tiny blows, a thousand tiny mistreatments, which slowly deaden the nerves.

Finally, I am free to go, and I begin riding towards the city centre in the muted afternoon light. It feels both odd and exhilarating to be back in Lebanon. This was where it all began, after all; where I first defied the naysayers to venture off in the saddle alone. Despite having cycled here before, however, I admit I still feel entirely unprepared. Perhaps not quite so unprepared as Freya Stark, I console myself, who arrived in the country in 1927 with just a fur coat, revolver and copy of Dante's *Inferno* to her name. But this does little to assuage my jitters as the shadows around me grow long. Tripoli at dusk is a dispiriting place, and I feel vulnerable and exposed as I navigate through the glut of traffic – a perplexing assortment of BMWs, Mercedes and rusty old bangers – attracting shouts and stares. Beside the road, sombre tower blocks rise like skeletal sentinels from a wasteland of debris, several of which appear to be sprinkled with bullet holes. It was only recently that the city was suffused in sectarian conflict between Sunni and Alawite jihadist groups, and I can't help but wonder if any pockets of unrest remain.

From the waterfront, I follow an avenue puddled with rainwater between rows of date palms sprouting sparse, stumpy fronds. At the end, a wilting Christmas tree stands in a square surrounded by a logjam of flatulently hooting cars. The city certainly seems a long way from its medieval heyday, when Ibn Battuta arrived here to find a kind of biblical paradise 'traversed by flowing streams and surrounded by gardens and trees, flanked by the sea with its copious resources and by the land with its sustaining bounties'. Right now, Tripoli's bounties feel distinctly scarce, while the only gardens and streams I encounter are filled with effluent, refuse and weeds.

Unable to reach my host, Bobby, I feel myself growing increasingly tetchy as I circle the darkening streets alone. But finally, to my relief, my phone rings. 'Sorry, hun!' a friendly Australian voice booms. 'I've been working. Come over now!'

Instantly, the city's edges seem softer, its shadows brighter, and within minutes I am happily ensconced in Bobby's carpet shop down the road. I can relax, he reassures me; the city streets are safe. I knew this – yet what has knowledge to do with nerves? It wasn't the reality that unsettled me but the unreality. An unknown world is a breeding ground of ghosts.

With Bobby, a playful twenty-something who moved here from Sydney seven years ago, the spectres of the subconscious have no place. 'I love Lebanon!' he cries as he gives me a tour of his showroom. 'I never want to leave.' Mostly, he enjoys the 'freedom' here, he says, which seems to boil down to driving without a licence and not paying taxes. I ask about the odd surfeit of BMWs and Mercedes I saw on the road, and he tells me it's due to people's desire to project an image of wealth and status. 'That's what makes my job easy. When I'm selling a carpet, I say, "You don't want that one, they're for ambassadors' wives" – and hey presto, it's sold!'

In Tripoli, curiously, this showiness goes hand in hand with a strong social conservatism. This has increased in recent years, Bobby says, though he stresses that generally everyone gets along well. 'Burkinis and bikinis mix together on the beach and nobody minds. But all people ever remember are the bloody jihadists splashed across the papers!'

Later, Bobby asks to hear some of my Arabic. '*Shukran lak ealaa alwajba*,' I say. '*Yislamo dayyetak*.' Thank you for the meal. May your hands be protected.

'Hmmm.' He raises an eyebrow. 'We need to work on that.'

The 'R' is pronounced as if gargling water, he explains, while for the 'G' I should pretend I have a peanut stuck in my throat. The 'Ayn' letter has no clear Latin equivalent but is best attempted while gurning like a frog and imagining I'm being stabbed in the ribs.

I have a few more attempts. 'You know,' Bobby says eventually, looking at me musingly. 'Maybe stick to English. Or French. Most people understand those here.'

'Really?' I reply. 'Both?'

'Yes. But particularly the elite. The Maronites.'

There's a clear cultural divide between the Christians and Sunnis, Bobby says, to the extent that many Maronites don't even see themselves as Arabs at all. 'They claim descent from the Phoenicians, who they see as more civilised.'

The division emerged with the birth of Lebanon, he explains. He gives me a brief history lesson. 'In the 1920s, when the Levant was being carved up by Europe, Greater Syria was taken by France and divided into smaller territories. One of these was the Maronite region of Mount Lebanon.' The Maronites demanded autonomy from the rest of Syria, he says, and – although this went against the wishes of the majority-Muslim population – France acquiesced. 'Tripoli, Tyre and the Bekaa Valley were added later to pad the region out a bit, meaning Syria lost half its coastline to a new, heavily Christian nation on its doorstep.'

Lebanon was, therefore, unique among the imperial mandates, in that it came into being not under duress but by request. While the Maronites were not a majority in their new state – they comprised around a third of the population – this didn't faze them. They had already prospered for centuries as a minority faith in the Islamic world and felt confident in their elitist credentials.

'It's amazing they survived at all, to be honest,' Bobby says, as he leads me through his shop to his flat at the back. 'The religion emerged from this weird little hermit in the fifth century, and its followers spent hundreds of years hiding in the mountains from the Arabs and Byzantines.' It was only when the Crusaders arrived that their fortunes improved, he explains. 'The Franks were basically their salvation. They formed a tight bond, which gave the Maronites a lot of clout. So, over time, they got rich.'

Nowadays, he says, the Maronites have lost much of their political power in Lebanon. 'But culturally, they're still the elite. And that feeling of entitlement isn't going away anytime soon.'

Exiting Tripoli proves a challenge. The traffic forms an angry skein of steel and smog, while spindly men on rusty bicycles dart between cars like fatalistic fruit flies. Eventually, however, the sea emerges like a beacon on my right, guiding me towards the south. From the outskirts of the city, I pass through a series of monotone towns, all cuboids and concrete shacks, until the buildings give way to bracken and grasslands and glistening mossy bluffs. It is an enjoyable ride, only slightly undermined by one small nagging concern lurking at the back of my mind: namely, a warning from Bobby that 'the biggest storm of the year' is due to hit today. However, it happens to be sunny now, and therefore – with the logic of someone who's never lived in Britain, or indeed anywhere – I reason it will most likely stay that way forever.

The reasoning proves unsound. I am barely thirty kilometres from Tripoli when the air begins to darken. Within minutes, the sky has engulfed the sea and night has descended like a kind of biblical retribution. Rain lashes down and the world around me swirls in a maelstrom of black and iron grey. Every so often, a guttural snarl erupts overhead, while buildings are stripped to their exoskeletons in electric flashes by my side.

And then Maud – of course – gets a puncture, sending us hobbled and dripping to the side of the road.

It is a miserable state of affairs. One entirely of my own making, of course, but miserable nonetheless. Depressed and half-drowned, I sluggishly change Maud's tyre in a neck-deep puddle and am just wondering what on earth to do when a car pulls over and two textbook serial killers climb out. One is wearing an oversized anorak with a hood that casts his face in shadow, while the other is bearded and beanpole skinny, and clutching a metal wrench.

As they approach, I instinctively grab my penknife and stand braced for combat.

'Hi!' the beanpole cries. 'Okay?'

'Okay!' I lie – before adding, perhaps redundantly: 'Bad weather!'

He gestures to Maud. 'You … help?'

'No, no!' I glance at Maud's undignified headstand and the mound of soaking panniers beside her. I can feel channels of icy water streaming down my back and coursing into my pants. 'All good!'

He seems unconvinced. He has kind eyes for a psychopath. 'Where … go?'

'Byblos!' I point in the direction they've just come from.

'Byblos?'

'Byblos!'

I assume that's the end of it. Nobody would take a stranger ten kilometres out of their way – or not unless they planned to do any number of gruesome things to them en route, that is. The men confer and the skinny one shrugs. Then he turns back, smiling.

'We Byblos! Come!'

We zoom off down the road, and shortly afterwards I find myself standing outside a restaurant in Byblos, entirely intact and un-murdered, exactly where I hoped to be.

'*Shukran!*' I holler, as the men turn the car to leave. But within seconds they are gone, and I am left damp and alone on the kerbside, marvelling at their kindness and the shameful irrationality of my fear.

Inside the restaurant, my friend Ramy greets me with a glutton's paradise of lamb döner meat, chicken shish and *makanek* (spicy sausages), plus a mountain of mezze delights that I devour too quickly to itemise. 'Welcome!' he cries in greeting. 'I hope you like kebabs?'

Ramy is a Maronite, like most people in Byblos, and is studying for a PhD in international relations in Beirut. As we eat, he gives me the benefit of his Sunday school teachings. 'Byblos shares its name with the Bible,' he tells me. 'The Greeks called papyrus *biblos* because the city was famous for it. This became their word for "book", *biblion*, which became the name of the Bible. *Ta Biblia!*'

Thousands of years ago, Byblos was the most powerful city-state in an advanced maritime civilisation known by the Greeks as Phoenicia, he continues. Expertly crafted 'Byblos ships' would sail from here to Greece, Libya and beyond – possibly as far as southern Africa, if you believe Herodotus – transporting glass, wine, faience (tin-glazed pottery), purple dye, cedar and silk.

'The Phoenicians were incredible people,' Ramy says. 'They even gave us the alphabet. Both the Latin and Arabic scripts came from it.'

Not everything they gave us was so beneficial, however, he admits. At least, not according to the Persians, who claim in Herodotus' epic record of the Greco-Persian wars, *The Histories*, that the Phoenicians bear responsibility for the initial breakdown of relations between Europe and Asia. It was they who abducted the princess Io from Argos, so the story goes, prompting the Greeks to snatch Europa and Medea in retaliation – which in turn incited Paris, the son of King Priam, to kidnap Helen of Troy. And the rest, as they say, is history. Or myth. Or, perhaps, as is often the case with ancient chronicles of the holy lands, a hazy combination of the two.

'Maronites actually have a special connection to the Phoenicians,' Rami says. 'It's believed we descended from them.'

'So I've heard,' I reply. 'But is there any proof?'

'Well, you can tell from our appearance. We look Mediterranean, not Arab.'

I examine him. To my untrained eye, he could easily pass for Sunni or Shia, but I decide not to press the issue. The idea of a genetic relationship between the Maronites and Phoenicians does seem dubious, however. Nearly a millennium passed between the decline of these powerful sea merchants and the rise of their alleged progeny, during which time their DNA was dissipated like the spray from their white-sailed *gauloi*. In the interim, Hellenic rule collapsed, the language shifted from Canaanite to Aramaic to Arabic, and almost all trace of Phoenician civilisation was lost.

The Muslim contention that Lebanon is actually an Arab country by heritage, historically aligned with Syria, appears to have a stronger basis. Since ancient times, Syria and Lebanon have been united in the minds of geographers and historians alike, bordered by natural frontiers on every side and known collectively as *Bilad al-Sham* or *Suriyah*. And, whatever their ancient genealogy, the Lebanese have undisputedly been Arabised since at least the ninth century, speaking in Arabic, adopting Arab customs and living under Arab rule.

'But what does Arab mean, anyway?' Ramy asks as I outline these thoughts, just as a heaving platter of *znoud el sett* (sweet pastry rolls) arrives at our table. Lebanon – Arab or Phoenician, Sunni or Maronite – has, it is safe to say, already won my heart. 'Originally, it meant the tribes of the Arabian Peninsula, but now it's basically anyone who speaks Arabic. That's a *lot* of people.' He bites into a pastry and an explosion of cream erupts volcanically down his chin. 'And you know what? I bet there isn't an awful lot that connects them all, if you dig deep down.'

The storm is still fierce when we finish lunch. The sea appears to have spread inland and is swirling at the restaurant door. 'Another Great Flood?' I ask. 'Seems a fitting place for it to happen.'

'You could do with a better ark, though.' Ramy gestures to Maud, who is standing under a sagging awning, looking glum. 'But don't worry. You can come in mine.'

In Ramy's car, we reach Beirut in an hour. While it is disappointing not to complete this coastal stretch by bike and relive that original seminal journey in December 2014, I simply can't cycle in this weather. I have no doubt that some people would: the truly mad ones who see risk not as a measured calculation but as a provocation to the gods. But not me. This winding seaboard route is dicey at the best of times; attempting it blind and in a kind of apocalyptic jet-wash feels like a step too far.

Ramy drops me on Rue Gouraud, the most bohemian-chic street in the trendy *haut monde* district of Gemmayzeh. My host is a friend-of-a-friend, Paddy, whose apartment combines Lebanese glamour, Parisian rusticity and Ottoman gilding to form my most stylish accommodation yet. Paddy, it turns out, is the grandson of Lebanese aristocrat and philanthropist Lady Cochrane (née Yvonne Sursock),[31] owner of the nineteenth-century Sursock Palace and descendant of a dynasty that helped transform Beirut into a major commercial hub with close ties to the West. It is an intimidating lineage, I admit – and one, I'm aware, that sits awkwardly alongside my rumpled clothes and overall tramp-like demeanour.

To add to my discomfort, tonight is New Year's Eve and Paddy has invited me to a party he's throwing in one of the bars he owns in town. Though grateful for the invitation, I admit what to wear poses a challenge. Having been instructed to 'dress up', I spend the next hour in a panic, trying to work out how to fashion a slinky gown out of some thermal leggings and a pair of padded underpants. It feels, at first, like a lost cause. But just as I'm reconciling myself to a night of sartorial humiliation (not my first, admittedly), I discover a silk scarf I bought in Gaziantep buried at the bottom of a pannier. Crushed and wrinkled, it is hardly Louis Vuitton, but beggars, as they say … So I wrap it around myself like a mini-toga, brush my hair, put on a lick of make-up for the first time in five months and hope I can just about pass muster with the Gemmayzeh glitterati.

It will be a tight call, I fear. Examining myself in the mirror, all I see is a charlatan. I feel like a cross between Patrick Leigh

---

[31] Lady Cochrane tragically died in August 2020 from injuries sustained in the Beirut port explosion.

Fermor and Eliza Doolittle, both of whom did their best to convince high society of their sham Austro-Hungarian gentility, the latter deliberately, the former deludedly. Admittedly, unlike them, my blueblood Magyar heritage happens to be real, but there is sadly little evidence of that long-diluted *noblesse* now. What I feel like, and what I'm sure all will see, is a vagrant imposter with watermelon thighs and a leathery arse – because that, when all the frills and trappings are stripped away, is of course precisely what I am.

When I arrive at the bar, however, it swiftly becomes clear my worries were all in vain. Everyone's already blind drunk. I could have come dressed in tinfoil and bubble-wrap and I doubt anyone would have noticed or cared. Bottles of spirits line the tables in vast troughs of ice, alongside trays of canapés and boxes of sparkling party paraphernalia. I meet an ex-Luton Town footballer who recounts salacious stories about the antics of Premiership players in hotel rooms and an American divorcee who complains about Lebanon's dearth of women's rights. 'It's *awful* here,' she says. 'There are hardly any women in positions of power.[32] And the laws are *hideous*. Women can actually be legally *raped* by their husband!' She wafts a perfectly manicured hand around the room. 'The only women who progress are the ones you see here. And even *then* it's a struggle.'

'So why do you stay?' I ask.

'I can't *help* it, darling. Lebanon's like an affair with a bastard. The more they fuck up, the more you go back for more!'

At 3am, the party moves to a house nearby. Beirut is a city where the music never ends, and the stamina of my fellow revellers is impressive. Here, people party until they're sixty, then move seamlessly into their second childhood. Middle age, like the middle income, has been squeezed into submission.

---

[32] She's right, as it turns out. Just 5 per cent of Lebanese MPs are female, ranking the country a dismal 180th out of 192 countries on the Inter-Parliamentary Union 'Women in Politics' index.

'Well, it's our way of escaping reality,' one man says by way of explanation, as he lights up a joint beside me. 'The government's so fucking corrupt, nothing functions anymore. We drink to forget what a shitshow everything is.'

Around twenty people have gathered here, seated in a circle amid a clutter of ashtrays, beer cans and vodka bottles. 'What needs to change?' I ask. 'Or is it beyond repair?'

'They need to tear down the shitty confessional system and start from scratch,'[33] he replies. 'It's all about *wasta* [cronyism]. The leaders have built up huge networks of patronage and there's no compromise or working for the common good. Half the time we don't even have a president!'

I ask the man, who works as a New York trader, if he's Maronite. He shakes his head. 'Greek Orthodox. But who cares? Sunnite, Shi'ite, Maronite … they're just names. It's nothing to do with religion. It's a bunch of warlords drunk on power.' He laughs drily. 'Believe me, God died in Lebanon long ago.'

I nod. Suddenly, I feel exhausted. I glance down at my diary, where I've been attempting to scribble notes before my last functional synapses dissolve. But already it's too late, it seems; the words veer madly around the page as if plotting the flight lines of a drugged mosquito. Putting the book aside, I instead listen to the murmur of conversation around me. Voices rise and fall, strident at times, then muted and rippling like a distant stream. *Country run by mafia … Economy of fools …* Most people speak English, but strains of Arabic and French are discernible too. *Those Solidere crooks ruined downtown … It all went wrong when Hariri died …*

---

[33] Lebanon's political system is bafflingly complex for such a tiny scrap of a country. Eighteen sects are recognised officially, all of which have seats in parliament in proportion to their size, while the leadership is split between the largest three: a Maronite president, Sunni prime minister and Shi'ite parliamentary speaker. The idea behind this rule, written into the 1926 constitution, was to ease sectarian tensions, but in reality it has often served to provoke them.

I lay back as the *azan* sounds for the 5am prayer. *Once the Paris of the Middle East ... Now more like Baghdad ... But Baghdad was powerful once ... Yes, Beirut was powerful once ...*

I awake curled in the foetal position in a cool, dark room. It feels like an odd and unfamiliar place to be. Then it emerges in a rush, like a *trompe l'oeil* picture coming into focus. Beirut! The storm! The endless terrifying buckets of gin! My eyes half-open, I squint into the murk with the dim curiosity of a newborn mole. Everything around me appears thick and mushy, as if cooked too long on the stove. I close my eyes again and groan.

I emerge from my cocoon at lunchtime, when a violent hunger takes grip. Outside, I wander down Rue Gouraud to a pizzeria – but it isn't until my return, when I notice the road labelled on a signpost, that the full implication of the name occurs to me. Rue Gouraud. *Gouraud* ... Described by the British as a highly devout, 'fiery, bearded, one-armed, heavy-handed' officer, General Henri Gouraud led France to victory in Syria in 1920 and proved the perfect successor to the medieval papal armies. 'Awake, Saladin, we have returned,' he crowed triumphantly while standing at the graveside of the Kurdish warrior who defeated the Crusaders. 'My presence here consecrates the victory of the Cross over the Crescent!'

Indeed, Gouraud was so universally despised by the Arab people that he even made the Brits look good – which, considering what we were up to in Iraq at the time, was no small feat.[34] '[The French] are making such a horrible muddle of the Near East,' Gertrude Bell wrote in 1919. 'It's like a nightmare in which you foresee all the horrible things which are going to happen and can't stretch out your hand to prevent them.' Eight centuries

---

[34] A revolt in Iraq in 1920, which briefly united Sunni and Shia against their British rulers, was brutally put down by 100,000 British and Indian troops and one of the first mass RAF bombing campaigns. Up to 10,000 Arabs died in the conflict: ten times the number of imperial casualties.

after their first 'civilising mission' to the region, the French picked up largely where they had left off: cities and farmland were devastated, civilians shot without trial, Maronites promoted over Muslims, and the most lucrative industries transferred into French control.

The ripples of this savage conflict can still be felt today. 'It was as though the Ba'athists had replaced the French,' the historian John McHugo wrote of the current Syrian War in his book *A Concise History of the Arabs*, 'and were determined to follow their example in crushing the rebellion by terror and overwhelming firepower.'

One morning, Maud and I stagger into the bedlam of Beirut traffic – which seems constantly paralysed yet faintly functional, reflecting perfectly the state of the country – and somehow make it intact to a bike shop on the other side of town. There, I buy the best tyres the city has to offer. They look distinctly flimsy to me, but I am reassured that they're '100 per cent puncture-proof'. And it turns out they are … for a full seven minutes. Considering my last set of tyres from Kona lasted four months and 5,000 kilometres, I can't deny that this performance feels a little disappointing. But with no better options available, I reluctantly patch up the hole and push on.

Muddied by a cheerless drizzle, the streets around me appear leaden, the buildings drab and unkempt. And yet, even amid the gloom, a latent energy in the city is palpable. With its battle-scarred walls and beleaguered past, Beirut has the aura of a wounded soldier, beaten down yet ever rising to fight again. I feel this in the teeming eateries of the Corniche, in the smiling, sagging faces of the bazaar, in the tumult and bustle of the rebuilt *centre ville*. I feel it too in the eucalyptus groves and woodlets of weeping fig – the pockets of natural beauty flourishing amid the decay.

When I was studying in California, 'Beirut' was the nickname given to a frat party game in which players would try to throw ping-pong balls into cups of warm beer. The balls were bombs, the thinking went, while the cups were the hapless crowds and buildings below. This was the impression that we, as students, had of the city: a pitiable wasteland comparable in appeal to a stale Coors or Bud Light. Yet it is an image that, now, I scarcely recognise. Beirut may be unstable, but it seems far from the war-torn wilderness of our imagination. A jihadist bombing killed forty-three people here in November 2015, but this was the first serious incident of violence since the end of the civil war in 1990. When compared to Europe, which lacks Lebanon's precarious geopolitics and yet has borne the brunt of multiple deadly terror attacks in recent years, this record feels nothing short of remarkable.[35]

As I cycle through the southern bowels of the capital, I remind myself of this fact. In these dark, deprived Shia districts, it is easy to feel vulnerable while travelling alone. Spiked bollards and husks of broken-down cars line the maze-like streets, while dogs sit in swampy puddles and furtively lick their balls. There are no weeping figs or *fêtes de la musique* here; the place, rather, has the aura of a sprawling refuse dump where inhabitants have been tossed like scraps.

The people I pass, however, prove nothing but friendly – and it isn't until another hour down the coast that I have my first unfortunate encounter. Pulling up beside me, a paunchy chap in a black Mercedes rolls down his window and announces, simply, 'Sex.' Not a question. Not even a command. Just a monosyllabic statement of fact, as if responding to an enquiry about grouting or descaling the kettle.

'Sorry?' I say, unsure if I've heard correctly.

---

[35] Indeed, Lebanon's endemic corruption has proved to be a far deadlier force than terrorism in recent years, as evidenced by the catastrophic port explosion in August 2020 in which 218 people died. Managed through a system of kickbacks and bribery, governance of the port was barely fit for purpose – yet to date no officials have been held accountable for the tragedy.

'Sex,' he mutters louder. He is sweaty and round, like a suet pudding.

'Ah,' I reply. 'In that case: *Tel has teezi!*'

'Eh?'

I smile sweetly and start backpedalling. Once at a safe distance, I cry as loudly as I can: '*Tel has teeeeeeezi!!*'

Kiss my ass! A handy phrase, as yet unused, which comes fresh out of its packaging, peppy and full of zest.

'Oi!' the pudding-man responds, once his initial shock has passed, before releasing a spew of words that now don't sound like anything related to grouting or kettle descaling. The space is too tight for a U-turn, however, and he is too lazy and spherical to chase me, so I leave him ruddy-faced and bellowing in my wake as I speed off triumphantly down the road.

The light begins to fade as I approach Tyre. Portraits of Ayatollahs Khomeini and Khamenei, the past and present rulers of Iran, appear overhead, alongside pictures of 'martyrs' killed by the Israelis. We are in Hezbollah territory now and Tehran clearly isn't shy to show its controlling hand. Lining the road are rows of armoured vehicles belonging to the UN Interim Force in Lebanon, which, since the 2006 Israeli-Hezbollah war, has been responsible for maintaining peace here. Then, with the swiftness of a flicked switch, the sky and road turn raven black, and I become hopelessly disorientated in what appear to be a series of interlocking construction sites filled with litter and dust.[36]

Eventually, I find my way to a tourist shop, where my concerns about Hezbollah are allayed. Rather than shunning foreigners, it seems they want us to buy their souvenirs. Keyrings adorned

---

[36] I admit that, during my brief stopover, I perhaps don't see Tyre in its best light. Revered in medieval times for its 'fountains of water', 'clean bazaars', 'lanterns of gold and silver' and 'quantities of wealth', according to the eleventh-century Persian traveller Nasir-I-Khusrau, the city today remains one of the most popular holiday destinations in Lebanon due to its white-gold beaches, UNESCO-protected Roman ruins and lively, cosmopolitan atmosphere.

with the face of Secretary-General Hassan Nasrallah are displayed among postcards of Tyre's sandy beaches, while the organisation's distinctive yellow-and-green flags can be purchased alongside those of Real Madrid. As I access the wifi to try to get my bearings, the shopkeeper voices his support for the Islamist group. 'They're the only ones strong enough to stop Israel,' he says. 'And they do much to help the poor. For me, they are the best hope for Lebanon.'

It feels strange hearing the man speak about Hezbollah as if it were just another normal political party. The organisation has long called for the annihilation of Israel and is believed to have been behind a series of bombings in the 1980s and 1990s that killed hundreds of soldiers and civilians. Because of this, it is on the terror blacklists of many countries across the world, including the US, UK, Israel, Gulf Cooperation Council and Arab League, while its military wing is outlawed by the EU.

Hezbollah nonetheless enjoys widespread support among the majority-Shia population of southern Lebanon. 'They don't try to steal from us,' the shopkeeper says. 'Not like all the rest.'

Money, it turns out, is his chief concern – not violence or terrorism, but the rising cost of living as expats move in and inflate prices. 'Before, I was fisherman, and life was peaceful and easy. But now I need shop like this to survive!'

'Yes, Hezbollah are popular here,' my friend Ailbe confirms later over a bottle of red wine, once I've finally managed to locate her flat. 'They've proved themselves against the Israelis and done a good job subsidising the health service. Without them, lots of people would struggle.'

Ailbe is an Irish doctor who provides healthcare for refugees through an international NGO. She describes her relationship with Lebanon, where she has lived for several years, as a mixture of fondness and frustration. 'I think Tom Fletcher [the former British Ambassador] put it best. He described Lebanon as being at the "frontline in the fight for tolerance" in the Middle East, where the real division isn't between religions but between people who want peaceful coexistence and people who don't.'

'And which side's winning so far?' I ask.

She considers. 'The rise of Hezbollah is worrying. They have a veto over government decisions so hold enormous power, and they basically rely on the corrupt elite to retain control.' And as long as Hezbollah – and Iran – remain so strong, she says, 'peace with Israel will of course remain a pipe dream.'

Indeed, the border with Israel is not only firmly closed but heavily fortified with barbed wire and electric fencing – which means, frustratingly, that there is no prospect of continuing my journey from here. Whether this is what the original draftsmen had in mind when, wielding their pens like rapiers, they cursorily dashed out the boundary a hundred years ago is unclear, but it seems safe to assume that they gave little thought to the best interests of the people who actually lived here. Instead, this shaky line was originally part of a broader plan to split the region into European 'spheres of influence' following World War I, granting Mesopotamia (Iraq) and Transjordan to Britain, and Greater Syria (including Lebanon) to France.[37] Cultural and geographical concerns were not discussed; every race, sect and creed was thrown together in various explosive permutations, with scant regard for contiguity.

One man in particular was dismayed by this turn of events. T.E. Lawrence had promised the Arabs independence in exchange for their help fighting the Ottomans, so when the British went behind their back to strike a secret deal with France, he was furious. 'I have decided to go off to Damascus, hoping to get killed on the way,' he told his station chief in 1917. 'We are calling on them to fight for us on a lie, and I can't stand it.' His compatriot Gertrude Bell was equally incensed. 'I think there has

---

[37] This plan was largely based on a secret pact – the so-called Sykes-Picot Agreement – made between Britain and France in 1916.

seldom been such a series of hopeless blunders as the West has made about the East since the Armistice,' she wrote from the 1919 Paris Peace Conference,[38] adding in a later letter: 'The credit of European civilisation is gone ... How can we, who have managed our own affairs so badly, claim to teach others to manage theirs better?'

Until her death in 1926, Bell pushed hard for a 'really liberal' government in Mesopotamia. But she was only ever 'a minority of one ... or nearly' and her clearsighted advice, like Cassandra, was destined never to be heeded. As both she and Lawrence predicted, Iraq today is a disaster by anyone's standards, and it seems safe to assume that the rise of jihadist groups such as Islamic State – who announced the abolishment of the Sykes-Picot line outside the Great Mosque of al-Nuri[39] in Mosul in July 2014 – would have come as little surprise to either of them.

'Militant groups fill the gaps where civil governance fails,' Ailbe says, filling my wine glass as yet another rainstorm rages outside. 'We see this across the Middle East: in Iraq, Syria, Yemen, here in Lebanon ... These aren't battles over faith, they're battles for identity and belonging. They're battles to be heard.'

My fixer, it is safe to say, is nothing like I expect. Dressed in a mini-skirt, tank top and *Dynasty*-style sunglasses, she resembles a young Joan Collins and can hardly be older than eighteen. Scooping me up from the kerbside in a black BMW with tinted

---

[38] This conference set the post-war peace terms and reconfigured the map of Europe and the Middle East. Yet nobody there except Bell, according to the colonial officer Sir Arnold Wilson, 'had any first-hand knowledge of Iraq or Nejd, or, indeed, of Persia.' Poorly informed decisions made at the summit went on to generate great bitterness among the Central Powers, Arabs, Turks and Kurds, while blowback for these decisions – including the outbreak of World War II – is still being felt today.

[39] This mosque is believed to have been built by a Muslim ruler named Nur ad-Din, who mobilised Arab forces against the Crusaders in the twelfth century, paving the way for Saladin's later victories.

windows, she says a brief hello, reapplies her cherry lipstick, then whooshes off at white-knuckle speed down the road.

With just two days left in Lebanon, I have made a last-minute trip to a refugee camp in the Bekaa Valley. The girl and I arrive at the settlement just as the sun breaks through the clouds and casts its cold rays across a sea of flapping tarpaulin. Clusters of children in a medley of multi-seasonal footwear – wellies, sandals, trainers, barefoot – chase pink balloons along the gravelly alleyways between the tents, while washing lines hung with damp mattresses sag limply overhead. Beside the entrance, a woman holding a baby sits atop a mound of broken timber crates, as still and expressionless as a statue.

The laughter of the children should feel redemptive, but instead only serves to highlight the bleakness of the surrounds. 'Look how we live,' one man says, opening his tent door to reveal a dark, fusty space the size of a large family bathroom. Damp rugs cover the stained concrete floor and an unlit metal stove stands in the centre. A small adjoining area contains a filthy fridge and a mound of clothes and tinned food. The man doesn't speak English, but the young Joan Collins translates. 'Everything is wet and ruined. My children are always sick.' He empties a box of tissues, toothpaste and disinfectant onto the rug. 'We need food, but what do we get? Cleaning equipment!'

Conscious of its difficult experience with the Palestine Liberation Organisation (PLO),[40] which moved its base here after being evicted from Jordan in 1970, Lebanon has not established official refugee camps. Instead, Syrians have been forced to build makeshift shelters like this one, or else seek sanctuary in cramped, dilapidated buildings. 'We have a stove but no diesel,' an older man says, whose family fled Daraa after being bombed. 'We

---

[40] The PLO insurgency against Israel was a key catalyst for the 1975–90 Lebanese Civil War, which began as a clash between the Palestinians and Christians before fracturing into a chaotic, multifaceted conflict of rapidly shifting political and religious alliances.

arrived nine months ago and our suffering worsens every day.' Lifting his shirt, he reveals a blizzard of blotchy scars across his back. Shrapnel, he explains. From Assad and Daesh.

'Who is worse?' I ask.

He smiles. 'I beg God to take them both.'

Three hundred people live in the camp. Rent for a tent costs $800 a year, subsidised by NGOs. Each one contains around ten people and receives five hours of power a day, plus a water tank a week. 'It's not enough,' a man in an incongruously smart but worn suit tells me, while his young son pretends to cook a pair of yellow wellies in a saucepan by our feet. 'We drink but rarely wash.' He is just thirty-six but has two wives and fourteen children – a fact that instinctively riles me, though my irritation is muted by the sadness of his story. 'We fled across the mountains after our village was bombed. The Lebanese army attacked us, so we paid traffickers $1,000 to get us here safely.' Now, however, they are stuck. 'We can't leave the camp because we're illegal. And the schools are all full, so our children cannot learn.'

As a refugee in Lebanon, it is easy to fall through the gaps. The country has declined to ratify the 1951 Refugee Convention, leaving the legal status of Syrians undefined, and instead relies on a series of ad hoc provisions to ensure their welfare. However, I am reluctant to criticise the state too severely. While the West has wrung its hands and locked its doors, Lebanon – along with Jordan and Turkey – has borne the brunt of the crisis, with Syrians now comprising an astonishing quarter of the country's population. Yes: a *quarter*. In Britain, this would be the equivalent of twenty million people turning up on our doorstep. In the US, it would be nearly a hundred million. Imagine that for a moment: a hundred million Syrians floating across the Atlantic, pouring into East Coast jetties and wharfs. It is a scenario almost impossible to envision.

The impact on Lebanon has, predictably, been severe. Public services are at breaking point; unemployment is soaring; wages have plunged. And all this in a country already teetering on the brink of collapse. When I was here in 2014, people's frustration was clear. 'We're flabbergasted at the lack of help from the international community,' Nayla Moawad, a politician and the widow of the former president Rene Moawad, told me. 'I'm simply revolted.'

Outside the camp, a café owner tells me that many people resent the Syrians because of their occupation of Lebanon from 1976 to 2005. Some refer to them as *musta'amarat*, he says: a term connoting illicit Israeli settlements on Palestinian land.

'But aren't they victims of the same regime that occupied Lebanon?' I ask. 'They hate Assad as much as you.'

He considers. 'Yes, true. But there will always be resentment, I think. We're like brothers, you see. We're so similar, but that's what pulls us apart.'

There are few groups in Lebanon worse off than the Syrians – but one is the Palestinians. Based in twelve official camps across the country, as well as multiple unofficial camps and communities, they have limited rights and freedoms and have never properly integrated. Granting them permanent residency would mean upsetting the fragile sectarian balance of the country, and there is little political will to do so.

'We're the forgotten people,' a young man, Malek, tells me, whose grandparents came to Lebanon in 1968. His dull, tired eyes seem out of synch with his zesty mop of curly hair. 'People only care about the Syrians, while our funds keep getting cut.'

Malek is showing me around Shatila camp in southern Beirut, which was established after the creation of Israel to house Palestinian refugees. Walking its streets feels like a form of slow suffocation. We meander through a warren of narrow, graffitied passageways, beside clapped-out mopeds and rows of jaundiced buildings slumped low on their foundations. A tangle of electricity cables and water pipes droops limply overhead, as ominous as an undetonated grenade. The water is brackish and undrinkable, I am told, and even corrodes the pipes. Power comes in fits and gasps, and shuts off shortly after I arrive. When I go to the toilet, I am given a candle to find my way.

Shatila was built originally for a thousand people but now houses upwards of 20,000 – exact figures are unknown – in a space four times as densely populated as Tokyo. With few open spaces, most homes stand in permanent shadow, yet competition over housing and services continues to grow by the day.

As we walk, I see a photograph of a young man hanging overhead. 'Killed by the Israelis?' I ask.

'Sort of,' Malek says. 'Electrocution from the cables. It happens quite often.'

'Sort of?'

'He died because he was evicted from his homeland. Anyone who dies here is seen as a martyr.'

Malek introduces me to some of the residents. Men generally work as labourers or traders, he explains, as Palestinians are banned from many professions and cannot own businesses or property. 'Muhammad makes $6 a day as a mechanic,' he says, gesturing to a man welding in a blaze of sparks, whose cherubic baby son is playing with a spinning rotary saw nearby. 'And he has four children to support.'

'How do they survive?'

Malek translates my question and the man smiles. 'By the grace of God. His eldest son is smart and studies hard, so his father has high hopes for him. Education is important to Palestinians. We know this holds the key to a better future.'

'Which school does he go to?'

'The UNRWA one. They run two schools here. They're terrible, but they're all we have.'

UNRWA stands for United Nations Relief and Works Agency for Palestine Refugees in the Near East: an anachronistic acronym created in the dying days of empire that gives a sense of the longevity of these people's suffering. In the absence of state support, the agency has worked on a shoestring budget to provide refugees with a lifeline of basic services.[41]

'Come,' Malek says. 'I'll show you the health centre.'

We approach a rusty, padlocked door with a circular red sign beside it stating that machine guns are forbidden. 'Beautiful, isn't it?' Malek says. 'It doesn't have much medicine, sadly. But it does give out special UN paracetamol tablets the size of frying pans. They're quite useful if you want to build a house.'

'This is the hospital?'

'No, we have separate hospitals. If we want to kill someone, we send them there.'

Beside the door is a poster of Yasser Arafat surrounded by PLO leaders. Similar pictures are strewn across the camp: a stark reminder of the militancy that is both cause and consequence of the refugees' plight. A sentence is scrawled across the portrait in red paint, which Malek translates: '"We will never forget the massacre".'

'Massacre?'

'After the 1982 Israeli invasion. The Phalangists[42] did it, but the Israelis planned it.'

I look up the incident later. In September 1982, following weeks of fierce battles, Israel successfully drove the PLO out of Lebanon and moved its troops into West Beirut. They then ordered their Christian allies to enter Shatila camp and destroy the remaining 'terrorists' inside. During the two-day slaughter, between 460 and 3,500 civilians were killed (depending on your source), including many women and children. In 1983, the Israeli Kahan Commission found that Ariel Sharon – the defence minister and future prime minister – bore 'personal responsibility' for the

---

[41] In August 2018, Donald Trump ended US UNRWA subsidies, slashing its total budget by a third and causing further misery for the millions of people who rely on its health, education and social services.

[42] Christian militants allied with the Lebanese Phalanges Party, whose conflict with the PLO precipitated the Lebanese Civil War.

attack, which is believed to have sparked the Middle East's first ever suicide bombing in Tyre in November 1982.

'What do you personally think of the Israelis?' I ask Malek as we exit the camp. It is a relief to be leaving. Walking outside feels like coming up for air.

'It's a hard question,' he responds, after a lengthy pause. 'Of course, I understand that they've suffered. But what I don't understand, after all they've been through, is how they can cause such suffering to others.' He emits a deep, drawn-out sigh. 'To be honest, I don't think I'll ever understand that.'

Chapter 5

MAN-WORLD COUNTRY

Jordan

'In the desert of life, the wise person travels in a group, while the fool travels alone.'

Jordanian proverb

On my bicycle, I am trapped inside Lebanon. The only land exits are illegal border crossings or a bracing dip in the Mediterranean, neither of which sounds particularly appealing right now. So, with some reluctance, I book a flight. From the plane, I watch the city lights below flicker and swirl like swarms of fireflies, until we pass from shore to sea and into the unifying blackness beyond.

When we disembark, I am instantly impressed. Amman airport has a gemstone gleam, and I purchase a visa, access the free wifi and locate a fixed-price taxi all within thirty minutes of arrival. After Lebanon's scatty inefficiency, Jordan's glossy functionality feels intimidatingly slick.

In the taxi, I receive my first lesson in Levantine Arabic. 'Guess how many words we have for lion?' the driver asks.

'Fifty?' I hazard.

'More.'

'A hundred?'

'More.'

'Tell me.'

'Three hundred! Big lion, small lion, African lion, Asian lion …'

'Wow,' I say, feeling a sudden renewed appreciation for adjectives. 'Impressive.'

The driver has a bushy beard and an aquiline nose that commands respect. He is a garrulous fellow and swiftly the conversation turns to religion. 'Christian?' he asks. Agnostic, I say. He seems puzzled. 'Married?'

'No.'

He glances over. 'You know, men can marry four wives here.'

'So I've heard.'

He understands that it's different in Europe, he explains. But it's not what people think. Men can only take another wife out of necessity – if a woman doesn't want sex, for example, or can't have children. And the man must provide for each of his wives equally.

'What if the man doesn't want sex or can't have children?' I ask.

He chuckles at the absurdity of the idea. 'Women's needs are different. They can't be with many men.' Besides, he adds, if his wife slept around, he couldn't be sure which children were his.

'What about trust?' I ask. He looks sceptical. 'Or a paternity test?'

'No man would take such a test.'

'So how many wives do you have?'

He grins. 'Just one. Any more and she'd kill me!'

My Warmshowers host is a twenty-eight-year-old computer engineer who lives in a large, bare, warehouse-style apartment with almost no furniture, a pungent stench of methane and panoramic windows that overlook Amman. We meet only briefly, due to my midnight arrival, and by the time I awake the next morning he has already left for work.

Shortly afterwards, I venture out too. On Rainbow Street in the central Jabal Amman district, artisan coffeeshops stand alongside boutique art galleries, while colonial-era shopfronts exhibit designer knitwear and exorbitantly priced antiques. Lively and cosmopolitan, this road acts as Amman's carotid artery, pumping oxygen into the economy and connecting the city's traditionalist east to its liberalist west. From a rooftop café, I can see a busy thoroughfare far below, winding its way through the urban sprawl like a river valley, the densely packed buildings appearing like tawny outcrops on its banks. For me, there's something both organic and dynamic about the scene. This is a city that grew from the desert, as nomadic tribes took refuge here from the parched wadis and wildlands beyond. But it is also a city of modernity and progress, known for its moderation, stability and socioeconomic ties to the West.

I turn towards downtown. Here, the streets simmer with a melee of Arabian cliché, from shisha pipes and *shawarma* to toasted sesame seeds and fried semolina. Battling through the crowds, I pass stalls selling embroidered *taqiyahs*, tweeting toy birds, bootleg perfumes and an inexplicable amount of leopard-skin clothing. There are old men in slacks and leather jackets, and younger men in jeans and dark hoodies. Looking around, I realise: there are an awful lot of men.

One man selling mobile phones offers me a cup of sage tea. His face is curiously droopy at the edges, as if his jowls were anchored to the ground while his mind were trying to drift off elsewhere. He fled Damascus last year, he says, but his wife and children are still there. 'I pay to go to Libya, then Italy and Germany. There, I hope my family join me.' He gestures to a bearded man in a wheelchair who lost his leg in a Baghdad bombing during the 2003 Iraq War. 'See how hard life is for us? We miss our homes, but we have no homes anymore.'

Around us, men are flooding into the square to pray at the Grand Husseini Mosque. Many buy sheets of cardboard from street vendors to use as prayer mats, and soon the crowds are cascading out of the mosque forecourt into the roads and passageways alongside. And then the *azan* begins, soft and mesmeric, spinning invisible threads to harness invisible souls, and I watch as hundreds of harmonised bodies stand and kneel and bow in one coordinated movement, all united in a common cause.

From the mosque, I make my way to the Citadel, which overlooks Amman from atop a lofty hill. From this vantage point, the city unfolds in all its desiccated majesty. Unusually for a capital, Amman has neither river nor coastline to provide form or focus, yet the shifting elevations evoke a tremendous sensation of space. Built on a series of rolling hills, the cityscape sinks and crests like a curdled sea, its scrummage of buildings jampacked Tetris-like into every available nook. In the distance, vastly outflanking the ocean of minarets surrounding it, the 416-foot Raghadan Flagpole can be seen flying the Jordanian flag: a mismatch of stature that feels faintly symbolic. This is a country less concerned about religious identity than national belonging, comfortable in its Sunni skin but lacking as yet a distinctive or confident sense of self.

In the foreground, littered about the vegetation, is a collection of ruins marking seminal moments in Jordanian history: the marbled arch of the Roman Temple of Hercules, through which the sun is framed at dusk; the rose-tinted columns of a Byzantine church, built from stone purloined from the temple; an eighth-century Umayyad palace, incorporating both a colonnaded Roman road and the cross-shaped Byzantine structure it replaced. These monuments span generations, yet all are inextricably linked. Sitting side by side like a curated museum exhibit, they create the impression of history not as a linear succession of events but as a unified whole, as if Amman's many pasts have been compressed and rolled into the present, which will then be rolled up in turn.

On my way home, I spot a door marked 'the oldest building in downtown'. The fact it can claim such a distinction despite being built in 1924 says everything about the fledgling development of this youthful capital. Intrigued, I venture inside – and discover a dusty jewel. Following a narrow staircase, I enter a charming, high-ceilinged villa filled with a wondrous array of colonial furnishings, impressionist paintings, calligraphic verse and watercolour sketches, all bathed in slanted sunlight. And standing at the centre, sporting a single woollen glove, is a tall black man with several missing teeth: Mr Jaffer, the caretaker.

This somewhat dreamlike place is run by 'the Duke of Mukhaibeh', Mr Jaffer informs me: the only duke in the kingdom. In 2001, he transformed the building from a hotel into a public space celebrating Jordanian heritage and culture, which anyone can access for free.

'The duke's real name is Mamdouh Bisharat,' an old man pipes up from the sunken folds of a floral armchair in the corner. 'It's said he was given the title after King Hussein held a picnic on his farm and it started raining. Mamdouh produced an umbrella, and the king was so impressed he granted him a dukedom in return!'

I smile. The story seems to fit the rabbit-hole surrealism of the place perfectly. 'This duke seems like a good person,' I say.

'Yes. He has a phrase: "We cannot enjoy modernity if we neglect our past." Lots of Jordanians are money-obsessed, but he understands we're more than this. We're a modern country built on ancient foundations.' He looks at me. 'Tell me, what do you think of our strange old-young country?'

I consider. 'I think there's a magic about it, though I can't quite put my finger on it.'

'I'm glad you think that,' he replies. 'That's what I think too.'

Jordan is 'repression light', Adam Coogle of Human Rights Watch (HRW) explains. King Abdullah II is the blueprint of a benevolent dictator, modernist and socially liberal, who has avoided the Islamism and pan-Arab nationalism of his neighbours. 'People don't fear him, but they don't criticise him either.'

Adam has kindly agreed to meet me in the foyer of the Marriott Hotel to help me better understand Jordan's thorny political situation. Jordan is 'a fake democracy', he says. The king is all-powerful, while parliament is a rubber stamp. 'When things go wrong, like with the Arab Spring, the king just scapegoats the government. He fires some ministers and does just enough to placate the public, but nothing that threatens the status quo.'

There was a moment in the 1950s when it seemed things might turn out differently. The popular leader Suleiman Nabulsi came to power in Jordan's first semi-free elections, and voters hoped he might be the one to implement real long-term reform. Like so many doomed free-thinkers of that era, however, Nabulsi turned not to the West but to the East and threw in his lot with the Soviets. The US pulled rank, Nabulsi was dismissed, political parties were banned and the CIA gained unfettered access to Jordanian intelligence in return for generous provisions of aid.

Since then, Jordan's gentle tyranny has endured – and the regime's grip appears to be tightening. 'Since Syria, there's been no pressure to do anything except provide security,' Adam says. 'Freedom's been put on the backburner.'

Later, I go to meet an American NGO worker called Verity. For her, Amman is reassuringly stable but lacks a spark. 'Things function, but it's pretty boring,' she tells me over a caipirinha in one of West Amman's many eye-wateringly extortionate hipster joints. 'Jordan lacks its own industry and is entirely reliant on aid. That's why it's taken in so many refugees: to keep the income flowing.'

The truth is that Jordan has never really broken away from its vassalage status under foreign powers. At first it was the British pulling the strings; now it's the US and Saudis. As a result, the country is both complacent and subservient, lacking not only the means but the will to address deep-seated grievances – of which, Verity says, there are many. 'Take the inequality, for a start. Don't imagine that West Amman has anything to do with Jordan.' She pauses to order a jug of sangria for the price of a small mortgage. 'Real life can be found in the east, in neighbourhoods westerners will never ever go into.'

Despite these issues, Jordan remains the 'safest haven in the region right now', Verity believes – just as it has been throughout the ages, in fact, since the Circassians flocked here from Russia in the mid-1800s and the Palestinians followed suit from the West Bank and Gaza a century later. More recently, it has been the Iraqis and Syrians who've arrived in their hundreds of thousands, settling in camps and cities across the country to escape war and persecution back home.

'There's a real mix of settlements here,' an aid worker friend called Peter explains, who joins us at the bar for last orders. 'At one end, you've got the gold-standard Emirati settlement, where residents live in caravans with satellite TV. At the other, there's al-Azraq out in the desert, where people's only greater fear than being stung by a scorpion is dying slowly of boredom.' In the middle is Zaatari, one of the world's biggest camps, which acts more like a sovereign territory than a community of exiles. 'It even has its own internal economy. We call the marketplace the Champs-Élysées.'

Jordan is doing its best in a difficult situation, Peter continues. Security personnel are not as bigoted or brutal as those elsewhere, and state subsidies are generous compared to Europe and the Gulf. 'Though, of course,' he adds, 'this still means huge suffering for the people involved.' It means sleeping in flimsy shelters and enduring hardship and disease. It means living with no independence and limited privacy or control. It means suffering the indignities of incarceration when you've committed no offence. 'Can you imagine living like that?' he asks. 'I mean *really* imagine it?'

For a moment, I try to. I try to imagine being driven from my home into such a place, with no escape and nobody on my side. But every time I reach for it, the image dissolves at the touch.

'No,' I admit. 'I can't.'

He nods. 'That's the problem. Nobody can – until it happens to them.'

Today, Jordan could be described as one giant refugee camp. The state may not admit it officially, but Palestinians now make up a significant majority of the population. As such, they constitute a political threat to both the dominant Bedouin community and the Hashemite rulers themselves. Should democracy ever take root here, the newcomers would no doubt give short shrift to this weak, autocratic dynasty parachuted into power by the Brits.

'Some say Jordan should be the new Palestine,' Muhammad, a Palestinian student, tells me. 'But this isn't our home.' In Palestine they're called Jordanian, he says, and in Jordan they're called Palestinian. 'We're stuck in purgatory, like ghosts.'

Muhammad is a member of a federation of medical students who fundraise for Gazan refugees. While most Palestinians from the West Bank have been granted Jordanian citizenship, those from Gaza are stateless and have limited legal rights. Together, the students have raised £12,000 to buy clothes, provisions and zinc roofing for a Gazan camp in Jerash, near the Syrian border in the north, and I have joined them on one of their visits.

'We want change, but many Palestinians worry that speaking out will make things worse,' Muhammad says, as we heave dozens of bags and cardboard boxes into a whitewashed concrete building. On the wall is a portrait of the king and queen looking every inch the modern Western couple, the king sporting a casual shirt and chinos, the queen a short skirt and blouse. 'This is how it's always been in the past.'

The Palestinians' plight is complicated by their association with militancy. Founded in 1964, the PLO used Jordan as a base for raids into Israel until being expelled in 1970 – at which point, as we have seen, it went on to cause mayhem in Lebanon. 'I'm against violence,' Muhammad says, when I ask his opinion of militia groups such as the PLO and Hamas. 'But people must understand it comes from desperation, not choice. Caged people will always fight to break free.'

After we have unpacked all the clothing, the residents begin to arrive. They wander slowly about the room, studying, selecting and trying on garments with an air of acute discernment, until an officious man clutching a clipboard ushers them out so more can enter and choose some for themselves. Around half the women wear niqabs, the others hijabs and abayas (full-length cloaks), and all emit a quiet, dignified reserve.

When the stream of visitors ends, we go to meet the families whose roofs need replacing. On the way, children scamper about us making victory signs and shouting *soura!* (photo!). One tiny girl, dressed in a beautifully absurd pair of leather stiletto boots, shrieks and scowls as I turn my camera her way, before stumbling like a newborn springbok down the road.

Perhaps due to its elevated hillside location, this camp of 30,000 people feels less densely populated than those in Lebanon. Beyond that, however, there seems little to distinguish between the settlements. The houses we enter are damp, their walls brown and mottled like used teabags. The entire camp appears to be cracked and flaking, in fact, as if suffering from an endemic skin disease. In one house, Muhammad points out the water tank lodged just inches below the fibrous cement ceiling. 'The water is often polluted by sewage or asbestos,' he says. 'It causes lots of health problems. Cerebral palsy, autism, hypertension ...' As if to prove his point, an elderly woman shuffles into the room as he speaks, hunched and wheezing and begging for help. She is half-blind and yellow, pus-filled lumps cover her legs. But no care is available, especially for older residents. 'All we can do is fix her roof,' Muhammad says. 'And keep out the rats and rain.'

I have an unexpected encounter as I am leaving Amman. Shortly after joining the main road out of the city, I hear a whistle from behind me and glance back to see a portly man in purple trousers running along the pavement. 'Lady!' he is shouting. 'Stop, please! Hello!'

Normally, I ignore such roadside invocations, but he is making such hullaballoo that I take pity and pull over. He rushes up, panting. 'Lady, hello! Name, please? Where from?'

'Rebecca,' I say, shaking his hand. 'London.'

'London!'

He looks pleased. Speaking broken, breathless English, he explains that he is about to qualify as a doctor and hopes to set up a sports medicine practice in Britain. Could I help with a visa? 'I know all the muscles,' he says, squatting and squeezing his thighs by way of corroboration. '*All* of them! And tai chi too.'

He demonstrates a few moves for my benefit, and I eye the speeding traffic to my rear with growing unease as his gesticulations become ever more exuberant. After a few minutes, I start mumbling my excuses to leave when he catches my wrist beseechingly. 'Lady, moment,' he says. 'I show you special thing. Please ...'

And with no further ado, he begins spreading his legs wide ... wider ... and wider still ... nostrils flaring, brow sweating, trouser seams stretching to the limit of their capacity ... until, on the pavement on one of the busiest highways of Amman, he finally succeeds in his heroic endeavour – and demonstrates the perfect sideways splits!

And if that isn't enough to convince the GMC to grant him a British medical licence, I genuinely don't know what is.

I am excited about my ride to the Dead Sea. This is partly because I'll be retracing one of the most timeworn Hajj routes through the Arabian sands, traversed by worshippers, pilgrims and merchants through the ages. But mainly because it should be downhill all the way. Located 400 metres below sea level, the Dead Sea is the lowest place on Earth, and I am looking forward to gliding down there with ease through the eastern peaks of the Jordan Rift Valley.

It is a good, simple plan with little room for error. But it fails to take into account one significant factor: namely, my uncanny ability to veer off a perfectly straight road, unintentionally and inexplicably, without any idea that I've done so. It is a talent I've had since I was young, and I recall the moment I first became aware of it – when, as a six-year-old, I disappeared from a small residential side street in Oxford, prompting widespread panic and a borough-wide police hunt. I remember the incident well, though to this day I'm unsure on the specifics of what happened. One moment, I was lining up my Care Bears and Transformers to launch an attack on my brother's army of Pterodactyls and Lego men; the next, I'd turned a corner and my surroundings were entirely unfamiliar. It was one of those seminal childhood moments that often build resilience and shape who you later become: e.g., I nearly drowned, so now I can swim; I got bullied, so now I'm a tai chi expert who can do the sideways splits, etc. But I got lost and continued to do so on a fairly regular basis for the next thirty years.

For someone like me, the satnav has proved a godsend. Due to this remarkable invention, I am finally able to know definitively where I am at any time and exactly where I'm going (physically, at least, if not always figuratively). I can attend meetings without carrying an *A–Z* the size of a coffee table and locate friends' houses without pulling into every petrol station en route to ensure that the motorway I'm travelling on is the same one I was on three minutes previously. This is an almost wholly positive development, I'm sure – even if, at the same time, I find myself questioning whether something along the way has been lost. Navigating by machine is to live in a plotted, predestined world; it is to remain inside one's comfort zone and to never stray outside the lines. Is this really, I wonder, the kind of life I want to live?

Or this is what I ask myself, at least, as I realise with a nauseating jolt that I have no idea where I am. At some point or other, although it's far from clear when, I appear to have ventured off the enormous thumping thoroughfare leading directly to the Dead Sea basin and onto a narrow, unpaved track. Baffled, I retrace my steps and attempt to locate the turning I must have made while semi-conscious. But it's no good. The original road has incomprehensibly disappeared – and I am indisputably lost.

Around me, all I can see are endless craggy hills, some parched and yellow, others clad in cypress groves and thorn. Pulling over, I try to collect my wits. With no map or phone signal, I feel stymied. But then, with a flash of inspiration, I have it – *of course*. Dismounting, I delve into my bags and, after considerable rummaging, find what I am looking for stuffed deep inside my rucksack: my plastic 95p compass! It's admittedly a little sticky from the milk explosion in Bulgaria, but it still seems to function. And I cannot deny that I feel distinctly intrepid – on a par with Shackleton, perhaps, or Stark – simply by holding it in my hand and staring at it.

After a short assessment, it appears that I'm going largely the right way. If I continue in this direction, I may not hit the sea quite head-on, as planned, but at worst I'll hit the West Bank and be able to journey south from there. As long as I don't inadvertently wander 200 kilometres north (to Syria) or east (to Saudi Arabia) – neither of which, I admit, is beyond the realms of possibility – I should still arrive at my destination by nightfall. So, with renewed spirit and focus, I remount Maud and continue.

Twenty minutes later, I pass an intriguing signpost for 'Iraq Al-Amir Handicraft Village'. Venturing inside, I find more curious signs: one for the 'Iraq Al-Amir Women's Cooperative Society', another for the 'Iraq Al-Amir Women's Association'. Perhaps, once upon a time, this odd, windswept compound was a bastion of feminist activism – though, today, the only resident appears to be a balding middle-aged man standing in a doorway. I decide to try out some of my best Arabic on him.

'My hamster escaped,' I say. 'I miss you.'

He looks puzzled, and I realise I'm confusing my phrasing. I try something simpler. '*Ayn albahr?*' Where is the sea?

This time, he appears to understand. He coughs, straightens and begins answering at length, gesturing in multiple directions at once as he does so, like a semaphore instructor or policeman directing traffic. He draws lines in the earth and spirals in the air; he bends down low and jumps high onto his toes; he grins and frowns and thumps the doorframe with his fist. Then, with all the timing of a *basso profundo*, he builds slowly to a fevered climax, pointing and waving and whirling his arms in a theatrical flourish – at which point I smile and thank him gratefully, having failed to comprehend a word.

I press on. The road is just a rutted track, dipping up and down in constant enervating undulations, and the landscape is grainy and bare. At one point, four sheepdogs encircle me with bared fangs, and a shepherd bearing a striking resemblance to Errol Flynn thrashes them back with a stick. On his head, he wears a purple US baseball cap wrapped in a green Bedouin scarf, which seems in one simple trope to sum up the searing incongruities of this peculiar old-young land.

After the hounds have retreated, I give the man a cigarette as a thank you, and for a few minutes we sit side by side, staring out across the bleak, serrated peaks beyond. Then I bid him farewell, lead Maud back onto the road and continue my jolting descent into the deepest bowels of the Earth.

The camp at Mujib Nature Reserve is not easy to find. Only a small signpost gives an inkling that anything exists here at all, and Maud and I tumble down a rocky slope, past an empty car park and onto an almost impassably sandy track without encountering any signs of life at all. Eventually, however, we turn a corner – and there it is, in all its surreal, preternatural glory: a constellation of domed clay cabins, silhouetted against a ruby sky, which looks not unlike a space camp on Mars.

Inside, the man at reception seems surprised to see me. I imagine, from the swarm of flies buzzing around the stacked chairs in the corner, that visitors in January are rare. This hunch is confirmed when he admits that they don't have a chef or any food, but I'd be welcome to share his dinner if I'd like to stay. I'd love to, I reply, and he bares a row of blackened teeth in a half-smile, half-grimace, before leading me back out into the darkness to escort me to my hut.

I am expecting something fairly primitive. Instead, what I am taken to is a cabin fit for a king. Pristine and modern with a gleaming glass frontage overlooking the water, the building feels as incongruous in these Martian surrounds as one of Gertrude Bell's linen tablecloths. 'Okay?' the man asks, looking over apprehensively. '*Jamil!*' I reply, smiling. Beautiful.

After dinner, comprising bread and humus the consistency of wallpaper paste, I retire to my terrace. Directly ahead, a deep blood-orange ribbon stretches across both the sky and sea, as if the world has been dipped in wet paint, folded and reopened to create an image of striking symmetry. It feels odd to imagine that the fractured city of Jerusalem lies just a few miles across this soundless expanse, and I feel a sudden surge of dismay at the bitter quarrel being played out in that most historic and holy of cities. How does it come to this, I wonder? That a place said to embody all that's best in the human spirit – compassion, enlightenment, tolerance, love – can be so easily and starkly debased?

I stare into the darkness, waiting for an answer, but nothing comes. All I see is water, that enduring archetype of life and rebirth, now black and mute and still.

There is no single catalyst for the suffering and turmoil being endured in Israel and Palestine today. It is a feud with no easy framework, no clear beginning or end. A clash that is not so much over territory as competing ideas of selfhood and belonging: ideas of protean shape and purpose that defy reason or logic alone.

However, it is easy to forget when watching images of this remote, shattered region broadcast across our screens at home that it is a conflict in which we Brits played a seminal role. At the height of our imperial power a hundred years ago, the Levant and Sinai were seen as indispensable assets that safeguarded access to British India via the Suez Canal – so, when Ottoman Palestine came up for grabs following World War I, we were determined to gain control over the territory at all costs. And the best way to achieve this, it was reasoned – at a time when the ideology of empire building was being replaced by a drive towards national self-determination – was to win Zionist support by endorsing their aspirations to return to the 'homeland' from which they were expelled 2,500 years ago.

It seemed, at first, like a winning plan. In 1917, Foreign Secretary Arthur Balfour made his famous declaration, and three years later Britain was awarded the Palestinian mandate with a 'dual obligation' to support the Zionists while protecting the rights of the Arab majority. While experts such as Gertrude Bell were adamantly opposed to the idea – Israel was an 'impossible proposition', she wrote in 1918, which would 'override every conceivable political consideration, including the wishes of the large majority of the people' – for Britain, the prize was worth the risk. French support was secured by endorsing their claims on Syria, betraying promises of independence made to the Arabs, while the Hashemite leaders Faisal and Abdullah, whose armies had helped defeat the Ottomans, were placated with the kingship of Britain's two other mandates, Iraq and Transjordan, respectively.

At the time, Transjordan was just a poor, sparsely populated country of tribal nomads, having been hived off the Palestinian mandate like a toenail clipping or flap of excess skin. The hope was that Abdullah – the plump, pliable great-grandfather of Jordan's current king – would be the ideal candidate 'to do His Majesty's Government's bidding', in the words of T.E. Lawrence,[43] and manage to staunch Arab anger as the Jews flooded in. But the hope was short lived. Britain had opened Pandora's box, underestimating both Arab resistance and Jewish resolve, and Abdullah was powerless to respond to the unfolding catastrophe. Tensions grew, clashes escalated, and it wasn't long before the Arabs were embroiled in a full-scale revolt.

---

[43] Indeed, Lawrence was not quite the steadfast Arab loyalist he is often portrayed to be. 'If properly handled,' he wrote in a secret memorandum in 1916, '[the Arabs] would remain in a state of political mosaic, a tissue of jealous principalities incapable of cohesion …' For many in the Middle East today, he is not remembered kindly.

Caught in the glare of the global spotlight, Britain knew it needed to change tack. In one of the most egregious historic examples of belated stable-door-shutting, it desperately tried to appease the Arabs by limiting Jewish immigration – all while, 3,000 kilometres to the north, the flames of the gas chambers burnt. Outraged, the Zionist terror groups didn't hold back. Declaring the British had 'dipped His Majesty's crown in Jewish blood and polished it with Arab oil', they bombed villages, massacred civilians, kidnapped soldiers and assassinated politicians. The tactics proved effective. In November 1947, the UN finally granted the Jewish people the homeland they'd coveted for so long, transforming the dynamics and demographics of the region forever.[44]

Since that time, the impact of the conflict on the region has been extraordinary. It has played a huge part in the emergent consciousness of the Middle East out of all proportion to the slender fragment of land involved. Yet it is important to remember that the dispute has never fundamentally been about faith. For the Arabs, Israel is not viewed simply as an enemy in its own right but as a creation and symbol of the post-imperial West; the racial and religious aspects of the conflict are just a sideshow. As the historian Bernard Lewis points out, after all, the two sides were never traditional enemies in the past. '[In Islam], there is little sign of any deep-rooted emotional hostility directed against Jews,' he writes in *The Jews of Islam*. 'Or for that matter any other group, such as the antisemitism of the Christian world.'

In the morning, I discover more punctures in one of Maud's puncture-proof tyres. I glue on three more patches, all to no avail. I add a fourth, then a fifth. Then a sixth – my last – atop the third. I pump the tube and it seems to hold. For about twenty seconds.

---

[44] Due to the ongoing building of illegal settlements, Israel now controls around 90 per cent of former Palestine, and its policy of land grabbing does not look set to change anytime soon.

And then I hear it, soft yet resolute, like the final exhalation of a soldier fatally wounded in battle. *Pfffft.*

Pfffffuck.

There is nothing to be done. The thorns have proved the iceberg to Maud's tender hull, and there are too many ruptures to keep the vessel afloat. Ever-resilient in such situations, I decide there's only one thing for it: I must take a dip in the sea and tackle the problem later. So, towel in hand, I scramble down the rocky shore to the water's edge – before immediately scrambling back up, going to the lodge and commandeering the company of the manager. Irrationally scared of open water, I am unable to bathe alone anywhere that I can't see the bottom – particularly a boggy, brackish swamp called something so macabre as the 'Dead Sea' – and require a little moral support to help me on my way.

The man has no idea why I've dragged him here, of course, and I fear he may have got the wrong impression. As I wallow near the shore, floating belly-up with all the languid elegance of a comatose manatee, he scoops up a handful of mud and approaches me with a tentative smile. When I shake my head, he looks momentarily confused before shrugging and lathering the gloop into his own hands, arms and neck. I am half expecting him to drop a portion down his shorts too, as this – according to my mother, at least – is apparently what male Dead Sea bathers do to ensure the high regional birth rates continue. But my friend has few concerns in that arena, it seems, as he keeps all his ablutions decorously above waist level.

I feel revived after my dip, and by 9am I have not only showered and checked out but have flagged down a truck on the highway to take me into town. The driver is tall and expressionless, with a drooping moustache that reflects his drooping eyes, and I snap a picture of him before we leave just in case anything goes wrong. I feel confident it won't, however; I've hitchhiked often in the past and it has always been fine.

And yet, almost immediately, this experience feels different. Off, somehow. The man is acting oddly, fidgeting and stealing twitchy glances in my direction while speaking in rapid gunfire bursts on the phone. He does this for several minutes – before, to my horror, he suddenly turns and blows me a kiss. It's not just one kiss, either. It's dozens. He keeps staring and puckering, his saggy eyes filled with a milky, torpid light. He accompanies this display with sporadic cries of 'love' (which, if I'm honest, feels a little quick off the mark after such a brief courtship), while attempting, with minimal success, to avoid steering the truck off the road.

Then, just as my bellows of fury seem to be quelling his ardour, he suddenly takes the assault to a whole new level – and reaches over to grab my left breast.

Shocked, I scream and bash his hand away, but he does it again, and then a third time. And by now I am panicking. While I've planned for a situation like this in my head, I never imagined it would happen in reality, and I run through my rehearsed motions in desperate, hurried succession. First, I brandish my fake wedding ring ('*Ana motazaweja!*' I cry. I'm married!), which stymies him briefly, but only for a moment. Next, I show him pictures of my fake children (my nieces) on my phone, which proves similarly ineffective.

Then, finally, I resort to my *pièce de resistance*: one unmistakeably un-fake penknife.

Instantly, I feel empowered. Pulling it like Excalibur from my bag, I hold it aloft so he can see it in all its sharpened, shimmering glory, before wafting it vaguely in the vicinity of his groin. The impact is immediate. For a man, I imagine there's something very sobering about the prospect of going a scrotum short. His expression shifts, first to angst and incredulity, then to a broad, nervous grin. 'Good!' he cries, jabbing his thumb at his chest. 'I good man!'

Could I stab him if I had to? I think perhaps I could. Fortunately, however, I'm not given the chance to find out. Within moments of seeing the blade, the man pulls over and drops me off – and seconds later he is gone. The town is another mile or so down the road, so I begin wheeling Maud along the pavement, her panniers swinging loose, her flat tyre flapping awkwardly against the ground. I continue for about ten minutes, then stop. The knife, I realise, is still clutched tightly in my hand.

I place it carefully back into my bag. Then I put my head down and take a series of deep breaths. I'm shaking. *Thank god*, I think. *Thank fucking god.*

The benefit of off-season travel is that you often have accommodation all to yourself. The downside is that many places have shut down altogether. In Kerak, the only guestroom available is in a gloomy, windowless dungeon with a cracked tile floor, bright white strip lighting and a curiously majestic bathroom caked with smears of brown scum. Just the kind of place Josef Fritzl might choose to vacation, I imagine, if he ever came to Jordan.

Once settled in this idyll, I venture out to see the Crusader fortress. This crumbling edifice, built in the 1140s from volcanic stone, stands on a glacis on the edge of town overlooking the gorge below. Known as *Petra Deserti* ('the Stone of the Desert'), the castle was once located on a bustling east–west trade route and was one of the 'most celebrated fortresses of Syria', according to Ibn Battuta. Its Western proprietorship was short-lived, however; just forty years after its construction, Saladin's nephew laid siege to its seemingly impregnable walls and, still reeling from their defeat to Saladin himself a year earlier, the Crusaders swiftly surrendered.

Despite this historic sectarian strife, Kerak has long had a reputation for tolerance. Indeed, even amid the throes of religious enmity that wreaked havoc here so many centuries ago, a spirit of inclusion seems to have endured. 'One of the most astonishing things that is talked of is that though the fires of discord burn between the two parties ... Muslim and Christian travellers will come and go between them without interference ...' the Arab traveller Ibn Jubayr wrote of the city in 1184 CE. 'The soldiers engage themselves in their war, while the people are at peace.'

'Yes, in Kerak people always respect each other,' the guesthouse manager tells me as I eat my dinner alone in the dank, foul-smelling dining room. 'For me, as Muslim, this very important.'

The word 'Islam' translates as 'peace', he explains. 'No force, no kill.'

'People must choose freely?' I ask.

'Yes. Qur'an very clear.'

'But what of the passages encouraging violence?' I ask. 'Like the ones quoted by ISIS?'[45]

He winces at the question. 'Daesh, they're … how you say, woof woof, *al-kalb* …?'

'Dog?'

'Yes, little dog. Puppy. They bark but weak. Just *woof woof*, always!'

'What they say isn't true?'

'No. Read the Qur'an yourself and you see.'

Later, on my Kindle, I do as he says. I find the following:

> There is no compulsion where religion is concerned. [2:256]
> You may fight in the cause of God against those who attack you but do not aggress. [2:190]
> If they refrain, you shall not aggress; aggression is permitted only against the aggressors. [2:193]

But there are other decrees too, often quoted by jihadists to justify their cause. 'Slay the idolators wherever ye find them,' Allah commands Muhammad [9:5], while to Muslims he instructs, 'Strike terror into the hearts of unbelievers' [8:12] and 'Fight those who believe not in Allah … until they pay the *jizya* with willing submission, and feel themselves subdued' [9:29].

---

45 In December 2016, Islamic State launched an attack on Jordanian security forces in Kerak in retaliation for their support of the US-led coalition fighting in Iraq and Syria. Having sought refuge in the castle during the shootout, the jihadists murdered seven police officers and three civilians before being shot and killed themselves.

It all comes down to interpretation, it seems. The Bible has brutally murderous sections too, after all, such as the *herem* passages referenced by the Crusaders to justify their campaigns, in which God demands the smiting of all heretics. Whether Islam is seen as a religion of peace or aggression, therefore, appears to be determined by the agenda of its adherents. For the jihadists, it is political and violent. For most civilians – so it seems to me from those I have met so far – it is not.

I fix Maud in the morning, having located a puncture repair kit, and afterwards I hit the road. Overnight, a bitter headwind has whipped in from the desert steppe, forming a blustery current along the Abarim foothills, and it is a tough, tiring ride. Yet the landscape helps to buoy my mood. Mountain ridges rounded like whalebacks billow in all directions, some a dull ochre in hue, others shimmering shades of umber, while the air feels as sharp and clean as cut glass. Occasionally, one of the peaks rises to pierce the wisps of cloud overhead, while those around it undulate in flaxen waves as if breathing against the sky.

Then, with startling abruptness, I tumble into a gulley. Down, down, down I race, fast and freewheeling, buffeted by puffs of dust and sand ... until, at the valley floor, I finally skid to a breathless halt. It feels remote down here, a kilometre deep in the Earth's crust, although the place is far from deserted. A cluster of black goatshair tents lie scattered amid the dunes, while several donkeys wander past carrying young boys perched on saddles of knotted rags. As I stop to get my bearings, a young girl emerges, swinging two dead rabbits by their feet, before spotting me and scampering off at a rapid canter down the road.

Marking the Old Testament boundary between the northern Moabites and southern Edomites, this colossal fifty-kilometre-wide canyon is the path reportedly taken by the Israelites during their exodus from Egypt – and, despite the difficult terrain, I can see why this route might appeal. The bare, yellowed rock may be bleak, but there is something undeniably soothing and protective about it too, as if I've nestled into the creases of a giant dun-coloured duvet.

Sadly there is no time to rest, however, so I continue across the base of the chasm and on and up the other side. The climb is no fun. It is, in fact, an agonising, interminable grind. This isn't how I imagined it would be after six months on the road. I imagined my relationship with hills would have transformed by now, and I'd approach each one like an old friend before dancing over its summit with a breezy wave and *ma'a salamah!* But sadly it hasn't worked out like that. I still hate hills, and the feeling seems to be mutual. What galls me most of all is their duplicity. At first they appear friendly: soft and meek and matronly. But the closer you get, the more their demeanour changes; their eyes narrow and that expression you took for tenderness morphs into a smug, sadistic smirk. *I've got you now*, they seem to cry. *And you're not leaving until I've made you curse the day you were born!*

All hills have elements of psychosis about them, but they're not all the same. In fact, I've learnt that there are specifically five types of hill, each with their own unique qualities. These comprise the following:

1. The bun-burner: a long, hot slog that sears the arse like a firebrand.
2. The false friend: a hill that doesn't seem like a hill until you realise it's been a couple of hours since you last felt your legs.
3. The masochist: a hill that gets gradually, imperceptibly steeper until all you want is to crawl into the foetal position crying for your mother.
4. The redeemer: a hill I can actually climb without too much trouble; more like a ripple in the road.
5. The up yours: basically a vertical wall with the words 'up yours' scrawled across it.

This particular slope begins as a three, before slipping seamlessly into a five. And although I have a sense of what wonderful, sweeping panoramas await me at the top, I still can't bring myself to enjoy the slog. I wonder, in fact, if anyone can. Are there crackpots out there who genuinely *enjoy* this kind of pain, rather than simply the pleasure of the payoff at the end? For me, and surely for most people of sound mind, there is no better hill than a retrospective one: a hill I've already climbed, lying deliciously and idyllically to my rear. I love those kinds of hills. In fact, I often weep at how beautiful they are.

Fortunately, this turns out to be one of the best retrospective hills I've encountered so far. The view at the top is magnificent. Caught like kindling by the dying sun, the tips of distant hills blaze in a conflagration of bronze, copper and gold, casting the valley in a radiant amber glow. Standing at the edge of the scarp, I stare at the scene, transfixed.

'Good, yes?' an old man says, who is loitering nearby.

'*Jamil*,' I say.

'*Jamil!* Yes.'

We stand for a few moments in silence. Then he turns to me. 'Husband?' he asks.

'Yes. Six children.' I hold up six fingers. I'm not taking any chances this time.

'Six?'

I nod, and he chuckles. 'That is busy lady – even for Arab!'

I awake at daybreak to the sight of a yawning sandstone gorge beneath a silken rose-blue sky. A strip of pale violet suggests a canopy of distant peaks, while the nearby craggy bluffs gleam a biscuity golden brown. It is one of the most devastatingly beautiful vistas I have ever seen. And I have it all to myself.

The rising sun provides my first proper view of al-Nawatef Camp, where I arrived late last night. A row of neat square tents perch on the cliff edge, each cosily furnished with a rug, stove and bed, while a small Bedouin-style hut laid with colourful cushions and rugs provides a communal gathering space nearby. The owner, Ali, apologises for the lack of electricity and running water. 'We don't have enough guests,' he explains ruefully. 'We had just 300 last year. Before 2011, we had 600 in November alone.'

Ali is a sweet dollop of a man with a bald head and beaming smile. He bought the site in 2006 and built the camp himself, he tells me as he lights a cigarette and instantly fills the shack with fumes. 'The buildings, balconies, wells. Everything.' By 2009, he was sold out, but in 2012 the flow of visitors stopped. 'It's very safe here,' he sighs. 'But people hear about Daesh and stay away.'

After a chilly bucket-shower, I pull on several layers of clothes and wheel Maud back to the road. I've now climbed to 5,000 feet and my skin tingles in the ice-whipped air. For hours, I journey up and down the crests of hills, pulled by a hidden current, my sails plump with wind. As I ride, toddlers give chase, teenagers holler and old women wave and invite me in for tea. I'm in Ma'an Governorate now, the most deprived and conservative district in Jordan, and I admit I'm relieved to find it so welcoming. Long known for its anti-establishment views, Ma'an has in recent years developed a reputation as a jihadist stronghold, harbouring Islamic State supporters and boasting its own homegrown militant Salafist[46] group. But there seems little to fear here today.

My cycle is not only entirely without incident but is a lovely, peaceful journey. In contrast to a few centuries ago, when this meandering thoroughfare – the King's Highway – formed a busy arterial passage between Egypt and the Euphrates, most traffic nowadays prefers the faster Highway 15 to the east, leaving this route to those who prefer a more leisurely pace. Loosely following the contours of the Dead Sea rift, the road winds its way south through history and myth, from the lush wheat fields of biblical

[46] Salafism developed in the Arab world in the late nineteenth century as a response to European imperialism. An outgrowth of the Wahhabi movement in Saudi Arabia, its adherents follow a puritanical form of Islam practised by the first three generations of Muslims. They can broadly be divided into three categories: the purists, who avoid politics (the largest group); the activists, who engage with politics; and the jihadists, who advocate violence (the smallest group).

Ammon to the ancient copper and maritime hub of Aqaba. Moses is said to have first glimpsed the Promised Land from a hill overlooking this route, while leagues of armies reportedly marched this way to fight the infidels of Sodom and Gomorrah. It is also believed to have been here that the Franks conducted their most vicious incursions against Muslim pilgrims travelling to Mecca, provoking the wrath of Saladin and spurring him on to victory on the battlefield.

Now pushing steadily uphill, I climb and climb until the land tips and spills like a treasure chest before me. Far below, I see my destination: al-Beidha (Little Petra), the mini-sibling of the resplendent Nabatean capital. After a hair-raising descent down a series of tight switchbacks, I roll into a cluster of concrete bungalows and track down the home of Ghazi, my Bedouin host – although the person who greets me at the door is someone quite different. 'Welcome!' a young Frenchwoman cries, ushering me inside with a sweep of her leonine mane. 'Ghazi's out, but he'll join us shortly.'

The woman, Odette, turns out to be Ghazi's girlfriend. They met when she hired him as her guide nine months ago, and they've been together ever since. 'Coming here is the only way I can see him,' she tells me. 'He won't go to Europe. He spent two decades as a physio nurse in Germany and found it really cold and unfriendly.'

She leads me into the living room. The three-room house is vibrantly decorated with eclectic bric-a-brac, from brass lamps and leather shoes to ornamental weaponry and Jimi Hendrix photographs, while multicoloured cushions and textiles cover every inch of floor and wall. Shortly after we sit down, Ghazi arrives, and within seconds he has vanished into the kitchen and re-emerged with a tray of tea, sweets and fruit. 'Hospitality is in our roots,' he says when I thank him. 'The Bedouin were the original Arabs, so the customs started with us.'

Ghazi is a tall, striking man with brooding features and a wild shock of black hair. His face is creviced with a cross-hatching of thick lines, as if it has been scrunched into a ball and then laid out flat again. As a child, he was brought up in the caves of Petra, he explains, but moved to a nearby village when Petra was converted to a UNESCO heritage site in 1985. 'The king visited and asked us where we wanted to go,' he says. 'We pointed to a place on the map, and the king agreed.'

'You like the king, then?' I ask.

He nods. 'Of course. The government is bad, but he is a good man.'

'You make it sound like he isn't in charge. But he can build you a village after you point to it on a map?'

'He is in charge, but he must deal with bad people.'

I ask what Ghazi's family think about his relationship with Odette. It's fine, he replies. 'Jordan is what I call a "man-world country". Men can do anything. For a local woman, it would be different.' However, times are changing, he stresses. 'A few decades ago, most Bedouin men lived in caves with many wives and camels. Now they live in bungalows with just one wife and wifi.'

'Lots of men still prefer their wives to stay at home, though,' Odette interjects. 'And women can't hold senior positions like sheikhs or judges.' This isn't just a Bedouin issue, she says. 'Jordan has really low numbers of women in the workforce. Worse than Iran or Pakistan. There's still an expectation that the top jobs are for men.'

I tell them about the truck incident, and Ghazi looks embarrassed. 'I'm sorry. Some men are very uneducated. They don't understand the world has changed.'

'He seemed to understand my knife at his balls,' I say.

'Yes.' He smiles. 'Of course. That's a language I think every man understands.'

A trip through the scorched wilderness of Wadi Rum is a voyage into deep time. Located on an elevated plateau, this stunning moonscape gained its striking, otherworldly appearance from eons of geological evolution. Giant mesas emerge like icebergs from the tidal dunes below, formed from prehistoric tectonic shifts that raised the bedrock high above the ancient ocean floor. Over millions of years, wind and winter floods eroded the stone into a wild array of geometric forms, from lofty columns and stocky buttes to elegant archways and sweeping ravines. All stand perched on a sweep of brick-red sand, rich with iron oxide, which has earned the site a starring role in almost every Mars-focused Hollywood blockbuster to date.

Surveying these remote, arid plains today, it is hard to imagine that any living creature could ever have made a home here. Yet trace the provenance of the etchings on the rocks and you follow the evolution of human thought itself, from the most primitive archetypal petroglyphs to the intricate cursive of Thamudic, Nabatean and classical Arabic. Guiding me through the epochs is my erudite Bedouin guide, Ayaan, who takes me clambering up towering rockfaces, staggering through narrow gullies and rolling down rippling sandbanks, before concluding the tour with a scramble to the pinnacle of a giant lopsided boulder. Here, we watch the sky soften into shades of pastel before erupting into a fluorescent flurry of magenta, pink and orange, as if the heavens were in the throes of a wild hallucinogenic rave.

As the sky cavorts overhead, Ayaan throws questions at me about my background and journey, which I answer as best I can. Then one of them floors me entirely.

'Please,' he says. 'Describe England for me?'

My mind immediately goes blank. What *is* England …? Is it butter pie and *Coronation Street*? Wellies and wax cotton Barbours? Sourdough and skinny lattes? Is it race riots or the rule of law? Richard Desmond or Robert Fisk? A deadbeat superpower or an enduring force for good?

'It's football and rain,' I say weakly. 'And soggy fish and chips.'

Back at camp, I turn the tables and ask Ayaan to tell me about himself instead. He was raised with five siblings in a Petra cave, he says, and walked seven kilometres to school every day. They had no running water or electricity, but the cave was always the perfect temperature, 'warm in winter and cool in summer', and contained everything his family needed.

'It wasn't claustrophobic?' I ask.

'No. We spent lots of time outside.' He gazes into the campfire. 'It was a good life. It's much harder now.' It's a lonely life too, it seems, as he recently separated from his Swiss wife. 'I tried living in Switzerland, but I couldn't. There was no nature or freedom there.'

The idea of Switzerland, with its sweeping glaciers and soaring mountain passes, lacking nature or freedom seems odd to me, but wilderness of course comes in different guises. From my limited time in Jordan, I feel perhaps I understand. The desert has a power that grips you by the craw. Stripped and bare, it casts a sheen of vulgarity on the trappings of modern life, as if nothing were more profound or cardinal than a billion motes of dust. 'In the desert I had found a freedom unattainable in civilisation,' Thesiger writes in his book about exploring the Empty Quarter, *Arabian Sands*. 'A life unhampered by possessions, since everything that was not a necessity was an encumbrance.' Thesiger's contentment, however, is tempered by his knowledge of 'the threat [his] presence implied' – namely, the spread of 'progressive' Western culture, which he saw as a danger to the traditional Bedu way of life.

Until now, Thesiger's words have always struck me as a romantic sentiment born of naive privilege. Privation is attractive only to those who enjoy it as an escape, after all, not those who endure it as a reality. But, speaking to Ayaan, I cannot help but recall Keira's comments during my stay in Geneva – *If I were Muslim, I'd be worried ...* – and wonder at the dual blessing and burden that Western society represents for those born into a warmer, less individualistic, more companionable world.

'Maybe one day I go back,' Ayaan says.

'To Switzerland?'

'No.' He visibly recoils. 'To the caves. I think I'll be happier there.'

* * *

I arrive in Aqaba in good time to buy my ferry ticket to Egypt. The ticket office proves difficult to locate, however, and by the time I find it I am in no mood for further delays. The boat is due to leave in two hours and I must catch it if I am to meet P in Dahab tonight, as planned.

'Yes, it's going,' the man behind the counter confirms. 'But not yet.'

'Not yet?' I say. 'Then when?'

He shrugs. 'It's as the wind.'

'But how do I know when to go to the port?'

'Come back in a few hours and I may know better.'

'A few hours?!'

I'm aware that my voice has risen a few decibels and assumed the peevish tone of a businessman denied an airline upgrade. I should be more zen about such things, I know. More Bedouin. But I can't deny that accurate timetabling is, for me, one of civilisation's more palatable evils.

'How do people manage?' I rant. 'It's impossible to *plan* anything!'

We finally board at 2am, twelve hours late. My fellow passengers comprise around 200 men dressed identically in jeans and black leather jackets, and we sprinkle ourselves liberally around the rows of seating in the main cabin. Once settled, tiredness overcomes me. Stretching out and closing my eyes, I find myself thinking back over the past week, much of which already feels like a dream. Mujib, al-Nawatef, al-Beidha, Wadi Rum … none were easily accessible, emerging after much effort and excavation like a series of uncut diamonds. The people, too, merge and blur in confusing drifts in my mind. Jordan seems a country of multiple identities – Palestinian and Bedouin; immigrant and indigene; altruist and chauvinist; democrat and autocrat – all clashing and contradictory, joined by arbitrary accord.

And yet there's something about the place. Something gentle and strong, which I like. Perhaps it's the soothing expanse of the desert, or the sturdy spine of the Great Rift peaks, or the depth of history anchoring this muddled land like heavy ballast from below. Stitched and shaped by the West, Jordan feels like more than a sum of its parts. It feels like a country slowly coming into focus: a place with a rich past and hopeful future, as its only duke once said, with a hint of magic at its core.

Chapter 6

THE LONG RIDE TO FREEDOM

Egypt

'Egypt was the first democracy in the Middle East ... It is a country of civilisation, of culture. It shouldn't be suffering.'

Ahmed Zewail, Egyptian scientist
and Nobel laureate, June 2011

I ring the doorbell at 7am, buzzing with adrenalin and a giddy sense of relief. I can't quite believe I've made it. I cycled through Jordan in just five days, running a gauntlet of mountains, valleys, sex pests and punctures, and made it safely out the other side. *I made it!*

P opens the door, looking sleepy. 'Oh hi,' he says, as if he may have been expecting someone else. 'You found it then?' And on that note, he turns and goes back to bed, leaving me to carry Maud and my bags into the apartment alone.

We make up later over an absurdly large Red Sea grouper. 'I'm sorry. You know I'm bad in the mornings,' he explains. 'And I'm knackered. I've had a tough week at work.'

'I've barely slept for three days,' I retort. 'I've cycled hundreds of miles across deserts and canyons to meet you. And you can't even say a proper hello?'

'I'm sorry.'

'I even came close to castrating a randy Bedouin.'

'I see.'

He doesn't, though, of course. Aching arse muscles and thorny shorelines and libidinous truck drivers are all outside his realm of experience right now. They exist purely in my section of the Venn diagram. On his side are work and chores and getting on with the everyday household duties that attract little glory or recognition but without which the world would struggle to turn.

In the middle section is … fish. And the simple pleasure of each other's company. Fortunately, however, this proves enough to salvage the short time we have together, and it turns out to be a blissful break. Dahab has long been a favourite place of mine, its former identity as a Bedouin fishing village evident in its simple, sandy backstreets, its mellow beachfront, its endless stalls of succulent, sizzling seafood. The sand is soft and white, the water calm and piercingly turquoise, and just twenty-five kilometres away the crimson peaks of the Hejaz glow like a bed of hot coals beneath a lucent sky.

Dahab means 'gold' in Arabic, and I hear different stories about the name's origins. Some say it derives from the Bedouin *al waqt min thahab*, meaning 'time is golden', while others believe it relates to ancient gold washed down from the mountains or to the regular floodwaters that deposit mounds of sand in the bay. For me, it's the first theory that feels most appropriate. Time passes here with molten ease, and it is hard to imagine more charming or peaceful surrounds.

Right now, however, they are perhaps too peaceful even for my and P's agoraphobic tastes. Dahab, once a thriving diving mecca, is now practically a ghost-town. Palmed gazebos lie wind-battered and abandoned, hotels dark and shuttered, and the skeletons of half-built buildings stain the inland steppe like washed-up debris from invisible tides. Everywhere we go, desperate shopkeepers and restauranteurs do their best to win our custom, rapidly deflating their prices like ruptured balloons as we pass by with an apologetic smile.

The problem lies not here but several hundred miles to the north, where a fierce insurgency has been raging since 2011. Led originally by impoverished tribesmen, the unrest escalated when jihadist fighters began pouring into the region after Sisi came to power in 2013 – jihadists who, in October 2015, caused havoc for the local tourist industry by shooting down a Russian passenger plane passing overhead.

'People hear about the Sinai violence and get scared, even though it's miles away,' Jimmy, a local businessman, laments. 'It's so frustrating!'

I first met Jimmy when I was here in 2011 reporting on the Arab Spring. A gregarious fellow, he owned a popular guesthouse and restaurant, and gave free meals to people who defeated him at backgammon. Now the guesthouse is gone, and he looks like a beaten man. 'We're back where we started,' he bemoans over a pot of tea, as two rangy tabby cats dangle from a peacock tree overhead. 'We've lost so much, for nothing.'

'So what now?' I ask. 'Should people return to the streets?'

'No, it's pointless.' His eyes are empty, his shoulders slumped. The flame that used to burn in him has died. 'Egypt can't be saved now. Too much damage has already been done.'

The Egyptian regime is a particular culprit where scaremongering is concerned. On the one hand, it wishes to convince people the streets are safe. On the other, it has dedicated tremendous energy to fomenting a climate of fear among the population at large. Its messaging is powerful and unambiguous: Islamist militants are an existential threat, and only a strong, ruthless state can keep the country safe. The fact that it is largely this strong, ruthless state that has galvanised the fanatics in the first place is somewhat glossed over in the marketing spiel.[47]

---

[47] Between July 2013 and December 2018, Egyptian security forces detained over 12,000 people in 'isolated and abysmal conditions', according to Human Rights Watch, many of whom were beaten, tortured and even killed.

Unfortunately for me, the state's zealous protectionism extends to cyclists too. Multiple entreaties fail to change the minds of the policemen guarding the roadways across the Sinai peninsula: I cannot cycle them. Not even after I pen a letter absolving them of any responsibility for my safety, inspired in part by Gertrude Bell's missive to the Ottoman authorities before her trek to Ha'il in the Nejd (a strategy that didn't work out especially well for Bell, admittedly, who ended up being extorted by hostile tribes, hammered by thunderstorms and imprisoned for a fortnight by the Rashid). The answer remains a firm, unshakeable NO.

I return to P, defeated. 'They don't care what happens to you,' he points out. 'They care about people *hearing* about what happens to you. It wouldn't look good for their image.'

As an alternative, P proposes that we travel to Cairo together. He's always wanted to visit the city, he says, and he too is worried about me tackling this leg of the journey alone. Considering that he is the main beneficiary in my will if anything happens to me, I admit I find this deeply touching.

'Okay,' I say. 'Deal.'

As soon as we make the arrangement, I know it's the right thing to do. My and P's relationship is certainly starting to feel the strain after so many months apart, so what better than a few romantic moonlit strolls through this magical 'city of a thousand minarets' to get things back on track?

'Uff!' a caliph reportedly snorted upon arrival in Cairo in the eighth century. 'She's the mother of all stenches!' The city may have entranced the world with its wealth and sophistication during its apogee in the Middle Ages, but there were clearly aspects of it that were less appealing.

Today, the odours remain as strong as ever: a steaming cocktail of diesel, sewage, spices and sweat. The second-largest city in Africa, Cairo heaves under the strain of its 20 million occupants, wheezing and farting like an over-pressurised boiler ready to burst. After Dahab, arriving here feels like a descent into the abyss. Chaotic streets tangle in helix-like contortions, rammed with a paroxysm of cars, donkey carts and mopeds, while overhead a sour yellow smog smothers the horizon like a fire blanket.

Relaxing and romantic it is not. Yet it is a fun break nonetheless, and for two days P and I wander the streets, invigorated and exhausted at every turn. We soak up the smiles of the street vendors, the dusty warmth of the back-alley cafés, the wondrous agility of the cycling bread-sellers with their two-metre baking trays perched precariously atop their heads. We walk and walk, the sun beating down, the endless hollers of passers-by echoing doggedly in our wake: '*Salam!*' 'Wilcom!' 'Where from?'

After P leaves, I slip into my usual fug and am grateful when a friend, Wael Hussein, suggests a distracting evening ramble through al-Azhar Park. Elevated on a hillside, this breezy expanse feels like a pocket of oxygen within the airless city streets. Wael is an Egyptian reporter for the BBC, and this is one of his favourite places to escape the pollution and crowds – not to mention the security agents. 'It's safer here,' he says, glancing around furtively when we meet. 'Less chance of being watched.'

'Is it less safe now than before the revolution?' I ask.

He nods. 'Much less. We've regressed sixty years.'

We walk on in silence. This feels like a damning assessment of a country that was only recently heralding a new era of democratic rule. In February 2011, millions took to the streets to declare '*'aish, hurriyya, 'adala igtima'iyya!*' – 'bread, freedom, social justice!' – and, just two weeks later, the regime of Hosni Mubarak came to a crashing, ignominious end. It was a thrilling turn of events, and I visited Egypt several times during those heady revolutionary days. On one occasion, in February 2012, I came to interview Mubarak's former foreign minister, Amr Moussa, the ex-chief of the Arab League and then-presidential frontrunner. Seen as moderate and level-headed, he had been viewed by many as a shoo-in – yet this was to underestimate the animosity towards anyone affiliated with the old guard. 'He *felool!*' my taxi-driver had cried when I'd asked his thoughts. A 'remnant'. 'He has big stomach. He was fattened by Mubarak!'

Ultimately, it was the Muslim Brotherhood that won both the presidential and parliamentary elections, but the bulging gut of the deep state found a way to be fed nonetheless. The Brotherhood were overthrown by the army after just a year in office, allowing Abdel Fattah el-Sisi – the sixth military-general to lead Egypt since it became a republic in 1953 – to assume control. The power-grab split the country. For some, it was a legitimate takeover after millions took to the streets to decry President Morsi's increasing authoritarianism. For others, it was a flagrant coup engineered by an industrial-military complex intent on maintaining its stranglehold over Egypt at all costs.

'The Brotherhood made mistakes, but they never really stood a chance,' Wael says. 'They didn't control the army, press, judiciary, anything. When they were in power, the electricity cut out constantly. People queued hours for petrol. Then, after Sisi arrived, everything was magically fine again.' SCAF (the Supreme Council of the Armed Forces) are master manipulators of public opinion, he explains. 'In 2011, they scapegoated the police for the protests, then stepped in afterwards to "restore order". It's the same with the economy. They destroy it through corruption and cronyism, then act as the saviours by building roads and selling cheap bread.'

In its paradoxical role of parasite and protector, SCAF's achievements are truly something to behold. Exempt from normal market forces and bolstered by tax breaks, cheap conscription labour and preferential access to state contracts, the Council dominates a vast range of industries, from retail, manufacturing and tourism to farming, fisheries and pharmaceuticals. 'SCAF probably controls at least a third of the economy, though nobody can say for sure,' Wael explains. 'Its accounts are a state secret. A black box in a black room.'

Like Erdoğan, Sisi has proved partial to elaborate vanity projects that do little to benefit the average citizen. The most extravagant of these is the construction of a shiny, sanitised new capital city, focused primarily on the rich, which aims to discard its ailing ancestor as a lizard sheds its skin. Privately developed at a projected minimum cost of $30 billion, the city looks set to be a superlative utopia, boasting a park twice as large as New York's Central Park and a fairground four times the size of Disneyland, as well as both the tallest building and the biggest Coptic church[48] in the world.

'And in the meantime, the rest of Egypt suffers,' Wael says. 'Thousands of civilians have been arrested and hundreds killed on Sisi's watch, and journalists and activists have been constantly abused and harassed.' He describes the 'torrent of death threats' he received after tweeting a picture of security agents allegedly accepting bribes to fast-track tourists' flights from Sharm El-Sheikh after the passenger plane shooting. 'If I didn't work for the BBC, I'm sure they would've arrested me.'

Whether Egypt would have fared any better under the Brotherhood, however, is debatable. Never a popular choice with voters, the group won the 2012 elections largely due to the absence of any viable opposition – and today their reputation lies in tatters, with many Egyptians believing them to be extremists, or even terrorists. This is despite the fact they've spent the past sixty years on a charm offensive, desperately trying to convince the world that they've renounced violence for peace and democracy. 'What we want to do is trigger a renaissance in Egypt, rooted in

---

48   Nowadays, only one in ten Egyptians are Copt, but what the sect lacks in heft, it makes up for in heritage. 'Copt' derives from the original Arabic word for Egypt, *qibt*, from the Greek *Aigyptos*, and was once used to refer to the entire population of the country. Heavily persecuted by the Romans and Byzantines, the faith continues to suffer severe social and political discrimination today, despite bold attempts by Sisi (such as the construction of this church) to convince everyone that he is their champion and protector. In the face of this persecution, the Copts have developed a strong sense of cohesion and identity over the generations. Many even deny they are Arabs – much like the Maronites in Lebanon – and instead lay claim to a more 'deep-rooted' lineage dating back to the pharaohs.

the religious values upon which Egyptian culture and society is built,' a Brotherhood member wrote in the *Guardian* in 2005. 'The objective must be to end the monopoly of government by a single party.'

While in the West, faith and politics can seem like a dubious double-act – the former permanent and inviolable by nature, the latter pliant and malleable – there doesn't seem, on the face of it, anything wrong with an Islamist party being elected fairly through the ballot box, as long as it can be voted out the same way. Whether the Brotherhood would have respected the democratic process in the long term is debatable, of course. But in the face of such a powerful propaganda campaign waged against them by the state, it is almost impossible to disentangle truth from fiction and judge them with an impartial eye.

'What do you think?' I ask Wael. 'Are the Brotherhood terrorists, like so many people seem to think?'

He considers. 'Well, there's not always a firm line between dissent and violence when you're fighting an innately violent system.' The movement has been repressed for decades, he points out, and a brutal crackdown since 2013 has seen thousands of Brotherhood supporters arrested, tortured and killed. 'If they weren't radicalised before,' he says, 'they probably are now.'

During my time in Cairo, I pass through Tahrir Square regularly. Each time, it engenders a sense of loss. Originally named Ismailia Square, the junction became a hub of protest against British rule after the 1919 Egyptian Revolution and was renamed Tahrir (Freedom) Square under Gamal Abdel Nasser. When I was last here, it was a frenetic place humming with energy and defiance, as residents of all persuasions amassed in protest against SCAF. One young doctor had shown me his torso mottled with purple lesions, which he'd said had been caused by soldiers who'd beaten him with electric batons and forced him to eat mud. 'All we want is justice,' he'd told me, standing beside a poster depicting images of anti-imperial revolt: 1917 Russia; 1936 Spain; the 1848 Springtime of the Peoples. 'Is that too much to ask?'

It was, it seems, for the square is now calm. No longer a fulcrum of unrest, it has slipped soundlessly from insurrectionary icon to obsolete relic. No tents or crowds remain; just a parched green disc rimmed by fencing and spindles of slow-moving traffic. 'Stability' has returned, muffling the cries and angry tears, crushing the drumbeat of revolt. Stilling the blood in the vein.

'He was a great man,' my companion Mustafa says as he leads me into a small roadside café. He orders two bowls of *koshari*: an odd mix of rice, pasta, lentils and chickpeas which reminds me of the experimental dishes I used to make at university from leftovers in the fridge. 'A great leader.'

The man in question is Muhammad Ali Pasha, the harsh but effective *de facto* founder of modern Egypt. We have just spent the past hour exploring the multi-domed, alabaster-embossed mosque he constructed in 1830 inside the twelfth-century Citadel,[49] and Mustafa has been waxing lyrical about the former ruler who exterminated the Mamlūks, crushed all opposition, and – inspired by the technology and Enlightenment ideals of Europe – attempted to catapult the country into a new age of industrialisation. For Ali, there was nothing incompatible between the values of East and West, Mustafa explains; in fact, he felt the Arabs had the *right* to emulate and exploit Western advancements, as it was merely calling in a debt from the Dark Ages.

'Yes, a great man,' Mustafa repeats, almost wistfully. 'But not great enough in the end. He was too arrogant. He got into debt. Lost control.'

'Maybe it's time for a great woman?' I suggest.

---

[49] The Citadel, built by Saladin, was Egypt's seat of government for nearly 700 years. It is located at the southern end of 'Islamic Cairo', a tilted rectangle of land that marks the original site of the present capital.

He smiles. 'Maybe. But I don't think so.'

'No?'

'Most women don't want to get involved in politics.'

'Rubbish!'

'It's true. Most Egyptian women just want to get a husband and his money.'

Mustafa recently left his fiancée due to her 'interfering family', he explains. 'All they cared about was my income.'

'But that's because of the society men have created,' I retort. Mustafa – a thirty-something friend-of-a-friend – holds two master's degrees and comes across as bright and thoughtful. His opinion dismays me. 'There's strong pressure on women to marry. They don't have the same opportunities as men.'

'Believe me, they do.'

Moments later, blind to the contradiction, Mustafa explains how virginity is the most valued asset for an Egyptian woman and that most are expected to live with their families until marriage. As we tuck into a plate of liver sandwiches, the conversation moves on to the subject of hymens, and I bite into the raw, juicy flesh just as Mustafa is divulging how some non-virgin brides choose to have hymenoplasties to 'prove' their chastity, while others purchase fake-blood capsules that explode on their wedding night like some cheap slasher B-movie.

I put the sandwich down.

'The easiest way, though,' he continues, 'is just to have anal sex. That's what my fiancée's mother told us to do.'

My mind immediately fills with an image of a prim Miss Brodie-type directing the couple's intercourse like the sex education teacher in Monty Python's *The Meaning of Life*. Suddenly, Mustafa's decision to flee the relationship begins to make more sense.

Later, when saying goodbye, I unthinkingly kiss Mustafa on the cheek. He jumps, then turns bright beetroot. 'I'm sorry,' I stammer. 'I wasn't thinking.' In Egypt, where shaking hands with a man can be deemed overly intimate, a kiss is akin to sexual assault.

Luckily, he just grins. 'It's fine,' he says. 'This is what you do at home?'

'With friends, yes.'

'I see. Just on the cheek?'

I laugh. 'Yes, Mustafa. Just on the cheek.'

A man starts playing 'When the Saints Go Marching In' on the harmonica. Another, hocking and glancing up from his backgammon board, tells him to shut up. A French couple raise their voices, seemingly in a fight, then stand up unsteadily and stumble, laughing, into the street.

'Stella?' Masud asks. 'Or Stella?'

Masud, a UN translator, has offered to introduce me to the city's nightlife. He has brought me to El Horreya Café, one of downtown's infamous *baladi* bars, which are apparently the only places you can booze in Cairo outside the tourist haunts. The room is large, with a high, corniced ceiling and faded French-colonial elegance, but its walls are tar-yellow, its bins are overflowing and the floor-to-ceiling windows are all part-frosted to prevent passers-by witnessing the awful depravity taking place inside.

The only beer available is Stella, and two 500ml bottles are waiting on our table when we arrive. It doesn't look like the Artois brand I know from home: less reassuringly expensive, perhaps, than encouragingly cheap. 'No, there's no relation,' Masud confirms. 'Actually, this one came first.' The beer is produced by the al-Ahram Beverage Company, which was founded in 1897 by a Belgian, he explains, before being nationalised under Nasser. 'Now Heineken own it and it's by far the biggest beer producer in Egypt.'

Al-Ahram was one of the companies involved in Mubarak's corrupt 1990s privatisation binge, Masud says. Sold for a pittance to an investment consortium run by a friend of Gamal Mubarak, and flogged five years later to Heineken for $1.3 billion, it was one of the most profitable corporate deals in Egyptian history.

'But this is what happens when you get your IMFs and World Banks trying to enforce their rules here. The rich get richer and the crooks more crooked.'

'How so?' I ask.

'You can't force privatisation and deregulation on a sector run by criminals. It just gives the bastards at the top more opportunity to steal our cash.'

Following a swathe of IMF-imposed reforms, he points out, $100 billion of state assets were sold to Mubarak allies for a fraction of their market value, while labour laws were weakened, land reforms revoked, food subsidies cut and tax benefits for foreign companies introduced. Mirroring trends across the region, Egypt's population soon began to thrash helplessly in the grip of this new gangster-capitalist class: inflation and unemployment skyrocketed, the number of people living on less than $2 a day doubled and inequality grew to levels unseen since the feudal days of King Farouk. In the meantime, Egypt became the World Bank's 'top Middle East reformer' three years in a row, while the IMF gushed about Mubarak's 'bold' and 'prudent' fiscal performance.

'You want to know what started the Arab Spring?' Masud says. 'Well, here you are. People marched in the street shouting, "We won't be ruled by the World Bank! We won't be ruled by colonialism!"' He plucks a packet of crisps from a bulging Sports Direct bag sitting beside us. 'Then, as soon as the revolution was crushed, Western leaders like Cameron and Obama shot off to meet SCAF with a load of arms dealers in tow. All while harping on about democracy!'[50]

Masud is a big drinker. As we talk, beer flows on and off the table like a conveyor belt, each bottle replaced by the waiter the moment it's empty with a sorcerer's flick of the wrist. I ask

---

[50] I look this up later and see that he's right. 'Egyptians have rejected both extremism and authoritarianism ...' Britain's then-defence secretary Michael Fallon declared chimerically in August 2015. 'Britain is offering our solidarity in return.'

how he reconciles being Muslim with drinking alcohol – but it turns out he doesn't. Being gay, he struggles with Islam's narrow views on sexuality and has long been a committed atheist. 'Not many people know that, though,' he tells me. 'Not many would understand.'

'Even the young liberals?' I ask. 'The educated?'

They comprise a small group in Egypt, he replies. 'For the majority, education is far from liberal. It's actually very traditionalist. Very old school. People are used to authority figures telling them what to think, whether it's their teacher, Allah, Sisi, whoever. They aren't encouraged to be open-minded and have their own opinions on things.'

Forced into living a double life, Masud turns to alcohol and antidepressants to cope. The stories he tells are tragic and harrowing. 'Once, I met up with someone who turned out to be an undercover cop,' he recounts. 'I got away from him, but he caught me, pulled me down and broke my hand.' The officer later tried to charge him with rape, he says. 'But in the end, luckily, he just accepted a massive bribe.'

We conclude the night in a cramped, murky hotbox called Jamaica Bar. A wave of sulphurous air buffets us as we enter and a dozen red, dewy eyes turn to look our way. The place is wildly grimy. A fiesta of food scraps, fag butts and unidentifiable liquids ooze stickily across the tables and floor, while tinsel and garish fairylights sag in anachronistic loops from the ceiling. Unspeakable things appear to have occurred in the loo.

The men all talk loudly over one another, and arguments rise and fall. One customer barks at the barman for forgetting his order, while others exchange convivial sexual abuse. *You're too flaccid! Your penis is like a worm!* Tucked into the corner, Masud and I drink 8 per cent Meister Max beer and order some whisky and brandy, which you can only buy in 300ml bottles. The whisky is thick, sweet and repulsive, and a vast improvement on the brandy, which tastes of diluted urine.

We drink and chat, and the room grows warmer and mustier still. 'Look around,' Masud says at one point, making a broad, sweeping gesture with his arm that appears to imply a world of inscrutable awe. 'Look. Look!'

I look, but all I see is a Nubian man belly-dancing and grinding his groin against a chair. 'Look at what?' We are both giggling, and have been for some time, but I'm no longer sure at what.

'Look!' he hisses again. 'I present to you – Egypt's *honest citizens!*'

I cackle harder, tipping the final drops of Vat 20 brandy into my glass. The sharp acidity that seemed so unbearable an hour ago has now mysteriously morphed into a pleasant fruity tang. 'Who?'

'*Honest citizens!*' he repeats. 'Egypt's finest. They love our country and defend it to the last. They weep and thump their chests and sing *baladi, baladi, baladi* to the sky.' He raises his glass as if making a toast. 'They get fucked and trampled and crushed ... but all they feel is *love!*'

At 4am, we decide to have a final sambuca. After lighting it, the blue flame carries up my hand and arm and sets the table on fire. Masud, almost apoplectic with delight, reaches over to stifle the blaze with a paper napkin, which flares alight in turn.

'Right,' he grins as the inferno rages around us. 'I think it might be time to go.'

The next day I wake up – and immediately wish I hadn't. Daggers of sunlight stream through the window as if trying to draw blood. Everything aches: my head, my eyeballs, my bronchioles. My breath is an abomination. What on earth happened last night? Did I really cause a fire??

I groan and roll over. I am desperate to leave this sandpaper city, slowly wearing me to the bone. It isn't just the cheap booze that's getting to me, I know. It's everything: the repression, the angst, the stressful, gridlocked streets. But sadly there's little I can do right now. I am currently a passport short, having sent it back to Britain (via Berlin) to receive my Iranian visa. So, until it returns, I am caged.

I pass my time exploring the city. Each day, I wind my way past rickety tuk-tuks and skittish cats, flayed carcasses and shrieking chicks, ululating *muezzin* and coffee-drinking goats. Workmen wield machinery amid a confetti of sparks, while Hyundai trucks lie shipwrecked among volcanic drifts of junk. The paradoxical impulse to both fleece and greet is evident at every turn – the first aimed at customers, the latter at guests – and I am at once pestered and protected, hounded and helped.

One afternoon, I walk to al-Qarafa, the sprawling City of the Dead, where the lives of past and present Cairenes collide. If Cairo is grey, al-Qarafa is the grey within the grey, the tissue within the bone. In this deeply deprived district, mausoleums and shrine-mosques lie in endless dense, jumbled rows, embodying nearly 1,400 years of history. Home to hundreds of thousands of residents, some of whom inhabit the actual graves themselves, this hulking necropolis was once described as one of the 'wonders of the world' by Ibn Jubayr, who marvelled at the tombs it contained of prophets 'of the kindred of Muhammad … of his Companions, of the followers of his Companions, of learned men and ascetics, and of saintly men renowned for their miracles'. Today, however, worn and weatherbeaten through the ages, the place has the aura of a Miss Havisham version of Montmartre, its passages crumbling and smog-black, its medieval lustre reduced to shadows and dust.

In this way, could al-Qarafa be seen as a metaphor for Cairo itself, I wonder? A city of haunted souls, staggering unsteadily on, looking forever back to lost splendours of the past?

Two weeks turn into three, then four. Still I wait, expectant. The city is making me unwell; it's all bristles and jagged lines. Everywhere I go, there's activity but no vitality, as cadaveric spasms give an illusory sensation of life. Crushed within Sisi's iron grip, the capital seems to be dissolving before my eyes:

the pharaonic Cairo of glory and pomp; the Islamic Cairo of intellect and pride; the colonial Cairo of glamour and unrest; the revolutionary Cairo of fury and flame. The fires have all died now and only ash remains.

There are embers, however. Pockets of light and hope. One of these, Lina Attalah, meets me in her office one morning. 'It's really a miracle we're still going,' she says as she passes me a cup of tea and gestures for me to sit. 'And I want this to continue. I don't want to get shut down.'

The founder and editor of *Mada Masr*, one of the few independent newspapers still operating in Cairo, Lina emanates a steely, headstrong grit. She launched the publication on 30 June 2013, three days before the military coup, despite having almost no money or equipment. '*Mada Masr* is not revolutionary,' she insists. 'It's independent. We don't want Sisi deposed; we just want accountability.'

Uber-modish and open-plan, the *Mada Masr* office could have been transplanted straight from the streets of Shoreditch. One of the walls has been converted into a giant whiteboard on which the cryptic phrase 'Tahrir is not a square' has been scrawled in the centre. Surrounding it are dozens of red and black words connected by spindles of violent lines, as if delving into the disturbed mind of the state: 'Anxiety & Representation / Speed & Demand / INSOMNIA + XANAX', one thread reads. 'Dust collecting on Terraces / Ideas / Cars & Leaves / Collectivities', says another. 'Were they *illusions*?'

Lina's courage is undeniable. Days after its launch, *Mada Masr* covered a vicious crackdown on protesters as most media outlets looked the other way. A month later, her journalists were dodging bullets once again to report on the shocking Rabaa al-Adawiya massacre, in which around a thousand Brotherhood supporters were killed.

'It was one of the bloodiest attacks in modern history,' she says of Rabaa. 'Most victims were just normal young men, not terrorists. But hardly anyone was reporting the facts.'

From the *Mada Masr* office, I make my way to a press conference where a group of equally tenacious women are making a statement after their anti-torture NGO, the El Nadeem Centre, was shut down by security forces. 'This decision came from the very top,' the four doctors declare to the packed room of reporters, as a man in my earpiece translates. 'We're being silenced because we're highlighting the abuse of the law occurring every day ... Nobody is talking about military violations and the people being tortured and killed.'

It is a bold and heroic spectacle. Aged fifty-plus and hijab-free, the women appear refreshingly subversive in this nation of adolescent anarchists and elderly patriarchs, and seem exactly the kind of foe to unsettle the cocksure patrons of the state. 'We will never stop,' they proclaim audaciously, 'until the violence stops.'

At the conference, I bump into Gasser Abdel-Razek, the head of the Egyptian Initiative for Personal Rights (EIPR), whom I first met in 2011.[51] 'The scale of human rights abuses right now is unprecedented,' he tells me. 'It's the biggest crisis Egypt's faced in recent history.' We discuss Giulio Regeni, a Cambridge PhD student from Italy who was recently tortured and murdered after being abducted from the streets of Dokki, the middle-class neighbourhood where I'm currently staying with a friend. 'There's no doubt security agents were behind it,' he says. 'But they'll never face justice.'[52]

Later, I go to meet Ezzat Ghoneim, a lawyer for torture victims and the head of the Egyptian Coordination for Rights

---

[51] In November 2020, Gasser and two other EIPR staff members were detained on a slew of fabricated security charges. While they were released on bail a few weeks later, they have been banned from travel and their assets have been frozen while the investigation is ongoing.

[52] It is believed Regeni – whose body revealed extensive bruising, burns, stab wounds and bone fractures – was murdered because of his controversial research into Egypt's independent trade unions. In Italy, prosecutors have charged four Egyptian security officials with the crime. In Egypt, however, the investigation has been closed and no charges brought.

and Freedoms. His words haunt me for some time. 'Regeni was a tipping-point,' he asserts grimly. 'The state is getting more paranoid and violent. Foreigners are no longer exempt.'

Ezzat doesn't look healthy. His face is gaunt and pale, his expression resigned. 'I know I'll be arrested soon,' he says. 'It's only a matter of time …'[53]

One evening, I go to a restaurant in Zamalek to meet the Egyptian-American activist and writer Mona Eltahawy. In this affluent district on Gezira Island, porticoed townhouses line broad, leafy avenues, while polished English and French accents ring out from art deco coffee houses. Half the island is taken up by the prestigious Gezira Club, which was founded in 1882 by the polo-playing colonial elite as a refuge from the Great Unwashed, before being nationalised and transformed into a series of youth centres under Nasser. Today, history appears to have gone full circle; while the club's doors are no longer closed to locals, its astronomical fees ensure that a respectable level of social decorum remains.

Beside the club is the Marriott Hotel, a terracotta monstrosity comprising two soaring towers that bookend a reconstructed version of Gezira Palace. Intended to resemble the Palace of Versailles, the original building was commissioned to celebrate the opening of the Suez Canal in 1869 and now stands more as a symbol of reckless profligacy than the refined opulence it was designed to emulate. By 1875, the euphemistically monikered Ismail the Magnificent had squandered so much money on his upgraded vision of Egypt – recentring the capital around a new 'downtown' area far from the muddle of Islamic Cairo, much as Sisi is doing with his new Cairo project today – that the coffers

[53] Ezzat's prophecy proved correct. In March 2018, he was detained and disappeared into a security black hole for five months. He eventually re-emerged, and currently remains in pre-trial detention despite a September 2019 court order granting him bail.

ran dry and Egypt's shares in the canal had to be hived off to the highest bidder (Britain).

At the restaurant, the conversation bounces like a pinball between Mona, her Canadian boyfriend, a male activist and a female journalist. They talk of revolution, globalisation and privatisation; feminism, Islamism and despotism; hymens, hijabs and human rights. They speak, at length, of the Ultras: a tempestuous, cross-demographic protest group united by their obsession with football. 'There are two places Sisi can't reach,' Mona says. 'Mosques and football stadiums.' The others nod in agreement. 'If religion is the opium of the masses,' the man remarks, 'football is the amphetamine.'

Liberal, Western and worldly, these people are far from the Egyptian everyman. But among them, I can feel the pulse of revolution still beating – faint and weak but unequivocally alive. 'There's a new power inside people,' Mona says. 'The fight's not over. It's only just beginning.'

I want to believe her. Historically, popular revolts have rarely provided a quick fix, after all. In France, often held up as an exemplar of revolutionary triumph, the cry of '*liberté, égalité, fraternité*' during the 1789–99 uprising – not that dissimilar from the cry of 'bread, freedom, social justice' during the Arab Spring – did not herald the beginning of democratic rule, but simply the beginning of the end of dictatorship. Perhaps Sisi is a modern-day Napoleon, I consider, seizing power and crowning himself emperor before democracy ultimately prevails?

On my way home, I am just mulling on this – perhaps wishful – sentiment when Maud and I are hit by a car swerving to avoid a bicycling bread-seller and sent reeling into the side of a tuk-tuk. Everyone is enraged: the car driver at the bread-seller; me at the car driver; the tuk-tuk at me; and the rest of the traffic at the tuk-tuk, which comes to rest at an awkward and obstructive angle across the road.

'You idiot!' I scream at the driver. '*Kun hadher!*' Be careful!

Red-faced and gasping, I disentangle Maud from the tuk-tuk

chassis and edge tentatively back into the road. I feel irate and indignant, and fired up for a row.

I feel – after five weeks in this volatile hotbox of a city – positively *Cairene*.

It is early March by the time I receive my visa and am free to leave Cairo. My original plan was to cross the Sahara[54] before winter gives way to the scorching heat of spring, but it is clear that this will now be impossible. I am venturing into the inferno.

Feeling not unlike the doomed mountaineers who take too long reaching the summit of Everest and subsequently come a cropper in the cheeringly entitled 'Death Zone' on their descent – if you'll allow me this brief foray into hyperbole – I set off at first light. Despite my anxiety at what lies ahead, it is a wonderful feeling to be back on the road. I love this time of day, as the sun raises its tousled head and stretches its arms towards the sky, and I meander silkily through the dormant streets, savouring the smiles and the *salams* and the scent of leavening dough. Cairo is stuttering to life, in all its shambolic, clamorous glory, and I nod a silent goodbye to the cars and cats, the street hawkers and salted potatoes, the tatty awnings and splashes of wilted green.

After much deliberation, I have decided to cycle the Western Desert route through Upper Egypt. This road, which weaves through a series of lush oases, is considerably quieter and more picturesque than the frenetic, crowded route down the Nile, though it is also far longer and more remote. Strapped to Maud's racks is enough food and water to sustain me for the hundreds of empty miles between villages, adding several kilograms to her already bulging load, and I already feel the extra strain in my glutes and legs as I pass through the outskirts of the city.

Soon the road begins to tilt gently uphill. At first, traffic hems me in tightly, the gaps between vehicles opening and closing just

---

[54]   The largest sandy desert in the world, which covers much of North Africa, including the whole of Egypt and the northern half of Sudan.

enough to let me through like a kind of gelatinous mire. But eventually I hit the desert highway and the cars begin to thin.

And then I encounter my first roadblock, fifteen kilometres outside Cairo.

'*As-Salam-Alaikum!*' I cry to the policeman, grinning with almost deranged zeal.

He doesn't return the smile. Instead, he requests my passport and proceeds to flick through it slowly and suspiciously, brow furrowed, nostrils flared. As he does so, I notice that he has just two stripes on his sleeve, marking him out as a low-ranking private. Then another man approaches. This one has three stars and an eagle on his uniform, designating him a brigadier-general: the second-highest rank.

'*Salam*,' the brigadier says, staring at me curiously and stroking his plump slug of a moustache. 'Where go?'

'Bahariya,' I reply. The first oasis, 350 kilometres down the road. I've been advised not to say Sudan.

'Ah,' he says. 'No.'

'No?'

'Bad road. Bad men. Kidnap, kill, steal.'

My heart sinks. Not again! Concerned about a repeat of the Sinai debacle, I decide not to argue this time. Instead, I produce my most winning smile – and a packet of Cleopatra Queen cigarettes. 'Please,' I say, holding it out. 'Smoke?'

He beams. '*Shukran!*'

Over the next twenty minutes, I pull out all the stops. I ask after the man's family and wax lyrical about his hair. I stare at him adoringly and squeeze his hand and flirt. I ply him with cigarettes and giggle uproariously at his jokes.

But it's all to no avail, as he still won't let me pass.

As I stand there, dejected, I spot another policeman raking through my panniers. Furious, I march over and demand an explanation. 'Security,' he replies curtly, as he continues digging. He then abandons the bags and picks up my camera. Tense with anxiety, I watch him scroll through pictures of Gasser Abdel-

Razek, Ezzat Ghoneim, the El Nadeem doctors, and a dozen or so other Egyptian *personae non gratae* ... but fortunately they're all just meaningless faces to him, and eventually he casts it aside with a grunt.

Moments later, the brigadier puffs up. 'Sorry, madam,' he says, having called his superiors at my insistence. 'You need permit from Giza.'

'Giza!'

I collect Maud and trudge despondently back to the road. Cairo is a cage indeed. And I am struggling to wrest free of these chains.

In Giza, I discover my bike lights are missing. I call the brigadier in a rage. 'Your officer is a *thief!*' I blast, as he stutters uncertainly in reply. 'Is this how you treat visitors to your country?'

But there's nothing to be done now; the lights are gone. And Giza is a bureaucratic shambles. A man at the entrance to the pyramids points me towards a man in uniform, who scratches his nose and waves over two further men, who appear to know even less than him. Then a young woman gets involved, who claims to speak English but who only knows two confusingly paradoxical phrases – 'stop please' and 'come now' – which together have the unfortunate outcome of leading to complete stasis. She eventually leads me in a circle back to the man at the entrance, who emits a big sigh and passes me on to the man in uniform. At this point, I ring Mustafa for help, who explains everything to a member of the tourist police, who directs me to the Archaeology Office, which transpires to be inside the pyramid complex and blocked by a guard who cries '*la la la!*' (no no no!) and refuses to let me pass. Then an entirely new man appears clutching a scrap of paper with a mysterious phone number on it, and the man in uniform – who by now has a harried look in his eye whenever he sees me approaching – reluctantly gives the number a call. He talks for a while, urgently, then jovially, then chuckling over a shared joke or two. Then he hangs up and hands the paper back. 'Wrong place,' he says. 'You must go Cairo.'

Eventually, much wrangling and foot-stomping later, the tourist police agree to deal with the issue. They take my letter, tell me to wait outside, confer for an hour – then announce their decision.

It's a no.

'But *why?*' I cry to the man behind the desk.

'Military zone,' he retorts.

'Your whole country is a bloody military zone!' I rant, all pretence at charm swiftly evaporating.

He looks up from under thick brows – brows that cry intransigence. Brows that, knitted together and arching upwards in the centre, appear to be trying to escape the sinewy landscape on which they've had the misfortune to germinate. 'No. Permit,' he repeats, louder and slower. 'Please. Leave.'

I consider trying a spot of the old *wasta*, in the shape of the wad of dollar notes stuffed into my pants, but have been advised that this may just make a situation worse. So, instead, I take the high road: I scowl, mutter a petulant '*shukran*', pick up Maud and begin the sluggish ride back to Cairo. It is now rush hour and the traffic is fierce. Campervan-style buses stop ahead of me every few minutes to allow passengers to leap to certain death in the middle of the dual carriageway, while hordes of schoolchildren pour into the remaining pockets of space like sand tipped into a jar of stones.

The driving is shockingly bad. So bad, I feel constantly amazed that everyone on the road isn't already dead. Traffic lights seem not so much instructions as suggestions, while roundabouts are a scrum of survival, a kind of accelerated Darwinism in practice. As I ride, I find my mind wandering. Could the traffic be symbolic of Egypt's attitude to democracy, I wonder? A sense that liberty is a free-for-all in which everyone takes what they want without control or compromise, rather than a slog of give and take governed by a framework of codes?

Perhaps. Or perhaps I've just been on the road too long. When the world begins to dissolve into endless allegory, maybe it's a sign that the mind is dissolving too.

I stay the night with a friend, and together we spend the evening discussing and amending my plans. A permit for the Western Desert looks unlikely to be forthcoming, we conclude, so my best option seems to be to try my luck on the busier road down the river.

The next morning, I leave early for departure mark two. From southern Cairo, there is no gradual transition into the country. There's Cairo and there's not-Cairo, where everything feels different. Tower blocks are replaced by tumbling shacks, concrete jungles by palm groves and bursts of cabbage green. While I cannot see the Nile from here, its presence can be felt in the sparkling irrigation channels bordered by blossom and fern, and the endless arable fields filled with cotton, sugarcane and soy. The Nile basin comprises the sole fertile strip in Egypt, unfolding like an emerald ribbon from the nape of the northern coast, and an astonishing 90 million people can be found clinging like drowning sailors to the lifeline it provides.

I stop at the first checkpoint, fraught with nerves. But, to my immense surprise, the officers wave me on after just a cursory exchange. Afterwards, I feel elated. I'm free! *Free!!* And suddenly I feel the power of that idea, *freedom*, as if I were experiencing it for the first time. As if it were not simply a concept or abstraction but a tangible entity with substance and weight – with *anti*-weight, in fact, raising me out of the saddle and releasing me into the sky.

Freedom … How rich and sweet it tastes. How pure. How can I have been so blind to its existence before?

I evade the police on the back of a moped driven by a trainee imam called Ahmed. 'Careful,' he cries over his shoulder as we career along a grainy track emitting puffs of black smoke. 'Bad road ahead!'

I met Ahmed on the outskirts of Beni Suef last night. After

helping me find a hotel, he invited me to join him at his village for lunch today – but when we reconvened in the hotel foyer this morning, I discovered the police already waiting. 'The manager called them,' Ahmed told me as we slipped stealthily out the back. 'All foreigners are meant to register with them, so they can spy on you better.'

The village is remote and riotously agrarian. A baying crowd surrounds us when we arrive, surging in wavelike formations like an army going into battle. The infantry plough in first, wielding pitchforks and trowels, followed by the cavalry nobly perched atop rickety carts and mules. At the back are the veteran rearguard reinforcements, standing firm among a sea of scrawny cattle. 'Wilcome! Sooo happening!' the older women cry, while the boys laugh and shout, and the girls recoil in terror.

In this community, I feel like I've stepped back a thousand years. A few dozen families live here, all of whom own livestock and modest patches of pastureland. I'm aware that it was *fellaheen* like this who first rose in anger against Mubarak twenty years ago, as rents surged by 400 per cent and the cost of living skyrocketed; however, there seems little evidence of such discontent today. Instead, my hosts are all smiles, and for several hours I find myself a prisoner of their goodwill, as I am hugged and pampered and taken on endless donkey tours around the sorghum field.

'Please eat, drink,' Ahmed remarks, as we sit on carpets dulled with age, eating *ful* (bean stew, the Egyptian national dish) and *koshari*. He is the only English-speaker here, but he speaks the language well. 'You are our honoured guest.'

Seated around us, the men are dressed in a mixture of *jalabiyas*, jeans and shirts, while the women wear flowery *abayas* and hijabs. The women in their twenties seem childlike, while those in their thirties appear ancient. There is no middle age, no soft segue into senescence. You're young and then – *boom* – your youth has fled and you must bear a world of responsibility on your shoulders.

We speak of religion. 'The West has Islam wrong,' Ahmed says. 'Muslims respect all faiths.'

I explain that I'm agnostic, and he seems mystified by the concept. When I say that P and I are unmarried, he's bewildered.

'But what keeps you together?' he asks. 'What stops you cheating?'

'Loyalty?' I say. 'Love?'

'You think he'll be loyal while you're away for so long?'

'Yes.' *I hope so.*

'You're very trusting!'

Later, I find myself assuming the role of reluctant agony aunt. As the women serve non-stop rounds of tea and sweetmeats, Ahmed murmurs a series of quiet confessions – one of which, he admits, has been worrying him for some time. 'I do something I shouldn't,' he whispers. 'I ... masturbate. A *lot*. But the Hadith says this will make me infertile.' His face is creased with anxiety. 'Is this true?'

I resist a wicked urge to lie. 'No,' I say. 'It's not.'

'Oh good!' He looks palpably relieved. He sits there for a moment, saying nothing. Then he leans in closer. 'Also, I must ask ...' His voice is so low now that I strain to hear him. 'I've, um, heard ...' He gestures to his groin.

My mind spins. 'Yes?'

'I've heard that maybe it's a problem ... if it's *small?*'

Entering Egypt has created new concerns, but it has also softened old ones. Surrounded by a constant frenzy of tuk-tuks and livestock, catcalls and chaos, stenches and shrieks, I live each moment on high alert, tense but terrifically alive. Now far out of my comfort zone, my days of maudlin naval-gazing are over.

A constant nuisance, however, are the police. At a checkpoint outside Beni Suef, I am forced to accept a security escort – and from now until Luxor, 600 kilometres to the south, I feel the officers' presence like a drift anchor. It becomes impossible to interact with passers-by in the casual way I could before, and I derive childish pleasure from making my companions' life difficult. When they ask me to speed up, I slow down; when they ask me to stop, I push on. At one point, they tell me to take the next right turn in order to avoid plunging through the crazed maelstrom of the village – so instead I turn left and crow with delight as their van gets bogged down amid the throng.

Small victories but important ones. I need to rattle these chains.

At my hotel in al-Minya, the police instruct me to fill in various forms and to inform them whenever I want to go out so they can provide 'protection'.

'But I don't want protection,' I say.

'You must take it,' they reply.

'Why?'

'This is the rule.'

'But *why?*'

They look nonplussed. It is the enquiry that always fazes them. Egypt is not a land of question and answer; it's a land of command and obey.

Later, however, I manage to slink out undetected to visit the Beni Hasan tombs. Four millennia old, these thirty-nine burial chambers represent al-Minya at the height of its prosperity, as tradesmen poured in from east and west to exchange gold, papyrus, linen and grain for cedar, metals, lapis lazuli and spice. Inside, a dazzling display of etchings provides a vivid window into ancient dynastic life, as thousands of miniature figurines can be found engaging in all manner of domestic activities, from hunting, trading and fishing to winemaking, breastfeeding and sex.

After a brief tour, I sit on the limestone scarp outside in the pumpkin glow of dusk, marvelling at the depth of history underpinning this damaged nation. For nearly 3,000 years, from its unification in 3100 BCE to its conquest by the Persians, Ancient Egypt was almost unrivalled in power across the globe. Its eminence was military, political, cultural and divine. It produced the first paper (papyrus) and one of the first forms of writing (hieroglyphics). It invented the solar calendar and published the first medical texts. It even created the first ever toothpaste out of eggshells, hooves and ash.

Its record on women's rights wasn't bad, either. Legally, women were viewed as equals, and a handful even ascended to the throne. Hatshepsut, who ruled Egypt for more than two prosperous decades and constructed a cavernous shrine to the goddess Pakhet here at Beni Hasan, is now viewed as one of the most successful pharaohs of all time. While pharaonic society was doubtlessly deeply patriarchal – Hatshepsut struggled to persuade her subjects of her legitimacy and was largely erased from history by her resentful male successors – it does suggest that the feminist cause has failed to make the kind of progress over the past five millennia that one might have hoped.

From my rocky outcrop, I look down upon a chequerboard of emerald, olive and jade cleaved by the silver-blue thread of the Nile. Without this great watercourse, Ancient Egypt would have been nothing. Since the first nomads began gathering along its banks 10,000 years ago, it has acted as a source of sustenance, a mode of transport, a lifebuoy, a god. I find something innately reassuring about its strength, but something, I admit, a little intimidating too.[55]

One of the guides comes and sits beside me. I want to ask about the corrupt security and government officials who, according to locals, engage in regular antiquities smuggling and illicit digging at Beni Hasan, but his English is limited and it's clear such an enquiry would prove futile. Instead, we make polite chitchat. 'Egypt good?' he asks, and I nod. He grins. 'Egypt best. Pharaohs. Pyramids. Very …' He struggles to find the word. 'Big.'

I smile. Egyptians' relentless patriotism can feel a little

---

[55] According to the thirteenth-century Arab historian and geographer Ibn al-Wardi, writing in his geographical treatise *Kharīdat al-Ajā'ib wa farīdat al-gha'rāib* (*The Pearl of Wonders and the Uniqueness of Strange Things*), the Nile is one of four world rivers that originated in Paradise. Two of these are visible (the Nile and Euphrates), while two are concealed (the Jaxartes and Oxus).

tiresome. But considering the puffed-up pride exhibited by those exulting in Britain's own paltry century or two of supremacy, it hardly seems surprising that people here hark back with tedious predictability to these halcyon days of yore. Three thousand years, by god ... That would take us to the year 5000.

'Big,' I reply. 'Yes. I think that's exactly the word.'

The further south I ride, the more I warm to Egypt, with its friendly faces, fresh perfumed air and languid pace of life. But sex seems ingrained in the soil, pollinating every encounter. The more it's denied, the more power it appears to have, like dammed river water that threatens constantly to burst its banks.

The journey to Asyut begins well. At 6am, the sun is hot but not uncomfortably so, and for the first few hours I encounter no real traffic, just the indigent and industrious in the shape of trucks, tuk-tuks and mules. A shimmering rivulet hugs close to my side, and I stop regularly to gorge on the harvested piles of sugarcane that burst with sweetness with every glorious bite. Soon, I find myself sinking into the meditative rhythm of the ride, and I begin to feel more energised and refreshed than I have for some time.

Then, suddenly, I am snapped out of my reverie by a hefty *smack* upon my arse.

Shocked, I turn and see a young tuk-tuk driver grinning lasciviously behind me. Instinctively, I lash out and attempt to return the blow, but the awful wretch just steers away from my flailing fists, cackling and hooting with glee. He does this again and again, clearly enjoying the chase, and I am just about to give up and admit defeat when a looming shadow emerges by my side. *Of course*, I think. *The police!* In my dogged endeavours to escape their clutches, it had slipped my mind that I'm essentially travelling with a retinue of personal bodyguards. As the vehicles thunder by, I watch in disbelief as the first van swerves into the tuk-tuk's path and the second drives it off the road. One of the officers then drags the boy out of his seat, throws him to the ground and starts pummelling him with thumps, slaps and kicks.

I pull over, my heart racing. The entire spectacle unfolds in a matter of seconds, and I know I should intervene. I'm a decent, liberal sort, after all, and vehemently opposed to this kind of brute physical violence. Whatever this randy young scamp has done, he doesn't deserve this.

And yet ... I hesitate. I simply stand there, watching, as the burly policeman rains down blow upon blow on this small, waif-like child. And I cannot deny that, after days of ogles, air kisses and bottom-grabs, I derive a certain amount of satisfaction at witnessing this Old Testament-style vengeance in action.

Eventually, however, I've seen enough. 'Please,' I say. '*Khalas*.' Stop.

The officer looks up, surprised. He is a grisly fellow with sharp, bullet-point eyes. 'Go,' he barks at me, before grabbing the boy and throwing him inside his van. Moments later, he screeches off in a cloud of yellow dust down the road, leaving the badly damaged tuk-tuk half-buried in the roadside brush.

I continue on, a little unsteadily. Now my anger has dissipated, I find myself pitying this young rapscallion, both villain and victim of the paternalistic state. Unlicensed tuk-tuks provide a precious and lucrative income for many struggling Egyptians, and it seems unlikely that he'll ever see this one again. His rash buttock-grab may just have cost him his ticket out of penury – and, satisfyingly voluminous though my rump may be, I very much doubt it was worth it.

Here is repression in action, I think: sexual, physical, political. A brutal system, barbarous and cruel, in which everyone loses except those who wield control.

All five of my hosts in Asyut are called Mohamed, confusingly.

'Yes, it's a problem in Egypt,' one of them explains. 'Too many Mohameds! So we go by nicknames or second names instead. I'm Ehab and this is Essam, Saad, Hesham and Ekbal.'

The friends, who I found on Couchsurfing.com, are all medical students at al-Azhar University, and it's immediately clear from their sparkling eyes and wry smiles that they're a bright and entertaining bunch. 'So you all want to be doctors?' I ask, as we sip sugarcane juice outside a shaded café.

'Yes,' Ehab replies. 'Well, sort of. We did well in our exams, so we were told to go to medical school. It's not really a choice. You don't get many choices in Egypt.'

They didn't choose their university either, he says. 'The higher your grades, the more likely you are to go somewhere local. Being close to home is seen as a blessing.'

The group all attended Islamic school together from a young age, but they are no fans of the Islamists. Nor Sisi. 'The Brotherhood were stupid,' Ekbal says. 'But they weren't criminals, like Sisi. So we're left with two options: the stupid or the criminal.' He smiles. 'Like Ehab says, you don't get many choices in Egypt.'

We speak of the Arab Spring, and they repeat Mona's assertion that the revolution isn't over. Another surge of unrest will take place soon, they believe, suddenly and without warning. This is, after all, how many revolts begin: not with discipline and leadership but with a sudden bursting at the seams. 'People are desperate,' Ehab says. 'Eventually, this will overtake their fear.'

At the boys' flat, they whip up a delicious meal of homemade *molokhia* (jute soup), chicken and rice. As we eat on the concrete floor of their oddly bare, garage-style apartment, the group banter with the casual wit of close friends. 'Egypt is very responsible,' Essam says, using their ironic term for 'idle'. He is the sweetest of the bunch, with a candyfloss beard that frames a shy, playful smile. 'It may be the most responsible country in the world, actually.' He shows me his bedroom, where the words 'Must avoid responsibility!' are emblazoned on the wall above multiple sheets of medical notes and diagrams. All the writing is in English, I notice to my surprise.

'Well, the Arabic textbooks aren't any good,' Essam replies when I ask the reason for this. 'So we use English ones instead.'

'That's amazing,' I say, as I try to imagine British medical students being forced to take their classes in Arabic. 'But what if you're brilliant at medicine but terrible at languages?'

He laughs. 'Then you're destined to become one of Egypt's great responsible citizens.'

The boys kindly wash my clothes in their electric washing machine, the hose of which must be placed in the bath to avoid flooding the room, and as the laundry churns away, they tell me that I will not be staying here but with their friend Aisha tonight. They cannot host me themselves, they explain apologetically, as men and women rarely socialise together in Asyut – and certainly don't sleep over.

'All relationships must be kept hidden,' Ehab says. He and Saad both admit to having secret girlfriends, but say that they've avoided sex because of the risk to the girl if they're found out. 'If an unmarried girl gets pregnant around here, her relatives might kill her. Secret abortions are common.'

In Islam, early marriage is encouraged so people can satisfy their lustful urges within wedlock, but this is apparently proving a challenge in the current economic climate. Weddings can cost two or three times the average annual salary, and few fathers are likely to entrust their daughters to a partner without a decent income. So Egypt's fiscal uncertainty has created a generation of impoverished, sexually repressed youngsters.

'Nobody even discusses sex here,' Saad says. 'All we get is a short talk from our fathers when we're twenty-five, and the advice never changes. Your father got it from his father, who got it from his father … It's all we ever know!'

We speak briefly about Britain – to the boys, it represents 'money', 'freedom' and 'the Queen', in that order of priority – before the conversation drifts back onto more carnal matters again. But this is inevitable in Egypt, I now realise, like heliotropic blooms that constantly turn to face the sun.

'Tell me,' Ekbal pipes up, apropos of nothing. 'What's better: sex first, then love? Or love first, then sex?'

The group all look at me expectantly. I can almost see them

sharpening their pencils and balancing notepads on their knees. 'Hmmm ...' I say noncommittally, suddenly struck with the disturbing notion that I seem to have become some kind of bogus Egyptian relationship guru. If the country wants to overcome its chronic fornicatory dysfunctions, I fear this might not be the best way to go about it.

'It's a good question,' I reply eventually, my mind entirely blank. 'But I think you may need to figure that one out on your own ...'

At the Asyut Dam, as dozens of young men enthusiastically hurl themselves off the forty-foot limestone edifice into the sparkling side-channel below, the Mohameds and I are drinking sweetened lemon juice and talking of faith. My admission to being an unbeliever has prompted the usual interrogation. Who created us, then? Why are we here? Why does beauty exist? And ugliness? And sin? I answer each question as best I can, knowing my replies are inadequate. I am open to the idea of God, I explain, just not the God prescribed in the holy books. Something less Manichean or anthropomorphised, perhaps. Something less austere.

The discussion continues for some time. Everyone takes part, offering their views with articulacy and listening without judgement. Around these boys, I feel the perceived gulf between our cultures narrow. With them, Islam and liberalism feel not just compatible but inevitable, and I am reminded of their al-Azhar compatriot Taha Hussein, a blind, penniless scholar who went on to become one of Egypt's most celebrated modernist thinkers. For him, Egypt's cultural heritage was both Islamic and Mediterranean, Eastern and Western, and 'all that nourishes the intellect' was shared evenly between the two.[56] Indeed, it was in Cairo during

---

[56] 'He had come to the Azhar with the intention of throwing himself into this ocean [of knowledge] and drinking what he could of it, until the day he drowned,' Hussein wrote in his 1948 autobiography *The Stream of Days: A Student at the Azhar* (referring to himself in the third person). 'What finer end could there be for a man of spirit than to drown himself in knowledge? What a splendid purge into the beyond!'

World War II, following a series of meetings with al-Azhar theologians, that Freya Stark came to the same conclusion. 'It was here that I came to realise ... on what democratic foundations the theory of Islam is built,' she wrote in *East is West*. 'Text after text they would quote, from the Qur'an, or tradition, or history of the first caliphs ... and this appeal, of the democracy of Islam, would time and again brush away all the arguments of our enemies.'

Aisha, my host for the night, meets us mid-debate. Clad in a black niqab and abaya, she doesn't engage with the conversation. As the banter flows, pulled along by a thousand unspoken smirks and smiles, frowns and sighs, it is impossible for her to participate from behind her self-imposed barricade. Instinctively, I find myself pitying her and the draconian social exile she has inflicted upon herself – as well as somewhat regretting that it is with her rather than with this group of lively young chaps that I am due to be spending the night.

Back at her flat, however, Aisha transforms. Removing her cloak and veil to reveal a casual t-shirt, jeans and an open, inquiring face, she chats animatedly as she potters about and prepares me a plate of cheesy chips and cucumber. She studied engineering at al-Azhar University in Cairo, she tells me, before switching to medicine and moving with her sister to Asyut. 'Our parents trust us, so we're very independent,' she says. 'We enjoy living alone.'

She brings up the topic of the niqab without prompting. 'I wear it because I love it,' she explains. 'I've worn it for ten years. It makes me feel precious, like a jewel.'

'It's not hard to communicate?' I ask.

'I believe communication is about the mind, not the face.'

'But doesn't the veil pre-date Islam by several centuries? I thought it wasn't even mentioned in the Qur'an?'

'Well, the Qur'an talks of the hijab, or "screen", which can be interpreted in different ways.'

Wearing a niqab isn't easy, she admits. Most Egyptians oppose it – including the Sisi regime, which sees it as a symbol of Islamist dissent – and even her parents tried to talk her out of it. But she knew she wanted to wear it after reading about her namesake, the Prophet's third wife, in the Qu'ran. 'She was clever and independent, and I fell in love with her. She wore the veil, so I felt it was right for me too.'

Aisha's young age when she married Muhammad – believed to be somewhere between six and nineteen – is often cited by critics of Islam as proof of the faith's inherent misogyny. While I have some sympathy with this view, it is worth bearing in mind that the marriage of young girls was just as common in Christian Europe as it was in the Middle East at that time. And although Aisha was young, she was clearly far from a repressed wallflower. The daughter of Abu Bakr, the first Sunni caliph after the Prophet, she was revered as a scholar and stateswoman, and even led a military campaign against Ali ibn Abi Talib, the fourth Sunni caliph and first Shia imam, following the death of her father's successor.

'Actually, the Hadith has thousands of amazing women in it,' Aisha asserts. Another favourite of hers is Muhammad's first wife, Khadija, an older, independently wealthy trader with whom he enjoyed a happy and monogamous union until her death twenty-five years later. 'People criticise the idea that Muslim men can marry four wives and receive more inheritance than women,' she says. 'But these things were originally designed to protect women, not repress them, and they were very progressive at the time. Byzantine women couldn't own property at all, and female babies were often killed!'

'I understand,' I reply. 'But haven't we moved on since then? These things aren't progressive anymore.' There are aspects of the Qur'an that trouble me, I confess – such as the infamous passage that states women are inferior to men and can be beaten (lightly) if they disobey. Aisha has already admitted that some of her married friends have been prevented from working or studying by their husbands. Is this not a concern?

'These issues are not about Islam,' she says. 'They're about culture. It's the same in Christian families. In Upper Egypt, most girls are poor and married by fourteen.' In Islam, she stresses, ideas about the role of women vary and can adapt with the times. 'Think about how many women the Bible has. Barely any! But look how Christianity has progressed.'

Aisha's main aspiration is not marriage or children, she tells me, but travelling the world with Médecins Sans Frontières (MSF). Somehow, I feel, she would do her namesake proud. 'I don't want to settle down anytime soon,' she says. 'But when I do, I just hope my husband is kind.'

'And handsome?' I ask.

'That's not so important.' She smiles. 'But maybe it would be a bonus.'

My arrival in Sohag is a bureaucrat's wet dream: a mindless orgy of officiousness, intrusiveness and ruthless inefficiency. Adel, my host, is summoned to the police station to speak to one of the officers. And then another. And then a third, while I am taken to a fourth. They take my details, his details and the details of anyone else in the vicinity. They scrutinise my passport and rifle through my bags. They smoke and belch and bark loudly on the phone.

'They don't understand,' Adel explains. 'They think us staying together can only mean one thing.'

Eventually, we are released and allowed to return to Adel's flat. But that isn't the end of the saga, it transpires. Having noticed my arrival, his neighbour takes it upon himself to ensure the good name of the apartment block isn't besmirched by the presence of such a brazen trollop and calls the police chief in a rage. He in turn calls Adel, and another long tussle ensues. Finally, Adel returns triumphant. 'I told him you were about to complain to the Embassy,' he grins. 'That scared him! I don't think he'll bother us again.'

A medical student at Sohag University, Adel has a shrewd intelligence and puckish charm, and clearly revels in the power games with the authorities. 'It's useful being a doctor,' he says as we take a stroll along the corniche. 'The police respect me.' He berates me for my carelessness when texting him earlier, however. 'You shouldn't have mentioned your job. I deleted the message, but they could still get it from the phone company. It could cause me real trouble.'

As we walk, we pass a giant globe on which all the countries are distorted. Canada is gargantuan, Antarctica minuscule, and South America bends back on itself so that Argentina falls in line with Mexico. Promoted by officials as a tourist 'guide and reference', the sculpture attracted ridicule when it was first unveiled and is viewed with embarrassment by the majority of locals. 'The thing Egypt was always good at was monuments,' Adel says scornfully. 'Now look at us.' For a bureaucracy blind to irony, however, he concedes it couldn't be a better symbol. 'It shows exactly what we've done to the world. Totally fucked it up!'

Later, Adel takes me to see the Abydos tombs, and two police vans follow us in convoy. In a village en route, we all become trapped behind a moving clump of foliage that's marching with stolid determination like the trees of Birnam Wood. A wisp of a tail suggests this might be less a case of ill-fated prophecy, however, than overburdened mule. 'Stuck between a police van and a donkey's arse,' Adel mutters as we crawl along. 'Actually, maybe *there's* a better symbol.'

I like Adel, but I can't say I entirely trust him. His eyes are shifty and he has an oleaginous charm that he switches on and off a little too seamlessly. At Abydos, he and a podgy police officer strut around the temple forecourt, backslapping and guffawing in a nauseating display of mutual sycophancy. 'You have to understand what it's like to live in a country like Egypt,' he tells me afterwards by way of explanation. 'We must play these games to survive. Please remember, when judging anything and anyone in Egypt, how big an impact the state has on our lives.'

To my relief, the police let us explore the monuments alone. Abydos is a historical jewel, ancient even by archaeological standards, and I've been looking forward to this visit for some time. The earliest pharaohs were entombed here, dating back 5,000 years, and in later times the site became a popular pilgrimage centre for Osiris, the god of fertility and the afterlife. It is among the most well-preserved necropolises of Egypt, and it amazes me that, unlike the tourist flytraps of Luxor and Aswan, there are no other visitors here.

'He lost his penis, you know,' Adel remarks as we enter.

'Who?' I reply, taken aback. 'That fat policeman?'

'No, Osiris.'

Osiris was the son of Geb (the earth) and Nut (the sky), and was one of Ancient Egypt's most revered deities. Forming a trio with his sister-wife Isis and son Horus, he wasn't short of sobriquets: Lord of the Underworld, Lord of Love, King of the Living, Judge of the Dead, Lord of Silence, Foremost of the Westerners.[57]

I was not aware, however, about his penis.

'That's one version of the story, anyway,' Adel continues. 'His brother Set killed him, chopped him up and scattered his body parts across the world. Isis managed to find them all and reconnect them – except for his penis, which had been eaten by a fish.'

The main temple, constructed by Seti I in the thirteenth century BCE, looks dull and squat from the outside, but through the entrance we walk into an enchanted world. Towering columns line the hallway, lit from below in a wash of cauldron green, and bas-relief carvings burst with a depth of colour and texture that seems impossible so many millennia after their creation. One vast hall leads into another, which opens to a gallery and series of smaller sanctuaries. Images depict Seti and his son Ramses II worshipping the gods, the gods presenting royal regalia to the kings, and the kings making offerings to each other. There are even images of uncertain provenance that suggest these ancient dynasties may have been curiously advanced for their time:

[57] In Ancient Egypt, the West was associated with the afterlife, while 'Westerners' were the souls of those who had died.

namely, a submarine, helicopter and military plane carved high at the top of some pillars.

Of most interest, however, is a famous relief carved onto one of the temple walls known as the 'Abydos King List', in which the cartouches of Seti and Ramses are depicted beside those of seventy-four of their predecessors. I study it carefully, searching, and then consult my guidebook. Afterwards, I turn to Adel.

'No Hatshepsut,' I say.

'No,' he confirms.

I look back musingly. 'Incredible, isn't it? They could worship a god without a penis, yet they still couldn't accept a queen …'

I disgrace myself with the *shattaf* again. One might have imagined, after several weeks in the country, that I would have learnt how to use the toilet facilities by now. But I have too many questions that I'm embarrassed to ask. Do you aim while sitting or standing? If sitting, how do you ensure nozzle and target are aligned? If standing, how do you avoid collateral damage? For me, it doesn't matter which method I try; the hose twists and turns like a dyspeptic cobra, always wide of the bullseye while saturating everything else in sight.

'But it's better than paper, no?' Manar says when I apologise for the mess I've caused. 'That never really gets you clean, I think.'

The sisters Manar and Amina are my hosts in Qena. I sit with the two trainee lawyers in the dining room of the most stylish Egyptian apartment I've stayed in yet – all high ceilings, burnished mahogany and marbled stonework – discussing love and relationships. Having spent the day cycling around town with two sweetly geeky boys pining for romance, I'm interested to hear their views.

'The films are silly,' Manar says, passing me a heaving plate of watermelon. 'Marriage is always the end, not the beginning. It's the wrong way round.'

Manar is twenty-six and exudes mature wisdom. Married with

two children, she lives down the road with her husband, while her younger sister resides here with their parents. 'I married with the head, not the heart,' she explains. 'Love came later.'

Her husband is the brother of her friend, she says, so she knew he was 'a good guy' when they met. 'We didn't speak before the engagement, but we spent a few months getting to know each other afterwards. At any point, if we chose, we could have split up.'

Her sister Amina wishes to follow suit. 'I've got all the romantic nonsense out of my head,' she asserts confidently. A twenty-one-year-old beauty, she has porcelain skin, enquiring eyes and – compared to the mottled fangs I've encountered in Upper Egypt so far – almost phosphorescently white teeth. 'I just want someone honest and reliable, who will be a good father.'

'Love', it appears, is a dirty word here. Love suggests romance, which suggests lust, which suggests sex. This is why, if a man shows interest, you cannot seem eager. Eagerness implies desire. And desire presumes sex.

'But desire's natural, isn't it?' I say. 'Why not strive for both desire and virtue, if you can get it?' I bite into a hunk of watermelon and feel its sticky juice dribble down my chin. 'After all, it's much easier being nice to someone you enjoy seeing naked.'

Amina smiles. 'Desire is a distraction. It can blind you.' That's why she and Manar could never live in Britain, she explains. 'It's all sex sex sex. We're looking for something deeper.'

I decide not to disabuse them of this rather exciting image of my countrymen, which, given enough oxygen, I suspect would provide a welcome boost to our tourist industry. Amina looks set to discover the unsordid truth soon enough anyway, as she plans to travel to Europe to explore the place for herself. Though she is traditional in mindset and prone to ventriloquising platitudes learnt from others ('if I wasn't born a Muslim, I'd die a Muslim'; 'men and women are equal but different'), an adventurous spirit and flames of free thought clearly flicker below the surface.

'Lots of Egyptians are scared of travelling alone,' she says.

'They see danger everywhere. Show them a piece of paper with a black dot on it and all they see is the dot.'

'But not you?' I ask.

'No. This is something that needs to change in Egypt, I think. Too much fear, everywhere.'

Before I leave the next morning, Manar admits that when I first arrived she assumed I was a spy. It wasn't personal, she explains. 'Many Egyptians think this about foreigners. We're suspicious people.'

'Don't worry,' I reassure her. 'If I were you, I'd probably feel the same.'

I would, too. Trust must be earned, after all, and Britain's legacy here is hardly a source of pride. Unlike other imperial territories, Egypt was not granted its autonomy by agreement but compelled to extract it by force – and the transition was far from smooth. After ousting Britain's portly puppet King Farouk I (a philandering, gluttonous kleptomaniac said to eat ninety oysters a day), Nasser had no intention of compromising with the old suzerains, whom he felt had exploited the nation for long enough, and instead took the drastic move of nationalising the Suez Canal.[58] In response, Britain and France didn't hold back: paratroopers were dispatched, bombs dropped, rockets launched and over a thousand civilians slaughtered. It was a savagely disproportionate attack – not to mention a deeply hypocritical one. The self-proclaimed saviours of the 'free world', fresh from victory against the Wehrmacht, were undertaking their tyrannical crusade in Suez just as Russian tanks were entering Budapest to crush the first serious revolt against Soviet rule.

Even my mother, an ardent Anglophile, couldn't forgive her adopted nation for this. She was just ten years old at the time

[58] In a mission named 'Project Fat Fucker', the CIA threw its support behind Nasser's overthrow of Farouk and his imperial patrons, earning America the momentary trust and gratitude of the Egyptian people (though it wasn't to last).

Two Bosnian builders who rouse me from my tent at 6am with a bottle of fearsome home-brewed *rakija*.

One of hundreds of half-finished houses I pass in the Balkans.

A filthy bedroom in the refugee camp in Harmanli, Bulgaria.

The set of terrifying hairpin bends that greet me after I summit the Prokletije (Accursed) Mountains on the Montenegro–Albania border.

Top left: A seven-kilometre queue of lorries waiting to cross from Turkey into Bulgaria.

Top right: Heavily armed Turkish police at an anti-Erdoğan street protest in Istanbul.

Posing with Maud in my new all-black, thermal cycling outfit, shortly before leaving Istanbul for the icy plains of central Turkey.

A balloon ride over the euphemistically named 'fairy chimneys' of Love Valley, Cappadocia, in central Turkey.

A frosty puncture shortly after beginning my ascent into the Taurus Mountains in southern Turkey.

A startlingly sudden change in climate on the far side of the Taurus Mountains, as I begin my descent towards the Mediterranean Sea.

Just one of many roadside rescues by kind locals after Maud gets a puncture during 'the biggest storm of the year', near Byblos, Lebanon.

A portrait of the former Supreme Leader of Iran, Ayatollah Khomeini, on the outskirts of Tyre, a Hezbollah stronghold in southern Lebanon.

An unofficial tented camp for Syrian refugees in the Bekaa Valley, Lebanon.

One of the dozens of young children living in the Bekaa Valley camp.

Shatila camp for Palestinian refugees in southern Beirut, where over 20,000 residents live in cramped, unsanitary apartment blocks.

Ominously entangled water pipes and electricity cables hanging in front of portraits of Yasser Arafat and Mahmoud Abbas, the past and present PLO leaders, in Shatila refugee camp.

The 416-foot Raghadan Flagpole overlooking Amman, Jordan.

A woman selecting donated clothing at a camp for stateless Gazan refugees in Jerash, northern Jordan.

A Jordanian doctor showing me the sideways splits beside the highway in central Amman (I desperately hope his British medical licence application is a success).

Lost again: a remote dirt road that I hope leads from Amman to the Dead Sea.

A young Bedouin goatherd I encounter at the bottom of a kilometre-deep canyon on the border of the Karak and Tafilah governorates in Jordan.

Al-Nawatef Camp in Dana, central Jordan.

The stunning moonscape of Wadi Rum in southern Jordan, where high levels of iron oxide turn the sand a striking Martian red.

Doctors from the El Nadeem Centre, an Egyptian anti-torture NGO, courageously denouncing the Sisi regime at a press conference in Cairo.

A cycling group I join for an early morning ride around Cairo.

Friendly villagers (and their friendlier camel) who insist on giving me lunch at their farm near Beni Suef in northern Egypt.

Egyptian police officers beating a young tuk-tuk driver who is spotted slapping my bum as he passes me on the road. I intervene to stop them – but not as quickly as I should.

A charming group of medical students from al-Azhar University who show me around Asyut in central Egypt.

Another medical student, Aisha, who hosts me in Asyut (pictured here with a friend). Her niqab brings her 'freedom', she tells me, and makes her 'feel like a jewel'.

The enchanting mud-brick Nubian village in Aswan, southern Egypt, where I stay for my final few nights in the country.

Peace at last: the Sahara Desert in Sudan shortly after crossing the border by ferry from Egypt.

Giant clay urns containing cool local water at a roadside rest-stop in northern Sudan.

One of the many Nubian families I stay with as I cycle down the Nile, pictured in the courtyard of their mud-brick bungalow.

The oddly flat-tipped Meroë pyramids in Sudan, reportedly decapitated by the Italian treasure hunter Giuseppe Ferlini in 1834.

My campsite under an acacia bush on my last night in the Sahara Desert (with my very poorly constructed snake barrier visible on the left-hand side).

The entrepreneurial tea-seller Awadeya Mahmoud Koko (pictured in green with colleagues), whose founding of a national workers' cooperative revolutionised the lives of tea-sellers across Sudan.

A poor, dismembered Maud following my flight from Khartoum to Muscat.

The road up Jebel Akhdar in the Al Hajar Mountains, Oman, open only to 4×4 vehicles due to its extremely steep gradient.

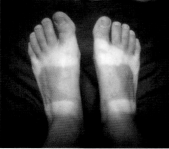

My grimy, chargrilled feet shortly before leaving Muscat for Dubai.

Smoking opium with a group of paragliders on a goat farm is not quite how I expect to spend my first day in Iran, but it's a common pastime among the youngsters of Bandar Abbas.

Bandari (port people), native to Homozgan province in southern Iran, who are known for their array of strikingly colourful, embroidered boregheh masks.

One of many generous Iranian drivers who stop to give me armfuls of wonderful, deeply impractical food to take with me on the road.

The breathtakingly beautiful nineteenth-century Nasir al-Mulk Mosque in Shiraz, Iran.

Posing with Maud in Yazd, central Iran.

The ancient mud-brick village of Aqda in Yazd Province, central Iran.

The majestic guesthouse in Aqda, which emerges with all the might and splendour of a Byzantine cathedral from behind a modest adobe façade.

The seventeenth-century Si-o-se-pol Bridge, the largest of eleven historical bridges on the Zayanderud River in Isfahan, Iran.

A brief rest-stop during an ill-judged shortcut through the Karkas Mountains in central Iran.

Rescue #782. Some kind farmers (pictured here weighing sheep for sale) who pick me up from the roadside after Maud gets a puncture in the Karkas Mountains.

A resident of the Sassanid village of Abyaneh, where most elderly women wear traditional colourful dresses and long, floral scarves.

My broken inner-tube, which explodes soon after I leave Qom and nearly scuppers my final 150-kilometre cycle to Tehran.

Success! At the finish line – Azadi Tower in Tehran – holding a somewhat risqué sign created by my fantastic friend Jo, who has flown all the way here to meet me.

Tehran, as viewed from a lookout point above Darband in the foothills of the Alborz Mountains.

of the 1956 Hungarian Revolution but remembers clearly how desperate her countrymen were for help. 'Thousands were dying,' she has told me on many occasions. 'But we were left to suffer alone.' The impact on my mother's family, and millions of others like it, was profound. The rebels were trounced, the Soviets emboldened and Yuppapa – as my brother and I called our grandfather, unable to pronounce the Hungarian word *nagypapa* – was imprisoned for several years as an enemy of the state.

The worst aspect of the whole sorry saga, however, was that Hungary was ultimately abandoned in vain. Far from buckling under the bombardment, Nasser turned the screws; the canal was closed, oil production shut down and the Anglo-French alliance forced into a humiliating retreat. For the British, it was the final nail in its post-colonial coffin. Close to being expelled from NATO, they could do little but watch in impotent disbelief as, one by one, states across the region wrestled free from their grasp in a surge of nationalistic, anti-imperialistic zeal.[59]

'When we think of Britain, we think of Suez,' Amina admits as we hug goodbye. But now, she adds sweetly, 'we will think of you too.'

My feet are a disgrace. They resemble strips of streaky bacon. I reverted to my sandals a fortnight ago and already the sun has seared my skin into deep russet stripes, while my soles have developed thick crusts like a pair of cloven hooves. It feels almost as if my feet and footwear are slowly merging into one, like the weeds and stonework of an old tumbledown ruin.

---

[59] 'The nationalisation of the Suez Canal in 1956 was one of the great moments in modern Arab history ...' the Palestinian writer Jean Said Makdisi wrote in her 2004 autobiography *Teta, Mother and Me*. 'If the whole Arab world reacted then with the exuberance of unity, the excitement of shared loyalty and pride, the self-assurance of supporting correct actions, those heady days of Suez stand in my personal memory, as well as in the collective memory, as a permanent reprimand to today's general indifference and corruption.'

A similar phenomenon appears to be occurring with me and Maud. My thighs, now the size of two pygmy hippopotami, are the texture of chromoly steel, while my body feels most comfortable contorted into a jagged 's' shape that mirrors her angular frame. Her rear rack is broken, while my lower back is sore, and the ruts on her paintwork reflect the calluses on my skin. If it weren't for her dastardly leather saddle – which still refuses to adapt to the delicate contours of my derrière with a stubbornness verging on the sadistic – I feel it would be almost impossible to tell us apart.

Despite my growing aches and pains, the ride to Luxor is invigorating. Explosions of cherry-red wildflowers ignite like firecrackers along the hedgerow, while a sodalite sky gleams with implausible brilliance overhead. When close to the city, however, my good mood ruptures in tandem with my inner tube. The puncture occurs just minutes after my security retinue departs, and it seems unfortunate that despite all the deities this region has to offer – Zeus, Amun-Ra, Osiris, Allah – it is Sod who appears to have assumed the role of guardian angel here.

The apartment of my Couchsurfing host, Asad, is located beside a banana plantation in a jungle of spinach green. When I finally arrive an hour late, he is waiting for me on his moped, looking rather elegant in his neat, grey *jalabiya*. 'Just leave your bike here,' he says jovially. 'I give you tour of the town!'

Minutes later, we're bouncing through acres of irrigated pastureland, past mud-brick buildings, scabrous concrete huts and scrawny children scrabbling in patches of dusty sun. Asad lives on the west bank of the Nile, far from the more popular theme-park Luxor across the water, and life here feels tranquil and slow. Buildings in faded pinks, blues and oranges depict scenic murals of temples and camels, while bright red tuk-tuks totter under mounds of tomatoes the size of pumpkins. In the distance, the sandstone Colossi of Memnon can be seen looming in all their shattering immensity against the flushed mountain tombs beyond, highlighting the humble rusticity of our own immediate surrounds. Once the gilded throne of Thebes, Upper Egypt's ancient capital is now a serene, impoverished township, subsisting on little more than memory alone.

Following a feast of *ful* and 'bird's tongue' (chicken and orzo pasta) soup, Asad and I retire to a palm-roofed café for shisha. Apple-scented whorls of smoke create lazy geometries in the spice-tinged air, and I sink contentedly into my bamboo seat as I feel my muscles decompress. Then, with startling abruptness, Asad leaps from his chair, strides across the room, shakes hands with another man – and announces we have to leave.

'What happened?' I ask once we've settled in another café down the road. 'Who was that?'

'A bad man. He beat my cousin in the last election by giving cash to voters.' He's surprised the man stood up to greet him, he says. 'It's a sign of respect. Maybe he feels guilty.'

'You left because you didn't want to be around him?'

'No. I left because I couldn't smoke in front of him. You don't smoke in front of your elders. It's another sign of respect.'

It strikes me that the more signs of respect there are, the less actual respect there appears to be. Egypt is a place where a spade is not a spade but a sceptre, a wand, a trophy, a sword: anything and everything that might paint reality in a more tolerable light.

Asad and I talk late into the evening. He is not entirely happy in Luxor, he admits, as his 'heart lies in Britain'. He lived there for twelve years after marrying a woman from Southampton, before returning to Egypt when they divorced. 'There's less judgement in Britain,' he says. 'And you can normally trust the police. Here, policemen can beat you up or rob you, or throw you in the cells for no reason. And, unless you know the right people, there's absolutely nothing you can do to stop them.'

Luxor's west bank may feel very different from the synthetic package-tour city I encountered on my last visit here, aged ten, but the heat feels all too familiar: those pools of skin-peeling sunlight that turn the earth to flame. Now, as March feeds into

April, the temperature hovers at a just-bearable 34°C, but I feel it creeping up hour by hour, day by day, taunting me with fiery prophesies of what's to come.

I stay for three days. Each evening, Asad and I talk and smoke in sweet havens of shade. He is a gentle soul, soft in build and demeanour, and on my final night he opens up about his relationship woes. The British woman was his second marriage, he says, because his first wasn't a success. 'It wasn't a love match. She'd had FGM,[60] so intimacy was a problem. We never got close.' The couple reconciled following his return from Southampton and now have four children, but he remains lonely. 'Most arranged marriages in small villages are like this. We don't have an engagement period, so people are often unhappy.'

So lust does have its virtues after all, I'm relieved to hear; Amina and Manar had almost convinced me otherwise. But it's interesting to note that what many Westerners may see as a baffling aberration – namely, the idea of coupling up without love or physical attraction – was, until recently, the norm across the world. Until the industrial age, 'love' in most societies was treated as a kind of disease to be cured, like BSE or rabies, as there were generally more important things to worry about such as milking the cows or planting the crops or fending off hordes of barbarous clansmen sweeping through your family allotment. Marriages were a means of status and security, while wayward loins, quite rightly, couldn't be trusted to keep the community safe.

Following the Enlightenment, however, attitudes began to change. People became more mobile and less tied to their communities, while land-grabs and the butchering of innocents began to lose their appeal. New concepts such as 'individual rights' and 'happiness' started to gain traction, and literature and the arts became a release valve for a torrent of repressed emotion.

---

[60] Around 90 per cent of Egyptian women aged between fifteen and forty-nine have undergone female genital mutilation, according to the UN, which usually involves the partial or complete removal of the clitoris.

Or they did for the elite, at least. For poorer communities still stuck at home, stability and security remained important considerations. If you didn't marry Cousin Bob the ploughman, it was a toss-up between Joe the blacksmith with the gammy leg or Jack the swineherd with the halitosis – and childbearing, swift and perfunctory, was top of the postnuptial agenda.

This continues to be the case in many Upper Egypt communities today, although times, slowly, appear to be changing. In a small, impoverished village near Aswan, a young entrepreneur named Asma explains how she is trying to change the mindset of local women. 'Girls often get married just to escape the family home,' she tells me. 'I want them to realise there's a whole world out there to be explored.'

The village is grimy and dilapidated, full of mounds of rubble and hollowed-out buildings as if recently devastated by war. Asma, however, is a ray of light, with a dimpled, pearly white smile and a hijab with an alluring leopard-print trim. Aged just twenty-one, she has set up an NGO with her own savings to provide business training for local women, and so far it has proved a success. 'It's all about independence,' she says, as she serves me sweet milky tea in her bare, whitewashed office. 'When women make money for themselves, they can choose whatever life they want. They aren't restricted to just one path.'

I ask about FGM, and she admits it remains a 'big problem'. 'It's now officially banned, but attitudes haven't really changed. Most girls are still being cut.' Around a quarter of operations are done with a razor at home, she says, and infections are common. 'The physical and mental harm is huge. It ruins women's lives.'

She stresses, however, that the procedure is nothing to do with Islam. 'It's an African tradition going back to the pharaohs. Most Muslim countries don't perform it.'

'What will it take to stop it?' I ask.

She doesn't hesitate. 'Education. A quarter of Egyptian women are illiterate. Until this changes, nothing will.'

* * *

By the time I begin my ride towards Aswan, everything is broken: my camera, phone, pannier racks, mudguards, spirit. My stomach feels queasy, my throat sore and the sun draws my energy like air from a ruptured tyre. Staying hydrated is now an ongoing concern, and I stop regularly at roadside cafés to glug down bottle after bottle of water, juice and lemonade, though I constantly feel thirsty for more.

Adding to my ill temper is my host, who turns out to be one of the least appealing characters I've encountered so far. Skinny and balding, with a wily, hawk-like face, he greets me on the roadside with a broad, lubricious grin. '*Sooo* good to meet you,' he says, shaking my hand. 'We'll have fun together, I think ...'

The man, Shafiq, evidently uses Couchsurfing primarily as a means to flirt with foreign women. He does this despite the objections of his pretty, docile wife, Kabira, who is busy laying out a feast of duck *molokhia* on the floor of their two-bedroom flat when I arrive. 'Welcome!' she exclaims, smiling with everything but her eyes. 'Please, sit! Eat!'

We sit and eat. The food is delicious, and I feel guilty that she's been forced to prepare it on my behalf – and even guiltier when I discover that I've been given the main bedroom while she and Shafiq are squeezing in with their two young children down the hall. 'No, it *fiine!*' she cries when I protest, her smile stretching across her face like the string of a crossbow primed to shoot. 'You *wilcome!*'

The couple are a rare love match, I learn. Kabira grew up in a village north of Cairo and met Shafiq on a train while she was studying here. Two years and hundreds of phone calls later, they met for a second time and got engaged. Within months, they were married.

After dinner, the wedding album appears. Flanking me on the sofa, the couple flick through page after page of garish, soft-focus pictures of the two of them posing against various staged backdrops, their painted expressions identical in each. Adorning each page is a clamour of hearts, flowers and excitable abstractions, all written in colourful, cursive English: *Love! Happiness! Peace! Joy!*

'Gosh ... Beautiful ... *Jamil* ...' I murmur at appropriate intervals. 'Oh, there's Shafiq with the doves again ... And doesn't grandma look like a *dream* ...?'

The album, along with the second and third, take up most of the evening and act as an excellent narcotic. The next morning, I awake fully refreshed and am immediately whisked off by Shafiq to see the Aswan High Dam. Kabira is clearly unhappy about the arrangement, but he brushes it off dismissively. 'She's just jealous,' he shrugs. 'All women are jealous!'

I resist pointing out that her jealousy appears entirely rational, judging by his behaviour. I've just discovered that Shafiq is an ardent Sisi supporter and have decided to pick my battles. 'Nasser built all of this with Russian help,' he remarks with conspicuous glee as we stand on the dam overlooking 43 million cubic metres of compacted dirt and rock that choke the urgent swell of the Nile. 'See that statue?' He points to a large stone edifice nearby shaped like a lotus flower. 'It's the Soviet-Arab Friendship Monument. It was our way of saying thank you. And fuck you to the West.'

'And you see Sisi as Nasser number two?' I say. 'Many people see him as a tyrant.'

He scoffs. 'He's just strong. But you British always want Egypt to be weak.'

I have some sympathy with Shafiq's opinion. Who, after all, can view their former colonisers with anything but contempt? But I admit I find his dogmatic views unsettling – not because he's uneducated and unintelligent, but because he's not. Every report I show him about the Sisi regime, no matter how credible or independent the source, he discounts as 'Western propaganda'. He is, of course, far from alone in his adoption of a comforting worldview from which he refuses to be swayed by inconvenient truths. But what hope is there for Egypt, I wonder, if even the tertiary-educated elite remain so susceptible to the newspeak and puffery of the state?

'Maybe,' I say. 'But we can't entirely be blamed for getting involved in Egypt.' Irritated by his lupine smirk, I feel a sudden uncharacteristic urge to defend my homeland. 'You got into debt. We bailed you out. We didn't intend to hang around.'

'But you did hang around.'

'And did some good.'

'And took what you could before we threw you out.'

He is right, of course. After taking control of Egypt in 1882, we arguably didn't begin badly. We ordered the country's finances, streamlined its administration and invested in infrastructure and public works. However, inequality was a problem from the start. The Europeans enjoyed privileges and immunities from which locals were exempt, while the Egyptian coffers bore the brunt of both the Sudan reconquest and World War I, leaving many citizens impoverished. In 1906, an infamous incident in the village of Denshawai appeared to sum up all that was wrong with the imperial system of governorship. During a pigeon shoot, a party of British officers accidentally hurt a female labourer, sparking a riot that left two of the officers injured. In the summary trial that followed, four of the rioters received death sentences, while several others were jailed for life: grossly unjust verdicts that provoked widespread anger and resentment, and created deep wounds that were never to heal.[61]

'Ok. You were probaby right to throw us out,' I say. 'But Nasser wasn't a saint, you know. Or a democrat. He had many flaws.'

Shafiq shakes his head and smirks. 'Well, you would say that,' he replies. His smile isn't lupine, I realise. It's musteline. Weasel-like. 'He made you look like fools.'

* * *

[61] 'If [England's] empire means ruling the world as Denshawai has been ruled – and that, I am afraid, is what [it] does mean to the main body of our aristo-military caste and to our jingo plutocrats,' the Nobel laureate George Bernard Shaw wrote at the time, 'then there can be no more sacred and urgent political duty ... than the disruption, defeat and suppression of the Empire ...'

I am no longer welcome at Shafiq's house. This is largely due to an unfortunate incident involving an open bedroom door and Kabira's naked rump.

'Knock!' she shrieks, as I stand frozen in the doorway mid-stride. The image of her fleshy buttocks remains emblazoned on my mind for some time, like a blinding light that endures long after you close your eyes.

I pack and depart within the hour. Before I go, as a peace offering, I give Kabira an Islamic prayer book I've been carrying around with me – and she's suddenly full of contrition. 'Stay, please,' she entreats, blinking her large, blank saucer-eyes. 'I make delicious food!'

But the offer isn't sincere, and I'm relieved to be leaving. Kabira's weakness fills me with pity and contempt, while Shafiq's lechery is nauseating. I have also found some lovely accommodation elsewhere: a colourful Nubian[62] guesthouse on the far side of the river, which stands like a rainbow regent among a hamlet of sandy roads and sun-baked villas. The place is run by a bald, plump, kindly soul named Karim – who, within ten minutes of arrival, has already invited me along to his friend's daughter's wedding on Elephantine island in the centre of the Nile.

'It's a love match,' he tells me. 'You must come if you're free!'

He runs through the programme of festivities. The invitations alone took three days, he says, during which time the couple visited neighbouring villages dressed in their full wedding regalia alongside an enormous entourage of family and friends. Today the couple were decorated with henna, and tomorrow the men will barbecue a cow and sign the marriage contract in the mosque, while the women cook the vegetables and attend the hairdresser to prepare for the evening's celebrations. On Thursday, another

---

[62]   Nubia is an ancient land that stretches along the Nile between Aswan in Egypt and Khartoum in Sudan. Once the seat of some of Africa's most advanced civilisations, the region was largely Islamised in the sixteenth century but retained a strong sense of cultural and ethnic singularity that continues to the present day.

cow will be roasted and more hair appointments booked, before a final climactic jamboree takes place that's expected to continue long into the small hours.

'Gosh, that sounds exhausting,' I say. 'When are we going?'

'Tomorrow.'

'Okay. I think I can handle that.'

'And Thursday.' He chuckles. 'You're with Nubians now. You need to up your game.'

The wedding is a fun affair. On Thursday, I am met on the island by a glamorous older woman called Betsy, whose dyed maroon hair and violet eyeshadow seem fittingly resplendent for these lively Nubian surrounds. 'We're foreigners, which means we're basically men,' she explains, leading me to a shaded gazebo beside the river. 'We can smoke and drink while the ladies get dolled up elsewhere.'

Betsy is the Dutch wife of the father-of-the-bride, Kamal, whom she met twenty years ago in Aswan. They now live together in Holland, although she admits it wasn't easy at first. 'He didn't do housework and didn't like me having male friends,' she says. 'But it's fine now. I trained him.' Since they married, the village has changed dramatically, she continues. 'Women don't put up with the shit they put up with before. They're more sociable and independent, and some even drink.'

Among the men, there are clearly no qualms about alcohol. Once the beer has run dry, several bottles of Red Label, Teachers and Smirnoff are produced – all purchased on the black market – alongside hunks of Lebanese hash the size of avocados. Before long, everyone is merry. 'My wife!' Karim exclaims, shimmying up to his friend. 'Dance with me!' They waltz together through the tables. As they do, Karim notices me talking to a man named Osama who is espousing his anti-military views. 'Brotherhood!' he cries as he jiggles by, his eyes shining with mirth. 'Dangerous man!'

All the men wear starched cotton *jalabiyas*, some with collars, some without. Osama has fifteen versions of the robe for summer and the same for winter, he explains, because 'it's important to look presentable'. They are Nubians, after all: the only pure race in Egypt. 'Other Egyptians have mixed with white-skinned people and diluted their genes. But Nubians descended from the pharaohs.'

'But aren't you married to an Italian woman?' I say. 'And Kamal to a Dutch woman? And Karim ...'

'Well, we can't help being irresistible!' he interjects, chuckling and downing his whisky in one.

At some point – perhaps midnight, perhaps later – our jolly party begins moving in jolts and starts towards the main square, where a huge marquee stands emblazoned in kaleidoscopic bunting and fairylights. In the centre, barely visible through the throng, the bride stands in all her iridescent, sequined glory, shrouded in layers of white lace that puff majestically around her waist. Part princess, part pavlova, she shuffles round and round in endless circular repetitions as the band wails in looping, rhythmic contortions from the stage. Clapping encouragingly, the women clustered about her exhibit an exuberance of sparkles, satins and silks, their faces plastered with black kohl, crimson lipstick and whitener. One woman wears head-to-toe red velour, another gold and silver crepe. The genders rarely mix, though the male dancers occasionally swoop in among the ladies, raising their arms like flapping macaws and expertly gyrating their hips.

The spectacle continues all night. While most of the guests appear to be enjoying themselves, the bride herself looks jaded to the point of comatose. I can empathise. By 4am, I can barely move too – so, when nobody is watching, I drift into the shadows, return to the quay and take a small wooden motorboat back to the main shore. Karim will be disappointed, I know. But he is a Nubian, descended from the pharaohs. And I know when I am outmatched.

Abu Simbel is not quite what it seems. Built in the mid-thirteenth century BCE by Ramses II, the two hulking rock temples erupt with breathtaking melodrama from the mountainside, suggesting both permanence and power. Yet this thrilling spectacle, it turns out, is an illusion. The mountain isn't real and the structures didn't originate here; they were moved fifty years ago, during the construction of the Aswan High Dam, to escape the rising waterline of the reservoir.

The operation was preposterously ambitious. Each twenty-ton sandstone brick was sliced, winched and repositioned in the blazing desert heat with no room for error. Comparisons with the pharaohs themselves were surely not lost on Nasser, the ruler at the time, who had always viewed himself as the rightful heir to Nectanebo, the founder of the last native dynasty of Egypt.

Indeed, the whole exercise, underpinned by brute strength and showmanship, feels distinctly Egyptian in character. This is a land where history is not fixed but fluid; if inconvenient, it can simply be revised, removed or realigned. And the same is true for people, it seems. As the dam floodwaters rose, 50,000 Nubians were uprooted from their ancestral lands and forcibly relocated elsewhere. And it seems highly unlikely – despite multiple agreements, campaigns and commitments – that they will ever be allowed to return.

At 8am, I go to the harbour. After buying a startlingly cheap 40p ferry ticket to Sudan, I sit at the dock lathering lotion into my feet and Proofide into my saddle (trying my best not to confuse the two), while looking out across the sparkling expanse of Lake Nasser. As I do, I think about the great eponymous ruler who brought imperial rule in Egypt to such a swift and irrevocable end. Nasser's socialist revolt was the cinder to dry hopes and dreams, igniting a new revolutionary age across the Arab world. Military coups followed in Iraq, Yemen, Libya and Sudan, bringing to power autocratic regimes that promised stability, social justice and independence from foreign control – promises that, when broken, ushered in a reactionary wave of Islamist militarism that continues to this day.

And so history turns: from ancient splendour to vassal

statehood to defiant tyranny to bloody insurgency. A long fight for power and respect from which few come out well. Not far from where I sit now, submerged beneath the surface of this pool of cobalt blue, lies one of the battle scars of this struggle: the Egypt–Sudan border, drawn by the British in 1899. As sharp and straight as buckshot, the line cries cavalier nerve. How must it feel to have your home forged by outsiders, I wonder? To have your identity altered through the casual stroke of a pen? As an island kingdom, our shape fixed by the tide, our borders coarse like hand-cut cloth, can we ever truly know?

Looking across the water towards Sudan, another former colony still bearing wounds of the past, I question how Britain can ever justify the freedom it seized from others. Our privileges have not been earned but expropriated, taken from those whose needs were always subservient to our own. Now, travelling through this region of fragile security and conflicted statehood, wielding my passport like a sword, I feel for the first time an acute awareness of how much I have benefited from this legacy – and how much others have lost.

Chapter 7

THE IMPRINT OF THE DESERT

Sudan

'No man can live this life and emerge unchanged. He will carry, however faint, the imprint of the desert ... For this cruel land can cast a spell which no temperate clime can match.'

Wilfred Thesiger, *Arabian Sands* (1959)

As the ferry departs, I feel myself relax. The water is soothing, lying flat and still like a steadying ballast against my pounding heart. Like Freya Stark, I am relieved to be leaving the messy crowds and exhausting 'pharaonic microbes' of Egypt – although I admit I feel nervous at what's to come. What I'll find at the far bank, I have no idea; I've made no plans and the map is tantalisingly sparse on detail. From the border, the Nile seems to be accompanied by just one solid road, while other paths meander, frayed and broken, into the empty, parchment-coloured expanse beyond.

On the small cargo ship, around twenty passengers sit squeezed along two wooden benches shaded by a corrugated awning. Within minutes, I have two invitations to tea: one from an elderly Nubian couple, the other from a young Egyptian doctor. The latter warns me to be vigilant in Sudan.

'Please watch out,' he says. 'There are many dangers.'

'What kind of dangers?' I ask.

'Oh, many things …' He trails off and I wait anxiously for him to continue. 'Well, there are scorpions,' he says finally. 'And the insects are quite big.'

He falls silent again and, after a few moments, I realise that's all he's going to say. For a police state renowned for violent conflict, ruthless repression and homegrown terrorism, these concerns seem manageable. 'Thank you,' I reply. 'I promise I'll take care.'

We disembark at an empty dock. There is nothing here at all: no people, no buildings, no shelter. Just pale dunes dusted by rubble, rimmed by the jagged outline of distant mesas. The heat is fierce, and I'm a little dismayed to discover that the official border lies another thirty-five kilometres to the south. In fact, studying the map now in more detail, I see the line is not quite as razor-straight as I first imagined but hiccups briefly across Lake Nasser before lurching east in two directions at once in a kind of hesitant, drunken stagger. This, I discover, is due to the drawing of two separate boundaries by the British in 1899 and 1902, the former granting the oil-rich Hala'ib Triangle to Egypt, the latter giving it to Sudan. For this reason, Egypt observes the 1899 border and Sudan the 1902 – leaving, in the middle, a tiny unclaimed enclave known as Bir Tawil, said to be the only true remaining *terra nullius* in the world.

Despite the beating sun, the ride is smooth and easy. It wasn't long ago that this route was just sand and grit compacted by millennia of moving feet, hooves and wheels. But now, to my delight, it is pristine, exquisite asphalt, and the journey takes less than two hours.

Crossing the border itself, however, proves somewhat less straightforward. Hundreds of people mill about amid towering ramparts of baggage, and I struggle to decipher any sense of order or logic amid the bedlam. Eventually, I learn that to obtain an entry stamp, I must join a baying mob around a kiosk and endeavour to scrabble my way to the front to slip my passport to the man inside. He will then pass it to another man, who will check it and give it to a third, who will stamp it and lob it back into the sea of waving hands. This, although I don't know it at the time, transpires to be one of the more efficient administrative procedures of this somewhat discombobulated authoritarian state.

An hour passes before my name is called, at which point I am hustled out of the crush into a small, dark side-room. *Here it comes*, I think: *the savage interrogation for which these border agents are renowned*. Steeling myself, I perch nervously on the solitary plastic chair and wait.

'Rebecca?' the man says when he arrives. He is tall and expressionless but doesn't look unkind.

'Yes,' I reply.

'Eenglish?'

'Yes.'

He begins leafing through my passport. 'Sudan ...' he says. 'Why?'

I smile. 'Sudan *hilwa*.' *Beautiful.* My trump card.

He continues leafing. Moments later, he stands and strides out of the room, leaving me alone for another nerve-racking twenty minutes. But then he's back – and he's smiling. 'Miss Rebecca,' he says. 'Wilcome Sudan!'

I'm in? I can hardly believe it. Sudan's notoriously porous borders clearly extend as much to foreign cyclists as they do to smugglers, bandits and jihadists, and I walk blinking into the sunlight in a kind of daze. The rest of the process is easy, and within an hour I am through the final gate and standing on Sudanese soil, overwhelmed with joy and relief.

As I prepare to depart, a young man approaches and introduces himself. He is a student at Khartoum University, he tells me, and he's very happy that I'm visiting his country. We exchange pleasantries, but quickly his tone shifts. 'Sudan is dangerous,' he warns, echoing the man on the boat. 'You must be careful.'

I nod. 'Yes. The scorpions.'

'The *deathstalker* scorpion,' he corrects. 'And, of course, the sand snake, which is very poisono—'

My ears prick up. 'Sorry, the what?'

'The sand snake. It hides in the ground with just its head showing …'

My heart starts thumping.

'… but you can't see it because its skin is sand coloured, so it's important to watch your step.'

I stare at him, aghast. I was aware there were snakes in Sudan. But *invisible* ones? That LURK WAITING FOR YOU IN THE SAND?? It's like my worst nightmare. Except it's here now, in real life, rearing its scaly, demonic head right in front of me.

Most people, I suspect, wouldn't be overjoyed at this news. But to me it comes as a particularly nasty shock because – as I've mentioned previously – I've had a deep-rooted snake phobia ever since I was young. Where it originated from, I've no idea. My brother believes it started as an attention-seeking measure inspired by my mother's fear of lizards, and he's probably right, but there's no doubt that at some point along the line, through a cruel form of wish fulfilment perhaps, it turned into something undeniably real. As a child, I would have to flatten all the lumps in my duvet before climbing into bed, just to ensure that they were indeed just lumps and not an errant python or salamander on sabbatical from the Amazonian jungle, and I would often check the arms of jumpers too, as a precaution, and the insides of slippers and shoes. Nowadays, I still blanch at bowls of spaghetti if I'm eating on my own, and there are moments when I'm out and about that I become so convinced there's a knot of wriggling serpents at the bottom of my handbag that it takes all my willpower not to catapult the thing into the nearest hedge and run in a howling panic down the road.

All of which I happen to think is extremely reasonable behaviour in the circumstances. After all, what kind of creature doesn't have any *limbs,* for god's sake? The whole idea is preposterous. And now I'm being forced to face my fear head-on. In the Sahara. All alone.

'Anything else?' I ask weakly, staring out in numb disbelief at the mass of inexorably reptile-ravaged sand stretching into infinity in front of me.

'No, that's it,' he chirrups jovially. 'I think you'll love our beautiful country!'

By the time I leave for Wadi Halfa, the sky has turned a deep navy blue and the shadows stretch with liquid ease across the ground. The road is empty and quiet, and only the occasional set of tyre tracks leading into the speckled dunes provide any hint of life beyond this central black artery. Cycling hard, I narrowly avoid overshooting the unsignposted turning, barely visible in the gloaming, and soon find myself cycling in the dark – still without bike lights – with just the spectral outlines of palm trees and breezeblock shacks to guide the way. Then the asphalt abruptly ends, and I find myself pushing through thick sand, slipping and sinking like a drowning swimmer thrashing towards the shore.

Sometime later, I manage to track down 'the best hotel' in town. This transpires to be a broad concrete bungalow located beside a sweeping pitch-black sandflat, where for £9 I receive a windowless cell with a bare bulb, a steel-framed bed and an asthmatic air-conditioning unit that gasps out deliciously cool air. I am also granted access to the communal bathroom, where pubes collect in the cracks like snowdrifts and the hole-in-the-floor toilets, blackened with grime, double as cold-water showers.

After a quick wash, from which I emerge slightly dirtier than when I went in, I go to charge my phone at the front desk and bump into a reporter called Aziz. He is on his way to Cairo to cover a story on human trafficking, he explains, which 'is not slavery, like Europeans think', but 'a kind of salvation'. Aziz himself once worked as a trafficker, he says, because he wanted to help people in need. 'You cannot stop this industry with penalties or by forcing countries like Sudan to solve the problem. We must change the global economic system, which creates such poverty and suffering.'[63]

Aziz asks what I think of Wadi Halfa, and I confess I've seen nothing of it so far. He laughs. 'Well, you haven't missed much.' Wadi Halfa, it turns out, no longer exists; it drowned sixty years ago in the floodwaters of the Aswan High Dam. Where we stand now is *New* Wadi Halfa: a poor replica; a city of walking ghosts. 'Wadi Halfa was rich and fertile, but the new town is a dump. There's no farmland, no industry, no past.' Fifty thousand Sudanese Nubians were forcibly uprooted, he says, some of whom were brought here, while others were taken 700 kilometres to the south. 'Many saw rain they'd never seen before. They complained they'd been put somewhere with a hole in the sky!'

The next morning, I see that Aziz's description is apt. New Wadi Halfa is a listless, windswept place spun from cobwebs of dust. A soaring bluff of debris looms over one of the streets, while heaps of rubble form edifices that seem more substantial than the buildings themselves. There are no proper shops, just metal kiosks hung with rags, and the roads are all sandy and unpaved. Everywhere I go, feral dogs limp between wisps of shade, their tongues red and swollen like hunks of raw bavette.

People are friendly, and sometimes a little nutty. A stallholder with goggly eyes and a twitch gives me a giant bear-hug before throwing a dozen tomatoes against the wall and catching them as they ricochet off unharmed (I decide against buying any tomatoes). Still in Egypt-mode, I haggle over the powdered milk.

---

[63] I have a great deal of sympathy with this view. In their bid to stem migrant flows from the Horn of Africa, the EU channelled around €180 million to Sudan between 2015 and 2018 through the 'Khartoum Process' under the guise of tackling the 'root causes' of displacement, while Britain set up a series of bilateral talks of its own. 'A young and diverse civil society in Sudan is raising its voice for change,' Lord Alton, Secretary of the All-Party Parliamentary Group for Sudan and South Sudan, told me during an interview for a *Guardian* article in 2018, 'but the UK and EU are instead focusing on engaging with a government committed to oppressing it.'

'Fifteen,' the boy says. 'Ten,' I reply with bold tenacity. 'Fifteen,' he repeats, confused. That's how much it costs. I fish out the notes, embarrassed, and go quickly on my way.

Having been told to register my presence in the country, I follow directions to the police station and find myself at a shack inhabited by two topless young men watching a pair of bush babies mating on TV. Leaping up when they see me, they hurriedly pull on their shirts and stumble outside to see what I want. Yes, they are indeed the police, they confirm once I explain the situation, but they are nonplussed about this 'registration' thing. They call their English-speaking friend to resolve the issue – who, as serendipity would have it, transpires to be the brother of a tourist guide I contacted in Cairo about helping with my visa, as well as the man who advised me how to change my dollar notes into Sudanese pounds at the border (I cannot access any money here due to the sanctions, so I'm forced to carry $1,000 of local currency with me).[64] It is my first taste of the sprawling matrix of *wasta*-based interconnectivity that silently greases the cogs of this vast and mystifying country.

The man advises me not to bother registering. 'It's Sudan,' he says. 'Don't worry.'

'But I was under strict instructions,' I reply. 'Couldn't it cause a problem?'

'Do the police look as if it'll cause a problem?'

I glance over. One of the men is lying topless on his bed again, while the other seems to have fallen asleep under a tree.

'Well, now you mention it,' I say. 'I think it'll probably be okay.'

* * *

[64] US sanctions were first imposed on Sudan in 1997 as a counter-terrorism measure, but have been gradually lifted since 2017. Sudan was finally removed from the US list of state sponsors of terrorism in May 2021, though sanctions and arms embargoes imposed by the UN and EU in response to the Darfur conflict and civil war remain in place.

For Churchill, Wadi Halfa marked the 'sharp line between civilisation and savagery'. Or it did in the mid-1800s, at least, before the genteel Brits arrived to liberate and edify the masses. The people to the south were 'virile' and 'simple-minded', the young subaltern wrote in his book about the British reconquest of Sudan, *The River War*, while the Arab-Africans of the north – though 'debased and cruel' – were undoubtedly superior in intelligence and genealogy.

There was one southerner who Britain could not so easily dismiss, however: a charismatic Nubian boat-builder's son named Muhammad Ahmad bin Abd Allah, who in 1881 declared himself the 'Mahdi', the messianic redeemer of Islam. By the time the British assumed *de facto* leadership of Egypt and Sudan in 1882, he and his devoted army of followers had already defeated the Ottoman Egypto-Turkish army in a series of bloody battles, and Britain faced a quandary. Should they try to subdue the Mahdi militarily, plunging Egypt's already beleaguered finances further into crisis? Or withdraw the Egyptian garrisons and attempt to strike a truce?

After much deliberation, they opted for the latter. Tasked with overseeing the operation was General Charles Gordon, a stubborn, gutsy, godly man not unlike the Mahdi in temperament, who, it was hoped, would evacuate the troops as swiftly and smoothly as possible. The hope proved short lived. Whether Gordon was unwilling or unable to carry out the orders is unclear; but left woefully unsupported by his army chiefs at home, he soon found himself trapped in Khartoum by the Mahdi's men – and, in January 1885, he was overpowered by the dervish rebels and killed.

Back in Britain, Gordon's fate caused a media storm. Enthralled by the tragedy, the press lost no time in depicting his stand against the Mahdi as a form of courageous, neo-imperialist Crusade, while Gordon himself was framed as a Christ-like martyr unjustly slaughtered by the infidel mob. It was a compelling, seductive narrative that instantly captured the public imagination. It was also, however, considerably wide of the truth. Despite his piety, even Gordon never saw religion as a key factor in the conflict. 'I do not believe that fanaticism exists as it used to do in the world, judging from what I have seen in this so-called fanatic land,' he wrote in his diary while stranded in Khartoum. 'It is far more a question of property ... like communism under the flag of religion.'

Churchill, for his part, agreed. 'Fanaticism is not a cause of war,' he posited in *The River War*. 'It is the means which helps savage peoples to fight.' The dervishes' list of 'legitimate motives' against their imperial chieftains was long, he pointed out: brutal repression, plundered wealth, stolen liberties, crushed identity. And the Mahdi, in his eyes, was no less than a 'hero' who 'freed his native land' from foreign rule.

If there's one way to get your mind off snakes, it's a story about crocodiles.

'This guy was washing in Lake Nasser when a stray dog came over and started sniffing around him,' the man tells me as I load up Maud in the hotel porch. 'The next thing he knew – bam! A crocodile leapt from the water and snatched the dog away.'

'No!' My heart, already fragile, thumps wildly in my chest.

'Yes! The guy was so shocked he spent two months recovering in hospital.'

Seeing my horrified expression, the man tries to offset the trauma of his tale with some practical advice. 'If a crocodile attacks, it will lock its jaws and try to drown you,' he says. 'The best thing to do is to tickle its nose.'

'Tickle?'

'Yes. Its nose is very sensitive.' Alternatively, I could try reaching into its mouth and grabbing the flap of skin in its throat so it chokes – but this, he concedes, 'might be harder'.

Assuring him that I'll do my best in the circumstances, I bid the man goodbye and begin to make my way back to the desert highway. Around me, the world feels wonderfully still. Only the occasional acacia bush punctuates the flat, featureless expanse, while the sky is so ablaze with blue that my eyes ache to look at it.

After an hour or so of cycling, I reach a police checkpoint. Who am I, the officers ask? Where am I going? Am I married? Do I have a phone? Each question is uttered with such unabashed indifference, it's a wonder they bothered to stop me at all. Rebecca, Khartoum, no, yes, I say, before being waved cursorily on. After the stifling intrusiveness of Egypt, Sudan's blithe dysfunctionality comes as a blessed relief.

I continue south, aiming towards the first settlement marked on the map: Semna. In 1800 BCE, this town marked the southern boundary of the Egyptian empire, its chain of mighty fortresses acting as a deterrent to the warring Nubian tribes beyond. Little of this former pomp remains now, I'm sure, but I'm curious to see what's emerged in its wake. Some crumbling ruins, perhaps? A thriving metropolis? An overgrown oasis fringed by baobab trees and palms?

Or a single shack, cuboid and squat, built from bamboo and straw?

Inside, the shade washes over me like a wave of iced water as I come face to face with a dozen men in *jalabiyas* and A.C. Milan shirts sitting around plastic tables. On one side there's a drinks bar, while at the back there's a wooden sideboard holding an ancient television and a collection of copper shisha pipes. Desperate for a cold juice or lemonade, I am a little disappointed to discover that all the bar sells is hot, steaming tea – which, considering the hot, steaming conditions outside, is just about the last thing I feel like drinking right now.

Grudgingly, I buy a glass anyway and collapse onto a chair. Outside, the sun is breathing fire onto the scorched earth, and my plan is to remain here until the worst of the heat has passed. As I wait, the men share their *ful* and snacks, then spread across the floor to perform their *Asr* prayer. I take the opportunity to lie down too, and for the next two hours I drift in and out of silken dreams, caressed by a light breeze that whispers under the bamboo. Is there any greater joy than this, I wonder? The sweet, simple pleasure of a rest hard-earned, when bean stew becomes a banquet and a patch of sand a feather bed …?

I make it to my final destination, El Beer, by nightfall. Sadly, its name proves misleading. There's no beer here. Or running water. Or even toilets ('Look around,' the caretaker, Mustafa, laughs when I ask. 'The Sahara is your toilet!'). But the hut is larger and livelier than Semna, and a sizzling stone barbecue emits a succulent feast of smells. At the back, where the porch dissolves into the dark recesses of the desert, a lone tree drizzles its prickly foliage over a mound of discarded car tyres, while chickens peck about for elusive scraps of grain.

About three dozen men sit scattered about the place. Most are gold miners, I learn, who leave at sunrise and return when the light wears thin. This shack is their refuge from the chemical pools and dead earth, from the noise and stress and bloated heat. As the power generator whirrs into life, I join them around a battered television to watch a soap that seems like a cross between *Desperate Housewives* and *Star Trek*, while devouring a plate of chicken liver and chips with all the grace and restraint of a hyena consuming a wildebeest.

Afterwards, Mustafa brings me some doughy *gorraasa* he's baked in the clay kiln. Speaking slow, hesitant English, he describes how the mining operations work, and how hazardous they are for the men. Car tyres are set alight to soften the rocky ground, he explains, before explosives are detonated to dislodge the tenderised turf. This is then mixed with mercury and cyanide to separate out the gold. 'The work is hard,' he says. 'Dangerous. Many get sick with cough and disease.'

The gold rush in Sudan began in 2012, when large reserves of the metal were discovered in North Darfur. The timing was fortuitous. South Sudan had seceded a year earlier, taking three-quarters of the country's oil supplies with it. For some, it felt like manna from Heaven itself, as if God had taken with one hand and provided with the other. Young men flocked to make their fortune panning in the dunes, and Sudan's gold industry grew to be the third-largest in Africa.

In reality, however, the discovery was less a gift than a curse. Little of the newfound wealth found its way to the public purse but was instead seized by the most nefarious faction of Sudan's ruling elite: the Rapid Support Forces (RSF), created by Omar al-Bashir in 2013 as a rebranding of his barbaric Janjaweed militia.[65]

'They devil-men,' Mustafa says, when I ask his opinion of the group. Janjaweed can be translated into English as 'devils on horseback', and he mimic horns with his hands. 'No God.'

After Mustafa leaves, I find an empty *angareeb* (string bed) in the courtyard and lay out fully clothed. Overhead, the firmament is on fire. The stars blaze in their billions, powdering the sky like icing sugar. I watch them, transfixed, breathless with the beauty of it, cupping my hands like blinkers and imagining I'm floating in space.

And then, gradually, the stars grow dull and soft, the air light and cool ... and I feel myself sink into the blackness and disappear.

The roadside huts prove my salvation. Each day, bruised from the heat, I crave each rest-stop as a free diver craves air. I soon develop a routine, rising before dawn and cycling until midday, before taking a lengthy break and continuing in the late afternoon. At present, the cycling is manageable, but it is now early April and I admit I'm fearful of what's to come. In just a few weeks, the

---

[65] The Janjaweed were formed in the mid-1980s to subdue the non-Arab rebels and forcibly Arabise the Darfuri population, and they became renowned for their savage campaign of torture, murder, arson and gang rape. While al-Bashir – who is still president as I travel through Sudan – did not create the conflict in Darfur (which originally came about due to competition over grazing land between the Arab nomads and indigenous African tribes), he manipulated and militarised it, turning a simple territorial dispute into a devastating conflict over race and identity.

temperature will reach its peak and all but the sand snakes and scorpions will be seeking sanctuary from the sun's bitter rays.

Giving me solace in the meantime is the Nile. Its power feels greater here even than in Egypt, for its banks are largely bare and there is little to distract the eye. Broad and calm, it is the uncontested commander of this land, with a rawness of strength that grips and dizzies the soul. Here, the river is not girdled and dammed like downstream but breathes slowly through the seasons: out in the summer months, as its belly expands to irrigate the riparian plains; in during winter, as it narrows and exposes the soil for new growth. It is an antidote to so much out here that concerns me – sunstroke, thirst, loneliness, loss – and I find myself constantly searching for it between the endless brown below and endless blue above, as if only this mighty watercourse had the ability to hold these two infinite worlds apart.

Near Abri, the Nile announces its presence with a shock of misty green. I follow its bank in a broad westward arc, past tussocks of dry pastureland and a lone grazing mule, then turn off the main road and aim directly for it, delving into the foliage as if plunging into an emerald lake. Bouncing across the sand, I pass a cluster of clay huts, a broken truck and a sleeping goat, before sliding to an unsteady halt beside a coppice of riverside palms.

Minutes later, careering into view in a cloud of black smoke, a clapped out old Morris Minor pulls up next to me. A tall, rake-thin man unfolds like a concertina from the driver's seat – which, like the rest of the car interior, is clad in an explosion of bright blue fur. 'Sorry I late,' he mumbles. 'Car need petrol.'

The man, Mahjoub, unlocks a gate nearby and leads me into a beautiful adobe courtyard. Built in the classic Nubian style, its ivory walls are decorated with clay pottery and woven wall-hangings, while half a dozen doors around the perimeter lead into a series of charming bedrooms. Mine contains a mahogany bed with blood-red satin sheets, a faded rug and, on the wall, the hide of what appears to be some kind of warthog or giant mongoose. Outside the window, the Nile can be seen just metres away, its sandy bank now a deep coral-pink as if its capillaries were relaxing in the fading light of dusk.

Mahjoub is thirty-one and soft-spoken, with a sharp, darting eye. Over a falafel sandwich, he tells me that he built the guesthouse after South Sudan seceded and he lost his job with the Malaysian oil giant Petronas. 'I wanted it to be Nubian,' he says. 'Traditional. It's important that we protect our culture.'

'You feel it's under threat?'

He nods. 'The Arabs have stolen it. Thousands of years ago, all this was ours.'

I look around. All I can see are a few crumbling huts and a donkey hollering like a creaky capstan. 'This?'

'The desert. I show you. I take you to the Kajbar Dam.'

Later, he does as he says. Or perhaps it's more accurate to say that I take him. Having accepted his offer to let me drive, I shuttle us across the sand, pounding dunes and ditches, dodging toddlers and goats. The car has no speedometer or seatbelts, or brakes to speak of, and its metalwork seems held together through force of will alone. To assist our safe passage, Mahjoub shrieks a stream of thunderous, hysterical instructions. '*Gears! Accelerator! Clutch!* Have you ever *driven* before?? Now *braaaake!!!*'

Ricocheting off a rock, we narrowly avoid plunging headfirst into the Nile as the engine, in a heroic act of harikari, issues a strangled groan and expires. It's a relief for both of us. Dying here would not only be ignominious, but preposterous. You don't cycle halfway across the world to perish in a Morris Minor plastered in blue fur.

'Out, please,' Mahjoub says, a little unkindly. 'No more driving today.'

Twenty minutes later the car is fixed ('it just need water!') and we are careering our way onwards once more. The further we go, the sparser and quieter the villages become, until only the odd tethered camel or flutter of laundry indicate that anyone lives up here at all. 'People go Khartoum,' Mahjoub explains. 'No school. No market. No jobs.'

We meet a group of Mahjoub's friends beneath a canopy of palms. While Mahjoub tends to his car, which collapsed again the moment we stopped ('it just need oil!'), the men tell me about the dams. Three are planned, they say, the Kajbar, Dal and El Shereik, all posing a threat to Nubian historical sites and homes. 'We'll die to stop them, as others have before,'[66] one man explains. 'Our land is sacred and our lives are by the river.'

'But doesn't Sudan need more electricity?' I ask, thinking of the clunking generators and power-cuts I've encountered here so far. 'I thought the Merowe Dam brought some benefits?'

'For some, yes.' Hydropower from the dam doubled Sudan's energy output, he says, but at great human cost. 'There are better, fairer ways to get power. But nothing was ever discussed.'

The waterline rose quickly in 2009 when the Merowe floodgates were closed. Dozens of Manasir, Amri and Hamadab communities were caught off guard, and some barely escaped with their lives. Overall, 60,000 people were displaced, their farmland submerged. Compensation was poor, sparking a spate of lawsuits, protests and UN statements of support – but the damage was already done.

'It was a good life before,' a visiting farmer named Khaled tells me as he grinds fava beans to make *ful* on a circular stone plinth. 'We never got sick, except from the dates. We caught fish with our clothes, looped and tied like a sack.' He remembers the day well when his family was forced to move far from the riverbank into the desert: the confusion, the tears, the dry sweetness of the air. Most of all, he remembers the aching wail of his aunts like the lowing of cattle being herded for sale. 'Our lives and homes were stolen,' he says. 'And we lost the river forever.'

Northern Sudan, comprising the sprawling tract of land between Khartoum and Egypt, is one of the few regions of the country that

---

[66] Three anti-dam protesters were killed by security forces at Merowe in 2006 and a further four here at Kajbar in 2007.

hasn't historically been plagued by war. Yet neglect here is almost as severe as the conflict-ridden south, east and west. Chronically centre-heavy, Sudan has long focused the bulk of its energy and resources on the capital, feeding the swollen belly of the state while bleeding the extremities dry.

The dams are a case in point. But they pale in significance when compared to one of Sudan's first great megaprojects – the Gezira Scheme – which set the trend for things to come. Devised by the British and run by the crème-de-la-crème of Oxbridge elite, Gezira was the largest agricultural irrigation venture in the world at the time of its completion in 1925. With the chief aim of producing cotton, it covered an area the size of Lebanon and, at its peak, was almost singlehandedly responsible for keeping the national economy afloat.

Whether Gezira ever truly benefited the Sudanese people, however, is questionable. As the main source of cotton for Britain's northern textile mills, the project was a critical asset for an empire stretched to the brink, and vast resources were focused on this one endeavour. A railway line was built solely to service Gezira, based a few miles south-east of Khartoum, while only a single track made the lonely journey through the marshy Sudd to the south. Indeed, residents of the south, who were mainly non-Arab and Christian – and who, in Britain's eyes, were little more than primitive swamp-dwellers straight out of the Conrad canon – were not only banned from working on the project but derived almost no value from it. They derived almost no value from *anything* in the north, in fact, as the imperial administrators were determined to keep the region as remote, impoverished and pliable as possible.[67]

[67] Following years of chronic neglect, armed unrest erupted in the south in 1955, leading to a lengthy battle for rights and autonomy that ultimately left at least 2.5 million dead and millions more displaced. In 2011, Sudan finally split in two, and the underdeveloped south – with its paltry fifty kilometres of paved roads and 75 per cent adult illiteracy rate – gained the unenviable task of creating a new nation almost entirely from scratch.

'Britain's legacy remains strong in Sudan,' Khaled says. 'We've had many governments. Democratic and military, socialist and nationalist, good and bad. But none have united us. The cracks run too deep.'

'And you feel we're to blame?' I ask.

He spits a date stone onto the sand. His face is streaked with sunlight filtering through the branches overhead, blacking out his left eye and giving him the look of a pirate. 'Yes,' he replies. 'And also no. We've had sixty years to put things right, and in all that time we've failed.'

Amara West is a disappointment. There are few obvious treasures here. No lofty battlements or faded frescoes or eroded colonnades lying shattered in the sand. Nothing, in fact, except a series of broad, square indentations carved like a chequerboard into the dunes.

At this ancient archaeological site, rainless storms can smother in a minute what diggers can unearth in an hour, condemning the area to an endless cycle of burials and exhumations. Right now, there is little to be seen. Yet burrow deep enough – so I'm told – and one would eventually unearth a kingdom. Founded by Seti I in the thirteenth century BCE, this shallow footprint of a city was once a soaring metropolis heralding Egypt's dominion over the Nubian Kingdom of Kush. Murals of military triumph were etched into the stonework, while hypostyle halls were adorned with swaggering pharaohs reigning supreme over their Nubian, Libyan and Asiatic slaves.

However, the story told by Amara West is double-edged – for it is not only a celebration of Egyptian power, but also its swan-song. A hieroglyphic dated 1126 BCE is said to be the last known royal inscription in Upper Nubia, marking the point at which the pharaonic armies were finally, devastatingly, expelled.

'Kush wasn't some poor servant to Egypt, like historians have always said,' my guide, Mohamed, explains. 'It was a mighty, sophisticated kingdom. They didn't just defeat the Egyptians; they conquered them. They reigned in their own right.'

The five Nubian 'Black Pharaohs' governed Egypt for a hundred years from the eighth century BCE, Mohamed explains, and were just as powerful and influential as the rulers who came before. Yet it wasn't until 2003 – when the Swiss archaeologist Charles Bonnet unearthed a cache of granite statues of the pharaohs that had been truculently destroyed by the Egyptians thousands of years before – that their story began to emerge. 'The Nubians have been forgotten,' Mohamed says. 'But as more discoveries are made, hopefully people will start to remember.'

These discoveries can be found layered in grainy heaps along the river, as temples, stelae and tumuli all emerge from the ground like custodians over the past. Each is a trove of hidden truths, exposing a chronicle of African achievement that sits uneasily with traditional narratives. 'The native negroid race had never developed either its trade or any industry worthy of mention,' the Harvard archaeologist George Reisner wrote in 1918, 'and owed their cultural position to the … imported Egyptian civilisation.'

Until now, the Nubians' ancestral pride has struck me as arrogant and misplaced. But their bombast is not plucked from the air, it seems, but from the ground. Their ruins may even be among the greatest historical treasures ever discovered, some experts believe, as vital to an understanding of world history as monuments from Ancient Greece and Rome. As Bonnet explained in a 2017 interview, 'There are no roots today in Africa, and we have to find those roots … This is the secret of Africa.'

My final night in Abri is a delight. I enjoy a sunset *sahlab* tea, very nearly work up the courage to bathe in the river (but don't) and wallow in a cool, open shower under a rhapsody of stars.

Afterwards, I call P and tell him about my near-success with the swim. 'I had a paddle,' I say, trying unsuccessfully to keep the pride from my voice. 'That's not bad, is it?'

'Define "paddle".'

'I … dipped a toe in. I didn't want to take any chances.'

'But I thought you said Abri doesn't have any crocodiles?'

'The locals *told* me there aren't any crocodiles. But maybe they're wrong?'

'These are the Nubians you mentioned?'

'Yes.'

'The ones who've lived there for thousands of years?'

'Yes.'

'You don't think, in all that time, they might've noticed the odd croc or two wandering around town?'

I pause, considering. He has a point. 'But what if the crocs aren't interested in locals?' I ask. 'What if they only eat foreigners?'

'Hmmm.'

'What if there haven't been any crocs until now, but a rogue one has broken away?' I persist. 'Remember that case I told you about – of that shark appearing in a freshwater creek in New Jersey and killing those two men?'

'The one from 1916?'

I don't like his tone. 'Yes, that one. The point is that in water *anything* can get *anywhere!*'

'Okay,' he says. Was that a sigh? 'Just stay on your guard. And if anything scary turns up – a crocodile or shark or aggressive seabream or whatever – just hold your nerve. You know what to do.'

'What do I do?'

'What that man said to do. You look them in the eye, grab them by the throat – and tickle them to death on the nose.'

At a rest-stop near Wawa, I meet a young student named Abdul. He serves me *ful* and fresh fish and a strange hard fruit called a *doum*, and urges me to stop at Kerma down the road.

'It's Nubian,' he says. 'Very special. Very old.'[68]

Abdul is Nubian too, but when I ask whether he believes that Sudan is really a Nubian, rather than Arab, country, he surprises

---

[68] Kerma was the capital of Nubia from 2500 BCE, and its ruins – known as the Western Defuffa – are said to be among the oldest in Africa.

me. 'No,' he replies. 'It's Nubian *and* Arab. And Beja, Fur, Dinka, Copt, Nuba … It's lots of things all mixed together.'

'Lots of things all mixed together' may be the best description I've heard of Sudan so far. This is a country of astonishing racial, cultural and linguistic diversity, with nineteen major ethnic groups and six hundred subgroups, each united by a complex conflation of culture, genealogy and belief. These intricate tribal cross-hatchings form the bedrock of the country, and in a different place and time could perhaps have formed a diverse yet cohesive whole. Under al-Bashir, however, Sudan's rich heterogeneity has been crushed by the militant enforcement of a single Arab identity. The result is a country shorn of texture and shade, in which diversity is replaced by spurious dichotomies: you're either Arab or non-Arab; part of the gang or abandoned in the peripheries to rot.

The impact of this has been devastating. Across Sudan, identity has become sharp and hard-edged. Ostracised from the centre, tribes have built walls of belonging, weaponising their ethnicity to survive. 'Al-Bashir has turned everyone against each other, but it's all rubbish,' Abdul says, leading me into a filthy, furnace-hot room to rest. 'Even he isn't pure Arab, like he says. I mean, just look at his green face! He's mixed, like everyone else.'[69]

I take his point. As Ramy noted in Lebanon, what does Arab mean anyway? Several self-identifying 'Arab' tribes in Sudan, such as the Shaiqiya and Ja'alin, are believed to have descended from the Nubians, while it's debatable whether contemporary Nubians share any genetic heritage with their Kushite ancestors at all. Even Sudanese Arabic is not wholly 'Arab'; it is its own unique dialect, with links to several Nilo-Saharan languages. Sudan is, at root, a country defined by transgression.

'Sudan is suffering right now,' Abdul says, as I sit on the saggy *angareeb* and feel my buttocks brush the gritty earth below. 'But soon we'll be free.'

---

[69] In Sudan, people's skin colour is often described (from light to dark) as 'white', 'red', 'green' and 'black'.

'Soon?' I say. I'm sceptical. The Sudanese have been fighting al-Bashir for three decades without success. Is anything really likely to change now?

'Five years.' He holds up five fingers. 'Believe me. Just you wait and see.'

Delgo is not what I expect. Described by Mahjoub as a 'big city full of thieves', I'd imagined something rather more gloriously nefarious than this bland adobe village barely visible through the sand-dusted air. Instead, it seems populated almost entirely by mad children. One of them, a lilliputian scrap of girl, dashes over to me as soon as I arrive, asks my name, demands money and then convulses with laughter so hard that she collapses spreadeagled onto the ground. 'Hi! Who? Where are? Dollar!' she chirrups deliriously from the floor. 'Eenglish! Me Eenglish! Who Eenglish? No!'

The girl insists on dragging me to her bungalow, where her long-suffering mother looks bewildered by the scenario with which she's been presented. 'I don't want to intrude ...' I say apologetically. I mean it. The girl's exuberance has a slightly sociopathic edge that concerns me. But the manic whippersnapper has other ideas. 'Please, sitting sitting!' she cries, scampering in circles like a malfunctioning robot. She has stumpy Minnie Mouse pigtails and a devious twinkle in her eye, while her scowling younger sister is clad in bright lilac with a snotty snail-trail streaked across her face. In the meantime, a crowd is slowly filling the courtyard around us. I eye them suspiciously. The girl has already requested money several times, while a woman has asked for my glasses and another my camera. Should I be worried, I wonder? Perhaps Mahjoub was right after all?

Feeling distinctly uneasy, I am seated on an *angareeb* while the usual phrasebook questions are fired my way. I am clearly the evening's entertainment for this crowd of listless onlookers, and once the lengthy cross-examination has concluded, my pint-sized nemesis has the inspired idea to fetch some henna. Off she bounds, returning moments later with what looks like an enormous slab of ginger mud. 'Sooo boootiful!' she coos, as the crowd shifts closer. I demur, but there's no escape. Taking my hands, she presses the gloop into my palms and fingers, coating every inch of flesh. Nobody else is doing this, I note, but the women all clap and nod excitedly. 'We frieeends!' the young Lucifer squeals. 'We frieeends forever!'

When the clay is removed, my hands are both radioactive orange. This is the desired effect, it appears. 'Booootiful!' the group howls, their ruby-eyes glinting like wolves. 'Today orange, tomorrow red!'

At 11pm, when the power shuts off and we are plunged into darkness, the girl starts entreating me to lie down. 'Sleeping, sleeping ...' she murmurs, stroking the cushions beside me as if it were the most natural thing in the world to doze off under the watchful gaze of two dozen strangers. I decline, stifling a yawn, and am deeply relieved when, at midnight, the guests finally begin to disperse. As they do, the remaining family members all start pulling their *angareebs* into the courtyard and laying them with pillows and blankets, while the girl drags her bed right up against my own. 'Best friends always,' she murmurs sweetly in my ear, before giving me a hug, asking for money one last time and curling into a ball to sleep.

And then ... peace. At last. Overhead, layers of stars recede endlessly into the inky black, some bulb-bright, others shimmering like fairy-dust. Their beauty feels overwhelming.

I will never tire of this sky.

Each day, I am dazzled by the strength of the desert. It feels like a living force, invigorating and devastating, breathing me in and out like a trifling mote of dust. In these temperatures, the wind doesn't dispel the heat but magnifies it, as though beating a wall of flames across my path. Near Dongola, a man tells me 'a heatwave is coming', and I can't help feeling bemused by the information. *A heatwave in the Sahara*? I think. *Like a frost in the Arctic?*

But he is right, as it turns out. There's heat and there's heat, and the next day I begin to struggle. I feel tired and sluggish, and my bare calves develop a mottled, itchy rash. In fact, my whole body is now a blotchy patchwork of pinks, reds and browns, wind-battered and sun-roasted, like a hunk of raw beefsteak being slowly barbecued on a spit.

At noon, the temperature reaches 44°C and I feel its weight on my chest. Sometimes, when all I can see is sand, I have the odd sensation that I'm drowning. There's no foliage here: no trees, no bushes, no shade. No safety buoys for when you lose your footing and sink. I remember scuba diving years ago in the Red Sea and becoming suddenly aware of the ocean of pressure on my tin-pot tank and crêpe-paper lungs. Humans aren't designed for such places, I recall thinking – and isn't there something hubristic and pitiable about our attempts to prove otherwise? Aren't regulators and rash-guards and buoyancy kits and neoprene suits a sign our skills may be better placed elsewhere?

Aren't four inches of sun cream and a swollen tongue? And a desire only to sleep as your eyelids sag beneath the sun?

Eventually, weary and parched, I reach the turning I am looking for. Following an unpaved track, I pass through a tangle of mango groves and *al-haraz* trees, jungle-thick, then burning, soupy sands where Maud sinks like a stone. I pass miniature cows and bulbous-nosed mules, and cross the river in a blue wooden boat. On the far side, I haul Maud up a sandy bank and then inch by inch, foot by foot, across a vast, mushy plain.

Around halfway, exhausted, I stop to rest beside a goat under a tree. And then I hear my phone ring.

It's Dad. 'Hello, darling!' he cries, his boomingly British timbre immediately recognisable. 'Is this a good time?'

'Dad!' I reply, almost weeping at the sound of his voice. But my mouth is so gummy with dryness that I find it hard to talk. 'Could I ring you back in a bit?' I ask. 'I'm stranded on a sand dune with a goat.'

By the time I return the call, I am ensconced in a large fuchsia house on the far side of the sandflat. About twenty people seem to live here and they invite me in without hesitation, fetching me water and biscuits and ushering me into a bedroom to rest.

'Sweetheart!' Dad says. 'I thought I'd see how you're getting on. Where are you exactly?'

'Well, I'm in a big pink house by the Nile,' I tell him, 'trying to find a buried city …'

'Ah,' he interjects, chuckling. 'So you're lost?'

Dad and I talk for thirty minutes. His voice sounds surreally incongruous in these torrid surrounds, like a Sunday roast or pint of warm ale. But I'm delighted that he's called. Last time I saw him, he was emerging from a lengthy delirium in his sickbed, blinking into the cold hospital light like a mole emerging from its burrow. Now he seems fully *compos mentis* and almost back to his old self.[70]

Before he goes, he relays a message from Mum, who is currently at aqua-aerobics. 'She said to make sure you drink enough in the desert. It's very hot! And please ring us if you get into trouble. BLAST will send the camel brigades.'

After the call, I set off to find the ruins of Old Dongola. The site lies an hour's trek from the house, across gritty dunes that resemble fields of crushed grain, and vine-like shadows creep from the roots of spiny shrubs as I take a looping walk across the sand. The first artefacts I encounter, dotted across the plateau, are dozens of large beehive domes resembling calcified space-pods, as if some futuristic civilisation has been incinerated by a fiery apocalypse. These turn out to be Islamic *qubbas* (tombs) from the 1600s, and each one is empty except for colonies of sleeping bats. Walking on, past hunks of stone and timber strewn like flotsam in a fossilised sea, I come to a cluster of tilting granite columns standing in a shallow depression: the surviving relics of Nubia's

---

[70] My father lived for several more years and finally passed away in April 2019, aged ninety.

largest church, constructed in the seventh century in the image of a Byzantine basilica.

Past the pillars, a trapezium-shaped fortress stands at the crest of a hill. Climbing to its summit, I feel like a fallen queen. Between the sixth and fourteenth centuries, I would have been staring out at a kingdom: first Christian, then Muslim, now ... well, only the spirits can say.

Although I'm going back in time here, it's a step forward from Amara West. Old Dongola was the capital of Makuria, the strongest of a trio of Christian kingdoms to emerge from the ashes of Kush. A formidable military power, Makuria proved more than a match for the mighty Muhammadan armies sweeping in from the north, forming an impregnable barrier that stoppered the tide of Islam across the eastern Sahara. It wasn't until the early 1300s that the empire was finally conquered by the Mamluks, and the palace where I stand now was converted to a mosque.

Soon the sun begins to set, and I lie back on a crumbling rampart looking out across the plains. There is something special about the evening light in the desert, which doesn't fade like in the city but softens and strengthens at once. Laser beams of carnation-red streak across the sky, while the ground takes on an entirely new hue, a little pinker than fawn, a little beiger than blush. Far below me I can see the Nile and the sharp slash of green and brown where the desert chokes the river foliage as if snuffing out a candle – and I find myself thinking about these snuffed-out people, these Nubians, forgotten by history and the ever-shifting lines in the sand.

By nightfall, I am back at the pink house waiting for a lift from an unknown person at an unspecified time to an undisclosed location. Writing this now, long after the event, I struggle to recall how this arrangement was made, but my impression of these liaisons is that they *just seemed to happen*, informally and organically, like so many things in Sudan *just seemed to happen*. On this occasion, I am collected by a stubbly man in a truck, who informs me that we're going to a house three kilometres to the north – and two hours and twenty kilometres later, we finally arrive at our destination, following a jolting, white-knuckle journey along the pitch-black riverbank, during which we have to dig out the vehicle three times from thick drifts of sand.

Where we are precisely, I have no idea. But my time at the house is brief. Having arrived around midnight, I depart at sunrise after accepting some biscuits from my kind hosts and a donkey cart ride back to the road. I decline the water they offer me, however. I can't drink local water without my filter-straw, which is maddeningly frustrating to use, so I've mainly been drinking bottled water bought from roadside pitstops. I still have one bottle left over from yesterday, which I reason should be enough to tide me over until I can purchase some more along the way.

It's a bad decision, as it turns out. I should have listened to my mother.

I lie on the edge of two deserts, beneath a sinking sun. On my left, pale Nubian sand sheets stretch to the horizon, unbounded and stark. To my right is the Bayuda, a broad volcanic bruise of acacia groves and baked wadis. Seen from above, they hug either side of a giant S: the 'great bend' of the Nile as it folds its way north towards the Mediterranean Sea.

Where am I precisely? No landmarks surround me, no tree or monument to provide a guide. Not even a crease marring the clean curve of the earth, which encircles me in a single sweep as if this bare patch of land comprised the entire globe. All I know is that I'm far enough from anywhere to feel afraid and close enough to feel a fool: two states of mind that have become troublingly familiar of late.

Half-dreaming, I think back to the morning. From the donkey cart, I joined a new road south, and at first I enjoyed the ride. It was early and breezy, and the world was beautifully still. But it wasn't long before I realised that this road was different from the ones I'd been on before; there were no rest-stops here, and all but the first of the roadside water urns were dry.

As the sun rose, my thirst grew quickly – and almost immediately I began to struggle. Far to my right, flashes of the Nile glinted and teased: an artery through cracked skin. *Plod on*, I thought as I rode. *Plod on. Plod on. Plod forever.*

Around me, the wind grew sharp and coarse-grained. It whipped up dust skeletons that skittered across my path. It pulled me off the road, across bristle and gravelly stones. *Plod on,* I kept thinking. *Plod on. Plod on. Plod forever.*

After a time, I thought of nothing but water. I saw it all around me, hovering like a Hades punishment out of reach. I watched it shimmering on the horizon in pools of curved light. I felt its silken touch on my tongue and crashing in foamy crescents over my head.

Plod on, I urged. *Plod on. Plod on. Plod forever.*

And then I saw it: a lone earthenware pot set back a hundred metres from the road. I recall the feeling as I stopped, the faint nausea of muted panic ... And I knew before I reached it and placed my hands upon its rim ...

That *of course* there was no water.

Back on the road, I retched: two, three, four dry heaves, ejecting flecks of acrid phlegm. Sinking to my knees, as if in supplication, I watched the sun turn electric pink and set both earth and air aflame. *Plod on*, I thought weakly. *Come ON.* But around me, everything seemed immense. I felt crushed by the Sahara's splendour and the crassness of its strength. I felt overwhelmed.

Fuck you, Fiennes. I can't.

It felt good to lie down. The ground opened beneath me, enveloping my sore back and legs. Here was my feather bed, my lotus field, and for just a moment I closed my eyes.

For just a moment.

* * *

I jerk awake with a start. Gasping like a swimmer surfacing, I take mad, hot gulps of air. I know I shouldn't be lying here. I need to get on the move.

Staggering unsteadily to my feet, I clamber aboard Maud and begin slowly to pedal. Cycling feels both inevitable and impossible. My tongue is bloated, my throat a thousand tiny knives. But the sky is growing dark overhead and I know I have to push on.

The air is cooler now, but the wind remains fierce. *Ten kilometres, nine, eight* ... Across the river, I spot the faint sodium-glow of a town, and I turn towards it as a turtle hatchling turns towards the sea. *Five kilometres, four, three* ...

On the bridge, I increase my speed, excited that finally, imminently, I'll be safe. But then, in my haste, I slip and lose control and feel myself falling towards the floor.

The crash winds me badly, and for several seconds I cannot move. I just lie there, dazed and dust-coated, as muffled footsteps draw near. And then hands appear, and faces, and bottled water to my lips. And I feel myself heaving again, and vomiting, as nausea rises in waves.

Some time passes. Then a donkey cart arrives, and more people, and I'm carried to a house nearby. There, I am taken into a dark room and brought sheets, water and juice. And then I am left alone.

For several hours, I lie on the bed, dozing in fevered fits and starts. The rhythmic cadence of the day continues to pulse inside my head. *Plod on, plod on, plod forever* ...

And then the room grows still, the rhythm dull and slow, and I fall deep into a dreamless sleep.

At 5am, I awake with the dawn. It's a morning I'll always remember because the thought hits me instantly, as clear and sweet as birdsong: *I'm okay.*

I still feel faint, but the delirium has gone. The world is sharp and steady again, full of colour and crystal lines. I drink three bottles of juice but pick tentatively at my food. My stomach remains queasy and I'm reluctant to disgrace myself again.

Outside, everything is quiet. I locate the bathroom, which lies open to the sun, and peel off my grimy clothes. Then I tip water from a bucket above my head, letting it slosh down over my body and form a puddle about my feet. It is deliciously cool, and the feeling of it fills me with pure delight and astonishment. I know I wash for too long, too wastefully, but the simple wonder of it thrills me – the enchanting touch of water under a dazzling pool of sky.

Afterwards, I see where I am. In the early morning light, this simple mud shack has a freshly laundered feel, as if the blustery night winds have scrubbed away the fervid impurities of yesterday. Three closed rooms surround the central courtyard, alongside a kitchen containing a fridge, stove and jumbled heap of pans. Outside, there's a water tank and a lone plastic chair. This is all they seem to have, the people who rescued me from the road and showed me such tender care.

By 7am, the household is stirring. Nine sweet young girls surround me, calling me Becca and Paprika and trying on my helmet for size, while five older women, draped in vibrant cloth, urge them to play outside. The women are all politely curious, asking questions from a dog-eared English phrasebook. 'You have husband?' one of them enquires, smiling. 'You ... leave husband?'

The women take me around the neighbourhood. The adobe buildings are pockmarked and crumbling, and plastic bags lie strewn like beached jellyfish across the sand. Stray dogs slump in mud-caked puddles, while emaciated goats lie in bony heaps in doorways and fusty pens. Inside one hut, I encounter an old, leathery woman surrounded by cobwebs, flies and litter. 'She says: welcome, God has brought you here,' her grandson translates, as she holds my wrists and murmurs hoarsely in my ear. 'He will guide you and keep you safe.' I thank her, feeling oddly reassured. 'And she says, you must meet her son,' he continues, as I feel her grip tighten. 'Maybe you can marry him?'

Back at the house, I prepare Maud for the road. I still feel weak but vow to take the ride slowly. I've now returned to the southern side of the Nile and know there are rest-stops along the way. Today, hopefully, the elements won't throw me to the wolves.

As I pack, the women press sugary biscuits and flatbread into my arms. They seem worried about me leaving, and I feel my eyes fill unexpectedly with tears. '*Shukran*,' I say. 'Thank you.' I try to give them money, but they refuse. Instead, I dig out a wooden leaf-shaped magnet and hand it to one of the girls. It feels like a pitiful token, but I hope they can see that to me it means much more.

Then, just as I'm leaving, an older lady rushes out clutching a bottle of water. 'Please!' she cries, thrusting it towards me. 'Good!'

I laugh and accept it gratefully, and everyone else laughs too. And then I turn and begin to pedal, and their laughter is lost on the wind.

Karima was once known as Napata, the prosperous capital of Kush, and it is here that I spot my first Sudanese pyramids. They rise on the crest of a slope, silhouetted against the hulking sandstone mesa of Jebel Barkal, huddled in a pack against the wind.

Considerably younger and smaller than their Egyptian cousins, these nine crumbling monuments lack the latter's brash bulk and majesty. Yet it is precisely their humility that, for me, contributes to their appeal. Grouped casually on the roadside with all the pomp and circumstance of a copse of English oaks, their heritage is not packaged and peddled for easy consumption but is carried lightly upon their shoulders, free and accessible, for any passer-by to see.[71]

Continuing into Karima, I pass whitewashed houses, languorous camels and splashes of apple green. Though larger

---

[71] Karima's earliest pyramids were built in the third century BCE, while those at Nuri across the river date back to the seventh century BCE. Egypt's oldest pyramid, in Saqqara, was constructed two millennia earlier.

and more developed than most Sudanese towns I've visited so far, Karima clearly has a way to go to recapture the Kushite splendours of antiquity – or this is how it seems at first glance, at least. Dig a little deeper and I've heard that there may, in fact, be something very special tucked away here, hidden behind high walls … Something that perhaps wouldn't have been so out of place during the city's gilded heyday 2,500 years ago.

Like a pearl lurking in sediment, the Karima Nubian Rest House is a rare and unexpected treasure amid these barren surrounds, and I admit I've been looking forward to tracking it down for some time. Almost entirely camouflaged from the road, the place isn't easy to find; however, once I finally locate it, concealed behind a locked wooden gate, I find myself walking into a fairytale. Arising before me is a secret garden, an anti-Narnia, in which spring blooms eternal. Low domed buildings form a pale yellow perimeter around a quadrangle of neat lawns and perfectly manicured flowerbeds, while sprinklers throw a mist of droplets across the foliage in a rainbow blaze of colour. The scene has such a fantastical, Potemkin aura to it that I can scarcely believe it to be real.

'Welcome!' the manager, Abou, cries as I enter. In his pristine white *jalabiya* and *taqiyah,* he looks to me right now like a kind of demigod or messiah. Leading me to a table on a large terrace overlooking the garden, he presents me with two jugs of iced liquid, one amber, one red, alongside bowls of nuts, crisps and popcorn. 'Baobab and hibiscus juice,' he says. 'Please, drink.'

I do – and I'm not sure I've ever tasted anything so heavenly. I finish both jugs in about three minutes, and Abou immediately replaces them. Afterwards, he sits down beside me.

'You seem tired,' he says, peering at me with his quiet, enquiring eyes. 'Where do you stay tonight?

My heart takes a small leap. *Surely not …?* Abou has been expecting my visit, as I contacted the Italian guesthouse owners several days ago, but I had anticipated nothing more than a drink.

'I don't know,' I say, exuding what I hope to be the right ratio of feebleness and stoic fortitude. 'I was thinking that maybe I'd camp ...'

'Camp?' A look of concern flutters across his face. 'Please, no need. We'll make up a room for you here.'

I stare at him, astonished. Rooms here cost upwards of ten times my daily budget, so I had never considered staying overnight. Resisting the urge to dive across the table and give Abou a big juicy smacker on the lips, I instead settle for a profusion of feverish thanks. 'It's nothing,' he says, bashfully batting my tirade away. 'This is what Nubian hospitality is for.'

He shows me to my room. Sumptuous and cool, it comes complete with two mahogany double beds, ornate wall tapestries and a soaring domed ceiling that rises temple-like overhead. It is, by any standards, sublime. While I cannot deny that the shocking incongruity of this plush European idyll with the arid, impoverished world outside discomforts me a little – highlighting, as it does, the contrived nature of my hobo status – I cannot truthfully say that *not* taking up Abou's offer ever crosses my mind. I may be aware of my privilege as a white, middle-class Westerner, but I am far from virtuous enough to refuse the gems it throws my way.

Later, over dinner with Abou in the pantry, the conversation turns to politics. 'Democracy will come to Sudan,' he asserts. 'But not through violence. It will be more like France.'

Considering the Reign of Terror that followed the French Revolution, during which tens of thousands of people had their heads lopped off, I wonder if this is the best analogy. But Abou is confident that, of all the Arab countries, Sudan has the best chance of reform.

'We're educated and experienced,' he says. 'We've had democratic governments before. If anyone can do it, it's us.'

The Nile road out of Karima continues for a few miles north before ending with the abruptness of a pirate's plank at the edge of the Merowe Dam. The only way to exit the city, it transpires, is to abandon the river and join a piston-straight highway that cuts directly across the Bayuda Desert.

I set off with a certain amount of unease. The Bayuda was formed several million years ago when a series of volcanic eruptions thrust the riverbed on a lengthy digression east, and its blistering climate today seems befitting of such a fiery birth. Temperatures frequently exceed 45°C – Levison Wood recorded a mind-boggling, if 'untrustworthy', reading of 58°C in 2014 – and the wind is bitter and strong. Reluctant to take any chances, I cycle slowly and stop frequently to rest and rehydrate. Since my collapse, I have a renewed respect for the desert – and also, I admit, a fear. The feeling sits low in my gut, gentle yet unmistakeable, purging me of any cocksure inviolability.

The Sahara has cracked its whip. I won't be testing its patience again.

Meroë[72] boasts more pyramids than the whole of Egypt. But this doesn't make it any easier to find. There is no road leading there, and all I have is a vague sketch of the location not unlike an X-marks-the-spot treasure map. Eventually, however, after much searching and backtracking, I locate a patch of tyre-flattened sand beside the highway which looks faintly promising – so, hoping my instincts are correct (which is rare), I leave the road and set off tentatively across the dunes.

Soft and duvet-thick, the sand is interspersed with hard, grainy patches that extend like an archipelago towards the horizon. Dragging Maud from island to island, I make slow, dogged progress, carving a deep, slug-like trail in my wake. The effort, I hope, will be worth it – because my intended destination, recommended by Abou, is another secret jewel of the desert: a luxury camp, currently closed to the public, owned by the same Italian couple who built the Karima guesthouse.

---

[72] Not to be confused with Merowe, where the dam is located, 400 kilometres to the north-west.

To my astonishment, the route does indeed prove correct. At the other end, I walk into a settlement of clay huts, mud-and-thatch bungalows and Bedouin-style tents, all interspersed with mounds of mortar and rubble that suggest construction is still ongoing. The site radiates comfort and charm – and isn't quite as abandoned as it appears, I realise, after I turn a corner and come face to face with a row of tethered camels. The boy leading them seems unfazed by my appearance and kindly dashes off to fetch me a jug of iced water as I wait on the terrace for the manager. From this vantage point, I have a clear view of the pyramids in the distance, their points curiously flattened so they resemble a row of jagged teeth. This odd appearance is reportedly due to the Italian treasure hunter Giuseppe Ferlini, who decapitated the structures in 1834 in order to scavenge the riches inside (only later to get his comeuppance when many of his patrons, believing Africa far too primitive a place to produce jewels of such exquisite beauty, denounced him as a fraud).

Looking at my elegant surrounds, it strikes me that the Europeans – myself included – have done rather well out of Kush to date. I've earned the privilege, I keep telling myself; I cycled all the way here, for god's sake! But the nagging feeling remains that, really, I haven't earned anything at all. And that maybe coming here and residing in such luxury, and accepting all these favours and kindnesses and gifts, is not really so very different from the likes of Ferlini at all.

As the sun dips low, I abandon my wait so I can make it to the pyramids before nightfall. The site, like Jebel Barkal, has no formal entrance or barrier, and I walk straight up to the monuments following a forty-minute hike across the sand – an ease of access I find both exhilarating and disconcerting. Around 200 tombs are located here, arguably numbering among the world's most prized archaeological artefacts, and they have been abandoned to battle the elements and desert storms alone. As I stroll about the windswept plains, I attempt to project myself into an imagined historical tableau two millennia ago, when the sand was a savannah of grasslands, sorghum and barley, the pyramids were sheathed in vivid polychrome plaster, and herds of elephants and gazelles grazed among the brush. Burials at Meroë peaked around the fourth century BCE, after the relocation of the capital of Kush from Napata, when the kingdom was at its prime. It would, I imagine, have been quite a sight to behold.

What most impresses me about Meroë, however, is not its former pomp and majesty but its admirable feminist credentials. Several powerful Kushite queens, or 'Candaces', are buried here, who were not simply wives or mothers but governed in their own right. One of the largest and best-preserved pyramids belongs to the first standalone female ruler, Shanakdakhete, who significantly expanded Nubia's wealth and territory, and personally led her army into battle. Nearby, another, smaller tomb is the alleged burial place of Amanirenas, who rallied her troops against Augustus Caesar and is rumoured to be the 'one-eyed' Candace cited in Strabo's *Geography*. Though ultimately defeated by Rome, Amanirenas managed to sweet-talk Caesar into highly favourable peace-terms – and had the last laugh, it seems, by burying a stone head of the emperor under her palace steps so people would trample over him every day. What a gal!

With no accommodation in sight, my final night in the desert is spent camping alone in the dunes. It is, I admit, far from the restful, ruminative experience I'd envisaged. Cripplingly terrified of encountering a snake, I pull out my tent and am distraught to discover a perfect serpent-sized hole in the side – a fear that is magnified tenfold when I realise I have neither glue nor fabric with which to repair it. Instead, summoning long-dormant skills from years of *Blue Peter* watching in the 1980s, I pull together a sizeable stockpile of sticky-tape, clothing, rocks and toiletries, from which I attempt to fashion the most effective makeshift barricade I can.

The result is disappointing. The barrier looks about as impenetrable as a net curtain. Horrified at the prospect of my safe haven being infiltrated, I lie awake for hours as darkness descends, staring at the sinewy shadows on the walls, listening to the gentle animal-rustle of the wind, beating back the rising spectres of my mind, and fervently wishing – not for the first time – that I hadn't decided to replace my thermos flask of booze with an emergency ration of water.

At sunrise, dazed from sleeplessness yet overjoyed not to find myself dissolving in the intestinal juices of a passing anaconda, I pack up camp and return swiftly to the safety of the road. There, a gusty tailwind propels me along as if I'd hoisted a sail, and I begin to think I might just reach Khartoum by lunch. But then, to my shock, the road stops. Or, rather, the asphalt does. The road itself continues as a broad expanse of sand, too soft and mealy to cycle, and I am forced to dismount from Maud and push.

I walk for several hours, searching for the tarmac as a stranded sailor might search for land. But ... nothing. So I simply *plod on plod on plod on* beneath the searing midday sun.

Then, just as I'm beginning to lose hope, my prayers are answered. Out of nowhere, a minibus en route to Omdurman rattles up the track, which – to my immense delight and disbelief – has precisely one seat spare, plus room on the roof for Maud. *Salam!* the passengers cry merrily as I board. *Welcome!*

I sink into my seat, exhausted. Then I turn and look back. Through the sand-encrusted rear window, the white-gold glare of the desert returns my gaze: unyielding, steadfast, calm. It could have crushed me if it wanted to; it could have ground my bones to dust. But it didn't. It took me in, beat me down and released me – and, in the words of Wilfred Thesiger, left its imprint marked upon me forever.

After a month in the Sahara, Khartoum feels intimidatingly cosmopolitan. Stumbling off the minibus, I am nearly mown down by an *amjad* – a Korean-made microbus – while its driver performs a dexterous juggling act of drinking, smoking and barking on the phone. The streets and buildings may be the familiar dirty beige

I've come to know well, but the latter are made of mortar, not mud, and do not stand broad and flat but rise several storeys into the sky. All around, the air thrums with vitality: the hollers of street vendors, the rumble of traffic, the competing strains of the *azan* from a medley of mosques nearby.

Maud now has two broken pannier racks, so I cycle slowly and gingerly, cradling her injuries as if stemming blood from a wound, until I spot a man waving from the roadside up ahead. It is a friend of the woman who has kindly loaned me her flat while she's away. 'Rebecca?' he says as I pull over. 'John. Welcome to Khartoum!'

The apartment, tucked inside a secure gated block, is elegantly furnished and beautifully cool. Aware suddenly of the grey desert crust caking me from head to toe, I do my best to acclimatise to this new idyll of civility as John, a British UN officer, gives me a brief overview of the political situation in the city.

'Things are fragile,' he says. 'Students are protesting, and two have been killed. The government is weak and paranoid, so at its most dangerous. You should be careful.'

'Careful?'

'All foreigners are watched. It could cause problems for people you meet.'

Later, over drinks at John's flat with a dozen or so diplomats, activists and journalists, more light is shed on the precarious security situation in Khartoum. Only recently, I'm told, a Western diplomat was jailed overnight for holding hands with his girlfriend while walking home from a party, shocking the expat community.

'It was bad luck,' Amjed Farid, a Sudanese activist, asserts as I feel myself begin to sink into the velvet softness of the evening. Just sitting on John's veranda, with beer and G&Ts on tap, feels impossibly decadent. 'A policeman on a power trip.' The danger posed by the security agencies is not so much their prowess as their unpredictability, he explains. 'One guy might beat you senseless, while another might offer you *aragi*.[73] It's a lottery.'

---

[73] The popular local firewater, brewed from dates.

Life is clearly growing harder by the day for the Sudanese people, and international agencies appear to be part of both the problem and the solution. 'Sudan's a patient in a coma and we're the life-support,' John says. 'If we pull out, the country dies. But staying just prolongs the status quo.'

'So let us die!' Amjed cries, smiling but serious. 'Nothing is worse than how it is now.'

'What about Syria?' I ask.

He throws up his hands. 'People always say this: "What about Syria?" But we're *already* Syria! Darfur's the size of France!' A few years ago hardly anybody was starving, he says. Nowadays, families hang bread on their doors so nobody goes hungry. 'Some people have even invented a new meal between lunch and dinner so they only eat twice a day. Things are getting desperate.'

The word 'Khartoum' comes from the Arabic for 'elephant trunk', and it is just about possible – with a squint and generous dose of artistic licence – to imagine that this refers to the plump proboscis of the White Nile as it joins with the Blue to form the animal's head and torso. While this interpretation makes for rather a spindly beast, with a skull of disturbingly mammoth proportions and a body that tapers feebly into the desert, it is perhaps not overly farfetched as visual metaphors go. Khartoum is the nerve centre of Sudan, after all, corpulent and overfed, while the peripheries have long grown weak and malnourished from neglect.

Such laboured symbolism works best from above. From eye level, the confluence of the White Nile with the Blue, known as *al-Mogran*, appears both formless and unimpressive. The rivers look neither white nor blue, for a start, but varieties of carbon-grey, while their meeting is greeted not with fanfare but with a cheerless, muddied bank. Despite this, to me, the seamlessness of the union does feel important. Here, two great contradictory forces come together – one thick, one thin; one from the east, one from the west – and blend in effortless harmony. One channel does not subsume the other, like the Rhone and the Arve in

Switzerland, or the Yangtze and Jialing in China, but instead they join as equals. In a nation of such violent discord and division, such a conjugation feels quietly aspirational.

Less cheering, however, is the history the site has witnessed. It was at this junction that the imperial forces congregated in January 1885 on their doomed mission to save General Gordon from the Mahdi's soldiers, and where Kitchener arrived to avenge the governor-general's death a decade later.[74] One of the fleet's gunboats, the *Melik*, is still on show today, though she is far from the formidable vessel she once was. In 1926, she was retired from government service, and in 1987, she was swept ashore by a flood, where she has since been abandoned in the sand to decay. On the day I visit, her walkways are cluttered with driftwood and debris, while bougainvillea and banyan trees grow tentacle-like around her hull. In my mind, the message couldn't be clearer if there were a tombstone stating 'British Empire RIP' perched up on deck.

'Well, actually, that might be misleading,' my guide, Mustafah, replies when I say this to him. 'Because Britain never really went away.' He doesn't just mean the institutions we left behind, such as the Blue Nile Sailing Club or Gordon Memorial College (now the University of Khartoum), but the very fabric of the capital itself, which was originally designed to resemble the Union Jack. Khartoum was not simply a reflection of Britishness, therefore, but an embodiment of it. 'All roads led to the centre, where the Brits were located,' Mustafah says. 'Next came the Egyptians in a ring around them. And finally the "natives" on the outside, spilling out into the desert.'

Khartoum remains similarly stratified today, he continues. The capital is really three cities in one: Khartoum, Omdurman

---

[74] After winning the Battle of Omdurman, Kitchener was made commander-in-chief of the Second Boer War, where he became notorious for his 'scorched-earth' policy of destroying crops and farms, as well as his management of horrific concentration camps in which around 28,000 inmates died from disease and starvation. He was subsequently promoted to Secretary of State for War.

and Khartoum North, all separated by branches of the Nile and speaking slightly different dialects. 'Many locals view Omdurman as the "real" capital because it was the home of the Mahdi,' he explains, 'while Khartoum is seen as the product of foreigners. Khartoum North is the poorest part, where the workshops and factories used to be before they all closed down.'

'And the black belt?' I ask. I've heard this term used but am unsure exactly what it means.

'Ah yes, the migrant slums in the outer suburbs.' The conditions there are said to be terrible, he says, although he's never seen them himself. 'No outsiders have, really. Officially, these places don't exist.'

Khartoum is a battle of busy contrasts. The city feels like a quilt patched from a thousand different materials, ruched and rough in places, shiny like satin in others. Sleek high-rises stand beside ragtag shacks, braying donkey carts beside gleaming sedans. Shops and restaurants bustle with industry, and a few demonstrate admirable creativity in evading US sanctions, including 'Starbox' and 'Kafory Fried Chicken', the latter of which has a picture of the owner's brother in the place of Colonel Sanders.

Compared to Omdurman, however, Khartoum is a model of order and urban planning. To me, the 'real capital' feels disjointed and amorphous, as if a giant has stepped on it from above and splurged it out at the sides. Just reaching it involves an *amjad*, two buses and a chaotic interchange of gridlocked traffic, and when I arrive I feel instantly disorientated. Walking for hours, I pass tumbledown huts and pillared porticoes, jaundiced tower blocks and sun-baked plains, yet on the map I see I've covered only a tiny thumbnail of this wild and incoherent district. The souq is particularly unwieldy, humming and hollering with rhythm but no rhyme, and looks not dissimilar to how it did a hundred years ago, I imagine, when it was said to be the largest and busiest market in Africa.

Situated by the Nile on the periphery of this melee, the Mahdi's tomb – along with the adobe villa of his successor, the Khalifa – is a picture of modest serenity. Indeed, both buildings are strikingly unostentatious considering the elevated status of their former occupants. They're also in surprisingly good condition, bearing in mind that Kitchener blasted in here not so long ago and put a whopping great hole right through the side of the crypt.

'He stole the Mahdi's remains, and then killed two of his sons,' Ateef, a local activist, tells me. 'Just one son – Sayyid Abd al-Rahman al-Mahdi – survived. He took control of the Mahdi's "Ansar" sect, and then in 1945 founded the National Umma Party, which went on to form one of the most prominent political power-blocks of Sudan.'

As he speaks, Ateef leans over and tops up my glass. We are at his flat tucking into 'the best *aragi* in town', which I have to admit tastes remarkably similar to all the other gasoline-orientated spirits I've tried in recent months – in that it tastes of nothing at all beyond an agonising burning pain at the back of my throat – but I appreciate the hospitality nonetheless. Ateef has offered to give me an overview of Sudan's complex political history and turns out to be something of a politics junkie. 'We've had three military regimes since independence and three coalition governments led by the Umma party and Democratic Unionist Party,' he says. 'The problem is always *rizg-alyoum-bi-alyoum*.' Short-sighted policies. 'Everyone wants to cling to power. We can't make democracy stick.'

I ask about the Muslim Brotherhood, which emerged in the 1950s and went on to dominate politics until the rise of al-Bashir. Many members, including Brotherhood leader Hassan al-Turabi, were educated in Europe, Ateef explains, and felt frustrated by the West's ignorance of the Arab world.[75] 'Turabi understood Western culture and connected with it. He wasn't solemn and fun-hating like

---

[75] 'Dialogue has to be two ways culturally,' al-Turabi remarked in 1994. 'Muslims know a great deal about Christianity because it is part of their historical heritage and tradition of Islam … The West knows so little about Islam generally.'

Bin Laden.[76] He travelled widely throughout Europe, and studied in London and the Sorbonne.' Al-Turabi even married the sister of former Umma Party leader Sadiq al-Mahdi, Ateef says, in a Romeo-and-Juliet-style alliance of rival powers. 'But that's the problem of politics in Sudan: these deep bonds of elitism and cronyism that underpin everything else, which started under the British.'

Ateef lights a Marlboro and stretches out his legs. Tall and rake-thin, he has a languorous air about him and his eyes flash frequently with mirth. 'The Brotherhood were a paradox,' he says. 'They were a product of the West, yet also fiercely anti-colonial.' But, of course, that's often the way, he surmises. 'The better your education, the stronger your sense of independence and desire for reform.'

He leans forward and clinks his *aragi* with mine. 'To democracy,' he says.

I clink his glass. 'And making it stick.'

We tip the drinks back and I feel my pharynx dissolve.

'Good, isn't it?' he smiles. 'You can really taste the dates, I think?'

'It was President Nimeiry[77] who ordered the September Laws in the early 1980s,' the man tells me, picking up Sudan's history where Ateef left off. 'But it was Turabi who wrote them. They struck fear into everyone.'

Bald, with a bushy, grey moustache and mournful eyes tucked behind tortoise-shell glasses, Nabil Adib emits the wise and reassuring aura of a barn owl. He has invited me to his office to help me gain a better understanding of how Sudan has got into the state it's in today, and I am extremely grateful to him for making the time. As one of Sudan's most prominent human rights lawyers, he is not an easy man to pin down.

---

[76] Osama Bin Laden despised Turabi, in fact, viewing him (astutely) as a corrupt charlatan whose government was 'a mixture of religion and organised crime'.

[77] A military officer who established a socialist one-party state in Sudan following a military coup in 1969.

'It wasn't just sharia,'[78] he continues, speaking through an interpreter. 'It was cruel and arbitrary.' Hangings and amputations were common, and you could even be jailed for thought-crimes such as 'intended adultery'. 'Meanwhile, moderate Islamists such as Mahmoud Mohammed Taha' – whom Nabil represented, and whose first period of incarceration was under British rule in 1946 – 'were executed.'

The September Laws horrified the population, and ultimately led to Nimeiry's overthrow in 1985. Four years of democracy followed, before Turabi and the National Islamist Front[79] – backed by a group of military officers led by an unknown former car mechanic named Omar al-Bashir – seized power for themselves.

'Under al-Bashir, the south was exempt from Turabi's laws,' Nabil recalls. 'But in the north, all of society was Islamised and Arabised. Education, public services, the courts, everything. Anyone who disagreed was sent to *Bayut al-Ashbah* [ghost-houses] to be tortured.' Women were hit hardest, he says. 'Polygamy was legalised and new dress-codes introduced. Even walking alone in public was banned.'

People were bewildered by what had happened. 'Where did these people come from?' the novelist Tayeb Salih famously enquired. Al-Bashir was not one of the *effendis* (educated elite) but appeared as if from nowhere. And Sudan was far from an extremist country. Its Islamic heritage was not Salafist, like Egypt and the Gulf, but had emerged from the mystical, liberal ideals of Sufism.

'Well, the *Inqaz* [Islamist revolution] was never about religion, of course,' Nabil remarks when I put Salih's question to him. 'Turabi and al-Bashir cared only about power, and Muslims were their main victims.' Indeed, Turabi ultimately became a victim too

---

[78] For most Muslims, sharia law bears no relationship to the gruesome penalties often associated with the term in the West – penalties, indeed, that most Arab countries have declined to adopt – but is used primarily to decide family matters such as divorce, inheritance and child custody.

[79] Later rebranded the National Congress Party (NCP).

after the two former allies fell out, he says. 'Al-Bashir jailed him in 1999, and he never held power again.'

Now, thirty years on from al-Bashir's power-grab, Nabil has never been so busy. His pro bono cases include the unlawful closure of *Al Tayyar* newspaper and the detention of student protesters, among many others. 'How do you do it?' I ask, in awe of this brave, bespectacled man who's never had a day off in his life. 'Aren't you worried about the consequences?'

He smiles his sad, sage smile. 'Well, the regime knows harassing me looks bad for them,' he says. 'So generally they leave me alone.'

Two days later, Nabil's office is raided. Armed officers arrest several staff members and students, confiscate files and laptops, and force Nabil onto the floor at gunpoint. The incident is unprecedented and, although it's highly unlikely to be related to my visit, I can't help but recall John's warning when I arrived: *All foreigners are watched. It could cause problems for people you meet …*

In the future, I vow to be more careful. But I admit it's hard not to be caught up in the energy of this embattled city, where rumblings of revolution seem to grow louder by the day. Unlike Egypt, where the population appeared dazed and enervated by the ferocity of Sisi's counter-revolution, here the streets fizz with a gentle but persistent tenacity. Khartoum feels like a kettle on the boil, rattling on its base and whistling hopelessly for attention as the rest of the world looks away.

One evening at the Pickwick Club – the Establishment enclave of the Foreign and Commonwealth Office, which I had imagined as all musty chesterfields, pipe smoke and pith helmets, but which looks more like a cheap school canteen – Amjed mentions casually that he has just been released from jail. He was detained when he drove to meet some student protesters outside Khartoum University and pulled up in his car to find the police escorting the youngsters away. 'I said I was the boys' cousin, and I was told to accompany them to the station,' he says. 'I then had to wait there while they beat the students for nothing.'

At first he thought he'd be released quickly, but then friends started posting about his detention on Twitter. 'The officers caught wind of this, so they realised I'd lied. But luckily their boss had already left, so all they could do was beat me for a while with sticks and a metal wire.'

'Are you okay?' I ask, amazed by his nonchalance.

'Yes, it's normal,' he laughs. 'Though we should probably rethink our social media strategy.'

Amjed is a former doctor, as well as the co-founder of two of the main activist movements, Girifna and Sudan Change Now. Generally, he says, he gets treated well by the police because he is well-connected and has *wasta*. But others aren't so lucky. He tells me about a detained Darfuri student who was doused in sulphuric acid, before later 'disappearing' alongside his father when his story emerged in the press. 'They were probably killed or taken to Kober Prison,'[80] he says. 'We may never know.'

Nahid Gabrallah sits in the doorway sheathed in sweat and fanning herself. 'The electricity's out,' she explains apologetically. 'The office is a furnace!'

I am aware of the power-cut already, in fact. On the way here, my *amjad* almost ran into a moped, a minibus and an old lady in quick succession after veering through a series of intersections with no functioning traffic lights. The reason most cars in Khartoum are white, my driver had reassuringly informed me during this suicidal steeplechase, is so they can be easily repainted following collisions.

---

[80] Built by the British in 1903 and nicknamed 'the Fridge' for its ice-cold conditions, Kober Prison has become notorious for its detention and torture of political detainees. During his many periods of incarceration, Amjed says he has noticed the British company name 'Cell Security Ltd' on doors and windows, so I agree to contact the firm for comment. They 'did not build this facility', a spokesperson confirms, but did 'export some cell doors and windows to a client (not the Sudanese Government) in 2008'. When I pass this information onto Amjed, he is sceptical. 'Sudan doesn't have any private prisons,' he responds. 'The contract was clearly with the regime.'

'It'll be like this every other day throughout May,' Nahid says, leading me into the stiflingly toasty building. But the electricity is far from her biggest concern. Over a meal of homemade *asida* – a kind of jellified sorghum porridge doused in okra that tastes far better than it sounds – she explains how the government has declined to renew her NGO licence, cutting her revenue in half. 'They know our sponsors can't donate if we're unlicensed. We're being deliberately suffocated.'

It's a saddening state of affairs. Nahid's NGO fights for the rights of women and children, and is a lifeline for many survivors of sexual and physical violence who have nowhere else to go. The name of the organisation, Seema, is formed from the initials of victims of abuse to ensure their memory is kept alive, including two girls who died of FGM and a four-year-old who was raped and murdered.

'The laws here are very badly enforced,' Nahid says. 'Domestic abuse and FGM are huge problems. A third of girls are married before the age of eighteen. We've come far, but we have a big fight ahead.'

Nahid is a deeply impressive woman. Politically active from a young age, she became the first female secretary-general of the Khartoum University Student Union in 1985 and has been pushing for social reform ever since. 'Well, Sudanese women are known for their strength,' she says, smiling, when I voice admiration for her passion and commitment. Like Lina Atallah in Egypt, she exudes both a softness and steeliness I find compelling. 'We were one of the first Arab nations to have a female MP, in 1965, and we've been leading the way in women's rights ever since.'[81]

---

[81] Indeed, even after thirty years of Islamist repression, Sudan generally ranks far higher than the US in terms of its quota of female parliamentarians (before the 2019 revolution, when statistics for Sudan were suspended, it was ranked 58th in the world, compared to the US at 87th). Several Islamist countries consistently rank higher than the US, in fact, including Egypt and Somalia: a reminder of how easy it is to judge foreign cultures while remaining blinkered to similar problems at home.

After lunch, Nahid arranges a meeting with a woman with similarly inspiring credentials: Awadeya Mahmoud Koko, a once-impoverished *set al-shay* (tea-seller) and sexual assault survivor, who greets me at one of her sleek, modern teahouses in southern Khartoum with a wide, toothy grin. 'A few years ago, we were selling tea for 1p on the roadside and were constantly harassed by men and the police,' she tells me, speaking through an interpreter. Draped in a radiant *thobe* of emerald folds, she sits enthroned at the centre of the room with an undeniable air of majesty. 'Officers would confiscate our stuff and charge us to get it back. But now we can work in peace.'

Awadeya's idea that revolutionised the fortunes of the *set al-shay* was a simple one: a national workers' cooperative. The pooled resources gave security to tea-sellers across the country, many of whom were poor migrants from Darfur and the other conflict states. Awadeya herself spent her teenage years in an internally displaced person's camp in southern Khartoum after being forced to flee her drought-plagued village in South Kordofan during Sudan's first civil war. But this early hardship, it seems, only served to strengthen her resolve.

'I was married in my early twenties and started selling tea to support my family,' she says. 'I'd get up at 3am to fetch water and then walk or hitchhike to Omdurman to start work.' Her only clothing was a single *thobe*, she recalls which she also used as a blanket at night. 'We sat in the sun all day, with no breaks. It was very hard. Eventually, I knew something had to change.'

The cooperative evolved in stages. At first, people gave just a few *piastres* for emergencies, but gradually the kitty grew. Soon Awadeya was not just buying clothing and tea equipment but funding legal aid, business courses and computer workshops. Now, nearly three decades on, membership stands at tens of thousands – and Awadeya has become a global sensation. In 2016, she even received the prestigious International Women of Courage Award from John Kerry in the US.

However, she hasn't let the fame go to her head, she insists.

She's still as focused as ever. 'I want to educate my daughters so they don't have to be tea-sellers,' she says with resolve. 'I want a better life for them.'[82]

The ululations pierce the air, echoing like the cries of skittish hyenas across the lawn. *Al Tayyar* newspaper has just reopened following Nabil's successful court appeal and the female reporters are clearly delighted.

'We were silenced because we wrote that al-Bashir's brother was corrupt,' one of the group, Fatima Gazali, explains to me once the howls have died down. 'But we refuse to be intimidated.'

An alumnus of the pioneering Ahfad University for Women,[83] Fatima comes across as highly confident and driven. However, she admits her career hasn't been easy. She is frequently harassed by the authorities, and was even jailed for five days in 2011 after writing about a rape by a security guard. 'This job has many risks,' she says. 'But this just makes me more determined to go on.'

Few are more aware of the risks than *Al Tayyar* editor Osman Mirghani. Not long ago, after publishing a series of articles about corrupt officials, twenty armed men stormed his office and nearly beat him to death with sticks and rifles. He spent five days in hospital, then a further two months seeking treatment in Egypt, and he still suffers problems with his sight. 'Since then, the paper's been confiscated fifteen times,' he says grimly. 'It's getting difficult to pay my staff.' Yet he remains undeterred. 'To impose change is a struggle, but we have no choice but to try.'

One man who's been trying for longer than most is the

---

[82] Awadeya, it is no surprise to hear, went on to take a front-line role in the 2019 protests that toppled al-Bashir and became known by many as 'the mother of the revolution'.

[83] Ahfad University emerged from a secular girls' school founded in 1907 by the Mahdist soldier and activist Babiker Badri, who was twice denied permission to build the facility by the British before finally being granted consent for a mud-brick classroom with seventeen pupils. The school grew steadily, and in 1966 was converted by Badri's son into a university.

octogenarian media stalwart Mahjoub Mohamed Salih, who founded Sudan's second-oldest newspaper *Al Ayyam* in 1953 and remains its editor today. With his warm, weathered face, snowy white turban and memory that spans the epochs, he exudes an almost seraphic aura. 'I remember the Queen's coronation shortly before independence,' he tells me. 'The grandeur, the crowds ... It was like nothing I'd ever seen.'

In 2005, Mahjoub won the prestigious Golden Pen of Freedom award from the World Association of Newspapers, and he has long been revered as one of the most powerful independent voices in the Sudanese press. When he began his career, however, he says he didn't even consider journalism a real profession. 'Under colonialism, the press was just propaganda. My aim was just to express my ideas about how to free our country.' This writing earned him several stints in prison, he says, although he remained undeterred. 'By the late 1940s, we knew the British were planning to leave. But we feared the mess they'd leave behind, like in India and Palestine.'

'And did we leave a mess behind?' I ask.

'You did,' he replies, smiling. 'And we have created our own mess too.'

But the mess can be cleared up, he believes. 'With compromise and broad alliances. We must start again from scratch.'

As a young city, Khartoum is neither beautiful nor historical. There are few obvious 'sights' to explore: no Phoenician forts or Abbasid temples or relics of ancient munificence. The capital could be seen, in fact, as a manifestation of failed aspiration. It is *not* Dubai; it is *not* Cairo; it is *not* Riyadh, although there are suggestions – not least the suppository of a hotel known as 'Gaddafi's Egg', which resembles a tubby Burj Al Arab Jumeirah – that it harbours ambitions to be all three.

And yet, despite this, I find myself warming to the city. Unlike Dubai, it feels real; unlike Cairo, relaxed; unlike Riyadh, alive. There is suffering here, and anger, and a constant bashing of heads against a thousand brick walls. But there is also humour and resilience and resolve. For a nation more splintered than any I've known, the human bonds of connection feel astonishingly strong.

The contrast between the vitality of the people and the heavy hand of the state makes for an intriguing atmosphere. Khartoum is both calm and frenetic, both dead and aflame. Filled with the tertiary-educated elite and largely detached from the fierce battles raging beyond its walls, it has the aura of a garrison city – and yet the ramparts appear, with slow inevitability, to be crumbling.

'Yes, something is happening,' Khalid Omer Yousif, the deputy leader of the opposition Sudanese Congress Party, confirms when we meet at Ozone café, a popular expat haunt situated on a busy intersection in central Khartoum. 'We're seeing the largest student protests since 1994. Change is in the air.'

'But you've been protesting for decades,' I say. 'Why is this different?'

'There are some ticking time-bombs,' he replies. 'The power-cuts. The attacks on the newspapers and Nabil. The doctors, who don't even receive basic supplies. We're reaching breaking point.'

Later, at the Pickwick Club, John approaches me with a thin smile. 'How's things?' he asks. 'Busy stirring up revolution?'

'What do you mean?' I reply, perplexed.

'Your tweets. They've been doing the rounds.'

'Oh!' I know the ones he means. 'In a good or bad way?'

'Bad. People aren't happy.'

The tweets in question referenced the raid on Nabil's office, cited 'chaos' on the streets and stated that 'something seems to be brewing' in Khartoum. Such messages are unhelpful, John explains. 'What you say reflects on the whole diplomatic effort here, and pissing off the Sudanese government can mean huge losses in time, effort and taxpayer funding. A spur-of-the-moment tweet can set back talks by a year.'

He has a point. I haven't put in the time and legwork to justify undermining sensitive negotiations. Yet John's issue is not simply with my rushed 280-character epistle, it turns out, but with hot-headed journalists and activists more generally, who he believes 'can often do more harm than good' in their vocal attempts to achieve justice. 'The noisy approach can work well, rightly targeted, but in my experience it can often prove counter-productive,' he says. 'Take Darfur. The activists may have raised awareness and got the International Criminal Court (ICC) to open a case against al-Bashir,[84] but they pushed the regime into a corner, talks broke down and the hardliners gained power. It didn't solve the deep-seated problems.'

'But even you said the UN is just a life-support machine,' I say. 'Maybe it's time for a new approach?'

'Maybe,' he replies. 'But overall I see it as a force for good. In regions of Asia and South America, its development work has been so effective that it's hardly needed anymore.' In Sudan, parts of the UN are now more than 80 per cent local staff, he points out. 'In my book, that's a pretty good success story overall.'

Conspiracy theories brew easily in a city such as Khartoum, where rumours ripen like summer fruit and falsehoods take to the air like dust. One particularly unhinged friend-of-a-friend piles riotous conjecture on riotous conjecture like a mad scientist concocting chemically unsound experiments in the lab. 'The CIA are everywhere,' he tells me as we wait in the Foreign Ministry so he can bribe an amenable minister to expedite his British tourist visa. 'They're in cahoots with Mossad. They probably killed the student protesters in an attempt to unseat al-Bashir.' After all, they've done worse, he says. 'They killed Sadat in Egypt. They started the Arab Spring.'

'Wasn't Sadat killed by the Islamists?' I reply. 'Why would the US assassinate an ally who'd just made peace with Israel?'

'To make it *look* like the Islamists.'

'That makes no sense ...'

---

[84] In 2010, the ICC charged Omar al-Bashir with crimes against humanity, war crimes and genocide, but he is yet to be taken into custody to face trial.

'Of *course* it does. Open your mind!'

I don't try to argue. The CIA's meddling hand is a favoured theme of the Sudanese, and conversations like this can get a little tiresome. But in a region where Western intelligence services have indeed been interfering for some time, such suspicions can perhaps be forgiven.[85] In Sudan, the CIA has had a close but uneasy relationship with the country's Islamist leaders since the 1980s, when the US was sending millions of dollars a year in military aid, while turning a blind eye to the state's growing tolerance of extremism. The blowback to this policy was severe. In the early 1990s, it came to light that al-Bashir was providing a safe haven for Osama bin Laden and other terrorists, and in 1993 al-Qaeda-trained militiamen killed eighteen American soldiers in Somalia, triggering a series of bloody attacks that culminated in 9/11.

'Look, I know the West has got up to some nasty tricks,' I say. 'But we're hardly unique in that.'

---

[85] This book lacks the scope to cover the extensive CIA shenanigans in the Middle East over the past seventy-five years, which have involved Syria, Iran, Iraq, Egypt, Sudan, Pakistan and more. But a note on the largest operation of all – Afghanistan – may give some indication of the enduring impact of such intervention across the region. For the first few decades of its existence, the CIA's main objective was defeating Soviet Russia, and all manner of unsavoury partners were cultivated in order to achieve this aim – including, most controversially, jihadist groups. In Kabul, the CIA was so desperate to oust the communist administration, which was doing such ungodly things as tackling inequality and building schools, that it threw its weight behind the local mujahideen militias. Vast sums were spent on cultivating the support of fanatical groups known for their savagery (including acid attacks and skinning people alive), and on the promotion of pro-jihadist USAID campaigns that promised children a place in Heaven if they 'plucked out the eyes of the Soviet enemy'. Soon militants began flocking into Afghanistan from across the Arab world, including an ambitious young chap named Osama bin Laden, and in 1992 the communists finally fell. Unfortunately, the nation then fractured into an internecine mess of tribal factions, giving rise to the Taliban and the chaotic mess that persists in the country today. 'What's more important in world history?' the former US national security adviser Zbigniew Brzezinski asked in 1999, starkly blind to the impending catastrophe of 9/11. 'Some agitated Muslims or the liberation of Central Europe and the end of the Cold War ... ?'

'Yes, of course,' he replies. 'But what's annoying is the *attitude*. You guys think you're the saviours of the world, when really that's just bullshit.'

'We're hypocrites?'

'Yes! That's the word.' He grins. 'You're all great big *hypocrites*.'

My flight is late, of course. 11pm passes ... then midnight ... then 1am ... The air murmurs with the sleepy restlessness unique to waiting rooms. Should I be leaving, I wonder? The soft thrum of the capital continues to beat in my mind like a distant call to arms. Could revolution really be looming? I'm hopeful, but doubtful. Unrest has been simmering for years, rising and falling with the seasons. Is anything truly likely to change now?

I am unaware that, soon, desperation will become unsustainable. I am unaware that the crowds will swell, dozens will die and the barricades will fall. I am unaware that, after thirty long years in power, the ageing tyrant that has ravaged this country so grievously will finally, triumphantly, be dethroned.

I am unaware that, after a brief spell of fragile, fractious democracy, the military will reclaim power once more.[86]

I know none of this. But I know the energy of the city, the vigour of the people, the courage on the streets. All suggest a country on the move, where injustice at the hands of the outmoded elite will no longer be tolerated. Something is brewing here, in this rainbow land of white, red, green and black, and everything in between: something momentous and thrilling and new. Perhaps they will succeed next time ... perhaps not. But what I know for certain is that they will never stop trying until they do.

---

[86] Shortly before this book went to press, on 25 October 2021, General Abdel Fattah al-Burhan overthrew the transitional government in a military coup, leaving the country's fate in the hands of the army, the Rapid Support Forces, a large band of mercenaries and old corporate cronies from the al-Bashir regime.

Chapter 8

BRAVE NEW WORLD

Oman

'But I don't want comfort. I want God, I want poetry, I want real danger, I want freedom, I want goodness. I want sin.'
Aldous Huxley, *Brave New World* (1932)

The plane stops unexpectedly in Riyadh to collect a new flight crew. It is a frustrating detour, though part of me is pleased to at least make contact with this mineral-rich titan of the Arab world. My original aim was to travel from Port Sudan to Jeddah by boat, but – much like Ibn Battuta, who trekked for two months from Cairo to the Red Sea, only to be prevented at the last moment from making the crossing – my plan was foiled. Unlike Battuta, however, this was not the result of a cranky Beja chief sinking all the ships over a tribal territorial dispute, but due to the rather more prosaic reason that the Saudis neither issue tourist visas nor permit women to cycle without a male guide. So, short of masquerading as a Bedouin sheikh and sneaking in as a stowaway – channelling the eccentric and wonderful Lady Hester Stanhope, perhaps, who spent much of her time in the

Middle East disguised in a male *thobe* and *keffiyeh*[87] – my journey across the sweeping sandflats of central Arabia will have to wait for another time.

When we finally touch down, Muscat instantly blinds me with its space-age sheen. The airport is pure gloss, and everything feels simple, convenient, clean. Buying my visa is easy; retrieving my luggage is easy; locating Hamed, my host, is easy. After the dusty dysfunctionality of Sudan, there is something almost sharp and acerbic about this ease, like the cloying scent of fresh paint.

Hamed is slight and awkward and drives a white SUV. As we exit the airport through a confounding cat's cradle of looping roadways, he throws out bullet points of information about Oman. It is liberal and tolerant, he says, with free healthcare and schooling. There's no income or property tax. Everyone loves the Sultan, who is currently the longest-serving ruler in the Middle East.

'I don't think he's gay,' he remarks, unprompted. I assume some people think he is. 'He doesn't have a wife or children, but that's probably because he deposed his father and doesn't want the same thing happening to him.'

The threat of patricide, I agree, could indeed prove a passion-killer. But before I have time to respond, we are already pulling up at Hamed's home. Here, the laundry-fresh ambiance of the city continues, and in the gleaming mirrored lift, I recoil at my reflection as if winded. The figure staring back seems shockingly sturdy, like a saddle or old shoe. Peering at it closely, as a *homo*

---

[87] Famed for her journeys across Turkey and the Arab world in the early 1800s, Lady Hester Stanhope, the niece of William Pitt the Younger, was one of the greatest explorers of all time. Her travels – which she undertook chiefly for the fun of it – were rife with peril and derring-do, and included shipwrecks, the discovery of buried treasure and the contracting of various deadly diseases (including the plague). The end of her life was far from happy, however, and she spent her final few years living as a poverty-stricken recluse in the Lebanese mountains, writing angry letters to Queen Victoria and raining invective on Britain, which she believed had 'made her accursed gold the counterpoise to justice'.

habilis might examine their face in a rockpool for the first time, I feel wonder that I was permitted entry to the country at all.

A bigger shock is forthcoming, however. After unpacking Maud in Hamed's living room, I discover that her derailleur hanger[88] has broken in transit: a tiny injury, but a potentially catastrophic one. I am carrying no spare and have only ten days to reach Iran before my visa window expires. There is no leeway in my schedule for delays.

A swift recce to Muscat's two main bike shops proves fruitless, so in a panic I contact Kona. To my delight and relief, they kindly agree to courier a new one from California – but the earliest it will arrive is a week. A *week*, by god!

Suddenly time is looking tight. And I am a prisoner in this city.

Now a bicycle short, I put a call-out on Warmshowers.org to find one to borrow. Three are offered: a single-speed with broken brakes, a foldable bike that doesn't fold and a steel monstrosity the size and weight of a combine harvester. Each seems certain to kill me on Muscat's cosmic superhighways in its own unique way, so the choice comes down to which seems likely to keep me alive the longest. After some deliberation, I punt for the third.

When I see it, I regret my decision immediately. The chain is loose, the gears rusty and the frame as plump as my forearm. It also has two flat tyres.

'I'll take it,' I say, lifting it with some difficulty from the man's car boot. '*Shukran*.'

He looks hesitant. 'Are you sure? It's not very good. I don't think it's even rideable.'

'Absolutely,' I smile. I'm not sure at all. 'It's perfect.'

After pumping up the tyres, I venture out for a test ride.

---

[88] For those who may not know (like me before this trip), a derailleur hanger is a vital component that connects the derailleur (the device that moves the chain between the sprockets) to the bike frame. In a collision, it is designed to break in order to prevent damage to the frame itself.

Moving with all the speed and agility of an army cruiser tank, I lumber through Muscat's sprawling network of eight-lane motorways and kamikaze intersections as Mercedes and souped-up SUVs – all, without fail, a sparkling, spotless white[89] – whip, bullet-like, by my side. As I cycle, I am struck by all the Sultan has achieved since he assumed power here fifty years ago. In the 1960s, under *de facto* British rule, this sequestered corner of the Arabian peninsula was in a deeply primitive state, boasting just one hospital, three schools and a 5 per cent literacy rate. One in four babies died before their first birthday, while decadent pursuits such as football, cycling and wearing sunglasses were banned. Order was maintained by the tyrannical Sultan Said bin Taimur through torture, executions and imprisonment in dungeon-like cells.

Today, Muscat is unrecognisable. It is not just the cars that are white, I realise, but everything: the buildings, the décor, the clothes. Everywhere I go, the city radiates a pearlescent, fairytale sheen. Oil has clearly made its mark here, though not with the brash fanfare and phallic swagger of other Gulf states, but with a modest, understated stealth.

Struck by its sumptuous beauty, I stop for a rest at the Grand Mosque. Constructed from snowy Indian sandstone, the building feels both serenely unpretentious and arresting in its grandeur. A vast complex of arched corridors and sweeping courtyards provides an overwhelming sense of space, while each opaline surface displays both a simplicity of form and a startling detail of artistry. In the colossal prayer hall, the world's second-largest chandelier hangs above the world's second-largest hand-loomed carpet, and it is no surprise to hear that it was the UAE – a country whose macho insecurities will never allow for second-best – that stole Oman's crown on both fronts.

As British meddling goes, the decision to unseat Sultan Said in favour of his son in 1970 was arguably one of our more forgivable

---

[89] It is – astonishingly – illegal to have a dirty car in Oman.

intrusions – even if the main reason for doing so, as outlined in a Foreign and Commonwealth Office memo accidentally released in 2005, was not so much the dismal state of the nation at the time as the worrying prospect of losing a secret war being fought in Dhofar that jeopardised our access to Omani oil and military bases. It was, without doubt, a risky move. At the time, twenty-nine-year-old Qaboos was living under virtual house arrest at the palace after returning from a period of study and work experience in Britain, and had almost no political experience. The coup must therefore have come as quite a shock to many Omanis – not to mention to his fellow town council interns in Ipswich, who were no doubt somewhat taken aback to open their newspapers one day to images of their enigmatic former colleague being saluted by a trumpeting guard of honour as his father was hustled away at gunpoint.

But the gamble paid off. While his father slowly expired in London's Dorchester Hotel, Qaboos began rebuilding the country from scratch. He banned slavery, released political prisoners, built schools and hospitals, and supported women's rights.[90] Most importantly, he repaired diplomatic relations across the region and achieved UN recognition for Oman as a member state.

'We owe the Sultan so much,' the woman tells me. 'He has made Oman peaceful and safe.' A religious teacher whose job it is to inform mosque visitors about Ibadism,[91] she ushers me to sit on the bench beside her. 'He is a true Ibadi – a unifier. He funds many Catholic, Protestant and Hindu places of worship, as well as mosques. He is very openminded. Very fair.'

The Sultan is also devoted to classical music, literature and the environment, the woman continues. Whereas other Arab

---

[90] In 1994, Oman became the first Gulf country to grant women the vote – though there remains a long way to go here.

[91] Ibadism, named after Abdullah bin Ibadh, is a moderate branch of Islam separate from both Sunnism and Shiism, which opposes dynastic succession and supports the free election of an imam who combines religious and political leadership. Ibadism emerged in Oman in the eighth century CE, and stuck.

countries have morality police to stop people having fun, Oman has pollution police to prevent people dropping litter.

'Before Sultan Qaboos, Oman was divided,' she says. 'It even had two names: Muscat for the coast and Oman for the *Dakhiliyah* [interior]. Now we're united. We're happy.'

'You're rich?' I ask.

She smiles. 'That has helped too, of course. But for Ibadis, richness of the spirit is the most important thing.'

Cleaved down the centre by the craggy Al-Hajar peaks, Oman has always been a land of two halves. However, it wasn't until the 1600s, as Muscat sailors learnt how to harness the monsoon winds and take control of east–west trade, that longstanding tensions began to escalate. For the traditional tribes of the interior, the coastal mercantilists were seen as avaricious heathens who had turned their back on Ibadism's spiritual ideals, while the merchants, for their part, saw the people of the *Dakhiliyah* as little more than primitive, insular fanatics with little understanding of the modern world.

Conflict inevitably ensued, followed by an uneasy peace. It was a ship owner named Ahmad bin Said al-Busaidi who, in 1749, succeeded in bringing the two regions together; however, while his leadership was accepted by the *Dakhiliyah*, that of his hereditary successors was not. The result was a fragile dual system of governorship in which a dynastic sultan ruled over Muscat, while a rival imam was elected to the interior. In the meantime, buoyed by British patronage, the power of the coast continued to grow, expanding its rule beyond the Persian Gulf to areas of East Africa and Iran.

'We love Britain!' the young man exclaims. 'You're our very good friends.'

I'm sitting outside a small, grubby café gorging on a *shawarma* wrap slathered in garlic paste. Three brothers sit opposite me, their variety of dress epitomising Oman's heterogeneous, multi-layered identity. One wears a cotton shirt and jeans, another a tight black t-shirt and *à la mode* flat cap, the third a white *thobe* (or *dishdasha*, as it's known here) and skullcap. All are in their twenties, and all boast a dusting of designer facial hair.

'What do you love about it?' I ask.

'Everything,' the man in the flat cap replies. His name, wonderfully, is 'Blessed Star' – or 'Bstar' for short. 'The history. The buses. The Queen …'

'The books,' the brother in the jeans interjects. He was 'amazed' when he visited Europe and heard people discussing novels, he says. 'Here, hardly anybody reads.'

We finish our *shawarmas* and Bstar gestures that it's time to leave. He likes the girl in the travel agency and wants me to deliver a gift he bought for her in Dubai: a glass paperweight containing a mini Burj Khalifa. He doesn't want to give it to her himself, he says, in case she turns it down.

At the agency, I take the present inside as promised. Two minutes later, I return with good news. 'She was delighted!' I tell him. 'I think she likes you.'

He lights up. 'Oh good! One day I hope to take her there. Dubai is a very special place for me.'

'Really, you think so?' The words come out before I can stop them, and instantly I regret their tone. The condescension is palpable.

'You don't.' He smiles. 'That's okay. Europeans will never understand the appeal of Dubai to Arabs. You're a developed place, but we had nothing for years. We didn't even have cafés until fifteen years ago. To us, Dubai is a sign of progress.'

I nod, and I feel bad for judging. Not just about Dubai but Bstar too, and all the other young 'trendies' I've met in Muscat so far. Clad in their Gucci shades and voguish apparel, with little apparent interest in culture or the arts, they've struck me as vulgar and shallow. But I take his point. It is only when you have easy access to material pleasures that they begin to lose their sheen.

'I'm sorry,' I say. 'Any girl would be lucky to visit Dubai with you.'

'You think?' He grins. Beneath his spray-on clothes and bulging body-builder physique, he is a sweet boy, childlike and earnest. His heart has been broken many times, he explains, and he's now on the lookout for a wife. 'Soon, I hope to take her number. And then, if her family agree, maybe we can meet.'

'And if they don't agree?'

'Then we can only speak by phone until we're engaged.' He laughs at my surprised expression. I somehow imagined Oman more liberal than this. 'That's good! Many Omani couples don't even meet until the wedding. My cousin didn't speak to his wife before they got married, and she didn't get any say in it at all.'

'That sounds very unfair on her.'

'Yes. But they're happy now. My cousin treats her well.'

I ask if women are generally treated well in Oman, and he nods. 'They have equal rights to men.'

'Except in marriage.'

He considers. 'Well, yes … I guess.'

'And in work? Do they have good, high-powered jobs, like men?'

'Um …' He thinks for a moment. 'Actually no. Not really.'

'And relationships? You say you've had sex, but it sounds like a single woman couldn't do that?'

He looks shocked by the suggestion. 'No! That would be very bad for her.'

'So …' I say. 'Maybe not completely equal then?'

He looks puzzled, and a little perturbed. 'I guess maybe not completely, no …'

We return to the brothers' flat. Their neighbourhood is noticeably poorer than Hamed's, with narrower, darker alleyways and scattered drifts of litter. Beside their block is a row of shops containing an electrics store, curry house and pharmacy, all staffed by Indians and Bangladeshis. Inside, the apartment is designed like a youth hostel, with colourful shell mosaics and abstract wooden montages splashed jauntily across the walls. I am given a large room to myself, and it isn't until I leave that I realise the brothers all sleep together in a single cramped bedroom at the back, squeezed into a messy crush of unmade bunkbeds, overflowing wastebins and mounds of dirty laundry.

Today is a Monday and, as Bstar helps me settle in, I ask why he's not at work. 'The company I worked for in Doha went bust,' he says. 'So now I'm trying to set up on my own.'

His plan, he explains, is to become a life coach and improve the work ethic of 'lazy' Omanis. He spent his early twenties slogging through a series of menial jobs before securing his dream role as a hotel manager, and he hopes to use his story to inspire and motivate others. 'I want to show people that if you try hard enough, anything is achievable.'

Taking Bstar's words to heart, I make a decision. I am going to attempt to cycle up Oman's highest mountain, Jebel Shams. I'm now as fit as I'll ever be, I reason, and I'm unlikely to have the opportunity again. It will also give me an excuse to escape Muscat and visit the Hajar mountain range, which stands as both a geological and political symbol of division across this fractured land.

Even my chief motivator, however, seems unsure about the idea. 'It's very steep,' he says doubtfully. 'I'm not even sure cycling is allowed.'

'Allowed? You think I care about what's *allowed*?' I shake my head and chuckle, bemused by the naivete of this fledgling young innocent. 'Bstar, take my advice: never do what's *allowed*. Cut those chains! Break that leash! The best adventures are the forbidden ones!!'

Cycling up Jebel Shams is not allowed, it turns out. Officially you need a 4×4. But this is a moot point anyway, as my death-trap bicycle collapses before I even begin.

'This wasn't a great idea,' Ryan, my Couchsurfing host, says as he examines my two flaccid tyres. It is just 4am, but he has kindly woken up to see me off on my heroic ascent.

'No,' I agree. Like my tyres, I feel deflated. 'It wasn't.'

We both stare at the bike. The tyres were definitely full of air before I went to bed. Perhaps if we look at them a little longer, I consider, they may revive to their former fleshy glory.

A few minutes go by.

'There definitely isn't a puncture?' Ryan asks, finally.

'No.' I checked the inner tubes last night. 'Not that I could see.'

We both continue to stare.

'Hmmm.' He squeezes the doughy rubber like a doctor taking the pulse of a dying patient. 'Well, it doesn't look good. Do you have a plan B?'

I confess that I don't. What self-respecting adventure *cognoscenti* does, after all? 'Just this one.'

The clock strikes 4.30am, and I am just reconciling myself to the miserable idea of returning to bed and having a long, leisurely lie in when Ryan suddenly turns to me with a look of inspiration. 'I know,' he declares. 'You should hike up Jebel Akhdar!' Shams is dull and inhospitable anyway, he explains, while Akhdar is just as steep and almost as high, and comes ornamented with wadis, pastureland and splashes of Damask rose. 'I can drop you off at the bottom if you like?'

'Great idea!' I say, forcing a smile. 'Thank you so much.'

An hour later, rucksack and tent strapped to my back and a bag of dates clutched in my hand, I begin my climb. Immediately, it's clear why only 4×4s are permitted to make this ascent. The road heaves itself up the mountainside in a contortion of corkscrew twists and turns, and is agonisingly steep from the start. Cycling would certainly have been impossible (for me, at least), and even on foot the gradient quickly starts to take its toll. But I am determined not to give up. Thesiger was fascinated by this 'unattainable' mountain, which he was prohibited from climbing by the local sheikh, and I admit that there is something quietly satisfying about succeeding where this dauntless adventurer failed. I share his perplexity, however, at the 'singularly inappropriate' name. Jebel Akhdar, or 'Green Mountain', is a misnomer; there is little green here, just swatches of scrubland amid a sea of mottled-brown. The hillsides are dun-brown, the road tar-brown, the foliage chestnut-brown. Meanwhile, erupting with sporadic zeal from the murk is the occasional alarmist flash of crimson hollering 'DANGER: Steep Gradient!'

The climb is tough. Why I only brought water and dates with me, I'm unsure. For the same reason I only brought a bike with flat tyres, I presume. Because I'm an ass. I don't even like dates; they're sticky and sickly and do unmentionable things to one's viscera when one least expects it. But, with no other sustenance available, I doggedly gnaw my way through them, waiting for the transformation of sugar to kinetic energy like the conversion of fuel in a combustion engine.

By 1pm, the heat becomes unbearable. My back aches, my legs throb and my eyes, sore with sweat and sleeplessness, struggle to stay open. But there is no shade in which to rest, so I continue trudging on … and eventually, to my relief, both the heat and landscape begin to soften. The bracken expands into flowering shrubs and terraced groves of olives, pomegranates and apricots, while the relentless expanse of swamp-brown separates into a delicate striation of pinks, yellows and reds. As I walk, dragonflies the size of birds murmur about my ears and freckled geckos skitter friskily across my path. The mountain is, at last, evolving into the verdant oasis its euphemistic name implies.

By mid-afternoon, the ground finally levels off and I emerge into an odd little tourist resort complete with playground, café and ice-white gazebos. This trite pocket of civilisation comes as something of a disappointment, I admit, and is far from the lush, untamed wilderness of my imagination. At the same time, the smell of beef burgers on the barbecue fills my heart with a joy so profound that I struggle to put it into words.

'One?' the chef asks, flipping the patties over in a pool of gloriously bubbling fat.

'Three, please. With extra cheese.'

I am just ordering my fourth when a Hyundai truck pulls up

nearby. '*Salam*,' a shaggy moustache announces from the driver's seat. 'You are visitor here?'

The moustache is just a front, I realise on closer inspection. Behind it is a plump, shiny pate and sweat-slicked brow. And behind the pate and brow are three wide-eyed children slathering themselves in chocolate-chip ice cream. 'Yes,' I say. 'Just exploring.'

'Ah!' he says. 'This my town. I show you!'

Minutes later, I am being whisked on a shotgun tour of the vicinity. Our first stop is a plunging precipice, where the man – Ahmed – points out tiny villages encrusted like limpets on the limestone ridges below. Tawny and flat-roofed, the buildings are distinguishable only by their sharpness of line from the folds of rock on which they perch. 'Empty now,' Ahmed tells me. 'People gone.'

Ahmed works for the Defence Ministry and has lived up here for three years. He speaks in breathy, truncated spurts, but I pick up the gist of what he says. Until fairly recently, the only way to reach these isolated clifftop villages was by donkey, he explains, and the *jebelis* (mountain people) were largely cut off from the world below. But after the road was laid a decade ago, everything changed; development erupted and a whole new micro-economy emerged. We drive past banks, a school, a police station and several state ministries, while further up the mountain, he tells me, a new ultra-luxury hotel has been built that boasts £1,000-a-night rooms.

'Before, all this very difficult, very far,' Ahmed says, handing me a thermos of saffron coffee as we pull up outside his square, white home. 'But now, you see. All is beauty.'

Britain is well aware how very difficult and far it used to be up here, in fact. Because, from 1954 to 1959, we were fighting a war right on this spot, trying with limited success to subdue an army of *jebeli* insurgents. SAS troops, two infantry companies and a squadron of armoured tanks all struggled to defeat the rebel militias, who engaged in an artful strategy of ambush, vandalism and sabotage. Sultan Said had recently ventured into the hostile territory of the *Dakhiliyah* alongside a caravan of armed *askaris*, turbaned dignitaries and Iraq Petroleum Company (IPC)[92] prospectors in order to seize the land (and oil) for himself – but the *jebelis* were determined to do everything in their power to stop him in his tracks.

It took the full force of the RAF to end the fight. Over a thousand tonnes of bombs were dropped on villages, crops and livestock, destroying the enemy's supply lines and killing vast numbers of civilians. The civilian attacks were deliberate, according to now-declassified files from the British National Archives, and by the end of the conflict around half the mountain homes lay in ruins. Afterwards, the UN didn't mince its words. 'Had it not been for the possibility of oil being discovered in the interior,' it asserted bluntly, 'the action taken by Britain might well have been less drastic and much damage, destruction, human suffering and loss of life might have been avoided.' The UN General Assembly went on to demand that the UK withdraw from Oman, halt its oppression of civilians and accept the country's right to self-determination.

The calls, predictably, fell on deaf ears. Britain may have recognised Oman as a fully independent state in 1951, but it remained a *de facto* British colony in everything but name – and Britain had no intention of letting it go. Oil had been discovered in the newly formed Kingdom of Saudi Arabia in 1938, and the Saudis had snubbed the old imperialists to grant a concession to the Standard Oil Company of California (now Chevron). By 1954, Britain's share of regional oil production was half what it had been in 1939, while America's quota had quintupled.

---

[92] A Western oil consortium, founded in 1925 as the Turkish Petroleum Company, jointly owned by a group of European and American oil giants, including the Anglo-Iranian Oil Company (now BP) and Royal Dutch Shell.

The pressure was therefore on to find oil in the *Dakhiliyah* – and, after years of fruitless searching, the Sultan's bolshy venture paid off. In 1962, prospectors hit the jackpot, and IPC profits soared.

Meanwhile, the Omani people continued to suffer. Under the indifferent gaze of his British advisors, Sultan Said grew more reclusive and despotic, and eventually abandoned Muscat altogether to hole up in Salalah, the capital of Dhofar governorate in the far south-west. It was not, perhaps, the wisest of moves. Once a rich trading post where pearls of frankincense were sourced from papery-barked trees to perfume the tombs of pharaohs, Dhofar was now little more than a neglected, impoverished powder-keg of unrest – and it wasn't long before the local people erupted in revolt.

At first, the rebels' grievances were parochial: to rid themselves of the double subjugation of Muscat and Britain, and assert their right to autonomous rule. Running on a ticket of social justice and equality, they built roads, schools and hospitals, banned slavery and polygamy, and gave generous subsidies to the poor. Soon, however, their ambition grew, and – supported by communist regimes in China, Saudi Arabia, the USSR and Yemen – they began mobilising support for socialist revolution across the region.

It was the situation Britain most feared: its own potential Vietnam. If Oman fell to Marxist forces, the rest of the region could fall too, they reasoned, handing Gulf oil – and Cold War victory – to the East.

Panicking, Britain didn't hold back. Employing the same tactics as they had in Jebel Akhdar, civilians were massacred, homes destroyed and pamphlets distributed promising to restore men's right to marry multiple women if they surrendered to the Sultan's rule. As many as 8,000 civilians may have died in the assault, according to investigative journalist Ian Cobain. This 'strategically vital war', he writes in his book *The History Thieves,* was one of the most ruthless and 'politically repugnant' on record.

The conflict lasted thirteen years, from 1963 to 1976. Throughout that time, however, the British public remained none the wiser. As the first media reports from Vietnam began to emerge, the Gulf remained cloaked in darkness. No reporters were allowed in and no information out. The Foreign and Commonwealth Office denied involvement, and Harold Wilson's 1971 book about his time in government makes no mention of it. Even when an occasional headline did appear, the details were strikingly sparse. 'Is the British government, like the Americans in Laos, waging a secret war without the full knowledge of parliament and public?' the *Observer* casually enquired in 1972. But the question hung in the air, rhetorical and unresolved, echoing soundlessly into the void.

After an uncomfortable night camping on the thorny Saiq Plateau, I hitchhike back to Ryan's flat. The process is smooth and seamless, as I've come to expect in Oman, and I am scooped up by a shiny 4×4 at the base of the mountain almost as soon as a lorry driver drops me off.

When I climb in, I see a Filipino woman already seated in the back. 'I do this almost every day,' she explains when I ask. 'It's cheaper than the bus.'

This neat divide – Omanis in their air-conditioned SUVs, immigrants carless by the wayside – feels almost figurative in its clarity. Since the 1970s, nationals from South Asia and the Philippines, as well as poorer Arab countries such as Egypt, Jordan and Sudan, have poured into Oman, nearly doubling the population and providing around three-quarters of the workforce. Reflecting trends across the Gulf, these migrants have become the cogs and wheels of this well-oiled machine, while the locals have reaped the rewards.

The woman tells me she works as a housekeeper in Nizwa. 'I get up at 5am and work thirteen hours without a break,' she says. 'But I can't complain. I am treated well.'

Thirteen hours without a break sounds like an excellent reason to complain to me, and I say so. She laughs. 'They have my passport, so I cannot. And I might end up somewhere worse.' She recounts some horrifying stories. A Bangladeshi woman beaten regularly with wire coat hangers. An Ethiopian woman raped for burning a shirt while ironing. 'You can complain, but the police won't help. They're always on the employers' side.'

I have written in the past about the exploitative *kafala* (work sponsorship) system employed throughout the Gulf, but hearing the woman speak about it directly, and so nonchalantly, still shocks me. I glance at the driver, intrigued by his reaction to these damning reports of his countrymen. His mouth is set in a grim line. 'It's true,' he says. 'Migrants are treated badly. My parents constantly shout at their cleaner for not working hard, but the house is always spotless.'

Ryan is a migrant too, having arrived here from Tehran several years ago, but he is a different category of expat. As a teacher, he receives excellent pay and benefits, and even a subsidised flat.

'It seems very unfair,' I say, as he welcomes me back with a delicious Persian banquet of *khoresh-e ghormeh sabzi* (lamb and bean stew). It turns out, to my delight, that he used to be a chef. 'Locals take it easy, while the foreigners do the work.'

'True. It's getting better, but slowly.'

'Seems like the Omanis have really nailed it.'

He smiles. 'In a way. Though actually they have their problems too.' There is severe corruption here for a start, he points out. 'If you know the right people, it's great. But not everyone does. I see this at work all the time. Wealthy students expect to get good grades without any effort, and it makes it very difficult for the rest.'

Anger at corruption was one of the key issues that sparked the 2011 unrest, in fact, along with frustration at price rises and unemployment, and a desire for greater social and political freedoms. While nobody was demanding the overthrow of Qaboos, only the most blinkered of votaries could have believed he was exempt from accountability. Indeed, a series of secret US diplomatic cables leaked in 2009 exposed the extent of patronage networks in Oman, stating that the private sector was little more than an oligopoly run by a clique of families with 'ties to the Sultan', who 'parlayed their privileged position and government ties into new business opportunities'.

'If things were so bad, why didn't the protests spread?' I ask.

'The Sultan was clever. He ditched a third of his cabinet, arrested a load of officials for bribery, brought in some reforms and created a ton of new jobs.' He pardoned the protesters too, Ryan adds, which helped to placate the crowds. 'That's part of Ibadi culture I admire, actually: the idea of compromise. You see it in the Sultan's foreign policy too. He's one of the few world rulers who's managed to stay on good terms with both Iran and the West. He's very practical.'

'Practical? Or lacking in principle?'

'You think any countries work on principle?' He grins. 'Come on.'

Even democracy isn't necessarily a principle to be encouraged, he believes. 'Look at Lebanon and India! A mess. Democracy means nothing when leaders are so corrupt. Here, there are no political parties, so they don't squabble in the same way. Everything is done by *shura* [consensus].'

My mind wanders to the Persian traveller Mirza Abu Taleb Khan, who visited England in the late 1700s and characterised the sitting of Parliament as like 'two flocks of Indian parakeets, sitting upon opposite mango trees scolding at each other' – a description familiar to anyone who has ever watched Prime Minister's Question Time, I imagine.

'You know,' I say musingly, as Ryan heaps another behemoth of *tahdig* (caramelised rice) onto my plate, 'you may well be on to something there.'

Maud is fixed!

I can hardly contain my joy. In recent days, with my window to enter Iran narrowing by the hour, I'd begun to wonder if my venture was destined to fail at the final hurdle. But all is well, thank goodness. All is *more* than well, in fact, because not only have the wonderful men at Oman Bicycle Shop reattached Maud's derailleur hanger – which arrived in the nick of time – but also repaired her luggage racks, rejigged her gears and scrubbed her metalwork from head to toe. Looking at her now, all spotless and gleaming and robust, I can't help but wish my own warts and flaws could be ironed out so easily.

'I can't thank you enough,' I say. 'How much do I owe?'

'Nothing!' the man replies. 'It was our pleasure.'

As ever, I am bowled over by the kindness here. I protest weakly, but he is adamant. 'We're trying to promote cycling in Oman,' he says. 'So please just tell people about us.'

With the clock ticking, I must leave Muscat immediately – and I am very happy to do so. During the last few days, I admit I've felt a restless urge to depart this city and its ubiquitous utopic sheen. Its bleached environment may project an aura of peace and equanimity, but for me it suggests, just as clearly, a sense of control and soulless apathy. Where is the life, the colour, the clutter? There is something curiously contrived about Muscat, I feel, as if the whole city were a museum exhibit curated by Qaboos. Even the traditional clothing was mandated by royal decree in 1970, it turns out, when a new national dress was introduced to harmonise the diverse regional styles of the past. Viewed through this lens, Omani identity becomes less an organic blend of the old and the new, and more an imposed homogeny designed to keep personal impulses in check.

While Qaboos has gradually opened Oman up over the years, the pace of change has been slow. At the time of my visit, he is gravely ill with colon cancer and looks set to pass away before any meaningful reforms have been introduced.[93] In the

---

[93] Sultan Qaboos died in January 2020. He was succeeded by Haitham bin Tariq, an Oxford University graduate who previously served as Minister of Heritage and Culture.

meantime, domestic woes such as youth joblessness, inequality and soaring debt remain serious concerns. Most worryingly, as oil revenue continues to dry up, there are signs Oman may fall prey to the same fiscal forces that have ravaged the rest of the region. Launched in 2019 with the aim of diversifying the economy, 'Oman Vision 2040' advocates the privatisation of public services, the reduction of subsidies and the introduction of new corporate tax incentives: all policies that, in a monocracy, have the potential to compound corruption and inequality further.

In such a climate, the equilibrium Oman has enjoyed for so long may finally begin to fracture. Perhaps this will rally people to the streets once more, banging the drum for change – although (in the near future, at least) this seems unlikely to me. A kind of inertia here is palpable, as if everyone has been feeding on the soporific lotus flowers of Greek legend. Political liberties will happily be foregone, it appears, as long as an acceptable level of security and comfort can be retained.

How I would react in such a situation, I'm unsure. As someone fortunate to have grown up with both security and freedom, it is not a dilemma I've ever had to face. But without liberty – personal, political, social, spiritual – I do feel that much of the beauty and purpose of the world is lost. 'But I don't want comfort,' the Savage cries in Aldous Huxley's *Brave New World*. 'I want God, I want poetry, I want real danger, I want freedom, I want goodness. I want sin.'

We are all savages at heart, I feel. But sometimes, weighed down by finery, we forget.

The Gulf coast has long been a hot place. In 1442, a Persian visitor reportedly lamented that the gems in his dagger had been reduced to coal, while the desert was full of 'dead, roasted gazelle'. Little has changed in the half-millennium since, it appears. On the air-conditioned bus to Dubai, I have the luxury of avoiding the worst of the midday sun. But Maud, trapped in the hold, is less fortunate. By the time we arrive, her tyres are both pancake-flat and her saddle is scorching to the touch. My thermometer, trapped with her, reads 69°C.

My first task in Dubai is locating the ferry ticket office. After leaving Maud at a hotel, I venture out to discover a world on high volume. Everything cries hyperbole, from the futuristic high-rises to the runway-wide roads to the burning white-blue sky that radiates waves of damp heat. There is none of Oman's temperance or tact here. Dubai is Muscat on amphetamines: neurotic, red-blooded and desperate to be heard.

Acting as a counterpoint to this dizzying spectacle, however, is the Dubai Creek. Sweeping crescent-shaped through the sheikhdom, carving off the centre from the sandy plains beyond, this shallow waterway softens the edges of its sharp, clamorous surrounds. Particularly charming are the traditional wooden *abras* that transport passengers and goods from shore to shore – all for a startlingly modest 20p a ride – and which seem to me a far more civilised form of travel than the suffocatingly jampacked metro underground.

Eventually, several *abras* later, I track down the ticket office among a tangle of backstreets minutes before it closes. Stumbling breathless through the door, I almost cry with relief when it turns out that the ferry not only exists but departs tomorrow afternoon as I've been told. '*Shukran!*' I exclaim to the somewhat bemused woman behind the counter, as I kiss the tickets in delight. '*Ante battalati!*' You're my hero!

The next day, I have lunch with a few members of a Dubai-based women's cycling club called the Velo Vixens. When I arrive at the chic brasserie, it's immediately clear that they're my kind of cyclists; it's just 1pm and all five are already on their second round of Hoegaarden. 'We ordered one for you too,' Emma, an attractive blonde British woman, says as I join them. 'Hope you don't mind?'

Founded by Emma in 2013, the Vixens prove to be a fun, tightknit group with a heart-warmingly collegiate attitude to cycling. 'We used to go out with the men, but they generally weren't too welcoming,' Emma explains. 'In the Vixens, we look after each other.' Nowadays, she laughs, they're often faster than the men who snubbed them before. 'They'll sit in our slipstream for ages, then try to overtake at the last minute so they don't lose face. It's quite sad, really.'[94]

Because of Dubai's brutal heat, the Vixens often rise early to complete a cool fifty kilometres before dawn. Most ride on the new cycle superhighway built by Sheikh Mohammed, which unfurls like a ribbon of liquorice into the dunes and looks incongruously sleek and modern against its blanched, thirsty surrounds. 'We lobbied the sheikh directly about the track, and he was very receptive,' another of the Vixens explains. 'He's a great cycling enthusiast. It's completely changed our lives.'

The Dubai ruler and UAE vice-president comes across at first as a highly impressive man. Under his stewardship, this once-sleepy fishing village has grown into a dreamworld of superlative wonders, boasting the world's grandest hotel (the 'seven-star' Burj al Arab), the world's fastest police service (led by a fleet of million-dollar sports cars) and the world's tallest building (the Burj Khalifa). Lacking the oil reserves of Abu Dhabi and other Gulf states, this sparkling emirate feels like a miracle of alchemy, having turned a valueless sweep of sand into an overflowing treasure chest of financial services, tourism, real estate and trade.

And yet, all that glitters ... There is much more to Dubai, it turns out, than the pomp and pageantry of its masonry. Scratch its gilded surface and it isn't long before the hidden sores begin to show.

---

[94] On this occasion, and this occasion only, I am prepared to admit that Miss Erskine's usually sage advice may be a shade off-base. 'Women are not, as a rule, fitted for club life,' she postulates. 'When in authority, [they're] apt to be arbitrary and tyrannical.'

'Yes, it can definitely be tough here if you're a woman,' Emma concedes when I ask. 'In politics, there have been some amazing reforms, and there's now a fifty-fifty gender balance in parliament.[95] But there are still a lot of social issues. Men still do better in family matters like inheritance and divorce, and it isn't against the law for them to beat or rape their wives.' Because of social and family pressure not to cycle, the Vixens have struggled to recruit local women to the group, she says. 'Numbers are growing slowly, but we'd love to have more.'

The situation for women may be far worse than any of us realise at this time, in fact ... because Sheikh Mohammed – the British-educated poet, entrepreneur, philanthropist and father of dozens of children from multiple wives – appears to hold secrets that would shock and sicken the world. Or he does according to his daughter Latifa, at least, who since my trip has accused her father of kidnapping and imprisoning her at the palace after she was caught attempting to flee Dubai in March 2018. In a sensational YouTube video posted after her capture, she doesn't mince her words. 'He's the most evil person I've ever met in my life,' she says, speaking in an emotionless monotone directly to camera. 'He's responsible for so many people's deaths and ruining so many people's lives.'

Latifa has spent much of her life under virtual house arrest, she alleges, banned from studying, travelling, working or even seeing friends. This is why she tried to run. And why her sister Shamsa also tried to escape back in 2000, before she too was captured and returned, never to be heard of again. 'Freedom of choice is not something we have,' Latifa says, as if channelling Huxley's Savage himself. 'When you have it,

---

[95] Because of this quota system, the UAE sits at an impressive fourth place on the Inter-Parliamentary Union's ranking of women in politics: forty places above the UK and a whopping sixty-eight above the US.

you take it for granted. And if you don't have it, it's very, very special.'[96]

For Britain, the scandal has caused a severe diplomatic headache. Since the seven emirates united to form the independent UAE in 1971 – the year that marked the end of the British Empire in the Middle East – the country, like other Gulf states, has proved a loyal and lucrative partner to the West. Whether acting as a conduit for secret CIA funds to the *mujahideen* in Afghanistan (as it did in the 1980s), or providing a thriving, deregulated economy in which Western financiers could invest (as it did in the 1990s), or helping to grease the cogs of our global arms industry (as it has since its founding),[97] the Gulf has done more than its fair share over the decades to strengthen Western power and influence across the globe.

In Britain, there is no denying that we, as citizens, have benefited handsomely from this cosy alliance. Nonetheless, for me, it cannot help but leave a bitter taste in the mouth.

---

[96] Since going public with her accusations, Latifa appears to have been permitted more freedoms, and in August 2021 she was pictured meeting her cousin in Iceland. However, she is far from the only female family member making serious claims against the sheikh. In 2019, his sixth wife, Princess Haya bint al-Hussein – the daughter of Jordan's former ruler King Hussein – fled to London following an alleged campaign of 'fear and intimidation' by her husband, and filed for divorce at the High Court.

[97] In 2018, almost 80 per cent of British weapons sales went to the region, allowing us to reclaim our ranking as the world's second-largest arms exporter. This commerce not only bolsters Gulf firepower but also buys its rulers an unspoken waiver from political opprobrium – the most egregious example of which occurred in 2006, when then-prime minister Tony Blair shut down a bribery investigation into a £43 billion contract between BAE Systems and Saudi Arabia following pressure from Riyadh. 'The reason the sector is so seldom investigated in the UK,' the arms expert Andrew Feinstein explained when I was reporting on this story for the International Bar Association, 'is because it always comes back to the heart of government.' (BAE was fined £30 million in the UK for 'accounting irregularities' and $400 million in the US to settle charges of false accounting and making misleading statements in relation to corruption. It has never been prosecuted for bribery.)

Undemocratic and opaque, the Gulf is as politically authoritarian as it is economically libertarian, and its material covetousness sits uneasily with its avowed spiritual ideals. In Dubai, niqab-clad women mingle with caviar-gorging tycoons, while migrant workers build diamanté palaces from the depths of impoverished ghettos. Smugglers and sanctions-busters launder their cash with impunity, while the Emirati elite go unchecked by oversight, censure or scrutiny. A brazen blend of conservatism and consumerism, the province is Thesiger's 'Arabian nightmare, the final disappointment': a place that knows the price of everything and the value of nothing, in which 'progress' is gauged by the pocketbook alone.

After just twenty-four hours in Dubai, I am relieved to be leaving. I am also delighted, and somewhat disbelieving, to discover the ferry may actually be departing *on time*.

'On time?' I say to the man in the kiosk. 'As in, the time it was due to be leaving? The time written on my ticket here?'

'Yes,' he replies, looking at me a little oddly. 'On time.'

'You're sure? You're not just saying that, only for me go to the dock and find it won't be here for another three days?'

'I'm sure.'

The man's beard is trim and has an aura of reliability about it, but I still can't quite bring myself to believe him. 'Okay,' I say doubtfully. 'We'll see.'

Inside, the waiting room is segregated: women on the left, men on the right. Some of the men are sporting knotted *keffiyehs* tightly bound about their head, while others are wearing the material loosely draped and fastened with a black *agal*. The men are courteous towards the women; old ladies are given preference in the ticket queue, while several men sacrifice their seats for mothers and young children. I watch enviously. Chivalry may simply be the acceptable face of chauvinism – marking men out, as it does, as gallant 'protectors' of the female species – but I can't say in all honesty that it doesn't have its appeal.

The ferry is on time. As I stand there marvelling at it in mute wonder, a woman in a colourful hijab comes over and introduces herself. She runs a property firm in Abu Dhabi, she says, and is travelling to Iran 'on business'. 'These women don't represent the whole UAE, you know,' she whispers, nodding at the black, shrouded figures surrounding us. More women are working and thriving than ever before, she asserts. More women – like her – are divorcing.

'More women are cycling?' I ask.

'Oh no!' She laughs. 'But that's nothing to do with gender. In Dubai, you have to have a death wish!'

Chapter 9

A TALE OF TWO COUNTRIES

Iran

'So turns the world: her favours are soon passed,
All whom she nourishes must die at last.'
Ferdowsi, tenth-century Persian poet, *Shahnameh*

The ferry lounge is basic but comfortable and cool, and I slide in beside a porthole and rest my head on the glass. Outside, I watch the final seeds of sunlight flicker and purl on the charcoal waves, before water and sky meld into a screen of pure black.

According to Google Maps, this ten-hour passage will cross the tapered southern end of the Arabian Gulf: a flyaway strand of sea that separates the Arabian Peninsula from the Iranian plateau. Should I check the site in just a few hours, however, it would tell me something quite different: that what we're passing through is in fact the *Persian* Gulf, its Arab pseudonym included like a guilty afterthought below. This digital sleight of hand is Google's way of navigating the sensitive geopolitics of the region, it transpires, allowing each side to see what they wish to see.

In this region of raw nerves and keen faultlines, the importance of names cannot be overstated. For the Iranians, there is no debate to be had; since the sixth century BCE, they point out, this shallow inlet has been known as the Persian Gulf. Almost every country across the globe views it as such, with the exception only of the Arab states. Even removing all modifiers is unacceptable, in their eyes; in 2006, the *Economist* was banned for calling it simply 'the Gulf', while in 2010, Iran threatened to close its airspace to airlines that failed to recognise the full name.[98]

On the boat, all is quiet. Beneath me, the water whispers across the hull, blithely unaware of the intense custodial battles taking place at the surface. Soon I fall asleep, and by the time I awake it is dawn and everyone is stirring. We have, to my astonishment, arrived precisely on time, and I dash out on deck to catch my first glimpse of the shore. At first, I see nothing ... and then, little by little, it appears, glowing soft and scenic beyond the prow: a deep pastel-grey smudge beneath a haze of silver-blue. For ten months, I've waited for this moment and – feeling a little like Odysseus approaching Ithaca across the Ionian Sea – I put *Ride of the Valkyries* on my iPod to endow the moment with a fitting dash of grandiloquence.

And yet the scene, as it emerges, proves something of an anti-climax. Faded turquoise and blush-pink fishing boats line the wharf, while slivers of reflected date palm glint in the sea-green glass of the buildings. Everything seems bright, cheerful, normal – and not, I realise with a jolt, anything like what I was expecting at all. What precisely I *was* expecting, however, I am unsure. Hordes of bellicose Quds wielding pitchforks? Proselytising mullahs beating infidels in the streets? Ayatollah Khamenei rising Kraken-like from the waves? Perhaps not ... But despite my pretensions to Knowledge and Enlightenment, the media machine has clearly been working in the wings. I was envisaging something darker, perhaps, physically and figuratively. Something more worn at the edges, epitomising years of global reclusion. Not this genial,

[98] The zeal to retain the term 'Persian' may seem odd when one considers the effort taken by Reza Shah Pahlavi to switch the country's name from 'Persia' to 'Iran' in 1935. Iranians had called their country Iran for millennia, he argued, while Persia was the moniker adopted by the Greeks and therefore represented a land occupied and degraded by outsiders. The fact that it is now the name 'Persia' that conveys an aura of poetry and romance, and 'Iran' that reeks of decline and decay, is a painful irony not lost on most Iranians.

sun-washed shoreline that opens before me like a friend spreading their arms in welcome.

Inside the customs building, I am ushered through passport control and told to wait beyond the gate. It is a tense half hour, during which my imagination toys playfully with my nerves. My main concern relates to the validity of my visa. Following months of calls and emails, the document was finally procured for a near-bankrupting sum – but it is not, you could say, 100 per cent kosher. This is due to a recent change in the law that banned British and US citizens from travelling through Iran unless accompanied by a guide or part of a tour. How the visa agent's 'creative' circumventing of this rule will bear up under the scrutiny of the Islamic Republic's notorious intelligence personnel, I am unsure. But I'm not wholly looking forward to finding out.

A short time later, I find myself standing in the street outside, my documents stamped and validated. I feel dazed by the ease with which I've been granted access to this pariah security state. Twenty minutes in an office for an interrogatory 'welcome to Iran'; three minutes collecting my bags, which are not even scanned; five minutes filling in an immigration card with highly patchy information – and that's it. I'm in. As I ride along the tree-lined avenue into town, the air baggy with saturated heat, I feel a sudden sense of triumph. *I've made it*, I think! *I'm here! I've cycled all the way to Iran!*

During these first tentative moments in the country, however, my triumph is tinged with caution. I am aware that several Westerners have recently fallen foul of the authorities on highly specious grounds, and I'm wary of being too complacent. Among the eighteen foreigners currently incarcerated are a British-Iranian woman, Nazanin Zaghari-Ratcliffe, detained for allegedly plotting a 'soft overthrow' of the regime, an elderly British-Iranian man, Kamal Foroughi, serving an eight-year sentence for spying, and a British-Iranian woman, Roya Saberi-Negad Nobakht, jailed for five years simply for writing on Facebook that Iran was 'too Islamic'. Such detentions usually have little to do with the law;

they are, rather, a form of geopolitical racketeering, used by the state as diplomatic leverage in negotiations. And while most cases tend to involve dual nationals, there are exceptions. US citizen Xiyue Wang was recently imprisoned for spying, while shortly after I leave Iran, an American and Australian-Briton both receive ten-year sentences for 'insulting the leader' and spying, respectively.

So, yes, I admit I am nervous. Journalists are a popular target for espionage accusations, and I have written regularly in the past about Iran and its dire human rights record. While I have removed what I can online, the thought circulates repeatedly: *What if they find out?* It is fortunate, perhaps, that 'Rebecca Lowe' is fairly generic as monikers go; had I been writing under my mother's maiden name – *Györy-Vajdaszentiványi-Vadasdy-Vadasdy* – the red flags may feasibly have been brighter.

I expect Couchsurfing.com to be blocked in Iran, but how wrong I am! It is not only accessible, in fact, but startlingly popular; a quick search brings up 6,000 members, a thousand of which are based here in Bandar Abbas, and I find a willing host in a matter of minutes. Making my way immediately to his flat, I meander sluggishly through the baking streets, past friendly passers-by who wave and shout hello, and a driver who pulls alongside me to show me his Instagram page dedicated to cycling. It is an easy, enjoyable journey, marred only by a young motorcyclist – my second most feared demographic after inquisitive children – who seems to follow me and linger with intent. He soon gets bored and moves on, however, after I stop in a layby and begin working my way with measured deliberation through an enormous bunch of bananas.

During the ride, I notice the cars are all small, dirty-white Peugeots, small, dirty-white Saipa Prides or small, dirty-white Paykans (Iran's old national car, modelled on the British Hillman Hunter). They are a far cry from the effulgent beasts of Oman and give a sense of Iran's struggling economy following decades of punitive sanctions. Despite this, I find myself quietly impressed by the level of development here. I see little of Egypt's grimy befuddlement or Sudan's raw deprivation, but instead a bustling, functional city touched by a delicate aestheticism. The streets are clean and fringed by flashes of rose, poppy and pittosporum, while the buildings range from concrete shacks to gleaming, glass-fronted office blocks. The traffic is neither maniacal nor paralysed, while patches of wall are covered in colourful street art reminiscent of Athens or Berlin. Named after the Safavid king Abbas I, Bandar Abbas has long attracted wayfarers and merchants from across the world and appears to retain its reputation as one of the most vibrant, cosmopolitan cities in Iran.

My host, Amir, greets me with a grin. He is jolly and stocky, with alarmingly voluminous eyebrows and an unwavering belief that everyone and everything is 'awesome'. I like him immediately.

'Want to watch me paragliding?' he asks. 'You can meet my friends.'

'Okay,' I say. 'Is it dangerous?'

'Not if you're careful. It's awesome.'

Amir is thirty-three and lives alone. He learnt English from television, I am impressed to hear, and it takes several hours before I realise he understands almost nothing that I say. But fortunately this doesn't matter too much as he does most of the talking. 'Eighty per cent of people hate the regime,' he tells me as we wind through faceless streets punctuated every so often by imposing portraits of Ayatollahs Khomeini and Khamenei. The former looks forbidding and austere, the latter elderly and avuncular, like an Islamic Father Christmas. 'But we're scared of being Syria, so no want change now. Change will come, but *yavash yavash*.' Slowly, slowly. 'We had chaos before and no want again.'

Amir speaks in a rush of cluttered consonants, as if throwing out as many words as possible to see which ones will stick. Most Iranians need second jobs to survive, he explains. He earns $500 a month as a teacher and recently set up an insulation business on the side, but the company is struggling. 'My office,' he says, pulling up outside a grubby concrete block. 'Two minutes. I get documents, please.'

Amir's office is a small, untidy cube within a larger, untidier complex. As he collects his papers, he takes a photograph off the wall and passes it to me. 'The Cyrus Cylinder. Cyrus is my hero.'

I examine the picture. Constructed from bisque-yellow clay, the cylinder is riven and cracked and barely a handspan in width. Over the years, however, this modest artefact has assumed an iconic position at the heart of the Iranian psyche. Dating from the sixth century BCE, the relic describes the conquest of Babylon by Cyrus the Great, the founder of the First Persian (Achaemenid) Empire, as well as outlining what some claim to be the world's first manifesto of human rights. '*I will respect the traditions, customs and religions of the nations of my empire ...*' it decrees in tiny cuneiform script. '*I will never let anyone oppress any others, and if it occurs, I will take his or her right back and penalise the oppressor.*'

While not all historians buy into this post-Enlightenment reading – the king was most likely trying to curry divine favour, they say, rather than offering a blueprint for progressive governance – in a sense this is to miss the point. It is less Cyrus the man than Cyrus the myth that interests Iran, and his evergreen legacy has proved as adaptable as it is enduring. In Xenophon's *Cyropaedia*, he is portrayed as the 'father' of the Persians, whose 'kindness of heart [was] always occupied with ... their well-being', while in the Bible he is depicted as a second messiah who freed the Jews from Babylon.[99] Nowadays, his image as a noble, principled proto-nationalist is as popular among the ruling Islamists as it is among the liberal elite, each remoulding his image to suit their own political purposes.

---

[99] Thousands of Jews continue to live peacefully in Iran today, I am surprised to discover, protected by a *fatwa* issued by Khomeini in 1979 that distinguishes them from 'the godless, bloodsucking Zionists': more evidence that tensions in the Middle East are fundamentally geopolitical, rather than religious, in nature.

'Fascinating,' I say to Amir, handing back the photo. 'Where can I see the real thing?'

'Oh, that's easy,' he replies, smiling. 'The British Museum. Maybe one day you'll take me there?'

The mountain glows crimson in the twilight and is entirely desolate except for a female goatherd who lives up here alone. While Amir assesses the wind, I join three paragliders smoking opium on a carpeted platform overlooking the valley. One of them burns coal on the *manghal* (brazier) and presses a lump of resin over a hole on the bulb, before taking a long, slow drag and passing the pipe on to me.

'*Khoobi?*' he asks, as I inhale the peppery fumes into my lungs. Okay? I nod, although in truth I feel nothing. Then, little by little, I feel myself sinking: a deep, full-body loosening that draws me into the cushioned boards below. Three or four tokes later and it starts to become clear why this cheap, mild drug is so popular in Iran, where thousands of tonnes are smuggled in from Afghanistan and Pakistan every year.

A second pipe is passed my way, but I decline. Though drowsy, I am still just about cognisant enough to recall what happened on the last occasion I decided to get blazed with a group of foreign men I'd never met before. It was a decade ago at La Bufadora blowhole in Mexico, where I was happily minding my own business when some friendly chaps had offered to share their *mezcal* and locally grown *mota*. All had seemed fine, until the next thing I knew I was waking up in my hostel at noon the next day with a splitting headache, no memory of the past twelve hours and the Mandarin symbol for 'bottoms up' emblazoned indelibly across my lower back – where it has remained as a cautionary tale to this day.

Fortunately, Amir returns before I have the chance to make a similar mistake again. 'Wind bad,' he says. '*Bezan berim.*' Let's go.

Driving in convoy, a group of us set off for a pool house nearby.

En route, I confess that I'm a journalist, and instantly Amir's tone changes. 'Don't tell anyone,' he warns. 'Risky right now.' Three months ago, the *Ettela'at* (intelligence services) cracked down on foreign guests and summoned him for questioning. 'It illegal to host foreigners, they say. They tell me tourists are spies.'

'But you weren't put off?'

He grins. 'No. Not me.'

We arrive to find the gathering in full swing. Most people are in their early thirties, with the exception of three younger Barbie-doll sorts with thickly applied make-up and perfect button noses.[100] Entering draped in black, they remove their hijabs and manteaus[101] to reveal an array of skimpy miniskirts, stilettos and boob-tubes, each a living metaphor for the secrets and hypocrisies of this fallacious Islamist state. It is unclear to me exactly where this group sits within the Iranian social spectrum. But they appear to be the millennial *bee-dean* (irreligious) whose values straddle East and West; the ones who drink and smoke and party in the mountains at weekends, straining but never cleaving the shackles of the state.[102]

'Tell people about us,' Hassan, an engineer, cries while clutching a tinned mojito and dancing with the kind of

---

[100] Iran is said to be the capital of the world for nose jobs, for both men and women, and plaster casts are often worn with pride. Pharmacists are even known to sell bandages to people who can't afford the operation, as a badge of wealth and status.

[101] Iran and Afghanistan are the only countries in the world where hijabs (headscarves) are mandatory for all women, including foreigners and non-Muslims. In Iran, clothing must be loose and hang below the groin, so most women wear either a manteau (long baggy top) or the more conservative chador (full head-and-body cloak). Penalties for non-compliance include warnings, fines and even imprisonment.

[102] Just as the protective shield of the Zagros Mountains once enabled nomadic tribesmen to enjoy lawless, independent lives beyond the purview of the authorities, 'going to the mountains' nowadays seems to suggest both a literal escape and an allusion to doing something subversive, whether drugs, drink, sex or simply socialising in peace.

impassioned gyrations that would make Miley Cyrus blush. 'Iran isn't what they think!'

Young people are now more liberal than ever before, he says, partly due to the growth of social media. Hassan and his powerfully coiffed hairdresser girlfriend, Laleh, met over one of the many dating sites now available, BeeTalk, while banned platforms such as Twitter and Facebook are accessed by millions – including, bemusingly, the regime itself – via VPNs.

Despite the rise of technology, however, traditional problems clearly remain in the dating world. 'We go out with girls, but it's complicated,' a young man named Parviz declares. 'They're obsessed with getting married.'

'Ha!' Laleh responds. She turns to me. 'Don't be fooled. It's the boys who are old fashioned. They pretend they're openminded, but they still want virgins as their wives.'

I ask about the hymenoplasty operations I heard about in Egypt, and Laleh admits they're popular here too. An eminent hard-line cleric, Grand Ayatollah Sadeq Rouhani, who opposes such depraved activities as playing chess and listening to music, is even said to have issued a *fatwa* permitting the operation. 'It's ridiculous,' she snorts. 'But welcome to Iran.'

'Here's a fact for you,' Parviz says suddenly, as if eager to change the subject. He taps into his phone. 'Did you know Iran had the first ever postal service? There's even a Herodotus quote about our mailmen at the New York post office. "Neither snow nor rain nor heat nor gloom of nights stays these couriers from the swift completion of their appointed rounds."'

'There's a Sa'di quote too at the UN headquarters in New York,' Laleh adds, as she googles the words. "Human beings are members of a whole, / In creation of one essence and soul." Sa'di!'

From censorship and sex to Herodotus and Sa'di ... the comet-like arc of the conversation, from the prosaic to poetic, takes me off guard. I didn't know about the post, I admit, though I can believe it. The Persians' startling range of invention over the past three millennia is well documented, spanning art, literature, philosophy, theology, physics and more. They engineered the air conditioner, battery, windmill, refrigerator and first monotheistic religion (Zoroastrianism). They produced algebra and backgammon, polo and chess, the carrot and domesticated rose. They gave gods to the godless Mongols, poetry to the illiterate masses and produced brilliant polymaths by the dozen – including Ibn Sina, whose *Canon of Medicine* served as the main textbook for medieval European doctors, and al-Biruni, who accurately calculated the Earth's circumference half a millennium before scientists in the West.

Parviz lists a few more names on his fingers. 'All Persians,' he says, '*Not* Arabs.'

'People get confused?'

'Yes! Even though Iranians are *nothing like* Arabs. We are civilised. Arabs are stupid and eat too much.'

I glance at his soft midriff and say nothing. He is smiling but only half joking. Both he and Amir prefer the Farsi word *dorood* to the Arabic word *salam* and clearly believe their language and culture to be superior. They are far from alone in this belief, I soon learn. Forged from 3,000 years of history and a troika of hulking empires, Iran is a deeply proud nation with a firm and unwavering sense of self. Fars, the province from which Persian civilisation emerged several millennia ago, remains largely at the centre of the country today: the cultural keystone to the bulging state that's grown around it.[103] While the Arabs may have occupied Persia in the seventh century – to the Iranians' bitter and long-lasting regret – they never truly conquered it, as they did with most other countries across the region. In fact, it was more the reverse; Islamised but never Arabised, Persia retained its own customs and dialects (albeit now translated into the Arabic script) and drew the invaders into its own mighty orbit. By the mid-700s,

[103] Fars was once known as 'Pars', from which the term 'Persia' originated. It changed after Iran's adoption of the Arabic alphabet, as Arabic does not have a sound for 'p'.

Persian bureaucrats dominated the Abbasid Caliphate,[104] and the capital was even moved from Damascus to Baghdad to be closer to the Iranian heartlands.[105]

'Anyway, can Arabs do this?' Hassan asks, suddenly running and launching into a high forward somersault into the pool, before emerging, laughing and spluttering, a moment later. 'No! No Arab can do that!'

The night staggers on, and at 3am Amir is finally ready to leave. It is at this point, as we are making our way down the road to the car, that I realise his ability to walk has somehow become compromised during the course of the evening's festivities. 'I'm *fine*,' he growls in response to a polite enquiry about the state of his mental faculties after he trips and plunges headfirst into a thorn bush. 'I'm *awwwesome*.'

Sliding into the passenger seat, I strap myself in and recite a short prayer, while Amir slumps behind the wheel and attempts with limited success to fit the key into the ignition. He then shoots diagonally across the road, brakes, curses and reverses into a lamppost.

'Right,' I say. 'Out. I'm driving.'

And this is how I find myself committing my second felony in Iran in the space of just a few hours. Not only do I have no licence or insurance, but I am certainly over the alcohol limit – should there be one, that is. As a teetotal state, drink-driving doesn't technically exist as a crime here; although, as Amir reassuringly informs me during our tortuously long, slow journey home,

---

[104] The Abbasid Caliphate (750–1517 CE) was the third Arab empire established after the death of Muhammad, following the Rashidun (632–661 CE) and Umayyad (661–750 CE). At its peak under the Umayyads, the Arab caliphate covered 11,100,000 square kilometres, making it the third-largest empire in history.

[105] This process of 'Persianisation' culminated in Ferdowsi's *Shahnameh* in 1010 CE: an interminable epic poem that retells Iranian history through a veil of anti-Arab mythology, and which continues to have a profound influence on Iranian identity today.

you can get a hundred lashes simply for alcohol consumption alone.

Several hours later, I am delighted and somewhat surprised to wake up neither in police custody nor under the charred remains of Amir's battered Peugeot. This feels like a stroke of tremendous good luck in the circumstances, and I resolve to make more of an effort to avoid criminal activity in the future. Or, at least, until I find someone more proficient at it than Amir, who I discover face down and snoring on the living room carpet, still wearing his trousers and shoes from the night before.

The next morning, my alarm sounds at 4.15. As it bleeps with its usual shrill persistence, it takes all my reserves of willpower not to hurl it out the window and sleep for another fortnight. But instead I wrench myself off my thin mattress on the floor – Amir's bedroom has no bed – and stumble blindly into my clothes. It is pitch-black outside, and everything already feels exhausting.

In the kitchen, I prepare a plate of bread, cheese and a KitKat, and I nibble at it slowly while attempting to steel myself for the ride ahead. I feel extraordinarily tense. While I always find entering a new country a little nerve-racking, here it feels different. The dangers seem more real, somehow. More intense. Perhaps because – as a foreigner, a Brit, a journalist, a woman – I am a walking sweet-spot of potential risk. And there are a good many people who said I shouldn't come.

After a year of anticipation, the reality of my predicament only sinks in now. I'm in Iran. *Iran*. On a dodgy visa containing bogus credentials. Was this really such a good idea? But it's too late to back out now, of course – so, at 5.15am, I take a long, deep breath, sneak past Amir asleep in the living room (we said our goodbyes last night, when he told me with touching sincerity that I was awesome), fetch Maud from the underground car park and make my way tentatively onto the road. Outside, flecks of moisture prickle the pre-dawn air, and I can already feel tremors of the violent heat to come. Adrenalin pulses through me in waves. I take a deep breath, and then another. *Plod on*, I murmur. *Plod on* ...

The highway out of Bandar Abbas is long and monotonous, growing ever broader and busier until I find myself in the city's industrial outskirts. Corrugated steel cubes, gnarled machinery and general detritus line the dual carriageway, as if the city has hurled up its innards onto the city's stark borderlands. Clinging to the edge, I grind anxiously along as speeding trucks rattle by on my left. A few beeps and hollers greet me as I ride, but the majority of drivers remain silent. What are people thinking, I wonder? Are they supportive, outraged, critical, confounded? Inspired? Indifferent? I simply don't know.

Gradually, however, steel blends to sand and the barbed edges of the city melt into pools of taupe, brown and blue. Traffic dies to a murmur, while intriguing masked women start appearing by the roadside, whom I assume to be the Bandari (port people) Amir told me about, native to Homozgan province. Their strikingly colourful boregheh face coverings range in design, from felt, embroidered headdresses to metallic, Kitchener-style moustaches, and act as a reminder that this region was once a key trading hub between India, China and Africa. While the roots of the costumes are unknown, some believe they originated during the Portuguese occupation of Hormuz Island in the sixteenth century, when women were known to cover their faces to disguise themselves as men and avoid being sold as slaves.

By lunchtime, I begin to tire. I am not yet used to this heat, which is not dry like the Sahara but thick and viscid like treacle, and there is no visible shelter from the burning midday sun. Around me, everywhere is just ashen, featureless sand. No sweeping dunes or foliage. No cacti or crumbling sarcophagi. Nothing at all, in fact, except an endless, empty expanse of craggy scrubland and thorn.

On the outskirts of a village, however, I finally spy a bush with a decent canopy. Pulling over, I dig out my sleeping mat and lay it out beneath the branches, delighting in the cool wash of shade that envelops me. For a moment, my world contracts to this modest smudge of shadow distilled among the muddied leaves and bracken – and closing my eyes, all I can think about is sleep …

'Hijab!'

Startled, I jump to my feet. Two police cars have stopped nearby, their roof-lights flashing. The cars are green and white, which can mean only one thing: the notorious *Gasht-e Ershad*, or morality police.

Four armed men approach me, looking stern. The voice repeats, gravelly and brusque – '*Hijab!*' – and I glance over to where my headscarf is hanging limply across Maud's handlebars. It should be on my head, I know, yet a wave of pique comes over me. How dare these beefy brigands tell me what to wear? More to the point, how dare they interrupt my nap to do so? The gall of it is infuriating.

But I know defiance is futile – and, in truth, I don't have the nerve to disobey. So, with a feeble sigh and nostril-flare, I fetch the scarf and drape it peevishly over my hair. Watching, the men say nothing. Then, to my surprise and confusion, one of them walks over and hands me a phone.

I put it to my ear. 'Hello,' a muffled voice says. 'Where you from?'

'Britain,' I reply, perplexed.

'Ah gooood!' The voice is odd, its vowels long and languid like molten cheese. 'You cycle Iran? The officer is my brother-in-law and we invite you to our home tonight.'

'Oh!' I say. This isn't quite the ruthless admonishment I was expecting. 'I see.'

'He will take you there now, and I will meet you after work. Please just wait for me. We are very happy you are here!'

The voice hangs up and I pass back the phone. The officer then returns to his car and motions for me to follow. For the next fifteen minutes, I am led down a series of ever-narrower, ever-sandier tracks – and, still feeling somewhat uneasy, I reach into my bar bag and press the location transmitter on my satellite tracker. If I am indeed being lured to the local *Ettela'at* interrogation chamber, at least BLAST will know where to send the marines.

When we arrive, however, it's immediately clear my concerns are groundless. Unless the Revolutionary Guard are disguising their security agents as buxom matrons with flour-dusted pinnies, it appears the invitation was sincere. After a brief exchange with the officers, the woman ushers me inside the compound – where, with a comforting flush of familiarity, I see the buildings are arranged around a central courtyard much like the adobe bungalows of northern Sudan – and leads me into a cosy, carpeted room. Largely empty, the space contains just a fridge and a bookshelf exhibiting an eclectic range of literature, including the Qur'an, *Teach Yourself English* and *The Hound of the Baskervilles*. Iced air pumps out in erratic gasps from a rusty unit on the wall, and I lie out blissfully, achingly, while my host busies back and forth with trays of tea, fruit, chicken and rice. As I eat, I reflect on the events of the past hour, which seem to embody one of Iran's most fundamental contradictions: namely, the clash between political ideology on the one hand, which views foreigners as a threat, and Persian hospitality on the other, which treats them as a friend. And in this instance, at least, it is clear which of the two has won out.

Later, the voice on the phone arrives. His name is Sadegh, and he is short and swarthy with a lustrous, sweeping quiff. 'Are you an early bird or night owl?' he asks. His accent is affected and precise, each word meticulously chewed and rolled around his mouth before being expelled. He speaks largely in bookish idioms. 'An early bird catches the worm, I think? Do you catch the worm?'

Sadegh works as an English translator in a factory and clearly feels trapped in this tiny, remote community where he earns just $300 a month. 'Marriages are arranged here, but I believe in love,' he tells me. 'I want to visit England and marry a British girl. I learnt English myself, to give me leverage in the job market.'

'Good for you,' I say, impressed by his use of 'leverage' and wondering if this is a marriage proposal.

'I dream of having my own fertiliser business,' he continues. 'Can you tell me, please, which British towns already have one?'

I confess I don't know, and he looks momentarily crestfallen. Then he brightens. 'It's okay, I'll google it. Where there's a will there's a way!'

Later, over a lamb *koobideh* (kofta), eaten on the ground on a traditional *sofreh* (tablecloth), I learn that this is a Sunni village. Sadegh declines to say whether they are treated well by the Khamenei regime, however, and I don't pursue the subject. Just one in ten Iranians are Sunni and many, like Sadegh, live in deeply deprived regions of the country. This has long been a deliberate strategy by the ruling Shia clerics, who pay lip-service to equality while doing their best to limit Sunnis' social, economic and political opportunities.

To the early Safavid monarchs, who instigated Twelver Shi'ism[106] as the state religion in the sixteenth century, this kind of dogmatic repression would no doubt have come as a disappointment. As originally conceived, Shi'ism was less doctrinaire than Sunnism and encouraged the reinterpretation of scripture as times and contexts changed. Shah Abbas I reportedly displayed a particularly inclusive spirit – initially, at least – inviting thousands of Jewish and Armenian families to settle in Iran and encouraging Christian missionaries to establish convents

---

[106] Twelvers are just one of a dizzying array of Shia sects. Following the initial Sunni–Shia schism – whereby Sunnis who supported the descendants of Abu Bakr, the Prophet's companion and father-in-law, split from Shias who backed Ali ibn Abi Talib, the Prophet's cousin and son-in-law – there were further divisions among the Shi'ites themselves. The Twelvers were the most significant subsect, followed by the Ismailis, or 'Seveners'. But there were also the Zaydis, or Fivers, who now comprise a hefty portion of Yemen, and the Nizari Ismailis, whose alleged penchant for hashish and murdering their opponents gained them the nickname the Hashashin ('Assassins'). Not to mention the Alawites, Druze, Bohras, Musta'lis ... and, well, I think you get the gist.

here. Indeed, Abbas was quite the guy by all accounts: a man of courage and quirky foibles who gutted his own game, addressed the Spanish Ambassador as 'grandpa' and revived Persian trade and culture across the world (the fact he later evolved into a paranoid psychopath who savagely punished his enemies, killed one of his sons and blinded two others is rather more glossed over in the history archives).

After Abbas' death in 1629, Persia slipped into a long and steady decline. Baghdad was lost to the Ottomans, while a series of dissolute rulers gradually relinquished control to the officious and illiberal *ulema* (clerics). For many Iranians, therefore, the haloed image of the Safavid era remains acute, bathed in the half-light of history and creative reimagining: a symbol of what they once were, and one day may be again.

'Yes, Iran was a great nation then,' Sadegh says. 'But now the tide of history has turned.' Every word he speaks feels like it has been dipped and glazed in liquid gold. 'And time, as they say, waits for no man ...'

At dawn, the desert has a kind of desolate beauty. A satin sky gleams overhead, while vermilion mountains glow like paper lanterns in the early morning light. I pass boarded-up huts, shepherdesses in emerald dresses and patchworks of twine and potato-sacking sculpted into disturbing donkey-shaped scarecrows. Slender clay domes appear every so often, graffitied and filled with pea-green water, which I'm told act as the entryways to a network of underground *qanats* (aqueducts) dating back thousands of years. Meanwhile, my tan lines fade and morph like a form of socio-political barometer, as my now-sheathed arms and calves, exposed and dark in Sudan, begin to turn an austere and puritanical white.

In a village called Latifi, a family kindly take me in after I appear at the townhall searching for lodgings. Their bungalow is large and flat-roofed, and the rooms are strikingly bare. No furnishings are evident at all, in fact, except elegant wall-to-wall carpets and two portraits of the Supreme Leaders who survey me broodingly from under sober, shaggy brows. The couple are clearly highly devout, yet exhibit no hint of judgement when I confess that I'm an agnostic. Instead, they rhapsodise about how overjoyed they are that I'm here. Would I like to stay for their daughter Donya's ninth birthday party? Mina, the woman, asks. They would so *love* it if I were there!

My curiosity piqued, I accept readily. It is only later that I become aware of the elaborate hospitality ritual of *taarof*, the rules of which dictate that you must decline an invitation at least three times before accepting it (except if *taarof nakon* is uttered first, that is, which apparently releases everyone from the edict's strictures like a magic spell). Ignorant of this custom, I obliviously say yes to almost every offer I receive during my first few weeks in Iran, unaware that in doing so I'm committing a grievous *faux pas* and no doubt forcing dozens of horrified hosts into fulfilling entirely insincere promises made solely for the sake of decorum.

Whether this particular invitation is genuine or not, I have no idea. However, exhibiting all the civility that three millennia of cultural hegemony will endow, the couple reveal no sign of being put out. In fact, they appear delighted – and I am too, for the party is a fun and lively affair. Mina busies about with trays of basil seed *sharbat* (cordial) and watermelon, throwing 50,000 rial notes into people's laps, while the mothers laugh and gossip, and the children dart about like gadflies. Most of the women wear floral skirts and vibrant hijabs that reveal a slender crescent of dark hair, though a handful are draped in black chadors that cloak their shirts and jeans. The smallest girls are more scantily clad and often heavily made up, as if keen to indulge in as much ostentation as possible before being hit by the sartorial limitations of womanhood.

This crossover, from child to woman, occurs at the tender age of nine. A ninth birthday is not simply a celebration, therefore, but a kind of initiation: *taklif*. At 10pm, as the room grows hushed, Donya appears in a virgin-white cloak and lays a mat in the centre of the room. She then recites an Islamic prayer, kneeling and stretching and touching her head to the floor in mesmerising, looping repetitions, as the women all encircle her and look on with encouragement and awe.

And then, in a flash, festivities resume. A tambourine and drum appear, and dozens of women take to the floor to dance. At regular intervals, Donya's mad grandmother seizes me in a kind of half-dance, half-wrestle, squawking *khoobi?* (okay?), to which the correct response appears to be *khoobam* (okay!). Meanwhile, in the room next door, the men sit in near-silence watching a game of football on TV.

By 2am, the party is over. After clearing up the debris, the couple, their two daughters and I all curl up on thin mattresses on the living room floor. I then set my alarm for 5.30am and fall instantly, exhaustedly, asleep.

Spanning the breadth of Asia, Iran is surprisingly large when examined on a map. Drop it into Europe and it could form a bridge between the Baltic and Black Sea, or the Channel and Bosphorus, while providing a topography of comparable beauty and diversity. The tropical northern woodlands provide relief from the searing southern dunes, while the ice-tipped coastal mountains shelter the arid inland plains. Stretching some 2,500 kilometres from tip to toe, this sweeping, variegated landmass dwarfs all seven of its neighbours and divides the historic global 'East' from Anatolia and the Arab world.

While I see little of this geological heterogeneity on my route – the central spine of Iran is largely desert, and bland, mealy desert at that – there is, nevertheless, a great deal about the journey that appeals. The deeper inland I ride, the safer and more serene I feel, as if rolling myself up in a giant feather duvet. Kindnesses eddy and flow around me, as pervasive as the summer breeze. Having lost my pump, I'm given one; having broken my sunglasses, I'm gifted a pair. On the road, so many drivers stop to offer me wonderful, utterly impractical food – watermelons, loaves of bread, bags of cucumbers – that much of it, to my dismay, must be discarded.

I know, anywhere I go, that I'll be looked after. In a village called Akbarabad, I am rescued from a night in a cow barn by a young man on a moped who insists I must stay at his home. And what a home it is! Tucked among the farm shacks and arable fields, his modest bungalow opens Tardis-like to reveal a vast, empty chamber that exudes the cool quietude of a mosque. Eight beautiful carpets line the floor and a single wooden crib sits tucked in the corner. The bathroom – like so many in rural Iran – wouldn't seem out of place in a medieval Ottoman hammam.

The man, Sajid, introduces me to his parents, sister and niece. The sister serves tea with cinnamon and pepper, while the twinkly eyed father bombards me with questions via Google Translate. I field them as best I can, like a batsman training in the nets. Am I married? Christian? Jewish? What do I earn? What does a British plumber earn? What do I pay for gas? An iPhone? A car? Do my friends smoke? Drink? Do sport? Do I visit my mother? Do I like the Queen?

I reply as honestly as possible, now secure in the knowledge that – despite being seated beneath the saturnine gaze of the twin Ayatollahs – neither my agnosticism nor marital status is likely to incur any hostility. As we tuck into a steaming banquet of lamb *koobideh*, I ask the family's opinion of Khamenei. 'Good,' is the answer. And Khomeini? 'Very good!'

I admit I'm surprised by the number of pro-regime people I've met so far. It's quite possible, of course, that they are simply wary of expressing dissent to a foreigner. But their support feels sincere, and it makes me question Amir's statistics. Are 80 per cent of Iranians truly against Khamenei? Or is he, like so many of us, trapped in a liberal bubble? Sajid's parents benefited from subsidies provided to poorer families following the 1979 revolution, he explains, and now feel more connected to their country than they ever did before. 'It isn't about money,' he says, 'but feeling you belong.'

I ask the family's view of Britain and am interested to hear that they distinguish between the British people, whom they 'love', and the British government, which they deplore: a distinction that we Brits, I feel, often overlook in our judgement of communities and cultures overseas.

'The West wants to keep Iran weak,' Sajid says, as he lights a mint-flavoured *qalyan* (hookah) and passes me the hose. 'That's why we don't use Facebook or watch the BBC. They're fake and full of lies.'

My instinct is to argue. The BBC is taxpayer funded, I want to cry. It is balanced and nonpartisan and serves the public good! How much this is true is a debate for another time – but there is no doubt that in 1950s Iran, BBC Persian was far from an impartial broadcaster. It was, rather, little more than a tool of imperialist propaganda designed to help Britain maintain control.

It is Iranians' knowledge of this and the UK's many other machinations over the years, rather than a sense of irrational paranoia, that has generated their deep-rooted cynicism today. We are the ultimate 'wily foxes' in their eyes, and a common joke when anything bad happens is to cry 'the British are to blame!': a phrase originating from the Iranian novel *My Uncle Napoleon*, which went on to become a national soap opera hit. Astonishingly, even Mohammad Reza Shah himself – a staunch Western ally and stooge – suspected we precipitated his downfall. 'If you lift up Khomeini's beard, you'll find MADE IN ENGLAND written under his chin,' he reportedly said in 1978, shortly before being toppled from his peacock throne.

British interference in Iran has a long pedigree. Whereas the US was a trusted friend until just seven decades ago, Britain has proved a frequent and bothersome meddler in Iranian affairs for the past 200 years. In the 1800s, during the so-called 'Great Game' in the Middle East, Russia and Britains fought over Iranian suzerainty like cats over a ball of wool, stymying development and the construction of roads and railways – as each power was concerned that the other may use them to their advantage – and creating chronic economic stagnation. 'What happens [in Persia] will be for the worse,' Lord Salisbury wrote as foreign secretary in 1879. 'Therefore it is in our interest that as little should happen as possible.'

As the Shah granted ever more lucrative oil and trade concessions to these encroaching chieftains, popular unrest grew – and, in 1906, culminated not in violent revolt but in the peaceful formation of a new constitution and semi-democratic parliament. This 'constitutional revolution' was an astonishing feat 'comparable ... to the signing of the Magna Carta', according to *All the King's Men* author Stephen Kinzer, and seemed to herald an exciting new future for Iran, free from foreign control.

Yet it wasn't to be. Determined to retain their iron grip, Russia and Britain did all they could to quash the endeavour. While Persia was never formally colonised, in 1907 it was carved into two zones of 'influence' by the superpowers and left 'lying between life and death', according to the British MP H.F.B. Lynch, 'parcelled out, almost dismembered, helpless and friendless at our feet'. A year later, when Iran became the first Middle Eastern country to produce oil, it was the Anglo-Iranian Oil Company (AIOC) that took the vast majority of the spoils while exploiting the local population for their manpower. According to the US diplomat and politician Averell Harriman, conditions at Anglo-Iranian's Abadan Refinery were 'shocking for ... employees of a large Western oil company'. While British workers enjoyed a luxurious lifestyle of manicured lawns, swimming pools and tennis courts, Iranian workers were denied holiday and sick pay, had almost no running water or electricity, and earned around 50 cents a day. In winter, their homes flooded with sewage; in summer, they transformed into rat-infested ovens infused with the stench of sulphur. 'Each family occupied the space of a blanket,' an Israeli worker told *The Jerusalem Post*. 'There were no lavatories [...] We often tried to show [the British] the mistake they were making in treating the Persians the way they did. The answer was usually: "We English have had hundreds of years of experience on how to treat the Natives. Socialism is all right back home, but out here you have to be the master."' The 'socialism' referred to was Britain's new welfare state, of course: Abadan was directly subsidising free education and the NHS, as well as the newly nationalised energy, transport and steel industries.

By the late 1940s, following decades of mistreatment, Iran was a tinderbox just waiting for a spark. However, that spark, when it came, was far from what anyone expected ...

Mohammad Mosaddegh, at first glance, seemed an unlikely saviour for the nation. Hunchbacked, aristocratic and eccentric, he looked like a cross between Gandhi and Uncle Fester, and was prone to fits of swooning and weeping at the least provocation. However, his uncompromising anti-imperialism and incorruptibility proved catnip to the population at large, and in 1951 – after being elected prime minister with a thumping parliamentary majority – he lost no time in making his mark. If the AIOC wouldn't match the recent fifty-fifty deal struck between the Saudis and the US oil firm Aramco, he declared, he would nationalise the industry and kick the Brits out on their ear.

Predictably, they wouldn't. So that's precisely what he did.

The drastic move made Mosaddegh an instant hero across the Middle East, as well as a global media star. *Newsweek* dubbed him the 'Fainting Fanatic', while *Time* magazine made him their Man of the Year. Churchill, predictably, was outraged. Iranian oil, he asserted, had played a pivotal role in the Allies' defeat of fascism, and the idea that Britain should surrender these reserves to some histrionic, hook-nosed demagogue was unconscionable. A barrage of embargoes, industrial sabotage and military threats ensued – followed, as a last resort, by a good old-fashioned coup.

The coup took two attempts. It also took the help of a new US security agency, still somewhat green about the gills, known as the CIA. Deeply concerned about the spread of communism, the CIA was convinced that Mosaddegh – a man who had banned forced labour, introduced sick pay and championed women's rights –

posed an existential threat to the West and must be stopped at all costs. Led by Kermit Roosevelt (the grandson of Theodore), the agency took on the project with gusto, forging a vast network of compliant, corruptible mercenaries to rally mobs, kidnap officials and spread fake news, while amenable Islamist leaders were bribed and courted for their support. In the meantime, secret codewords were transmitted to the Shah via BBC Persian to keep him up to date and ensure his ongoing commitment to the scheme.

The first coup attempt failed, but the second took Mosaddegh unawares. In August 1953, as anarchy raged on the streets, soldiers raided his home and chased him in his pink pyjamas over the back wall of his garden – and Iran's brief dalliance with democracy came to a piteous and insalubrious end.

Mosaddegh spent three years in prison and the rest of his life under house arrest guarded by SAVAK officers, the Shah's ruthless secret police.[107] When he died in 1967, the hope of a free, egalitarian Iran died with him. 'If the US had not sent agents to depose Prime Minister Mohammad Mosaddegh in 1953, Iran would probably have continued along its path towards full democracy,' Kinzer writes in *All the King's Men*. 'Over the decades that followed, it might have become the first democratic state in the Muslim Middle East, and perhaps even a model for other countries in the region and beyond.'[108]

Shiraz hits me like a truck, almost literally. The road widens and separates into multiple lanes, while lines of wheezing traffic choke

---

[107] SAVAK was funded and trained by the CIA using methods 'based on German torture techniques from World War II', according to the former CIA analyst Jesse Leaf.

[108] The Mosaddegh coup set the blueprint for future CIA operations across Latin America, Southeast Asia and Africa, in which brutal, dictatorial regimes were frequently supported in a bid to defeat their socialist opponents and secure Western corporate interests. Roosevelt didn't hang around for these, however; he left the agency in 1958 to take a lucrative position with Gulf Oil, one of the five US petroleum firms granted a 40 per cent stake in the AIOC concession following the coup.

the streets like clogged arteries. Around me, soaring high-rises and glass-fronted office blocks contrast with low, stumpy bungalows sitting in clouds of dust. As the birthplace of the great Persian poets Hafez and Sa'di, it is not quite the peaceful, poetic idyll I envisaged, although there is admittedly something about the city's grubby vivacity that appeals.

My host is an architecture graduate called Maziar, who is tall and angular and emits a delicate melancholy. He clears a space for me to sleep among the junk and old mattresses in his parents' garage, then serves me tea with *nabat* (rock candy) in their living room. The house is the most modern I've encountered so far, boasting a busy miscellany of styles that contrasts markedly with the chic austerity of the villages, and we sit on the floor among a confusion of chintzy violet sofas, shiny tasselled curtains and gaudy polka-dot lamps as Maziar describes his visceral hatred of the regime.

'I was beaten and jailed for ten days in 2002 after joining some street protests, and my nose was badly broken,' he tells me. 'Then, during the Green protests,[109] a group of us were arrested and beaten again.' He is now desperate to travel but cannot get permission to do so due to his former activism. 'I'd love to have a British passport,' he says, his sad eyes full of longing. 'It's like a golden key.'

Later, I go to Bagh-e-Eram (Paradise Garden) to meet Salma, a friend-of-a-friend who has invited me to lunch. The verdant grounds are pristinely ordered, built in the eleventh century by the Seljuqs and recrafted afresh by each successive dynasty. Orange, pine and persimmon trees create perfumed enclaves for covert trysts, while an orgy of Qajar verandas, mosaics and marbled columns reflect in a dazzling Hockneyesque pool at the centre.

---

[109] The Green Movement arose after the 2009 presidential election, when up to 3 million Iranians took to the streets to protest against alleged vote-rigging and the election of Mahmoud Ahmadinejad. Green was the campaign emblem of opposition candidate Mir-Hossein Mousavi, but later became a broader symbol of unity for the movement.

But this landscaped beauty comes as no surprise. Iranians have long been passionate horticulturists and even gave us our word for 'paradise' from the Old Persian term for 'walled garden': *paradaida*. Evoked with breathless frequency in Persian art and literature through the ages, gardens are seen as a paradoxical embodiment of both purity and passion, the corporeal and divine.

I find Salma waiting beneath a row of swaying cypresses. She drives us to her home, where she proceeds to pile dish upon dish of aromatic delights onto the *sofreh* as I talk to her husband, Mohamed. 'Khomeini was an educated, thoughtful man,' he tells me. 'He read Ibn Sina and Ibn Rushd, and all the great philosophers. He was a mystic, not a fanatic.'[110]

Mohamed's character proves similarly contradictory. A religiously devout research biologist, he believes in science but not evolution, and supports gender segregation while encouraging Salma in her work and studies. He is sanctimonious and pious, yet respectful and polite. He is single-minded, however, about the Baha'is. 'They're dangerous,' he says. 'They're controlled by Israel and want to destroy Islam.'

The hatred towards the Baha'is in Iran has always bewildered me. Heavily persecuted since the religion's founding in 1844, this group of gentle peaceniks, who preach such retrograde values as love, tolerance and gender equality, continue to be banned from state jobs and higher education, and live in constant fear of arrest. Propaganda against them is fierce, and even the most freethinking of Iranians seem to believe that the sect has sinister secrets to hide.

'I believe you're wrong,' I say, as Salma's mother heaps another

---

[110] In Michael Axworthy's *Empire of the Mind*, I come across an astonishing, censorious letter written by Khomeini to a group of hyper-conservative clerics in 1989 that seems to provide some evidence of this. 'This old father of yours has suffered more from stupid reactionary mullahs than anyone else,' the missive begins. 'Learning foreign languages was blasphemy, philosophy and mysticism were considered to be sin and infidelity... Had this trend continued, I have no doubt the clergy and seminaries would have trodden the same path as the Christian Church did in the Middle Ages.'

juggernaut of lamb and courgette stew on my already overflowing plate. 'I know many Baha'is and they're good, decent people.'[111]

'That's not my experience,' he replies, holding out a hand to halt his mother-in-law as she swoops in, torpedo-like, with a follow-up sortie of saffron rice.

'Have you met any?'

He pauses. 'No.'

I survey the Everest of food before me. Even Ranulph, I suspect, may have met his match here. 'You said earlier that you thought Britain publishes a lot of fake propaganda about Iran,' I say. 'And you're probably right. But you have to accept that your government may do the same.'

I expect him to argue. But he just looks at me, saying nothing. Then, eventually, he replies. 'I understand what you say. And I agree we must all be willing sometimes to question our beliefs.'

I take Mohamed out of the box I've put him in and wonder where to place him now. There are no easy binaries in Iran, it seems. No comforting presumptions fulfilled. Just smudges where clear lines should be, and light in the darkest of shades.

The booze is quite something. Litres of Absolut vodka, Lebanese wine, Indian whisky, Ukrainian schnapps and homemade cognac cover every inch of table like the laboratory of a mad chemistry professor. The room itself, with its velvet chaise longues, Georgian furniture and geometric rugs, feels like a cross between an art deco gallery and Louis XIV drawing room, while at the same time still expressing its distinct Persianness as if this were a dominant gene that can never be repressed.

'Drink is special to Shiraz,' my host, Bijan, explains, while

---

[111] It was through a Baha'i friend that I met Maziar Bahari, whose film *To Light a Candle* documents the severity of the persecution against Baha'is in Iran. As a *Newsweek* reporter, Bahari was detained in Iran for four months in 2009 on false spying charges. His book about the experience was made into a film, *Rosewater*, by the US comedian Jon Stewart.

pouring two glasses of rust-coloured claret. 'The vineyards are all brown now, but it still runs in our blood.'

A technician friend of Amir's, Bijan is small and stocky with an intense manner and plump helmet of hair. As we work through this platter of inevitable liver failure, he gives me his rundown on Iranian society. There are four categories of people, he asserts: religious people who support the regime, religious people who oppose it, non-practising Muslims and 'agitators' who actively rebel. Ninety per cent of people fall under the last three categories, he says, and want Khamenei gone.

'They're lying,' he responds when I mention all the pro-regime families I've met so far. 'They're scared.'

'They don't seem scared.'

'Trust me.'

Khamenei has enormous power, he insists. 'He controls everything: the president, media, judiciary, Sepah …[112] Khomeini was a tyrant, but he at least led a quiet life. Khamenei is rich. He's built a huge mansion for himself, Beit-e Rahbari, and sees Iran as his own personal property.'

Following a little research, I discover there's a lot of truth in what Bijan says. Unlike Khomeini, who had a shoestring staff, Khamenei employs hundreds of people at Beit-e Rahbari and enjoys access to an extraordinary amount of wealth via a shadowy agency named Setad. Originally established to manage the seizure and sale of properties abandoned after the revolution, Setad has expanded to become 'a massive network of front companies hiding assets on behalf of … Iran's leadership', in the words of

---

[112] Sepah, or the Revolutionary Guard, is a special military branch with far-ranging powers. Designated a terrorist organisation by the US and some Gulf states, it has been linked to global smuggling rings, kidnapping scandals and bombings, and one of its most senior commanders, Qasem Soleiman, was assassinated by an American drone strike in January 2020. Sepah has its own media wing and intelligence service, and – much like SCAF in Egypt – is believed to control up to a third of the Iranian economy through a sprawling empire of corporate interests.

the US Treasury, with stakes in everything from oil and real estate to contraception and ostrich farming. According to a Reuters investigation, the agency was worth an eyepopping $95 billion in 2013 – and probably considerably more now.

'Khamenei's a criminal,' Bijan stresses. 'Believe me, most people hate him.'

Later, when I'm gathering my things to leave, Bijan presents me with a bottle of clear liquid. I assume it's water and accept it gratefully, but he corrects me. '*Aragh*,' he says: the local moonshine, derived from raisins. The Armenians are permitted to make it, he explains, and some secretly sell it too. But I should watch out for dodgy varieties made by amateur vintners in their living rooms, some of which may contain methanol rather than ethanol and make me go blind.

'So if some random guy offers you any,' he warns, 'don't drink it.'

'Okay,' I nod. 'So, who made this?'

'A guy I know.'

'In his living room?'

'Yes.'

I place the bottle gingerly in my bag, as if it were a Molotov cocktail or canister of Novichok. 'Thank you,' I say. 'I'll bear that in mind.'

Celebrated for centuries for its beauty, Shiraz to me feels like the heart of Iran, epitomising its contours and contradictions. Mosques built by Europhile khans stand beside walls of graffiti feting Allah and inebriety, while residents celebrate the Epicurean polymath Omar Khayyam[113] as much as they do the Qur'an. In

---

[113] Born in 1044, Khayyam was an astronomer, mathematician and poet, whose elite status allowed him to say things a normal man could be hanged for, according to Iranian literature professor Ahmad Karimi Hakkak. However, his poetry, which often questioned religion and tradition, was banned from the public sphere during his lifetime and did not gain wide readership in either Iran or the West until the Victorian poet Edward FitzGerald translated his quatrains into English in 1859.

1280, the Mongols reputedly stopped their riot of slaughter at the doors of the city, so bewitched by its charms that they began memorising verses of the *Shahnameh* as the embers of conquest still burnt. '[Shiraz] has elegant gardens and gushing streams, sumptuous bazaars and handsome thoroughfares ...' Ibn Battuta wrote of his visit in 1347, a century after the Mongol occupation of Persia. 'In the whole East, there is no city except Shiraz which approached Damascus in the beauty of its bazaars, fruit-gardens and rivers ...'

I would love to stay longer to explore the place properly, but sadly my time here is curtailed. On my second day, Maziar calls me in an agitated state. A policeman keeps phoning him and asking awkward questions about me, he says. 'I told him you weren't staying here, but he'll probably come to check.' His voice is thick with anxiety. 'I'm so sorry to tell you this – but I think you need to leave.'

To my surprise, Persepolis proves a disappointment. Constructed as the ceremonial capital of the Achaemenid Empire in the sixth century BCE, this ancient fortress-city once sparkled in a cosmopolitan mosaic of Egyptian ebony, Lebanese cedar and Bactrian gold, attracting tribute bearers from across the globe. Now its skeletal remains lie like an open casket at the base of a hill, its bones fractured and scattered, its flesh long decayed. Limestone columns stand in clumps and stunted lines, throwing into relief the wide, empty expanses where marble porticoes, resplendent tapestries and winged griffins gleamed long ago.

Viewed from above, the layout of the original settlement is still clearly delineated in a cross-hatching of low walls and ramparts, as if Persepolis was never a real structure at all but just a blueprint or etching in the sand. But perhaps this is apt, in a way, because even in life Persepolis was more masquerade than functional metropolis: a symbol of grandeur rather than a living, breathing city. Nowadays, the value of the place lies less in what edifices remain than in the imaginative spaces in between – spaces that hark back to a mythological golden age with roots in classical antiquity. Since Alexander the Great destroyed the site in 330 BCE, its martyred spirit has endured, stronger in death than in life. It lives on eternally as an icon in the heart of the people, a mirror to their values and goals. For some, it represents sovereignty and liberty from foreign rule; for others, a secular, pre-Islamic ideal.[114] For this reason, Persepolis and Iran's other ancient monuments have long posed a dilemma for the religious establishment, acting as a reminder of both an ungodly era of avarice and a time when Persian hegemony reigned supreme.

In a village called Pasargad[115] nearby, I stay with some friends-of-friends. The family comprises a middle-aged couple, their parents, their two adult sons and their young daughter, and I like them immediately. 'Hijab, no!' the mother cries as I enter, and I tug it off with relief. The house, I note, is a perfect balance between tradition and modernity, with sofas and a Western toilet but also wall-to-wall carpeting and rolled mattresses for beds. I am beginning to read the political code of soft furnishings now, and it comes as no surprise when my hosts reveal that they are 'semi-Muslims' who rarely attend mosque and feel indifferent towards the regime.

On their insistence, I stay with the family for the weekend.

---

[114] For Mohammad Reza Shah, Persepolis appeared to represent luxury and hedonistic wealth, bearing in mind the tone-deaf festivities he organised here in 1971 to celebrate the 2,500th anniversary of the Persian Empire. As the Iranian population starved, he invited dozens of world rulers to a three-day, multi-million-dollar feast of caviar, lobster mousse and peacocks stuffed with foie gras. 'What do they think I should feed fifty heads of state?' he is rumoured to have retorted when eyebrows were raised about the cost. 'Bread and radishes?'

[115] Pasargad lies on the site of Pasargadae, the first dynastic capital of the Achaemenid Empire. At that time, the city was the economic and cultural hub of the world, brimming with luxuriant gardens, stuccoed palaces and basalt mausoleums to ancient gods. Today, all that remains are some crumbling ruins and a thirty-foot tomb said to belong to Cyrus the Great, which stands lonely and unprotected on the roadside (and which, to me, feels like a more fitting symbol than Persepolis for the state of Iran today).

Friends and neighbours drift in and out with such smooth constancy over this period that I find I can look up and discover an entirely new group of people in the house before becoming aware that anything has changed at all. Among these visitors is the requisite mad old granny, a version of which seems to exist in every household, who sporadically skips over to squeeze me like a lemon before miming riding a bicycle and cackling with maniacal glee. On the first night, we play a kind of charades in which we each act out words for the group – 'flower', 'Englishman', 'penicillin' etc. – and the woman, having been given the word 'insanity', points at me with a long, bony finger before collapsing in a fit of toothless hysterics on the floor.

It soon becomes clear that political opinions among the guests are wildly mixed, along with people's sense of religious devotion. Some women decline to remove their hijabs yet speak bitterly of the 'corrupt' or 'useless' mullahs, while others pay only lip-service to religion but speak with grudging respect for the regime.

The weekend slips by, slumberous and serene, punctuated by regular naps, food and drink. For hours we sit munching on cucumber in the garden, or watermelon in the desert, or noodle soup on the *sofreh* indoors. I am amazed by how well the family members get along, all squeezed together in this modest four-room bungalow, and I struggle to imagine my own relatives enjoying such cosy intimacy for so long. Not while sleeping in the same room, at least. And certainly not while sober. It is truly a marvel to behold.

As each day passes, my sense of ease and security grows. The Islamic Republic may be a cold, dark place, but Iran feels awash with light. It is as if the idea of 'Iran' – or 'Persia', perhaps, with all the weight of romance that attaches to the term – permeates the soil itself, rarefied and undefined, oblivious to the shortcomings of those who speak in its name. What creates this sense is hard to pinpoint, but it seems at once both personal and aesthetic, contained both within the people and the poetic charm of the surrounds. Perhaps, in part, it is our common Indo-European heritage that inspires this cultural kinship, and our shared linguistic roots. Farsi certainly feels familiar at times, like a covert nod between members of an ancient club; words like *dokhtar* (daughter), *nam* (name) and *tondar* (thunder) need little interpretation, while 'I am Iranian' translates as the immediately recognisable *Irani-am*.

One day, on the brow of a steep hill, a driver pulls over to hand me a bottle of water. Accepting it gratefully, I am just dwelling once more on the wonders of Iranian hospitality when he smiles and motions for me to join him in the car. I hope that I've misunderstood, but the offer is followed by a series of gesticulations that allow for no ambiguity. This crude display, the first I've encountered in Iran, comes as such a shock that at first I'm rendered speechless. But then, with a heave of fury that feels like a dam breaking, I find my voice. '*Gom shoo!*' I cry, backing away. '*Pedar sag!!*' Go away! Your father is a dog! Two insults, as yet unused, that I picked up from Bijan in Shiraz. They fail to have the desired impact, however, as two minutes later the driver stops again to entice me with a bag of plums. '*Goozidam too cheshmet!*' I scream (the impactful, if anatomically challenging, 'I fart in your eye'). The man adds a nectarine to the haul, and I vow to work on my pronunciation.

As I stand there, flushed and indignant, I realise that I've fallen into the trap of romanticism. The kindnesses I've received have all but blinded me to Iran's deeply embedded misogyny. As if to ensure the first wake-up call hasn't gone unheeded, I have two more unsavoury encounters shortly afterwards, neither of which dwells on foreplay. 'Iran *ziba*?' one man asks. Iran is beautiful? 'Sex?'

The road to Yazd is no fun to cycle. Descending for 190 kilometres into a broad depression between Dasht-e Lut and Dasht-e Kavir, Iran's two hyper-arid deserts, the highway is long, dreary and blisteringly hot. In 2005, NASA registered a world-beating ground temperature in Lut of 70.7°C, and although the mercury creeps only to a relatively glacial 45°C here on the elevated western ridge, that is quite toasty enough for me. For hours, I beat my way on through a torrid wind, head down, eyes closed, as a sand storm swirls about me and a white-gold sun beams down overhead. Every part of me is tired now: my back, my limbs, my bones.

Yazd appears like a mirage, a cinnamon town in a blizzard of dust. Pulling up, exhausted, it takes some moments before I hear a voice calling with growing persistence from the roadside. 'Rebecca, Rebecca, *khosh amadid!*' Rebecca, Rebecca, welcome! 'Ahmad, from Couchsurfing, your host!'

An ancient Zoroastrian city first settled five millennia ago, Yazd doesn't feel like a thriving metropolis of 600,000 people. Constructed almost entirely from mud, its architecture feels organic and elemental, its skyline soft and low. 'It's a very relaxing place to live,' Ahmad says as we sip lemon juice on a rooftop terrace staring out at a tawny landscape of sandy courtyards, *ab anbars* (domed reservoirs) and *badgirs* (windcatchers) reminiscent of mini-Athenian temples. 'It's very friendly, very traditional. Though, to be honest, also a bit boring if you're young.'

Yazd may be dull, but it exudes ingenuity. Through its complex system of *ab anbars, badgirs* and *qanats*, air is captured, clay moulded and water diverted, all with trademark Persian style and efficacy. It is largely due to this self-sufficient harnessing of natural resources that the town has been able to repel invaders through the ages and provide a refuge for people fleeing persecution and war. 'Lots of Zoroastrians came here after the Arab invasion,' Ahmad explains as he takes me on a lengthy drive into the desert to an odd little village named Chak Chak. 'And it remains the last surviving centre of Zoroastrianism in Iran today.'

Encrusted like a limpet on the side of a cliff, Chak Chak at first doesn't look like much. Yet hidden high on the rockface, tucked among these simple, balconied apartments, lies the beating heart of the Zoroastrian faith. It is here, in a shallow cave concealed behind two bronze doors, where the mountain cracked open in

640 CE to save the Sasanian princess Nikbanou from the invading Arabs, so legend goes, and a permanently dripping spring – producing the *chak chak* sound from which the village derived its name – is said to symbolise her tears of grief.

As we enter this sacred grotto, I can't help but feel a frisson of excitement. Zoroastrianism, for me, has always been the king of the faiths. While its provenance is shrouded in mystery, its long-term influence has undoubtedly been profound. Long before Christianity, Islam and even the ancient philosophers, Zarathustra was teaching about the nature of free will, the importance of virtue and the eternal conflict between good (Ahura Mazda) and evil (Ahriman). Fourteen hundred years after the Muslim invasion, the religion remains firmly rooted in Iranian culture today, retaining an indigenous spirit and purity that the state-sanctioned version of Islam seems increasingly to lack. In the West, its impact runs almost as deep, casting its shadow over a vast canon of cultural works from classical music and Enlightenment philosophy to contemporary fantasy dramas (*Game of Thrones*) and car manufacturers (the Mazda).

'The mullahs are always trying to ban Nowruz,'[116] Ahmed says, as we return to Yazd across the blustery sands. 'But they'll never succeed because it's so popular.'

'I can imagine,' I say. 'Iran feels more Zoroastrian than Islamic to me, in a way.'

'Yes.' He opens the car window to flick out his cigarette ash, letting in a whoosh of fiery air. 'After forty years of the Islamist Republic, I think a lot of Iranians would probably agree with you.'

As Ramadan begins in mid-June, I feel nervous about what this month of enforced abstinence will mean for my journey. It is apparently against the law to ignore the fast, but if I don't regularly shovel food and drink down my gullet like a stoker on

---

[116]   An ancient Zoroastrian feast day celebrated on the spring equinox.

a steam engine then I know my days of survival in the saddle will be numbered.

It swiftly becomes clear, however, that my worries are in vain. Shirking Ramadan appears to be a national pastime. Excuses to avoid it remind me of the school locker-room before gym class: women are on their period, men too infirm, unfit or unwell. There are special dispensations for travellers too, it seems – so everything, to my relief, continues much as it did before. Shops stay open, food remains plentiful and people continue to feed me, insistently and incessantly, like a goose being fattened for slaughter.

Iran is a country that sparkles with secret treasures like gold flecks sifted from clay. In the sleepy adobe village of Aqda, I wheel Maud through an unassuming guesthouse gateway to discover a vast, vaulted chamber reminiscent of a Byzantine cathedral. Constructed entirely of mud, the cruciform room exudes both splendour and serenity, its transepts hung with jewelled lanterns, faience and batiks, its stained-glass windows filtering a wash of rainbow light onto the flagstones far below. Who the clientele are is a mystery – the rooms are empty at present, and the cook must be fetched from home to prepare my food – but the place, so incongruous in these barren, unobtrusive surrounds, is truly a wonder to behold.

According to the guesthouse pamphlets, Aqda is one of the oldest villages in Yazd Province and possibly dates back 6,000 years or more. Yet the neighbouring town of Naein – where an archaeological feast of Safavid mansions, Qajar *mosallahs* and medieval mosques sit alongside Parthian ruins, pre-Islamic *qanats* and Zoroastrian caves – may be even older, I'm told … though nobody can say for sure.

Having now been in Iran for several weeks, I have learnt to take such claims lightly. Not because I don't believe them but because history has such ubiquity here that its presence seems as the air. Time is Iran's currency: a tangible asset of national pride, like cars to the Germans or wine to the French. It is found heaped in centuries and millennia in the way it's sprinkled in years and decades at home, and I feel myself constantly lost within it as I wade deeper into the country each day.

I have a visitor! I see her in the distance, squinting towards me into the sun. Then, spotting me, she rushes forward. 'Bex!' she cries, waving. 'Here!'

One of my closest friends, Jo, has flown from London to see me. As a dual Greek-British national, she is exempt from Iran's strict visa protocols, and I was delighted when I heard she planned to make the trip. After a jubilant embrace, we fall swiftly into the familiar rhythms of friendship, exchanging news and gossip and fond, affectionate abuse. It feels like a long time since I've felt so entirely at ease in someone's company, with no linguistic or cultural barriers, no formalities of etiquette, no forced politeness or misconceptions of *taarof*. It is, of course, a wonderful thing to meet new people and discover new cultures and beliefs. But it is equally joyful to fall back on the consoling comforts and tropes of home, and feel momentarily anchored amid one's ambulatory existence on the road.

Sadly, however, we have just one evening in Isfahan together before we part ways. Jo is more a bus than a bicycle kind of girl, so she plans to explore Yazd and Shiraz before joining me again in Kashan. 'Try not to get killed while I'm here,' she counsels wisely as we say our goodbyes. 'My flight is non-refundable, so it'd be quite inconvenient for me.'

After Jo leaves, I move in with a couple and baby. The woman, Sara, is a Persian literature student at Tehran University, while her husband runs a tour company.[117] Brought up in the religious city of Qom, she is a devout Muslim while her husband rarely

---

[117]   Surprisingly, despite being banned from seventy-seven fields of study in dozens of universities, female university graduates in Iran frequently outnumber men.

prays. Yet it is he who admires Khomeini and Khamenei and she who despises them both. 'They are ...' – she searches for the word – 'oppressor.'

Later, after settling her son in bed, Sara removes a book of Hafez from the shelf. She then sits beside me on the sofa and begins reciting from it with her eyes half closed, murmuring the lines like a canticle or psalm. I watch her, transfixed. For me, English translations of the fourteenth-century poet's works have always felt flat and clumsy, somehow, as if forced into an alien habitat where they don't belong. In Persian, however, the beauty of his verse is undeniable.

'Hafez is my favourite poet,' Sara says when she's finished. She looks bleary eyed, as if emerging from a trance. 'He sees the divine in everyday things.' She often reads his work for guidance, she says: an Iranian custom known as *Fal'e Hafez*. 'Your Queen Victoria, I think, did this too.'

Born in the period between the Mongol and Timurid invasions, Hafez emerged like a rose between thorns. His mystical, sonnet-like ghazals remain as popular now as they were then, tapping into an ancient, elemental Persian psyche that the Qur'an struggles to match. Deeply interwoven with symbol and subtext, his *Divan* seems to contain something for everybody, quoted by the devout and secular, old and young, traditionalists and progressives alike.

Sara's recitation does little to dispel my romantic notions about Isfahan, which of all Iranian cities seems most to embody the mythological Persia of my imagination. It feels dreamlike just being here, and I struggle to view my surrounds with a dispassionate eye as I make my way along the Zayanderud river towards the centre. To my side, pools of evaporating water lie in silky abstractions along the riverbed, endowing even drought and decay with a kind of grace, while the fortress-like Khaju and Si-o-se-pol bridges both glow with muted majesty in a velvety, amber light.

At Chahar Bagh Boulevard, I let my fancies loose. Sheltered

by bowing plane trees, Chahar Bagh was once one of the most glamorous avenues in the world, cleaved down the centre by a sparkling onyx channel and bordered by thickets of jasmine planted by Shah Abbas himself as he scattered gold coins among their roots. Transporting myself back 400 years, I imagine the aristocracy walking this way for their daily promenade, listening to the cooing doves overhead and breathing in the heady scents of lavender, juniper and rose. I picture them visiting the imperial zoo to see the tigers and featherless ostriches, and humouring the merchants hawking their goods from the backwaters of Armenia and Amsterdam. I see a few of them even entering the Shah's personal harem, where hundreds of women were rumoured to reside inside a 'pleasure house' of gilded passageways and mirrored glass.

'Shah Abbas chose Isfahan as his capital and went crazy building bridges, palaces, gardens, hammams ...' a young man called Hormuzd explains, who offers to show me around after spotting me looking lost near Khaju bridge. 'It was so amazing, it was known as *Isfahan nesfe jahan*: "Isfahan is half the world".'

Describing himself as the 'king of the square', Hormuzd is a sinewy, shifty character, somewhere between the Artful Dodger and Uriah Heap in demeanour, and I can't say I feel entirely at ease in his company. However, he turns out to be an excellent guide. The square in question is Naqsh-e Jahan, a giant quadrangle bordered by resplendent Safavid monuments, and we walk there together past stalls of craftspeople creating works of exquisite charm: jewellery boxes forged from tessellated filaments of rosewood, camel bone and mother-of-pearl (*khatam*); copper plates engraved with arcadian wonderlands of ibex and deer; miniature portraits painted in delicate strokes of bronze, silver and gold. 'Welcome to my kingdom,' Hormuzd says as we walk. 'I know everyone, and everyone knows me.'

We pass some rental bicycles, and Hormuzd tells me how lucky I am to be able to cycle alone through Iran. These bikes are just for men, he explains, and women are often stopped by the *Gasht-e Ershad* from riding unchaperoned in the streets. 'In cities like Shiraz and Tehran, it's fine, but it's more traditional here. Women cyclists are rare.'[118]

At Naqsh-e Jahan, Hormuzd robes me in a chequered chador and escorts me through the resplendent turquoise iwan[119] of Sheikh Lotfollah Mosque into a beautiful prayer room emblazoned in a carnival of indigos, ochres and greens. From the *mihrab*, a mullah is speaking in a low voice to a handful of male congregants, while a huddle of black-cloaked women sit beyond his eyeline on the far side of a makeshift barrier. To me, the scene feels oddly incongruous: the open democracy of the space, with its soaring dome and melodies of pattern and form, alongside the segregated bigotry of the floorplan, in which some people are clearly more equal than others.

Outside, I ask Hormuzd why women seem always to be relegated to the periphery inside mosques – but he doesn't hear me. He is too busy ogling a young woman in a glitzy hijab nearby, his expression somehow both languorous and beady-eyed.

'I brought a Swedish girl here last week,' he says suddenly, as if answering a question I never asked. 'She *loved* it. And so did the French girl who came before.' He has relationships with many foreign women, he explains. 'I used to be religious, but then I started meeting Europeans through Couchsurfing. Now I drink and have sex all the time!'

'Wonderful,' I reply. 'How proud that makes me.'

---

[118] In September 2016, Khamenei attempted to clarify the situation by issuing a *fatwa* banning women from cycling in public anywhere in the country. However, this merely prompted thousands of women to take to the saddle in protest, posting images of themselves with the hashtag #IranianWomenLoveCycling.

[119] Believed to have been invented by the Parthians around 2,000 years ago, iwans are large, rectangular, usually vaulted spaces, open on one side, which frame the gateway to ceremonial and religious buildings (particularly mosques).

He laughs and drapes a stringy arm across my shoulders. 'Good! So ... where now?'

'Nowhere!'

I remove his arm with a glare. After a year on the road, my tolerance for creeps is precisely nil.

'Sorry.' His grin falters. 'Just being friendly.'

'It's not friendly, it's harassment. Anyway, I thought touching wasn't allowed here?'

'It's okay these days.' He puts his hands in his pockets as if stuffing weapons into a holster. 'I mean, it's possible you might be arrested, but it's all a bit of a joke.' Iran isn't like it used to be, he says. There are even sex parties where guests pay $10 each to attend. 'You don't read about that side of Iran, do you?'

I ignore the bait. 'So, if the police are getting soft, does that mean there's hope for change?'

He nods. 'Revolution is coming. Ten years, tops.'

'But I thought nobody wanted revolution?'

'They don't. But it'll happen.' He stops to light a cigarette. 'It's like me and that Swedish girl. I didn't want to have sex with her, but somehow it happened anyway.'

I stare at him, awestruck. How he's managed to shoehorn sex back into the conversation in the space of thirty seconds is quite extraordinary.

'Yes, it's just like that,' I tell him. 'Now, if you don't mind – please take your greasy hands and *gom shoo*!'

On Google Maps, a slender white thread runs shakily through the Karkas Mountains between Meymeh and Kashan. Juddering its way across a spider's web of contour lines, it unspools all the way to Abyaneh, a mud-brick Sasanian village that's said – yes, here we are again – to be one of the oldest and most beautiful settlements in Iran. My hope is that it signifies a road, although my host in Meymeh is sceptical. 'Absolutely not!' she says, chuckling at my foolishness. 'Just grass and goats!'

I know I should heed her words. But there is an obstinacy deep within me that's always had trouble taking advice from people more knowledgeable than myself (namely, most people). So, at 5.30am, I say my goodbyes and set off towards the smudge of distant peaks. Bleak grasslands surround me, straw green and henna red, sprouting in grainy tufts as if the land were slowly going bald. Then, as I start to climb, the foliage fades away and soft folds of rock begin to encircle me in waves, lapping at the roadside in a swirl of lavender, burgundy and beige.

As I approach the place where the turning should be, I hold little hope of success. But then, with a burst of excitement and vindication, I spot it: a narrow, unpaved track, barely a donkey cart in width, nestled among the roadside scrub. Whether it could be categorised as a 'road', precisely, I'm unsure, but I feel deeply relieved to have found anything here at all. From this spot, Abyaneh lies just twenty kilometres to the east, and I am hopeful I can make it there by lunch.

At first, the terrain is gravelly but manageable, and I set off at a slow but steady pace. As it continues, however, the path begins to deteriorate. Rising ever steeper, it dissolves first into rock, then rubble, then sand, and my progress slows to a crawl. Soon I cannot cycle at all, so I dismount and push, the strain tearing into my shoulders, glutes and thighs as rivulets of sweat course in a steady torrent down my back.

On I go, up and up and up. At the crest of a small hill, I look out at a dry depression surrounded by speckled indigo peaks. Far below, I can just make out a cluster of red-roofed outhouses, but they appear dark and abandoned. It is swelteringly hot now, and my throat feels cracked and sore.

After four hours, I have travelled just ten kilometres and am desperate to stop and rest. But there is no shelter in sight, so instead I dig out my final three energy gels and swallow them in quick succession. One of them splits in my haste, leaving a fluorescent pink residue down my chin like the trail of a particularly flamboyant snail. *Come on, you pussy*, I mutter, imagining Dervla Murphy's disapproving gaze. *It's hardly the Khyber Pass!*

Then, just as I feel the sugar seeping into my pores, I hear it. The sound I always dread, which has plagued me in fits and bursts – literally – since Beirut.

Pfffft.

Emitting a wail somewhere between a sob and the howl of a strangled cat, I drop Maud and slump down beside her onto the sand. *Now?!* The situation is especially galling because these inner tubes, bought in Muscat, were meant to be slime-filled and self-repairing. But it feels somehow fitting that they're not. What better accompaniment to puncture-proof tyres that get constant punctures, after all, than self-repairing tubes that fail to repair?

The hole proves impossible to mend. My glue is almost finished, and what remains appears to have congealed in the heat. Feeling a mild tremor of panic, I wonder what to do. My options seem worryingly limited. One: attempt to push Maud the remaining ten kilometres and hope the road improves. This may be possible, although I fear such an effort may be beyond me, and I am likely to damage Maud's wheel rim in the process. Two: have a nap and hope for a miracle.

I punt for two. And, to my astonishment, it works!

Just as I curl up by the roadside, about to nod off, a battered truck appears in the distance. Seeing it, I feel such a rush of exhilaration that I forget to put on my hijab and instead dash madly along the track, arms outstretched, hair flying in grimy straggles like some kind of crazed mountain sasquatch. The driver, faced with such a sight, could hardly be blamed for ignoring me entirely and continuing on without a second glance. But instead, he pulls over and nods a calm hello, as if half-feral female cyclists were a regular and tiresome phenomenon out here in the remote Iranian boondocks, and helps me lift Maud into his truck without uttering a word.

'*Merci, mamnun, sepâs!*' I gasp. And then, as none of these expressions feels quite sufficient: '*Ghorbun daste shomâ!*' I sacrifice myself for your hand![120]

The man takes me to his farm, which appears to comprise little more than a windowless stone hut, a barrel of *doogh* (fermented milk), various mounds of bricks and detritus, and several hundred grazing goats and sheep. Inside the hut are two dirty mattresses, some cooking equipment and a pile of packaged food. To me right now, the place looks like the Shangri-La.

Two farmers live here. The one who picked me up wears a pristine white shirt and dark trousers, and has a rather distinguished air to him, while his partner appears somewhat more grizzled at the edges, with capaciously baggy slacks and a lugubrious demeanour cast into shade by a stained cotton sunhat. Neither seems particularly enthused by my presence; they simply continue with their work as if I were not here at all. Through a mixture of pigeon-Farsi, semaphore and charades, I try to persuade them to drive me the remaining few miles to Abyaneh – but they, understandably, pay no heed.

Shortly before dusk, just as I'm beginning to worry about spending the remainder of my days rearing ungulates with this pair of phlegmatic goatherders, a car appears. A man and young boy have arrived to buy some sheep. The man, Atash, speaks a little English and tells me, to my immense relief, that they will happily give me a lift to Abyaneh when they leave – though I must wait for their transaction to be completed first. Over the next hour I watch, enraptured, as the sheep are all painstakingly

---

[120] I love how many ways there are to express gratitude in Iran. *Merci* and *mamnun* seem the most common, though *sepâs* is popular too as it's a Persian word without an Arabic root. Then there's *moteshakiram* (more formal), *tashakoor mikonam* (I thank you), *lotf dârid* (you are very kind, often used in reply to compliments), *daste shomâ dard nakone* (may your hand be free from harm), *sharmande hastam* (a kind of embarrassed thank you when any response feels inadequate) – and more. If language is the key to understanding a culture, Iran is nothing if not a nation of unabashed civility.

weighed in pairs in a small wire basket, their eight hooves stuck ludicrously and indecorously in the air so that they resemble a set of fluffy bagpipes, before they are grabbed and hurled like sacks of flour into the back of a truck. I feel quite sorry for them, but as someone who devours lamb *koobideh* with wild, greedy abandon at every opportunity, it seems a little hypocritical of me to object.

We then load up the car – Maud, my bags, the man, the boy, a tiny lamb the boy's taken as a pet, several barrels of *doogh* and me – and, after a heartfelt thank you to my smallholder saviours, we set off. As we do, the lamb stretches out sleepily on the back seat, its head resting on the boy's lap, its downy rump on mine, and I feel a sudden surge of giggly euphoria that only a misadventure and miraculous rescue can engender. This giddiness is heightened by the manic bumpiness of the drive, as we race along the rutted, scabrous landscape, thrashing our suspension on rocks and puffing up clouds of dust that blot out the sky in our wake. I realise now why the car chassis is more dodecahedron than classically cuboid in shape. Every time we encounter a new obstacle, such as a gaping crevasse or gang of rabid hounds, Atash grins and cries 'Iranian road!' with a helpless sigh, as if he were a mere innocent bystander to this unfortunate state of affairs rather than the person with their foot welded permanently and inexplicably on the accelerator.

Eventually, bruised and ragged, we pull into the charming terracotta town of Abyaneh. Here, Atash drops me at a local hotel that appears to have been designed by a drunk Aladdin – all antique lamps, mini tomahawks and porcelain dolls dressed in sequined Azari robes – and helps me to negotiate a half-price deal before returning to the car to continue on his way.

'*Sepâs!*' I holler, as he slides behind the wheel. '*Moteshakiram!*'

He smiles, winks and attempts several times to close the misshapen door. He then laughs, throws up his hands and pronounces a final sheepish cry – 'Iranian car!' – before disappearing in a cloud of russet dust down the road.

* * *

Jo and I meet again in Kashan. The city turns out to be one of the jewels of this already heavily bejewelled nation, with an exquisite array of villas, gardens, mosques and hammams built in the time of the Seljuqs, Safavids and Qajars. At the eighteenth-century Agha Bozorg Mosque, we enter a building more reminiscent of a royal mansion than a place of worship. With its five floors of sand-coloured brick and two towering turquoise minarets, the sense of space is overwhelming. The eighteen-metre brick dome overlooks a double-tiered courtyard in which the centre has been excavated to create a subterranean *madrasah*, while the prayer hall is based in a large, open cloister where the inside and outside coalesce. As is traditional in Islamic architecture, emptiness here assumes a material significance, articulating an unknown world beyond.

It is Bagh-e Fin, however, a beautiful walled garden built originally for Shah Abbas, which most piques my interest – though it is not so much the leafy avenues of cypress, pine and cedar trees that intrigue me as the smaller of the two hammams tucked into the shadows in the corner. This is said to be the spot where the former prime minister Amir Kabir was murdered in 1852 after attempting to implement a series of controversial political reforms, and a montage of somewhat surreal, sorry-looking mannequins has been arranged inside a plexiglass case to mark the occasion. Distinctly 'Persian' in style – i.e. more meditative than murderous – this odd display depicts Kabir kneeling serenely on the floor as a curiously wizened hitman delicately slashes him on the wrists. Beside them lie some scattered tankards and sweets, because in Iran, as Freya Stark points out, 'anyone you meet understands the pleasures of a picnic' – even those in the midst of a political assassination.

The overall impact of this peculiar memorial-slash-shrine-slash-*tableau-vivant* may be somewhat underwhelming, but Kabir himself certainly was not. Believed by some to be Iran's first great moderniser, he balanced the budget, sacked corrupt officials, overhauled the tax system, supported clerical minorities (with the exception of the Babis, a precursor movement to the Baha'is, whom he ruthlessly persecuted) and founded a higher education facility that went on to become the University of Tehran. He also, more audaciously, took measures to limit the influence of Russia, Britain and the religious authorities, and thereby wrong-sided almost everyone with a vested interest in the entrenched power dynamics of the state. His death was a tragedy, if hardly a surprise, and serves as a stark reminder of the almost insuperable challenge of reforming a system riven by nepotism, patronage and foreign control.[121]

When exiting the garden, Jo and I encounter some posters promoting the hijab. 'The Islamic veil is for women the equivalent of the oyster for the pearl,' one reads. 'The oyster keeps the pearl safe from the hazards of the ocean. Therefore the Islamic veil must be seen as a protection and not an imprisonment.'

'Well?' I ask Jo. 'Convinced?'

She considers. 'I do have certain pearl-like qualities, it's true. But when you need to defend your dress code as "not an imprisonment", it's probably a bad sign, isn't it?'

'If we don't fast, God will punish us,' the mullah proclaims, staring at us with an air of solemn condescension. 'If we pretend to sicken with heart disease, Allah will sicken our heart.' Moments later, his train of thought shifts to more pressing aesthetic concerns. 'Women with dyed hair are *jendehs*.' Whores. 'The dye will enter their brain and cause a fatal haemorrhage.'

Fortunately, I stopped highlighting my hair a year ago, so should hopefully be safe unless the damage has already occurred.

---

[121] The Qajar king who ordered the killing, Naser al-Din Shah, was quite something. In power for forty-eight years, he kept hundreds of concubines, enjoyed burning people alive (and occasionally shooting them from cannons), and assumed the modest title 'Shah of Shahs, Asylum of the Universe, Subduer of Climate, Arbitrator of His People, Guardian of the Flock, Conqueror of the Lands and Shadow of God on Earth'. Clearly impressed by such credentials, the British in 1873 appointed him a Knight of the Order of the Garter, the highest order of chivalry.

I worry for the other guests here, though. Nobody is fasting, and at least one looks suspiciously flaxen about the fringe. Mehdi, our Couchsurfing host, who is translating the cleric's words from the television, justifies his own lack of abstinence as evidence of his hospitable nature. 'I look after travellers,' he asserts. 'And it's important for travellers to eat.'

Mehdi is plump and middle-aged with a toothy grin that never quite meets his eyes. Jo and I arrived at his flat this evening to find the place already packed full of Couchsurfers eating, drinking and watching PressTV.[122] The reports this evening are focused on the Great Satan's legacy in Iraq, with much discussion of Guantanamo Bay and waterboarding. A series of American talking heads with dubious credentials are drafted in to present their views, each one appearing as a pixelated, stuttering blur that suggests they've been patched in from underground cells or via dial-up connections from the 1990s.

As we watch, Mehdi tells us how much he admires the West and how he does Couchsurfing to 'meet interesting people and learn about foreign cultures'. This all sounds very heart-warming, and especially so when he reveals that he's moved his family into tents in the garden in order to accommodate all his guests. But it isn't true, it turns out. He does it for the cold, hard cash – as we discover early the next morning, when he dashes outside as I am leaving to demand money for an 'orphan charity' he runs but oddly can provide no paperwork for. While I am happy to pay for accommodation, the devious nature of the request riles me, and under questioning the truth soon emerges.

'You slept in our bed,' he says. 'You ate our food. These things cost money.'

'Of course,' I reply. 'But why not just say that instead of inventing a fake charity?'

---

[122] A state-funded English-language news channel banned from UK broadcast in 2012 after it aired a 'confession' from the Iranian *Newsweek* journalist Maziar Bahari obtained through torture.

'Many people ask for money. It is not much for you.'

Keen to avoid a row, Jo and I grudgingly give him as much as we can. In fact, Jo gives him rather more than just money. After I cycle away, she realises I've forgotten my bike pump and chases me down the road in her pyjama shorts, pulling her t-shirt above her head to act as a makeshift headscarf while exposing her entire naked back to Mehdi and half a dozen neighbours who have piously arisen at dawn to perform their *fajr* prayer. Dashing towards me, her hair covered, her midriff and legs bare, she has the air of a disgraced nun caught *in flagrante* and forced to jump from a window and flee.

'You should ask Mehdi for a refund,' I gasp, wiping away tears of laughter. 'That was surely worth a week's free accommodation alone!'

In Qom, I eat at the first table I have sat at since arriving in Iran. Nobody is fasting except the woman, Maryam. Her husband is exempt due to ailing health, while their nephew, Afshin, suffers from 'medical complications' related to an intolerance of spicy food.

This is a devout household, although that comes as little surprise. Qom is the second-most sacred city in Iran and the world's largest centre of Shi'ite scholarship. It was here where Fatimah bint Musa, the daughter of the seventh Shia imam and sister of the eighth, was buried in 816 CE, and where an orphaned Islamist scholar named Ruhollah Khomeini took up residence a thousand years later, stirring up public anger against corruption, colonialism and mistreatment of the poor.[123]

---

[123] In their bid to distance themselves from the rich, decadent West, Khomeini and his fellow clerics took great pains to appear as poor and humble as possible. 'What are these chairs?!' one of the senior officials, Ayatollah Taleghani, reportedly shrieked when they arrived at parliament in 1979 to find a room full of Edwardian furniture. Outraged, they all sat cross-legged on the floor for several days, until finally conceding that the comfort of the cushioned seats may be worth God's opprobrium after all.

Despite their conservatism, however, everyone here despises the regime. Afshin – the cousin of Sara in Isfahan – feels particularly strongly on the matter. A twenty-five-year-old English teacher with a gentle manner and luxuriant bushel of a moustache, he has both a childlike naivety and independence of spirit I find endearing. While critical of Iran's lack of freedom, it is not sex or drink he hankers after, or even ideological reforms such as democracy or free speech, but simpler pleasures such as 'nice cafés', 'amusement parks', and 'prettier-coloured chadors'. Most importantly, he wants to travel to Europe and fall in love, although he worries about how some of his more 'traditional' ideas might be received.

'I wouldn't want my wife wearing a bikini,' he tells me. 'Could this be a problem?'

Possibly, I admit. 'Generally, women don't like being told what to wear.'

His face falls. 'I thought so. I know it's my issue, but it's how I was raised.'

He looks pensive for a moment. Then, suddenly, he brightens. 'I know, I'll find a girl who can't swim!'

While we eat, the television crackles with images of Tel Aviv and Washington DC, while hirsute pundits speak with monocratic conviction about the 'Greater Israel' conspiracy between the Western powers and their regional proxies. A cleric with baggy jowls and officious nostrils comes onto the screen, speaking with a sense of bullish urgency. I ask what he's saying, and Afshin flashes scarlet. 'He's saying it's *haram* for, erm,' – he hesitates – 'for, well, married men to masturbate. Because it might stop them having children.'

'He's saying that? On national TV?'

He laughs. 'That's normal. Khomeini once said that if you have sex with a camel, you shouldn't drink its milk because it would be impure.'

'I don't believe it.'

'Really!'

I look it up and am stunned to discover he's right. It's one of

3,000 'everyday' issues that the former leader addresses in his religious treatise *A Clarification of Questions*, it turns out (which I admit does make me wonder whether his social life may have been rather more interesting than he let on). But even Khomeini doesn't win the prize for the most obscure, or intriguingly specific, advice from the ruling clerics. That award must go to Ayatollah Mohammad Mohammadi Gilani, who once opined that a naked man who fell through his bedroom floor during an earthquake and accidentally impregnated his aunt would not need to worry about incest because the child would be legitimate and all would be forgiven.

'As you can imagine,' Afshin says, 'it was very reassuring to hear.'

As darkness falls, Afshin and his aunt take me to see the shrine of Fatimah bint Musa. The place is quite extraordinary. With its caramel-gold dome, diamanté iwan and rocket-like minarets that glow witch-green at the tip, the building looks less like a place of worship and more like a fantastical fortress from a Hans Christian Andersen tale. In the vast forecourt, a dense throng of people are shopping, socialising and enjoying their *iftar* meal, while a handful of mullahs scurry to and fro among them in their dark, flowing robes.

After draping me in a heavy chador, Maryam pulls me tightly beside her and smuggles me into the shrine. Inside, we enter a crush of black, writhing figures, all of whom are doing their best to hustle their way towards the tomb at the centre, elbows pointed, bodies doubling as battering rams. Many are wailing theatrically, clawing at their chests as if trying to expel centuries of Shi'ite persecution and pain that originated with the dual martyrdom of Imam Ali and his son Husayn. Such rituals comprise a core element of Shia spiritual identity, and the death of Husayn continues to be commemorated each year with the festival of Ashura, during which processions of men flog themselves with whips in the street while onlookers howl in ostentatious displays of grief.

How a cynical Westerner should react to this kind of scene is unclear. To admit to indifference feels contemptuous; to feign admiration, condescending. When I finally reach the casket, which gleams gold and silver beneath a canopy of mirrored emerald, I do my best to lose myself in the moment. But this proves tricky while wedged in a musty stronghold of armpits, bellies and breasts, and instead all I feel is a sense of deep claustrophobia and panic.

Back outside, I opt for a kind of cheery ambiguity. It seems to work, as my hosts are all smiles. 'My aunt is so happy you went inside,' Afshin says. 'She could see that you were moved.'

Tehran is in my sights! Five years of hoping, one year of planning, eleven months of cycling … and my holy grail finally, inconceivably, seems to lie within my reach.

Buoyed by a new surge of adrenalin, I make preparations for this last valedictory ride. Already, I know it won't be easy. Over 150 kilometres lie between me and my finish line at Azadi Square, and Maud's tissue-paper tyres are a growing concern. The night before I leave, two kind men from the local bicycle shop insist on changing her (newly punctured) inner tube and giving her a general all-over spruce. But both she and I are clearly ailing from our lengthy stint on the road, and I admit a small part of me wonders – daren't wonder – if we'll make it healthy and intact to the other side.

The new tube is pencil thin, but it is the only one available so I grit my teeth and hope. The hope is short-lived. At daybreak, I make it barely a mile before I hear a loud *pop!* and Maud slumps heavily to the floor below me. Pulling over, dismayed, I go through the now-automated motions of repair, and I am just inflating the tyre when I receive a text from Jo. 'May the force be with you!' she writes encouragingly. A split-second later, the tube explodes.

I am not a believer. I never have been, and I feel it's unlikely I ever will be. But at this point, I can't deny I experience a momentary glimmer of doubt. I should have been more deferential at the shrine, I consider; I should have shown Fatimah the reverence and respect she deserved. But it's too late now. Whether due to simple bad luck or something more ominously prophetic, I am snookered.

Just as I'm contemplating turning back and delaying the ride, however, a flash of inspiration seizes me. Holding my breath, I delve into my bags and start burrowing through them with a kind of fevered desperation. *One pannier, two, three …* As the pile of debris around me grows, I start to lose hope. But then, at the bottom of the fourth and final bag, my fingers make contact with something long and lumpen and rubbery. I pull it out in a rush of excitement, disentangling it from my bungee cords and clothes and the folded legs of my camping stool, until it is hanging before me in all its flaccid, disfigured glory.

My old inner tube from Jordan!

Having patched it to within an inch of its life following its run-in with the Dead Sea thorns, I decided to keep it as a kind of battlefield souvenir – and thank goodness I did, as I hope it might now prove my salvation. Feeling a little like an army medic carrying out a surgical operation in the field, I begin tracking down each remaining hole, slowly and methodically, until, bit by bit, minute by minute, the tube grows firm and airtight. It is a slapdash job, and had the tube been an actual patient, I fear they may not have survived the ordeal. But I don't have time right now to be precious about my handiwork; I just desperately hope that it will hold.

By now, a small crowd has gathered around me, clearly mystified by this unkempt creature hunched and hobbled by the roadside. One woman gestures at my dislodged headscarf and shrieks 'Iran, Iran!' while running about in circles, while a man offers to hold Maud as I pump up her tyre and promptly drops her onto her side. It is, I feel, time to go. The sun is already high in the sky and I have a long, tough ride ahead.

I have imagined this final leg of the trip for some time: how I'd be so magnificently fit by now that I'd soar effortlessly across the dunes, buoyant and weightless, like a hawk or peregrine falcon. It would be my lap of honour, my triumphal march, during the course of which – after a year of bruises and sores, obstacles and frustrations – I could finally wallow in the glow of a lifetime's ambition fulfilled. Sadly, however, the journey doesn't quite work out like that. After its inauspicious start, the day gets steadily worse from there. Even leaving Qom proves a challenge, as the rush-hour traffic sucks me in like a swamp, churns me up with the diesel and smog, then casts me out, soiled and trembling, into the sallow desert plains beyond. There, the wind picks up where the traffic left off, stronger and more scorching than I've known it, flinging me like a ragdoll between the lorries, the crash barrier and the prickly roadside thorns.

For several hours, the wind and heat continue to rise, beating and burning in unison. Downhill feels almost as hard as uphill, and I lean into the gale like a quarterback braced for a scrimmage. By noon, the mercury has crept to a fearsome 48°C – the highest temperature of the trip so far – and I feel myself beginning to wilt beneath the sun's scalding rays. The bleak scenery does little to assuage my misery and is far from the poetic landscape of my imagination. 'Oh the desert around Tehran!' Gertrude Bell gushed in a letter to her cousin Horace Marshall in 1892. 'Miles and miles of it with nothing, *nothing* growing ... it is a very wonderful thing to see ...'

At 3.30pm, I stop at a service station sixty kilometres from Tehran and lie down for a brief rest. Two hours later, I wake up. *Oh no*, I think. *Jo!* I arranged to meet her at Azadi Square at 5pm, but there's clearly no hope of that now. *Sorry, running late,* I text, thinking it best not to mention the snooze. *See you 8pm?*

Then, just as I attempt to leave, my tyre finally gives way.

It proves a nightmare to mend, and afterwards I stare at my hatchet job in bemused disbelief. Gnarled and disfigured, the tube is now more patch than rubber and seems an appropriate metaphor for my physical and emotional well-being. I just hope by some miracle it remains intact.

It doesn't. Two hours later, a smattering of gravel lacerates the rubber like shrapnel: two more punctures, two more patches. I'm then back on my way – but as the sky darkens from ice-blue to burgundy to cinder-grey, I can tell the tyre is deflating, making it increasingly difficult to steer. Should I stop, I wonder? The crazed maelstrom of Tehrani traffic is tough enough to navigate in the daytime; cycling at night, with no bike lights and a flat front tyre, feels like insanity. However, fuelled by adrenalin and nerves, I press on. Neon signs and unseasonal fairylights flash by overhead, as six or seven lanes of cars swirl around me and sweep me like a burst water main into the centre. The ride is thrilling, petrifying, electrifying. As I cycle, drivers regularly and hazardously pull up beside me to pass me grapes, apples, a banana, a plum. Meanwhile, at the other end of the civility spectrum, young motorcyclists whisk past crying 'sex!' while attempting to grab my rump.

Finding Azadi (Freedom) Tower[124] isn't easy. But eventually, in the distance, I spot its distinctive sweeping form, lit up a diabolical blood red. Built in 1971 to celebrate 2,500 years of Iranian history, the monument has come to be seen as an icon of national unity, combining architectural styles from both the pre- and post-Islamic eras, and acting as a backdrop for both anti-Shah and anti-Ayatollah unrest. As such, it feels like a fittingly harmonious place to be drawing my journey to a close.

At 10pm, staggering across the final intersection to the square, I spot a familiar figure waving. She has been waiting patiently for five hours, braving the wrath of the *Gasht-e Ershad* with a huge canvas sign that reads: '10,000km and 2 sexy thighs!' (Later, I work out that it's nearer 11,000km, but who's counting?) Falling into her arms, I feel overjoyed to see her, to be here, to be alive,

---

[124] Recently, I discovered that Azadi Tower was designed by my friend's uncle, an Iranian-Canadian Baha'i named Hossein Amanat, who fled the country during the 1979 revolution.

and we cling to each other for several minutes, laughing and gabbling like lunatics.

Then, finally, we let go – and she breaks the bad news. 'When my friend discovered that you're a journalist, he decided he couldn't risk hosting us,' she tells me. 'So I'm afraid to say that we're homeless.'

Chapter 10

SECRETS AND DREAMS

Tehran

'Drink wine and look at the moon and think of all
the civilisations the moon has seen passing by.'
Omar Khayyam, eleventh-century
Persian polymath and poet

Of course, it's impossible to be homeless long in Iran. As Jo and I discuss our predicament beneath the splayed wings of the tower, we're approached by a family who have overheard us talking. We cannot possibly stay in a hotel, they insist. Expensive, lonely places. Not to mention the *food*. We must come with them.

This may be *taarof*, but fortunately neither Jo nor I are aware of this custom yet. So, after the briefest of deliberations, we say yes. A flash of surprise follows this ready acceptance, then a ripple of bemused mirth. Whether the laughter denotes delight at our refreshing disregard for convention or (more likely) nervous alarm at the prospect of having to follow through with their offer is unclear. But whatever the truth of the matter, this genial group could not be more gracious. Together, we bundle into their tiny Peugeot, three in the front, five in the back, oozing out of windows and doors like excess meat from an overstuffed sausage. The boot door is lashed half-closed with bungee cords and headscarves, Maud squeezed precariously inside, while our manifold limbs interlock in a clammy confusion of clothing, sweat and flesh.

The family live in a small flat in southern Tehran. The home is modern yet distinctly Persian, filled with Louis XIV-style furniture and layered draperies adorned with golden arabesques. The kitchen is folded into a dark alcove beside the living room, while the shower and toilet are compressed into a single cubicle with barely space to turn. Qur'anic verses hang on the walls, alongside a brooding portrait of Imam Ali. With his lustrous beard, dark-rimmed eyes and ruby lips, all cast in an astral sheen, the Shia leader seems both transcendental and faintly transsexual in appearance, as if embodying all of humanity – the masculine and feminine, warrior and thinker – within one platonic form.

Jo cannot stay, sadly. Her flight leaves tonight, so we say an emotional goodbye as the machinery of Persian hospitality whirrs into motion around us, dispensing tea and Coca-Cola and mounds of oaky, sizzling kebab. It is hard losing her so soon, and after she goes I feel like a leg brace or crutch has been removed and I must learn to walk all over again on my own.

A little later, I retire, exhausted, to bed. I don't wake again, unprecedentedly, for another eight hours – but when I do, I feel entirely refreshed. It is a long time since I've felt so content in the morning, rather than restless and alert like a soldier primed for battle. There is nowhere else to go now; I've reached the end of the line. Staring drowsily at the ceiling, I drift in and out of sylph-like dreams. *Tehran ... Tehran!* The refrain twirls and reels about me, spiralling to a clamorous roar. *Am I really here?* It already feels improbable, like the night-time phantasms of a delusional mind. But the evidence is clear, in my aching buttocks and thighs, my sun-baked skin, Maud's front wheel leaning dusty and deflated against the wall ...

I stay with the family until lunch. Nobody is fasting for a range of implausible reasons, and the mother serves me an enormous portion of *abgoosht* – a thick tomato-based stew accompanied by a cannonball of crushed chickpeas and lamb – which, still parched from yesterday's endeavours, I struggle to finish. Instead, I consume water and non-alcoholic beer by the gallon. When I ask if anyone drinks the alcoholic version, the group appear shocked. 'No alcohol, no boyfriends,' Sana, the daughter, explains, speaking through Google Translate. An anthropology graduate from Tehran University, she is immaculately made up, her lips plump and glossy, her eyes thickly rimmed with kohl. At the mention of men, her mother pulls a comic grimace and slides a finger across her throat. She does the same when we speak of Khamenei, and everyone collapses in giggles. 'We all hate him,' Sana says simply.

Mahshid and Sassan – my new hosts, arranged through an Iranian friend of my niece – arrive after dessert. Together, we lash Maud's poor fractured body to the car roof like a patient on a stretcher and, with a final grateful farewell to the family, I am whisked forever out of their lives, out of their cramped flat and litter-strewn street, out of the pipe-cleaner alleyways and breezeblock shacks of southern Tehran, into the chicer, sleeker, neater neighbourhoods of the north. Moving in this direction, we traverse layers of hidden contours towards the cooler foothills of the Alborz, ascending physically and socially above those left adrift in the steamy depression below.

Mahshid, Sassan and their four-year-old son live in an elegant apartment block built originally for widows of the 1980–88 Iran–Iraq War.[125] 'Foreign guests are *haram*,' Mahshid whispers as we replace our shoes with *roo-farshi* (house slippers) at the door. 'My neighbours will be shocked, but it's none of their business.' They would be even more outraged if they knew she had alcohol, I presume. Once inside, she leads me into the dining room, where a

---

[125] Iran never fully recovered from this bitter, eight-year conflict – in which chemical weapons were used (with America's knowledge) by Saddam Hussein – and portraits of 'martyrs' killed in combat are a common sight along Iranian streets. It was during this war that President Reagan was discovered to be secretly selling arms to Iran so he could funnel cash to right-wing militants in Nicaragua and secure US commercial interests in the country: the infamous 'Iran-Contra' scandal.

bottle stands on the table with a glamorous gold label: *Shumpain, 28 per cent.*

At first, I assume the couple are non-practising Muslims, like so many people in Iran. But they are actually Kurdish Yarsanis from the western province of Kermanshah, it turns out. 'We're different from Muslims,' Mahshid explains, pouring me a glass of yolk-coloured fizz. 'We're more liberal. More openminded.'

A mystical, syncretic sect that originated seven centuries ago in the Kurdish provinces of north-western Iran, Yarsanism is viewed by many senior clerics in Iran as a 'deviant faith'. Because of this, Mahshid admits that they often feel like outsiders here. 'We don't have many friends,' she confides as she flicks the television to the 'Kermanshah channel', on which Rouhani can be seen giving an interminable address to an audience of bleary-eyed Kurdish ministers. 'We don't really belong.'

Mahshid is thirty-eight and a schoolteacher, while Sassan, a few years older, works as a charity administrator. They are comfortable, though not rich, and I soon become aware of a latent *ennui* hanging in the air, intangible but pervasive. Outside, the sun wields its power like a prison guard, driving us into the cool sanctuary of the flat until nightfall, at which point we venture out for tea with the extended family or a picnic in one of Tehran's many elegant parks. From Mahshid in particular, I sense a simmering frustration at a life that's failed to take flight. As a Yarsani, she is isolated from Muslims; as a middle-earner, from the *haut monde*; as a woman, from the everyday liberties so many of us take for granted. Spiritually, socially, sexually, the odds seem stacked against her.

'I would never leave Iran, as it's my home,' she says one evening as we take a stroll among the pristine flowerbeds and modernist sculptures of Mellat Park. One curious abstraction depicts a woman spinning balletically inside a contortion of wire mesh: a tacit commentary, I wonder, on the ban on public female performers? 'But sometimes I feel so trapped, I find it hard to breathe.'

* * *

My cycle ride may now be at an end, but my journey, I feel, is not. Not quite. Not until I gain at least a tentative understanding of this prodigious and bewildering country that has captivated me from afar for so long. And Tehran – chaotic, confounding, inscrutable as it may be – is surely the place that holds the key.

I stay a month in the city. Much of this time is spent travelling along Valiasr Street, the central artery that gives the capital life. Sweeping unhindered for eighteen kilometres from north to south, the road connects two very different Irans and acts as an enduring emblem of the country's stark dualism and diversity. From Mellat Park, I wander south under a canopy of bowing sycamores, through a swirling crush of Tehranis and traffic, past public drinking fountains and metre-wide *joobs* (gutters) that gush with mountain run-off. A woman with bleached hair and pneumatic lips steps over a one-armed man hawking razors and live chicks; loved-up youngsters flirt over barberry juice and *faloodeh* (rice-noodle sorbet); tattooed skateboarders clatter past a huddle of mullahs clutching Qur'ans. And I walk and walk and walk, enthralled and befuddled at every turn.

The symbolic significance of Valiasr is not just geographic but semantic. Built by Reza Shah in the 1920s in the mode of the grand 'garden streets' of the Safavid era, it was originally called Pahlavi Avenue in honour of his royal dynasty, before being renamed Mosaddegh Street for a brief interlude in 1979. Finally, after the Islamists hijacked the revolution a few months later, it converted to its current moniker, which translates as the 'expected one' or 'Mahdi'. Through this metamorphic identity, the road becomes not just schismatic but prismatic, wrenched not just between two polar extremes but scrabbled over by tsarists, leftists and Islamists; *chadoris*, intelligentsia and nouveau riche; *Basijis*,[126] Yarsanis and trendies.

From Valiasr, I meander from road to road, intersection to

---

[126] The much-hated street militia, run by Sepas, mainly composed of vulnerable youngsters enticed by excellent perks and wages.

intersection, trying to orientate myself in this jumbled helter-skelter of a metropolis. Without a waterway or obvious 'centre' as an anchor, however, the city feels bafflingly loose and baggy. Looping parabolas of asphalt knit the districts together like frayed threads on a Persian carpet, sometimes tangled in clumps, sometimes ballooning sixteen lanes wide. Tehran's rocketing growth has been a problem since the 1960s, when the oil boom and a wave of urban migration created new ghettos of rich and poor, and its population – now 9 million strong – continues to expand at a startling pace. A grim rectangularity of tower blocks dominate the skyline, interspersed by a jagged mishmash of minarets and hydraulic cranes that together create a fitting visual metaphor for the pseudo-pious, development-hungry brigands pulling the strings behind the scenes.

Today, almost anyone can build a hideous high-rise here if they pay the requisite 'fee', I'm told, and Tehran's once prolific gardens have been disappearing at a startling pace. Meanwhile, huge murals depicting lush meadows and pastoral idylls have been sprouting up throughout the city as part of a scheme overseen by the Orwellian-sounding 'Bureau of Beautification', as if the capital were slipping from reality into myth before our very eyes.

'The mullahs seem to think we won't notice they aren't real gardens,' my guide, Basir, says scathingly. 'They're so blinded by lies, they think they can build a whole city on them.'

I met Basir in Abyaneh, where he gave me his number and offered to show me around Tehran. Having taken him up on the offer, I now find myself being whisked into the vast Sa'dabad palace complex in the far north of the city, where once upon a time, so I hear, Kermit Roosevelt conducted his clandestine meetings with the Shah. As we pass along the lengthy driveway into the sprawling, hundred-hectare grounds, I try to imagine what it must have been like for the American agent sneaking this way seventy years ago, concealed under a blanket in the back of an unmarked car: a journey he took regularly and diligently until, on 19 August 1953, suddenly he no longer had to hide. 'I owe my throne to God, my people, my army, and to you!' the Shah is reported to have declared as the men raised a toast of vodka to Mosaddegh's fall. In retrospect, perhaps his gratitude was a little premature.

'It's actually pretty sad what happened to the Shah's family,' Basir tells me. 'Two of his children who used to live here committed suicide recently. I don't think they ever recovered after '79.'

Indeed, with the power of hindsight, the whole compound radiates ominous hubris. Built by the Qajars and expanded by the Pahlavis, the site's eighteen palaces are intemperately ornate, their plasterwork brocaded with gold leaf, their furnishings layered with taffetas, satins and silks. In the fifty-four-room White Palace, crystal chandeliers hang above Italian Baroque oil paintings, while French gilt candelabras shimmer beside opaline Rosenthal tables. A statue of Mohammad Reza Pahlavi is striking for the painful improvidence of its caption: 'The Shah's and the People's revolution has no ocean, mountain or river borders. It fixes an exalting start of human civilisation's third millennum [sic] which will be marked everywhere by the thought of His Imperial Majesty.'[127]

It is out in the palace grounds, however, where the most enduring icon of this fallen empire can be found: a pair of giant bronze legs, haplessly truncated mid-thigh, which once held aloft the brawny torso of Mohammad Reza's father, Reza Shah. One of the early casualties of the revolution, the limbs now stand in sad, comic isolation, without even a hint of burnished manhood to salvage the old patriarch's pride and self-respect.

'Poor guy,' Basir says, leaning against one of the shoulder-high Cossack boots. 'He was ruthless, but at least he was strong.

[127] The Shah's bombast is perhaps unsurprising given the praise lauded on him by his Western allies. 'Surely he must be one of the world's most far-sighted statesmen,' Margaret Thatcher effused in April 1978, nine months before the country erupted in revolutionary fervour. 'He is leading Iran through a twentieth century renaissance ...'

Maybe if you guys hadn't thrown him out, we wouldn't be in the disastrous position we're in today ...'

Ah yes, the pre-coup coup. It tends to be glossed over when discussing the West's shenanigans in Iran, overshadowed by the more colourful events of 1953. But its impact was profound, if only for the consequence of propelling Reza Shah's weak, avaricious son into power, whose craven servility to his foreign masters helped to set in motion the catastrophic events that followed.

Reza Shah, as Basir notes, was not a wholly ineffectual leader. Tall and strapping, with an uncouth manner and gritty resolve, he moved swiftly up the ranks of the Cossack army brigade and eventually onto the Persian throne. Fed up with the incompetent Qajars, Britain actively supported him all the way and was therefore somewhat taken aback when he proved to be far from the loyal, pliable lackey it had presumed. Citing Atatürk as his hero, Reza Shah lost no time in implementing a series of audaciously nationalistic, anti-imperialistic reforms, including changing the name of the country from 'Persia' to 'Iran', banning foreigners from buying property, and renegotiating lucrative British concessions. Meanwhile, he earned the support of the masses through his populist rhetoric and extensive construction of hospitals, railways and schools.

Yet Atatürk he was not. Reza Shah was a tyrant – and a fairly old-school tyrant at that. He murdered opponents, censored the press, oppressed minorities, destroyed the nomadic tribes and looted vast amounts of public wealth. He wasn't one for diplomacy; when he heard that bakers were stockpiling wheat to inflate prices, he is said to have thrown one of them into an oven and burnt him alive. Fiercely anti-mullah, he banned the hijab and massacred those who protested in a mosque. By the start of World War II, when he declared Iran neutral in the conflict, it wasn't just the British who wanted him gone but the nationalists and socialists, Islamists and liberalists alike.

In 1941, following a joint Anglo-Soviet invasion, the Shah was finally cast aside. Two years later, as a mark of their renewed grip over the country, Churchill, Roosevelt and Stalin met in Tehran to declare the opening of a second front against the Nazis. During the meeting, more importantly for Iran, they made guarantees to recognise the nation's post-war independence and to help rebuild its shattered economy.

'And a decade later, the Mosaddegh coup happened,' the woman says, wafting her cocktail flute in an airy manner that seems to suggest both apathetic indifference and unabashed contempt. 'So much for promises!'

I am at a party in a flat that feels like an art gallery. By the time I arrive, everyone is drunk and talking floridly about art, politics, sex and other favoured topics of the beatnik glitterati. 'Sepah make it difficult for artists to work freely,' the host, Sadie, tells me as she plucks a pimiento-stuffed olive from a buffet of bruschetta, salchichón and prosciutto. 'They come weekly to examine my work. Nudity is banned, and anything political. Once I did a painting of a girl in ripped jeans with a nose-bandage and cigarette. That was a definite no!'

A haven of debonair grunge and contrived eccentricity, the apartment bursts with surrealist oddities: six-foot plastic flowers shaped like hearts; papier-mâché oxen with serpents for horns; hallucinogenic gazelles contorted in suggestive poses. One woman tells me she designs 'wearable sculptures', while another specialises in 'transgressive spaces' through the medium of 'durational installation'. I feel extremely un-trendy in my ragged black shirt and trousers – and also, as a foreigner, entirely unremarkable. Several people here hold American passports, and a couple own galleries in Paris and New York. My status as exotic, anomalous Westerner has at last, it seems, been revoked.

Many of the guests appear to have had politically active pasts that have since been cast aside. An older 'reformed Marxist' recounts how he was jailed for a year in 1980, only to emerge, disillusioned, to find that many of his former comrades had fled.

'We just go endlessly in circles,' he says. 'Rafsanjani, Khatami, Ahmadinejad, Rouhani … We'll have another asshole zealot next, you'll see.'[128]

This crowd lie at one end of the spectrum of Tehrani elite: the one encompassing the intelligentsia, students and ex-Qajar gentry, exemplifying liberalism and class. At the other lie the mullahs, nouveau riche and state officials, who represent tradition and wealth. Between the two, it is clear, there is little love lost.

'My god, you should just *see* inside their *houses*,' a woman splutters as she rolls a joint beside a platter of bresaola. 'Hideous chandeliers and laminate gold floors and fake synthetic antiques. Worse, even, than the *Arabs!* Take those Gulf sheikhs and multiply them by ten …'

The next fortnight is a whirl of boozy parties, country mini-breaks and genteel soirées. I have crossed to the other side. At these gatherings, I admit I feel a sense of relief at no longer being a cultural curiosity to ogle and plump like a fatted calf. However, there is clearly less warmth here too – and, perhaps, a looser sense of belonging. Where is the essential *Persianness* I experienced before? These people speak and drink and joke like Americans. They even wear their shoes indoors: the ultimate sign of modernity.

One weekend, I am invited to join a group camping in the Alborz. We depart at 4am, travelling in a convoy of SUVs and Toyota trucks, churning up dust on the gravelly mountain pass. Steep ridges surround us, sparse of vegetation yet soft of edge, and we twist through ruts and furrows enveloped by a cool, dense mist. As we ascend, wisps of cloud collect in the creases of the land like candyfloss, gradually forming a thick, fleecy ocean that

---

[128] He's right: the hardline cleric and prosecutor Ebrahim Raisi was elected prime minister in June 2021. A deeply controversial figure, Raisi has been accused of being part of a 'Death Committee' set up in 1988 that oversaw secret death sentences for around 5,000 political prisoners (a charge he denies).

rolls and foams like waves. 'You mustn't tell anyone where we're going,' one of the girls insists en route. 'Once, a French reporter wrote about an island near Bandar Abbas that we secretly used to visit, and the police arrived and raided it. She ruined it for everyone.'

Several hours later, we arrive at a clearing filled with lush greenery and roaming livestock, where we stop to make camp. Over the next two days, under bursts of rain and sun, we talk and walk and nap during the day, and drink and smoke and dance as darkness falls. Cocaine and MDMA are passed around, alongside joints, vodka and beer, and suddenly the Iran I've come to know – the country of brutal heat and sober recreation and intrusive *Gasht-e Ershad* – seems a very long way away indeed.

One evening, five of us decide to hike up a nearby hill to watch the sunset. On the way, we encounter several families picnicking under some trees. The women all wear headscarves and chadors, and a few of them are dancing, singing and playing volleyball. 'They wear a hijab and yet they're happy to jump about wiggling their asses,' Yasmin, a graphic designer, snorts as we pass by. 'I wish I could speak to them and understand how their minds work.'

'Why can't you?' I ask.

'We never mix. We're like different species.'

The schism is striking. Two worlds under one flag, hanging loosely by a thread.

'What hope is there for Iran if the people are so divided?' I ask.

'I don't know. There are big divides in the West too, of course. But you still have shared values that unite people. Democracy, free speech, etc. It's different here.'

'Bullshit,' her friend interjects. 'Our culture unites us. Nobody wants a theocracy.'

We emerge from the spiky brush onto a high embankment, where golden sunlight pools like melted toffee across the grasslands. Yasmin turns to me. 'Believe me, most Iranians aren't ready for democracy yet. They're not as openminded as they seem.'

Later, by the campfire, I gain a better understanding of the source of Yasmin's cynicism. Her story horrifies me. 'Not long ago, I went on a minibreak to a small village with some friends,' she begins, her face flickering a phantasmal red as she stares trancelike into the flames. 'We were staying at a chalet with a high wall around it, so it seemed private and safe.' One night, however, they heard a noise outside and, before they knew what was happening, fifteen armed men had stormed the compound. 'They locked the guys in a room and took the girls to a house nearby. They said they were going to rape us.' Fortunately, one of the villagers called the police, she says, so the men released them. But in the street, nobody came to their aid. 'We were running in bare feet and torn clothes, crying for help. But people just turned away.'

The perpetrators, she explains, were part of a criminal gang released from prison by Ahmadinejad during the Green protests to harass and beat activists. Two of them were convicted, but the ringleaders got away. 'The judges were paid off,' Yasmin says, 'and probably thought we deserved it anyway.' These ideas filter down from the very top of society, she believes. 'Friday prayers are the worst. A mullah in Mashhad recently said it would be the equivalent of going to Mecca twice if a woman slept with soldiers fighting in Syria.' She shudders. 'I mean, seriously – how fucked up is that?'

By midnight, the party is in full swing. Bottles of Smirnoff and Johnnie Walker clutter the tables, and a convulsive mob of dancers thrust and gyrate around a DJ thumping out pyretic beats. There is almost no furniture in this dark, smoky hotbox, though not as a nod towards the kind of modest minimalism found in rural homes but because, as it turns out, the apartment was never designed to be lived in at all. 'This is a party flat,' a man explains. 'Some wealthy guys rent it for $3,000 a month so they can have a place away from their parents to hang out with friends.'

We are in a neighbourhood overlooking Jamshidiyeh Park,

an affluent enclave in the most northerly reaches of Tehran. The invitation came from the former roommate of a lawyer I met through a journalist I stayed with in Kosovo (as I continue to test the elasticity of my contacts list to the limit), and I snapped up the opportunity to see how the 1 per cent of the 1 per cent live. In the event, the bash proves disappointing – more school disco than *Great Gatsby* bacchanal – but the scent of privilege is clear. These are the *bacheh pooldars* (rich kids) who walk in different elitist circles from the heterodox *chapis* (leftists) I've met so far. The men wear tight Calvin Klein t-shirts and emit wafts of zesty cologne, while the women strut about as bare-legged, button-nosed coquettes in various states of undress.

'This is the top of the top,' one young man explains as he mixes me a cocktail at a black marble bar. 'Nobody else would risk having parties like this in central Tehran.' He takes a sip of the viscid concoction and grimaces, before adding another huge glug of vermouth. 'Even here, they never have more than thirty or so guests.'

Later, the man approaches me again. Dancing up, he slurs in my ear that he's planning to have a sex-change operation so he can 'see what it's like to be a woman'. 'It's legal, y'know. The state will even pay for it!' However, this is not because they're *nice*, he stresses, leaning in closer and hitting me with a briny waft of bergamot and Brylcreem. 'It's because they hate the *gays* ...'

I have a lucky break. Hashem, an Iranian-American I met at the party, is going abroad for a few days and kindly invites me to stay at his parents' house in Jamshidiyeh Park while he is away. When I arrive, I am delighted to discover that his 'bedroom' comprises an entire separate studio apartment built in the style of a Scandinavian ski chalet tucked into the corner of his family's spacious garden.

For this privilege, I don't just have Hashem and his parents to thank, it turns out, but the notorious Setad bailiffs. After the revolution, many homes in this neighbourhood were seized and reoccupied by regime officials – including the house next door, I hear, which is now reportedly occupied by one of the assassins of Shapour Bakhtiar, the last prime minister before the revolution – but this one was left untouched.

'I think my parents just weren't big enough opponents to worry about,' Hashem's father, Durant, surmises – although he admits their connection to the Pahlavis was an 'intimate' one. Durant's father was the gynaecologist to Farah Diba, Mohammad Reza's third wife, and delivered all four of her children. 'He was close to the family, but his role wasn't political. So he wasn't seen as a threat.'

I ask Durant if he's hopeful about Iran's future. Many people seem to have given up, I say. Compared to Khartoum, which trembled with revolutionary fervour, Tehran feels disappointingly inert.

'Don't be deceived,' he replies. 'We've seen the damage revolutions can do. We're playing the long game. Swift change means swift collapse.'

From the northernmost metro station, Tajrish, I am flushed down into the bowels of the city. The station was built only recently and, while it was welcomed by most, there are those who lament the mobility – physical and social – it has provided for those based further down the line. 'Now *anyone* can travel up here if they want to,' a woman at the party had lamented, pouting her puffer-fish lips, as if the southerners were wild animals trapped in a pit and the metro a rope-line designed to help them escape. 'It's just not *safe* anymore!'

As in Cairo, the Tehran metro is a tool of democracy. Journeys cost as little as 10p, opening it up to every tier of society. Black-shrouded *chadoris* sit beside balloon-breasted *palangs*,[129] Versace-garbed fashionistas beside dishevelled, grungy teens. Most days,

---

[129] Literally, 'panthers', referring to women who have overdone their make-up or plastic surgery.

I opt for the female-only carriage, identified by a depressingly apposite symbol of a hijab-clad woman with no face, though its feminine credentials rarely translate into a gentler ride. Getting on, it is every woman for herself, elbows crooked, acrylic nails primed – although, once this initial cut and thrust is over, I admit I am quietly impressed by the human warmth on show. Personal space is public space in Iran, and people happily talk and smile and make eye contact in ways that would seem oddly importunate at home.

From Tajrish, the train plummets down down down, dropping from gullet to gut, shedding occupants as it goes like a rapidly sinking ship. My destination is Shoush, a deprived district in the far south of the city – and when I arrive, I emerge into a different world. It is noticeably warmer here, the air thicker. Porridge-coloured tenement blocks line the streets, while tired patches of greenery are framed by cave-like workshops swimming in grease. Around one in three Iranians are reported to live in 'absolute poverty', surviving on only a few dollars a day, and many can be found in areas like this, scratching out a living as mechanics, construction workers or tradesmen. Wandering into a weather-beaten park, I pass waxen-faced *sheesheh* (meth) addicts sprawled on cardboard sheeting and a group of security guards beating a skeletal old man on the ground. I swiftly wander out.

My destination is a dilapidated apartment block at the centre of a filigree of knotted alleyways. 'Thank you for coming,' the woman says who greets me. 'We don't get many visitors here.'

The woman, Nabila, and her husband, Jafar, are among three million Afghan migrants living in Iran. They reside with another Afghan family in this cramped, four-room apartment, living on a combined salary of $150 a month. This couple is unusual among the community, however, in that they have no desire to leave. 'We tried and failed,' Nabila explains through a translator, clutching a tiny, sparrow-like child to her chest. 'Now we think it better to stay.'

For them, Europe was once the promised land. They left their village in Helmand Province after Nabila fell pregnant and Jafar's cousin was killed by the Taliban, hoping to provide a better future for their child. They would travel to Germany, they decided, and try to start a new life there.

From Khoy in Iran, the couple paid a trafficker $1,500 to take them across the border to Turkey. It was a gruelling fifteen-hour journey through rugged, mountainous terrain, and there were several moments when Jafar desired to return. 'I got painful sores and blisters, and at one point the mule Nabila was riding almost fell down a gulley. I thought we should stop, but Nabila urged me on.'

They reached Edirne in western Turkey, where they paid another $2,500 to be led through dense woodland to Greece. Nabila, round-bellied and nauseous, toiled through rivers and heavy brush, hacking a path with a knife. But soon after they arrived, they were stopped by police. 'We were arrested and put in a compound,' Jafar recalls. 'A hundred of us shared two toilets and a sink. There was barely enough space to sleep.'

For six weeks they remained there, waiting, hoping, surviving. As May turned into June, the cell grew so hot that they found it hard to breathe. But when they were finally moved, their situation barely improved. 'The new place was filthy, and we both came down with fever,' Nabila says. 'But we weren't locked in there, so after a month we decided to leave.' They spent two months in Eleonas Camp in Athens, paying $200 to squat in one of the prefab containers designed for registered refugees, before being discovered and evicted by guards. 'I was huge, the size of a bus. But they treated me like a dog.'

The couple had $1,000 left, but lost it all when their trafficker took it from them and disappeared. Destitute, they slept in parks and doorways, begging for scraps to survive. They sought help from Médecins Sans Frontières and were both diagnosed with Hepatitis C. As autumn approached, they began to fear the deepening cold. 'We registered for asylum, as we knew our Germany dream was over,' Jafar says, wiping his hand across his mouth. 'We thought: better that than nothing.'

Nabila smiles weakly. 'But, actually, that was worse.'

Nabila and Jafar moved into a tent in Elliniko camp, based on the site of an old airport terminal on the outskirts of Athens. A week later, Nabila went into labour. She gave birth alone in a hospital with almost no assistance or pain relief. 'I could feel the baby tearing me,' she says, rocking the child in her lap. 'There was so much blood. I cried and cried, but nobody came. I felt like I wanted to die.'

A few months later, their asylum application was rejected and they were deported back to Afghanistan. From there, they returned to Iran. 'We've come full circle,' Nabila says. 'We've lived a whole lifetime and arrived back at the start.' But they're content now, she asserts. Here, in this airless hole, where a stygian spider's web of cracks vein the walls, they feel safe.

'Europe is a dream, but it isn't real,' Jafar says. 'Here, we have a home, an identity.' He reaches down to scoop up his daughter, who is tugging playfully at his cuff. 'Here, at least, we are free.'

Gzing and Arman divorced two months ago. Nobody knows except them – not even their teenage children. 'We did it because, in marriage, we weren't equal partners,' Gzing explains in Farsi, as Arman translates. 'A man holds all the power. I wanted to take that power back for myself.'

Friends of Mahshid, the couple have invited me to stay with them at their home in south-west Tehran for a few days. These days prove to be among the most fascinating of my time in the city, as a beguiling array of tough but troubled women drift in and out of their apartment, seeking solace and support. The atmosphere, on occasion, is curiously sexually charged. Gzing, an attractive forty-something with a penetrating gaze and tactile sensuality, is like nobody I've ever known. For these women, she appears to be a form of mentor or counsellor – and perhaps, for some, a lover too.

'The problem in Iran isn't the law,' she says, as she nestles onto the sofa between two blonde women, Sara and Suzanne.

'It's society. Iran won't change until people start being honest about themselves.' For Gzing, these aren't loose words. After years of blogging about women's rights, she recently came out as a bisexual online. 'I lost many friends and loved ones, but I knew I had to do it,' she says. 'The greatest pain is caused by a life of deceit.'

As Gzing speaks, she, Arman, Sara and Suzanne form a human chain on the sofa in which each person is massaging the neck of another. I watch with slight discomfort, wondering if this is a social gathering or an orgy. My concerns are compounded moments later when Gzing shows me a photograph of her kissing another woman. 'Ziba,' she tells me. A German-Iranian writer who came to stay. 'She taught me how to live true to myself.'

Ten years ago, one in eight Iranian marriages ended in divorce. Today, it's more like one in three. There's less stigma now, Gzing says, and more women are asserting their right to break free. But there's a long way to go. She sees several women a week, all trapped inside a system in which men reign supreme. Sara is a hairdresser who for years was stuck in a loveless marriage until Gzing helped her to muster the courage to leave, while Suzanne fled from her violent husband a decade ago but has been unable to obtain a divorce despite seven years of court hearings. 'Her black eyes weren't enough,' Gzing says. 'Her husband just told the judge she'd fallen down the stairs.'

Men seek Gzing's advice too, although they're often confused by her motives. 'Many assume I just want sex. One man rang Arman and asked permission to sleep with me. He said his wife knew, though of course she didn't.' Gzing soon resolved that issue: she exposed the man on Facebook, revealing his intentions to the world. 'Men are used to doing as they please without consequences,' she says. 'And women are used to accepting it.'

One evening, Gzing reveals the truth about her own troubled past. She was just six years old when she was touched sexually for the first time, she says, and it tainted her view of men forever. 'I felt from a young age that men's instinct was not to respect female beauty but to abuse it,' she explains. 'It made me very cynical. Very hard.' She recounts a tragic story from her youth about a young girl who was raped as a punishment for an unpaid debt. 'The man did it as revenge, to destroy the family's honour. But everyone just blamed the girl. She became withdrawn and bitter, and lived a deeply unhappy life.'

As a teenager, Gzing decided she never wanted to marry, so 'no man could control her'. However, when she met Arman, a fellow Kurd from Mahabad in north-west Iran, she felt immediately that he was different. 'He surprised me,' she says. 'He didn't want to dominate or domesticate me; he just wanted a friend.'

Gzing was twenty-five when they married. On their wedding night, the couple decided against the normal custom of having sex while the family waited outside for bloodied proof of her virginity. Instead, they spent their first night together in private. 'I was lucky,' Gzing says. 'Arman had been in Japan and had learnt about sex from TV. Many men believe women are just there for their pleasure.' This is a serious issue in Iran, she believes. 'There are times when men are actually assaulting their wives, and this can turn women against sex for life. This then leads men to stray.'

From the beginning, she and Arman enjoyed an 'honest, intimate relationship', Gzing says. However, it was only when Ziba came to stay that she truly began to understand what it meant to live a truthful life. The two women began to provide emotional support and advice to other women – including social outcasts, such as drug addicts and prostitutes – and, with Arman's blessing, Gzing found the courage to write about her own confused sexuality online. 'People thought I was ill,' she says. 'They're used to living in a hidden world. They didn't understand that there's no harm in actions that don't harm other people.'

Honesty, however, had its price. Someone filed a complaint, and Sepah accused the women of adultery, prostitution and spreading indecent information. Ziba was deported to Germany, while Gzing was ostracised by her family and friends. One cousin even said she should be killed. 'I kept telling myself that this was part of the challenge: to put my reputation aside and tell the truth. But it was very, very hard.'

She wasn't scared of Sepah, however. 'All they did was demand that I delete my blog,' she says. 'If you're a gay man, it's much worse. You'll lose your benefits, your job, everything. If there's evidence of a sexual act, you can be put to death, though this is very rare. Women are not viewed as sexual beings, so lesbians are not such a threat. They're not seen as real.'

The next few months were a 'very dark time', she admits. 'I didn't know if I was heterosexual, homosexual or bisexual. I didn't know if I was with Arman because of the marriage or because I loved him. As a woman, my concept of sexuality had been corrupted from a young age, so everything was very confused.' The marriage 'felt like a pair of shackles' that stopped her from thinking straight, she says, and she knew it had to end. 'It was hard convincing Arman, but afterwards I knew it was the right decision. Our relationship felt more equal and free, and I lost the mental load I'd been carrying. I realised I truly loved him.'

Now Gzing is trying to encourage others to forge their own paths too – not necessarily through divorce, she stresses, but through questioning the strictures of both society and the state. 'The relationship between the people and regime is like the relationship between a husband and wife, or a lord and his slaves,' she explains. 'People need to learn how to think for themselves.'

Around Gzing, the enigma of Iran deepens. The country does not simply hold secrets, it seems, but is fed and borne by them, from its gnostic faith and mythical pasts to its clandestine liaisons and the shadows of the ruling cabal. The key to understanding is *Irfan* (spiritual awareness), Gzing believes, not as preached by the clerics but in the broader mystical sense of truth or self-knowledge. 'Our country is built on shame,' she says. 'Until we admit and address that, we'll never truly be free.'

I emerge onto Valiasr enveloped by the dense mantle of afternoon heat. Doing anything at this time of day feels twice as enervating as it does at dawn or dusk, and not for the first time I find myself wondering whether our imperial success as Brits was due less to our naval skills and economic prudence and more to the simple fact that our climate neither bakes our brains nor freezes them, and we can (on the whole) make it through the day without the need for a snooze.

It is not the heat, however, that chiefly concerns me now. It's my nerves. I am on my way to meet Nasrin Sotoudeh, one of Iran's most prominent human rights lawyers, and I admit I'm feeling anxious. Is the *Ettela'at* watching me, as I've been warned? Is it watching her, or monitoring her emails or calls? I am aware of the potential repercussions of being caught together – for myself, certainly, yet more significantly for Nasrin. She has already spent several years behind bars, and has long been a prime target of spurious investigations by the security agencies. This has particularly been the case since 2012, when she was awarded the EU's top human rights award, the Sakharov Prize for Freedom of Thought, while incarcerated in Evin Prison.[130] However, she is highly aware of the risks, of course, and – unlike so many others – has readily agreed to meet me. So I have decided to trust her judgement.

From Valiasr, I walk quickly to Nasrin's apartment, head down, hijab pulled low. When I arrive, I am surprised by the slight, pale figure that greets me. 'Please, come in,' she says, ushering me into her airy dining room. 'It's good of you to come.'

'It's good of you to see me,' I reply. I mean it. I know Nasrin through the human rights lawyer and Nobel laureate Shirin Ebadi, whom I interviewed after she fled Iran for London following a series of death threats in 2009, and thought it was unlikely she

---

[130] This notorious prison, built by the Shah in the 1970s, is renowned for its inhumane conditions and appalling treatment of detainees. Inmates have reported endless interrogations, sleep deprivation through noise and bright lights, lack of medical care, solitary confinement in tiny, windowless cells, threats of execution and dismemberment, and forced consumption of concrete mixed in with their food.

would find time to meet. Plastic files and notes cover every inch of desk in her office, alongside a megalith of a filing cabinet and a small bronze sculpture of Lady Justice brandishing a pair of scales. 'I know how busy you are.'

She smiles. 'I just feel I need to be working.' There is no hint of arrogance about her, just a soft, irrepressible strength. 'There's so much that needs to be done.'

'It's such dangerous work, though,' I say. 'You're not worried about the consequences?'

'Well, I've heard the Revolutionary Courts are opening a dossier against me. Soon, I'm sure I'll be called.'

Her courage astonishes me. The repercussions for advocates who take on political cases can be grievous. After being released from Evin in 2013, she and a group of fellow lawyers were barred from practising law for a decade – though, incredibly, she later managed to overturn the ban following a series of sit-ins and protests. 'I don't know why they backtracked,' she says. 'The government is a mix of conservatives and reformists, so all outcomes are unpredictable.'

This unpredictability is one of the state's most effective weapons, she explains. 'The intelligence agencies project an image of power, but nobody knows how strong they really are. The red lines are always unclear.' Where her own situation is concerned, she believes her phones are tapped but is unsure how rigorously they're monitored. 'All I know is that if they want to get me, they will.'

Despite the risks, Nasrin hasn't flinched from taking on the most politically sensitive clients possible, including religious minorities such as the Baha'is, women protesting the mandatory hijab and minors facing death sentences. 'The poorest prisoners tend to suffer the most in Evin, as they are lower profile,' she tells me. 'But it is extremely hard for everyone. Imagine: no phone, internet or contact with the outside world. Eventually, your spirit is drained.'

For her part, Nasrin remains unreasonably upbeat considering the extraordinary stress and pressure she faces every day. 'The future looks positive,' she says, smiling her small, steady smile. 'Change is possible, if only we don't stop trying.'[131]

Tehran feels like a city at war with itself. It exudes tension, like a tug-of-war rope pulled taut. Half the people do not know or understand the other half, and many refuse even to look across the divide. In a ceramics shop in Tajrish, an elderly couple visiting Iran for the first time since emigrating in 1979 to Los Angeles – or Tehrangeles, as it's known to some, due to its large Iranian population – lament the loss of cabaret bars, billiard halls and glitzy French boutiques. At Mellat Tower, a coffee-drinking technician tells me he has nothing in common with his tea-drinking compatriots and longs to return to Stuttgart where he used to work. At Golestan Palace, a retired cobbler who requests help with some taxing English vocabulary in the novel he's reading ('what is a "barn-like outfit", please?') explains he doesn't recognise the so-called 'freedoms' desired by the young because, for him, the concept means 'freedom from foreign rule and outsiders who want us weak'.

'The country is so divided, it's hard to gauge how much support the regime really has,' Ben Fender, the British Acting Chargé d'affaires, explains. He has invited me to lunch at the British Embassy, and we sit at a table heaving with silverware on a shaded terrace, overlooking acres of perfectly manicured gardens. 'It's extremely difficult to access the villages to hear what people are thinking.' I am 'almost certainly the first British woman to have cycled alone through Qom since the revolution, if not ever', he continues – which is cheering to hear, if a little unsettling, and

---

[131] In March 2019, Nasrin was tragically handed a thirty-eight-year sentence, plus 148 lashes, for a variety of trumped-up offences. She is currently being held at the women's prison of Qarchak: an overcrowded former industrial cow barn with windowless cells, revolting toilets, salty drinking water and a permanent stench of sewage, referred to by inmates as 'the end of the world'.

I admit that I'm somewhat relieved to have found out about my potential place in the history books only after the fact.

Built in the 1870s and designed in a neoclassical style by the British architect James William Wild, the embassy is a freeze-frame of colonial-era Britain, exhibiting a musty, decorous elegance that suggests topcoats, smoking jackets and neat Ascot ties. I find it easy to imagine the consular elite poring over sepia maps on the lambent mahogany bureaus, or Churchill and Stalin quaffing Scotch on the chaise longue under Roosevelt's disapproving gaze. Despite its efforts at stately *hauteur*, however, the building hasn't always managed to retain a sense of regal detachment from its turbulent surrounds over the years. In 1906, it provided sanctuary to 14,000 protesters calling for democratic reform, while in 1981 the name of the avenue outside was provocatively changed by local activists from 'Winston Churchill' to 'Bobby Sands' Street, in honour of the famous IRA hunger-striker. Most recently, in November 2011, a group of *Basijis* and regime supporters broke into the compound in response to a new wave of nuclear sanctions,[132] smashing windows and furnishings and setting the chancery on fire. While not as consequential as the 1979 hostage crisis at the US Embassy – during which fifty-two Americans were held for 444 days in revenge for the US providing asylum to the Shah – the incident nevertheless sent shockwaves across the world.

'We were closed for four years,' Ben says, as he points out the building where the protesters gained entry. Charred and boarded up, it looks oddly incongruous amid our otherwise immaculate

[132] The nuclear sanctions imposed on Iran over the past four decades comprise the most stringent global sanctions regime ever implemented on a country. Many were lifted following the 2015 nuclear deal between Iran and the P5+1 (the US, UK, France, China, Russia and Germany), but the future of the pact remains uncertain following America's withdrawal in 2018. While concerns about Iran's nuclear ambitions appear justified, it is hard for the West to escape accusations of hypocrisy; it was the US that first encouraged Iran to develop its nuclear capabilities in the 1960s, after all, and there are reasonable questions to be asked as to why it's only regional allies of the West, such as Pakistan and Israel, who are permitted to have a bomb.

surrounds. 'Though we did keep the gardeners on. Otherwise we'd have returned to a jungle.'

Almost nobody I meet in Tehran admits to being politically active anymore. Yet I feel I can detect a murmur of dissidence nonetheless, a hum of muted iconoclasm, as if they were not really retired at all but simply dormant, biding their time until they storm the barricades once again. Perhaps Durant was right, I consider. Perhaps everyone really is just engaged in a clever waiting game after all.

Indeed, there are places where the rumble is more pronounced – where I hear not just a whisper of insurrection but a guttural growl like the threat of distant thunder. One such place is the Hayyan Cultural Institute, where I've been invited by the academic Sadegh Zibakalam to attend the launch of his new book, *How the West Became the West*. A living oxymoron of Islamist conformity and activist critique, the institute thrums with heretical fervour as the two Supreme Leaders overlook proceedings with their usual moody gravitas from the walls. On the stage, speaking alongside Sadegh, is the reformist Islamic scholar Mehdi Khazali, the renegade son of the hard-line cleric Ayatollah Abolghasem Khazali, who has been jailed several times in Evin due to his ongoing criticism of the regime.

A Tehran University professor, Sadegh is one of the few dissident voices not to have seen the inside of an Evin cell. Largely tolerated by the establishment, he is often interviewed by the conservative media to give a veneer of credibility to their conspicuously partisan rhetoric. Before the event begins, he escorts me backstage so I can watch proceedings alongside his assistant. 'Sadegh believes that many of Iran's problems are because we're stuck in the gap between tradition and modernity,' the assistant explains as the panellists begin their discussion. 'And we always blame others for our issues, such as the Arab states or America.'

Over the years, Sadegh has become a master of creative subversion, he continues, flirting with the red lines without crossing them.[133] His new book is a prime example of this. 'It looks at how the West turned into the political and scientific powerhouse it is today. In Iran, we're told it was all extortion and plunder. But it was also the product of intellectual thought spanning centuries, through Descartes, Kepler, Newton, Locke.'

'At home, I feel we have the opposite problem,' I say. 'We learn about the Enlightenment but less about the plunder.'

'Hmmm.' He nods musingly. 'Yes. The truth probably lies somewhere in between ...'

I learn about *taarof* precisely forty-eight hours before I am due to leave Iran.

'You did what?' the young woman cries in alarm when I mention that I accepted a lift from Hashem's housekeeper to the Tajrish metro station.

'I ... took a lift,' I stutter. 'She offered.'

'No, no, no.' The woman, Bita, shakes her head. A friend of Hashem's former roommate, she has invited me to join her in Darband, in the far north of Tehran, for the evening – although it seems she may already be regretting it. 'She didn't mean it. You shouldn't have accepted.'

'She *seemed* to mean it,' I insist.

'She didn't. Trust me.'

With horror, I think back to all the kindnesses of the past two months. The meals, the gifts, the endless offers of assistance and accommodation. Could they all have been just an elaborate ritual of hospitality? 'Don't worry, I'm sure many were genuine,' Bita reassures me as we walk together up Darband Street, which winds high into the hills a few miles west of Jamshidiyeh Park. 'Though they might have been surprised by how quickly you accepted.'

---

133 There are signs, however, that this may be changing. In 2018, Sadegh received an eighteen-month jail sentence for 'spreading lies and propaganda', while in 2019 he was given a further year for 'publishing lies to terrorise the public'. He has appealed both sentences and currently remains at liberty.

An Iranian-Canadian dual citizen, Bita grew up in Toronto and returned to Iran several years ago to learn about her roots. As a magazine journalist, she is 'taking a big risk' by meeting me, she says, but kindly agrees to do so anyway – and I am grateful that she does. In the honeyed light of dusk, Darband is alive with music, crowds and colour. In this favoured elitist hangout, lips are full, heels are high and hijabs remain fixed on the backs of fulgent manes through some magical adhesive known only to Persian women. Walking up the slope, we pass popcorn machines and candyfloss looms, snow-white goats and clairvoyant canaries, Burberry-clad fashionistas and dogs in designer handbags. The aromas are rich and sweet, the air clear and fresh, and beside us a waterfall cascades through moss-covered rocks into the cool, damp darkness below.

Our walk ends on the mountaintop. From a small plateau, Tehran spreads before us in a haze of coral grey. Laid out like this, exposing its cupolas and steel scaffolds and stripes of blush-pink smog, the capital's naked ambition is plain to see. Scant greenery is visible, just a frenzy of ballast and building work snaking like stretchmarks into the foothills in a web of pallid scars.

Tehran is a flawed, ugly city – of that I have no doubt. And yet there's something about it. Something ... compelling. Perhaps it's because I don't know it yet. Perhaps it's because, like an elusive lover, it defies being known. But deep in the cracks, beyond the surface brume and grit, I can sense the city thrumming. A softer city than the one we see in the headlines. A kinder, more enigmatic one, in a million contrasting shades.

By the end of July, I feel ready for my journey to end. Iran, gracious and open in so many ways, is a land of broken eggshells. Meeting people is rife with risk, and I've grown weary of whispered trysts and cancelled appointments and constant vigilance every time I venture onto the street – not to mention the burden of covering my hair and skin under the blistering sun, the injustice of which sends me into daily paroxysms of muted rage.

In truth, however, I've also grown weary of myself. I've now been with myself for a whole year, enduring thousands of long, lonely hours in the saddle, and I'm thoroughly bored of my own company. I've exhausted all my best jokes and anecdotes, and have an unnerving sense of every physical and psychological shortcoming – of which, I am depressed to discover, there are many. I miss P, my family and my friends, all of whom have patiently tolerated such shortcomings for so long. I miss my home and my routine. I miss my bed.

I also miss my country, I am surprised to find. I long to go to the pub, wear a strappy top, howl anti-state slogans in the street: all things unthinkable out here but eminently achievable at home. In fact, knowing I can do these activities in Britain without fear of judgement, abuse or arrest makes me view my homeland with a newfound appreciation. For the first time, I have some understanding of the unabashed Anglophilia of my mother, who fled Soviet-controlled Hungary for the UK in 1967 and has always described the freedom she encountered upon arrival as 'like a dream'.

A life of freedom in Europe remains a dream for millions today. They arrive in boats and trucks and planes, exhausted and inspirited, risking everything in the hope of a better life. Yet alongside hope is frustration: at the antipathy, the Islamophobia, the borders slamming shut like a series of prison doors. In the West, our memories are short. We look east and we forget it bears our imprint. We forget how it came to this and how the liberties we cherish were earned.

In the meantime, the world keeps spinning, the centre shifting. We lock our doors and avert our gaze, but how long will it be before our own cloistered refuge grows cold? How long before we start to regret this world we've created, in which sovereignty trumps humanity and arbitrary lines become fortress walls?

At the airport, the check-in queue extends in tangled coils and loops across the floor. I heave my boulders of bubble-wrap behind an Afghan family, who tell me they've been visiting friends in Tehran after fleeing Kabul for Helsinki in 2012. They enjoy their new life, they say, although they struggle with the weather. 'We'd never seen snow before,' the mother smiles. 'Now it's everywhere!'

Behind me, a man leans forward and murmurs something in Farsi to the woman, and she laughs. He then turns to me. 'Classic Iran,' he says, glancing dismissively at the bustling crowds around us. 'The place looks all cool and modern, but actually it's a mess.' His parents left Tehran for Pennsylvania in 1981, he tells me, and every time he returns, he notices more absurd attempts to mimic the US. 'Yesterday, I saw an ambulance with the word "ambulance" written in mirror-writing on the back,' he snorts. 'And look at the roof here. It's basically the Washington airport roof inverted!' It looks like a normal curved roof to me, I confess, but he's on a roll. 'They hate America, but they want to follow it all the same.'

I don't know if what he says is true, but there is something about the idea of the American and Iranian buildings fitting together, jigsaw-like, which appeals. The countries seem like worthy complements to me – not through the kind of gauche aping suggested by my East Coast friend, but through a mutual give-and-take born from generations of cultural and social exchange. Both are lands of generosity, charity and gluttony; both are consumerist and materialist, patriotic and proud. Both take their Gods seriously, one bowing to the cross, the other to the crescent moon. Both are divided, both insecure. Both skittish, in their way, while maintaining a strong and durable core.

After checking in, I spend my final cash on a packet of pistachio biscuits, before remembering that I'd hoped to hold on to a little currency for posterity. 'No worry!' a fellow customer exclaims, plucking some notes from his pocket. 'Please, take some of mine.'

A final kindness, a final goodbye ...

It is hard to leave Iran. It is hard to leave the *Middle East*, which has kept me safe and healthy and fleshier than I ever imagined I'd be after twelve months on the road. Here, among the hundreds of Muslim homes I have visited, I have come to know the religion shorn of its political armoury. Islamists may steal the headlines, but Islam is reticent and rarely makes the front page. It is not concerned with jihadist militants, theocratic ayatollahs or tribal revolutionaries; it is not enamoured by power. It is gentle and hospitable and unwaveringly warm.

As I board the plane, memories of the past year flicker through my mind: the passion of Tahir Elçi, shot and killed in Turkey for his beliefs; the chutzpah of the El Nadeem doctors, persecuted in Cairo for their courage; the vitality of Amjed Farid, laughing off his beatings by the Sudanese police. The hundreds of people displaying tenacity, spirit and compassion in the face of a world that's turned its back.

Not everyone I met was a hero, of course. Many were unremarkable, a handful difficult. Several were indifferent, wary or suspicious. Yet nobody was cruel or hostile, and almost everyone, everywhere, was kind. Almost everyone, everywhere, was *human*, with all their flaws and whimsical variation – doing what human beings do.

AFTERWORD

On 13 September 2022, six years after I left Iran, a young Kurdish woman named Jina 'Mahsa' Amini was arrested by the *Gasht-e Ershad* while visiting her brother in Tehran. Her headscarf was too loose and her jeans too tight, they declared, and violated government regulations. Bundling her into the back of a van, they informed her she was being taken to a detention centre for 're-education' and would be released after just a few hours.

But Mahsa was never released. She died in hospital three days later, still in police custody, after collapsing and falling into a coma. The regime claimed she had suffered multiple organ failure due to a pre-existing health condition. But her fellow detainees told a different story: she had been viciously beaten about the head and body while being transported in the security van, they said, and had lost consciousness as a result of their brutality.

Mahsa was just twenty-two years old when she died. She wasn't an activist or agitator. She wasn't interested in politics. She was an ordinary, happy, healthy young woman to whom millions of families across Iran could relate. And her murder hit a nerve unrivalled by any other event since the founding of the Islamic Republic in 1979 – not simply among women or Kurds or the feminist liberal elite, but among men and women, the rich and poor, traditionalists and progressives alike.

Driven in part by the Kurdish freedom movement, with its decades of grassroots activism, protests erupted like wildfire across Kurdistan and Tehran, and eventually the country as a whole. Women tore off their hijabs, chopped off their hair and took to the streets in their hundreds of thousands chanting 'Women, Life, Freedom': a slogan that soon went viral throughout the world. After forty-four years of humiliation, subjugation and abuse, the women of Iran had finally had enough, and they were adamant their voices would be heard.

In a sense, this was nothing new. Renowned for their passion and courage, Iranian women have been at the forefront of pioneering reformist movements for generations, from the time of the 1905–11 Constitutional Revolution, when female nationalists played a seminal role in the fight for democracy and autonomy from foreign control, to the drive for female suffrage in the 1950s and 1960s, which thrust women's rights to the heart of the political agenda. In the 1979 revolution, vast numbers of women joined the uprising to demand an end to corruption and autocracy under Mohammad Reza Shah – only to return to the streets just weeks after his fall to protest against the shock imposition of the compulsory hijab by the new Islamist regime.[134]

Under the Islamic Republic, women continued to find innovative ways to resist the oppressive strictures of the state, tirelessly chipping away in the shadows to expose those elusive chinks of light. Subversive online movements such as My Stealthy Freedom and White Wednesdays, launched in 2014 and 2017 respectively, encouraged women to post photographs of themselves defying the mandatory dress code, while solitary acts of civil disobedience – such as Vida Movahed's removal of her headscarf while standing on a utility box on Enghelab (Revolution) Street in Tehran in December 2017 – inspired thousands of other women to carry out similar acts of rebellion of their own.

So, in many ways, what we are seeing now is simply a

---

[134] 'It took scarcely a month [...] to realise that, in fact, I had willingly and enthusiastically participated in my own demise,' the Iranian human rights lawyer and Nobel laureate Shirin Ebadi writes in her memoir *Iran Awakening*, describing the moment she realised the true devastating consequences of the 1979 Iranian Revolution. 'I was a woman, and this revolution's victory demanded my defeat.'

continuation of all that has gone before. And yet it is also a departure. It is unprecedented. Women are no longer banging the drum on the periphery or being subsumed into a broader activist campaign. They are front and centre, the heart and the soul. They are not fighting simply for women's rights, but for the rights of their country as a whole. The female body symbolises the civic body, and its emancipation means freedom for all.

As I write this, in February 2023, the protests have been ongoing for five months. While exact figures are uncertain, the US-based Human Rights Activists News Agency reports that around 20,000 people have been arrested and over 500 killed (including scores of children) since the first gathering took place outside Kasra Hospital in Tehran, where Mahsa died, on 16 September 2022. Four people have been executed following closed trials in the revolutionary courts, while dozens more are facing the death penalty for crimes such as *moharebeh* ('enmity against God') or 'corruption on earth'.

Due to this ruthless *sarkoob*,[135] or crackdown, the momentum behind the unrest has slowed in recent weeks. Yet, even as the crowds disperse from the streets and relative normality returns, the clarion call for change remains very much alive. In 2009, the Green protests were largely driven by the urban, educated middle class, while the demonstrations of 2017 to 2019 were triggered by rising food and fuel prices rather than a desire for meaningful political reform. In contrast, the 2022–23 protests have drawn together an inclusive, intersectional alliance that cuts across ethnic, religious, gender and economic divides. Leaderless and uncoordinated, they have provided no easily identifiable figurehead to be targeted and crushed by the regime, instead drawing their strength from a kind of egalitarian solidarity. And they have galvanised youngsters in their teens and twenties like never before, turning classrooms into some of the most vocal

---

[135] Literally 'the pounding of the head'.

arenas of dissent and suggesting an ongoing issue that will only worsen in years to come.

Not everyone supports the protests, of course. Iran remains a deeply divided country, and there is undoubtedly a section of society – albeit a dwindling one – that retains a sense of loyalty towards the regime. In 2018, the office of former president Hassan Rouhani released a survey, based on 2014 figures, which showed the population to be split almost equally in its attitude towards the mandatory hijab, while around a third of respondents said they thought women should be compelled to wear the more traditional chador. Over the past few months, I have received several texts from hosts I stayed with in Iran downplaying the demonstrations and voicing their support for Ayatollah Khamenei (although whether they felt they could speak freely to me is questionable, of course). 'All you have heard about girls and women in Iran is inaccurate and everything is OK,' one – unsolicited – message read. 'Most people love our regime and our unique ruler [...]. You may think the regime treats the women in a bad way, but as a matter of fact in Islam a great attention is paid to women and their freedom as long as it doesn't affect Islamic society.'

The lack of an obvious leader, while benefiting the movement in the early stages of unrest, means that the Khamenei regime is unlikely to be overthrown anytime soon. There is currently no viable opposition to establish a transitional route to reform, while most Iranians have little appetite for a chaotic, Arab Spring-style revolt. However, the spark of revolutionary fervour ignited by the protests seems only likely to grow. Shortly after taking office in August 2021, Iran's hard-line president Ebrahim Raisi was busy Islamising the population, ramping up morality patrols and introducing a new national 'Hijab and Chastity' day to take place every July. Now, just eighteen months later, the picture looks very different. In September, a group of clerics from seminaries across the country released a statement officially rejecting Khamenei's religious 'guardianship' due to the atrocities committed under his rule, while in December the attorney general, Mohammad Jafar

Montazeri, announced the abolition of the controversial *Gasht-e Ershad*. In January, in a sign of his weakening grip on power, Khamenei began to adopt a more conciliatory tone towards women who fail to observe the compulsory dress code. 'A weak hijab is not a good thing,' he told a group of conservative, pro-regime women, coining a phrase that will likely enter common parlance soon. 'But it should not cause that individual to be seen outside of religion and the revolution.'

Whether the regime has a genuine desire to reform the system and relax its oppressive morality laws remains to be seen. It has remained vague and noncommittal, and has taken no concrete steps so far. However, whatever action it takes now will clearly no longer be enough. Today, thousands of women are boldly walking the streets of Iran with no hijab, their heads held high beneath defiantly resplendent manes, in a manner that was all but impossible just a few months ago. The female body, branded for so long with the regime's most conspicuous symbol of masculine, Islamist hegemony, has thrown off its shackles and weaponised itself with searing fortitude against the state. The climate of fear has broken – and there is no turning back now.

'This protest was different from all the previous protests in Iran since 1979,' a male friend I met in Tehran messaged me recently. 'This time, people saw how the regime killed protestors, how they shot at protestors' eyes, how they raped girls, how they lied on the news. This time, the people outside Iran united with the people inside Iran.

'This time was different, I tell you. Most Iranians know this regime will be gone very soon. Trust me, Rebecca. We just need time.'

Rebecca Lowe
February 2023

BIBLIOGRAPHY

Abdoh, Salar, *Tehran Noir*, Akashic Books, 2014

Anderson, Scott, *Lawrence in Arabia: War, Deceit, Imperial Folly and the Making of the Modern Middle East*, Atlantic Books, 2014

Arnold, Sir Thomas Walker, *The Preaching of Islam: A History of the Propagation of the Muslim Faith*, Wentworth Press, 2016

Asher, Michael, *Khartoum: The Ultimate Imperial Adventure*, Penguin, 2006

Axworthy, Michael, *Iran: Empire of the Mind: A History from Zoroaster to the Present Day*, Penguin, 2008

Barr, James, *A Line in the Sand: Britain, France and the Struggle That Shaped the Middle East*, Simon & Schuster, 2012

Battutah, Ibn, *The Travels of Ibn Battuta: Explorations of the Middle East, Asia, Africa, China and India from 1325 to 1354, An Autobiography*, translated by H.A.R. Gibb, Pantianos, 1929

Bell, Gertrude and Howell, Georgina, *A Woman in Arabia: The Writings of the Queen of the Desert*, Penguin Classics, 2015

Bell, Gertrude, *The Letters of Gertrude Bell Volumes I and II*, Benediction Books, 2009

Blow, David, *Persia (Through Writers' Eyes)*, Eland Publishing, 2007

Churchill, Winston, *The River War: An Account of the Reconquest of the Sudan*, Dover Publications, 2007

Cobain, Ian, *The History Thieves: Secrets, Lies and the Shaping of a Modern Nation*, Portobello Books, 2017

Cockett, Richard, *Sudan: The Failure and Division of an African State*, Yale University Press, 2015

Davidson, Christopher, *Shadow Wars: The Secret Struggle for the Middle East,* Oneworld Publications, 2017

Davison, Anne, *The Ottoman Empire*, CreateSpace Independent Publishing Platform, 2017

Ebadi, Shirin, *Iran Awakening: A Memoir of Revolution and Hope*, Rider, 2007

Elliott, Jason, *Mirrors of the Unseen: Journeys in Iran*, Picador 2007

Erskine, F.J., *Lady Cycling: What to Wear and How to Ride*, The British Library Publishing Division, 2014

Ferdowsi, *The Epic of Kings: Shahnameh*, translated by Helen Zimmern, 2020

Fermor, Patrick Leigh, *A Time of Gifts: On Foot to Constantinople: from the Hook of Holland to the Middle Danube*, John Murray, 2004

Fermor, Patrick Leigh, *Between the Woods and the Water: On Foot to Constantinople from the Hook of Holland: The Middle Danube to the Iron Gates*, John Murray, 2004

Fiennes, Sir Ranulph, *Where Soldiers Fear to Tread*, Mandarin, 1995

Frankopan, Peter, *The Silk Roads*, Bloomsbury Paperbacks, 2016

Geniesse, Jane Fletcher, *Passionate Nomad: The Life of Freya Stark*, Modern Library, 2001

Gordon, Charles George & Hake, Alfred Egmont, *The Journals of Major-Gen C.G. Gordon, C.B. At Kartoum*, Franklin Classics, 2018

Guppy, Shusha, *The Blindfold Horse: Memories of a Persian Childhood*, Tauris Parke Paperbacks, 2009

Hemingway, Ernest, *In Our Time*, Perfection Learning, 1996

Herodotus, *The Histories*, translated by Aubrey de Sélincourt, Penguin Classics, 2003

Hourani, Albert, *A History of the Arab Peoples*, Faber & Faber, 2013

Howell, Georgina, *Queen of the Desert: The Extraordinary Life of Gertrude Bell*, Pan Books, 2015

Hussein, Taha, *The Stream of Days: A Student at the Azhar*, translated by Hilary Wayment, Longmans, Green & Co, 1948

Huxley, Aldous, *Brave New World*, Vintage Classics, 2007

Ibn Jubayr, *The Travels of Ibn Jubayr: A Medieval Journey from Cordoba to Jerusalem*, translated by Ronald Broadhurst, I.B. Tauris, 2019

Ibn Tuwayr al-Jannah, Ahmad, *The Pilgrimage of Ahmad, Son of the Little Bird of Paradise: An Account of a 19th Century Pilgrimage from Mauritania to Mecca*, translated and edited by H.T. Norris. Warminster, Aris & Phillips, 1977

Jones, Jeremy and Ridout, Nicholas, *A History of Modern Oman*, Cambridge University Press, 2015

Khayyam, Omar, *Rubaiyat of Omar Khayyam; Rendered Into English Verse by Edward Fitzgerald*, Andesite Press, 2015

Khusrau, Nasir-I, *Diary of a Journey Through Syria and Palestine*, Forgotten Books, 2018

Kinross, Lord, *The Ottoman Centuries: The Rise and Fall of the Turkish Empire*, Sander Kitabevi and Jonathan Cape, 1977

Kinzer, Stephen, *All the Shah's Men: An American Coup and the Roots of Middle East Terror*, John Wiley & Sons, 2008

Lawrence, T.E., *Seven Pillars of Wisdom*, Penguin Classics, 2000

Lee, Laurie, *As I Walked Out One Midsummer Morning*, Penguin Classics, 2014

Lewis, Bernard, *The Jews of Islam*, Princeton University Press, 2014

Lewis, Bernard, *The Middle East: 2000 Years of History from the Rise of Christianity to the Present Day*, Phoenix, 2001

Macfarlane, Robert, *Mountains of the Mind: A History of a Fascination*, Granta, 2008

Mackintosh-Smith, Tim, *Travels with a Tangerine: A Journey in the Footnotes of Ibn Battutah*, Picador, 2002

Maclean, Rory, *Stalin's Nose: Across the Face of Europe*, Flamingo, 1993

Makdisi, Jean Said, *Teta, Mother and Me: Three Generation of Arab Women*, W.W. Norton & Co, 2006

Manley, Deborah & Abdel-Hakim, Sahar, *Egypt (Through Writers' Eyes)*, Eland Publishing, 2007

Marks, Isabel, *Fancy Cycling, 1901: An Edwardian Guide*, Old House Books, 2013

Massoudi, Cyrus, *Land of the Turquoise Mountains: Journeys Across Iran*, Tauris Parke, 2018

McCarron, Leon, *The Land Beyond: A Thousand Miles on Foot through the Heart of the Middle East*, Bloomsbury Publishing, 2017

McHugo, John, *A Concise History of the Arabs*, Saqi Books, 2016

Miles, Hugh, *Playing Cards in Cairo: Mint Tea, Tarneeb and Tales of the City*, Abacus, 2011

Molavi, Afshin, *Persian Pilgrimages: Journeys Across Iran*, W.W. Norton & Co., 2002

Morris, Jan, *Sultan in Oman*, Eland Publishing, 2002

Murphy, Dervla, *Full Tilt: Ireland to India with a Bicycle*, Eland Publishing, 2010

Nafisi, Azar, *Reading Lolita in Tehran*, Eland Publishing, 2010

Navai, Ravita, *City of Lies: Love, Sex, Death, and the Search for Truth in Tehran*, PublicAffairs, 2014

Phillips, Christopher, *The Battle for Syria: International Rivalry in the New Middle East*, Yale University Press, 2020

Pryce, Lois, *Revolutionary Ride: On the Road in Search of the Real Iran*, Nicholas Brealey Publishing, 2018

Raban, Jonathan, *Arabia: Through the Looking Glass*, Eland Publishing, 2018

Rogan, Eugene, *The Arabs: A History*, Penguin, 2018

Ruskin, John, *The Stones of Venice*, Penguin Books, 2001

Russell, Bertrand & Feinberg, Barry, *The Collected Stories of Bertrand Russell*, George Allen & Unwin, 1972

Salibi, Kamal S., *A House of Many Mansions: The History of Lebanon Reconsidered*, I.B. Tauris, 2005

Seal, Jeremy, *A Fez of the Heart: Travels Around Turkey in Search of a Hat*, Trans-Atlantic Publications, 1995

Shenker, Jack, *The Egyptians: A Radical Story*, Allen Lane, 2016

Stark, Freya, *East is West*, John Murray, 1945

Stark, Freya, *The Valleys of the Assassins and Other Persian Travels*, Arrow Books, 1991

Stewart, Rory, *The Places In Between*, Picador, 2014

Sweis, Rana F., *Voices of Jordan*, C. Hurst & Co Publishers, 2018

The Qur'an, translated by M.A.S. Abdel Haleem, OUP Oxford, 2008

Thesiger, Wilfred, *Arabian Sands*, Penguin Classics, 2007

Thesiger, Wilfred, *Desert, Marsh & Mountain*, Flamingo, 2011

Thubron, Colin, *Shadow of the Silk Road*, Vintage, 2007

Watney, John, *Travels in Araby of Lady Hester Stanhope*, Gordon & Cremonesi, 1975

Wood, Levison, *Arabia: A Journey Through the Heart of the Middle East*, Hodder Paperbacks, 2019

Wood, Levison, *Walking the Nile*, Simon & Schuster, 2015

ACKNOWLEDGEMENTS

Writing a book is hard, it turns out. Harder than cycling through the Middle East, and without the wonderfully steely buttocks to look forward to at the end (in fact, its impact on the rump is entirely detrimental, I can report). I certainly could never have made it this far without the assistance and encouragement of a fantastic group of family, friends and supporters, to whom I owe a huge debt of gratitude and more beers than the sales of this book could ever feasibly cover.

First, I must thank my friend Jo Skoulikas, who not only heroically jetted all the way out to Iran to cheer me on for the final leg of my bike ride, but whose detailed, eagle-eyed reading of the work-in-progress was invaluable and saved me many an embarrassment over typos and rogue grammar. Ever selfless, she is the type of person who always makes time, whether she has any to spare or not, and I'm not quite sure what I would do without her.

Second, thank you to my partner Patrick – my rock – for tolerating both the indulgence of the journey itself and the subsequent book writing with such patience and good humour. Not everyone would have stuck by me so loyally throughout, and I dread to think how many brownie points he's earned from the whole endeavour. Suffice to say, if/when he announces his plan to fulfil his dream of a Big Wave Surf Safari across the world, I fear I'll be in no position to object.

Next, I must thank my poor, long-suffering mother, who I know far from relished the idea of her only daughter disappearing over the horizon for twelve months with just a bike and bellyful of kebabs to sustain her, but who ultimately went on to prove my biggest champion during the course of the trip and beyond. Thanks to her too for taking the time to read and comment on my draft manuscript with such care, and for strong-arming everyone she's ever met into buying multiple hardback copies when they must doubtlessly be sick and tired of hearing about the whole bloody thing by now (I'm so sorry, everyone).

It strikes me at this point that I should probably thank my daughter too. Having a baby during the closing stages of writing a book is definitely not something I'd recommend – and Frankie's editorial suggestions, I admit, were not always gratefully received. But I can reliably report that there are few things more effective at focusing the mind than an imminently wakeful, hungry baby! Without her presence curled on my chest, acting as my own personal human timebomb, this book arguably may never have seen the light of day. (Though if I ever try to do this again, please shoot me.)

Thank you to my brilliant agent Carrie Plitt, from Felicity Bryan Associates, who not only sold the book here and abroad, and expertly negotiated the contracts, but who steadfastly stood by me throughout the highs and lows of the pitching, writing and publishing process. And a huge thank you to Hannah MacDonald and Charlotte Cole at September Publishing – as well as their talented team of editors, marketers and designers – for their tremendous support and enthusiasm for the book, and for bringing it to publication with such commitment, care and finesse. I couldn't be happier with how it turned out.

Thank you too to my good friends Ben Clement, Romilly Holland and Saleem Vallaincourt, and my brother Rob Lowe (no, not that one), for reading chapters of the book and providing their insightful and valuable comments. I'm also most grateful to my old college supervisor Robert Douglas-Fairhurst for not only reading and commenting on several chapters but doing so with his trademark astuteness, thoughtfulness and eyewatering efficiency.

As my father always used to say: if you want something doing, ask a busy person.

Thank you to my fellow cyclist and writer Kate Rawles, who was stumbling in the literary rushes at the same time as me and whose witty, supportive emails always provided a much-needed boost when motivation was low (please do buy her book too when it's out – it will be superb!). And thank you likewise to my experienced tour-cyclist friends Max Goldzweig and Emily Conradi, who not only gave me excellent advice and tips before the trip but provided much-needed reassurance – when so many were doing the opposite – that I would (almost certainly) come out alive and well the other side.

Thank you to the following country and regional experts, who read excerpts from the book and provided valued feedback (in alphabetical order): Manu Abdo, Reza Afshar, Mutaz Alkalbani, Ian Bancroft, Nasrin Behtoyi, Alexander Christie-Miller, Mohammad Ehab, Muhammad Ekbal, Mohamad Esam-Salem, Mohammad Essam-Salim, Amjed Farid, Ben Fender, Fatima Gazali, Pascale Ghazaleh, Gzing Ghazi, Kathryn Harrison, Hamza Hendawi, Valerie Hopkins, John Jaeger, Emma King, Ben Lyons, Marko Matijevic, Emad Mekay, Asmaa Moustafa, Osman Mirghani, Boris Mrkela, Arthur Mühlen-Schulte, Mary Nazzal-Batayneh, Natasa Posel, Hasna Reda, Kiran Roest.

Thank you to all my sponsors, without whom the journey may not have been possible at all: Kona, for their Kona Sutra bicycle; Lightwave, for their Firelight 250 sleeping bag and G15 Raid tent; Garmin, for their Edge 1000; Lenovo, for their ThinkPad X1 Carbon Ultrabook laptop; Arkel, for their four Orca panniers; Berghaus, for their Vapour long sleeve t-shirt, Explorer Eco cargo pant, Kinloch hoody, Vapourlight shorts, Spectrum gilet and Velum GORE-TEX Active shell pant; and Pedros, for their ICM Multitool. None of the companies requested anything in return, and their generosity in providing equipment to a person who could have been (and arguably was) a complete charlatan was quite remarkable. I am particularly indebted to Kona founder

Dan Gerhard, who agreed to donate one of his best tour bikes – Maud – barely moments after the email left my outbox, no strings attached. What a guy.

Last but certainly not least, thank you to the hundreds of people who looked after me so generously and unconditionally on the road, of whom there are far too many to list here. Some of you made it into the book; many did not. But please know that your warmth and hospitality lies at the heart of this story, and I will always be grateful for your kindness.